The working of econometric models

M. Morishima Y. Murata T. Nosse M. Saito

THE WORKING OF
ECONOMETRIC MODELS

CAMBRIDGE: at the University Press 1972

Published by the Syndics of the Cambridge University Press
Bentley House, 200 Euston Road, London NW1 2DB
American Branch: 32 East 57th Street, New York, N.Y.10022

© Cambridge University Press 1972

Library of Congress Catalogue Card Number: 79-184901

ISBN: 0 521 08502 0

Printed in Great Britain at the University Printing House, Cambridge
(Brooke Crutchley, University Printer)

Contents

Preface

This volume is based mainly on empirical studies which I have done with my colleagues in Japan. It is devoted to applications of the general equilibrium models, the theoretical, or qualitative, examination of which has been one of my main concerns for the last fifteen years.

Applications have been made to the United States of America, the United Kingdom and Japan at different degrees of aggregation. The US model (with Professor Saito) is primarily a growth model which explains the development of the American economy in the first half of this century. Although it is highly aggregated, it discusses such problems as the existence and stability, or instability, of the state of long-run growth equilibrium maintaining full employment and of the state of balanced growth with constant prices and the incompatability of the two states. It is also concerned with the quantitative evaluation of monetary and fiscal policies as two short-run measures for achieving full employment of labour. An experiment with a hypothetical investment function of the Adaptable Acceleration Principle type successfully generates a depression, as expected by Sir Roy Harrod, of a magnitude comparable with that of the Great Depression.

The theoretical models underlying an application to the UK economy and two applications to Japan are of the mixed Leontief–Keynes type. The UK model (with Professor Nosse) is a fiscal policy model, and is used to estimate the effects of an increase in government expenditure. It is found that these vary significantly according to the channel by which the government expenditure is injected. It would be desirable for the public authorities to plan expenditure so as to maximize its effect on the national income. The global and marginal criteria for the optimum allocation of government expenditure are given in terms of the first and the last of the Samuelson–LeChatelier sequences of multiplier effects respectively. Calculating these for the UK in 1954, we examine the UK budget in that year for efficiency, from both the global and local points of view. Our study also contains contributions to the theory of the balanced-budget multiplier due to T. Haavelmo and to the estimation of short-term and long-term built-in flexibilities of taxes due to R. A. Musgrave.

An application to Japan (by Professor Saito) is made in order to investigate the interdependency of prices and outputs. It is found that the

Jacobian matrix of the estimated excess demand functions is dominated by gross-substitutability, so that it is quantitatively confirmed that the Hicksian laws of prices of substitutes, theoretically established to hold globally in my *Equilibrium, Stability and Growth*, are satisfied in spite of the existence of complementary goods. The price changes experienced in 1906–1 are analysed into the effects caused by shifts in demand, supply and imports. The multiplier effects and the Musgrave–Miller measure of the effectiveness of built-in flexibility are estimated, for purposes of comparison with those obtained for the UK economy.

Another Japanese model (with Professor Murata) is a model for estimating disguised unemployment in Japan. In this country, which has so many Marxian economists, it has often been pointed out that there is an enormous amount of disguised unemployment accumulated in agriculture and traditional domestic industries. But no rigorous estimate of this unemployment has yet been offered, and no econometric work has been attempted on its movement through time. Our model for the first time provides estimates of disguised unemployment in various industries for the four years for which input–output tables are available; it is found that the general drift of the results is consistent with the qualitative information which is available. Then the disguised unemployment thus found is analysed into the effects of relative wages, exogenous demand, marginal propensities to consume and the technological structure of the economy, of which the effects of relative wages dominate the others. In addition, the multiplier effects on disguised unemployment are estimated and distinguished from those on normal employment.

The final model (with Professor Murata) is concerned with international multipliers. The multipliers calculated from the other models are of a 'one-way' character, in the sense that they allow for leakages of purchasing power to foreign counties but not for feedback to the country where the original impulse occurs. Therefore, they should be compared with the true foreign multipliers. Aggregating the world into one exogenous and eight endogenous regions, we calculate the short-run and long-run multipliers and the Brown–Jones supermultipliers and analyse the actual GNP of each region into a dissipative part, a stationary part determined by the long-run multipliers, and a trend-part determined by the Brown–Jones supermultipliers, among which the long-run multiplier effects are dominant.

Finally, I should add that Part I is a complete revision of a paper originally published in *International Economic Review* and then reproduced in *Readings in Economic Statistics and Econometrics* edited by Arnold Zellner (Boston: Little, Brown and Company). Part II includes parts of Nosse's D.Phil. thesis (University of Oxford), and Part III is a revised version of M. Saito, 'An interindustry study of price formation', *Review of Economics and Statistics* (vol. 53, 1971). Thanks are due to the editors of these journals for permission to include the papers in this volume. We would like also to acknowledge the supervision which Nosse and Saito received from Lady Ursula Hicks and Professor L. R. Klein.

M. M.
September 1971

NOTE: 'Billion' is US usage throughout.

The Leontief inverse refers to $(I-A)^{-1}$, where A is a non-negative square matrix.

PART I

A dynamic analysis of the American economy,
1902–1952

by M. Morishima and M. Saito

1. *Introduction*

Once upon a time, there was a Japanese priest named Noh-in, who was notorious for his eccentricities. After having sat at a window of his hermitage in Kyoto for several months and acquired a suntan, he pretended to have come back from the Far North of Japan, and published poems singing of the journey. We are like Noh-in, in that we are writing a story about the American economy, although deriving the formula of the Turnpike theorem was all one of us did in a sunny bungalow when he was in California, while the other, now in the United States, had never been there when he engaged in this econometric study. We are, however, much emboldened by the historical fact that even the greatest traveller, Marco Polo, wrote about Japan without having been there.

We have constructed a log-linearized macroeconomic model of the Keynesian type on the basis of time series data for the United States over the period 1902–52. Our system consists of seven stochastic and two definitional equations, one of the smallest Keynesian models which has ever been subjected to econometric treatment. Compared with the monumental Brookings model of Duesenberry, Fromm, Klein, Kuh and others, the present model may be called a midget. But the world was not made only for giants.

In Chapter 2 the theoretical foundations of the model are given, and our estimates of the structural parameters are compared with those obtained by other econometricians. The model is examined from two points of view, short-run and long-run. Chapter 3 is devoted to evaluation of monetary and fiscal policies as two short-run measures for achieving a satisfactory level of employment. Chapter 4 deals with long-run properties of the model such as the existence and stability, or instability, of growth equilibrium, and the contradiction between price–wage stability and the maintence of full employment of labour.

In Chapter 3 we estimate various multipliers: fiscal and monetary multipliers for income and employment, and impact and dynamic multipliers. It may be conjectured, as it was by Keynes, that the multipliers at a high level of economic activity are different from the multipliers at a low level, so that the effectiveness of the alternative policies varies with phases of business cycles as well as with stages of economic development. We therefore compute the multipliers for each year in the sample period, from which we

[3]

conclude that an empirical law operates, namely that the effect on employment of an increase in investment becomes smaller as the employment ratio
becomes greater, while the effect of an increase in real cash balances on
employment is almost independent of the employment ratio; and hence the
excess of the former over the latter becomes larger as the employment ratio
decreases. The Keynesian idea that in depressions public investment policy
has an advantage over traditional monetary policy as a measure to promote
full employment is thus confirmed econometrically.

In Chapter 4 we present an empirical analysis both of the state of long-run
economic growth maintaining full employment and also of the state of
balanced growth with constant prices, the former having recently received
much attention from neoclassical economists such as Solow, Uzawa, and
Meade and the latter having been discussed by many von Neumannians,
including Joan Robinson and Sir John Hicks. Our econometrics show that
price stability and perpetual full employment cannot be achieved simultaneously unless we have powerful anti-inflation policies. That is to say,
price stability produces severe unemployment, while a serious inflation
accompanies full employment. This is one of the dilemmas of present-day
capitalism.

Another dilemma concerns the stability of growth equilibrium. Sir Roy
Harrod has argued that a reasonable investment function of an acceleration-
principle type would imply the instability of long-run equilibrium, so that
a capitalist economy could at best proceed along an unstable path of
equilibrium growth. On the other hand, neoclassical economists insist that
the Harrodian instability disappears when the price–wage–interest mechanism works, if there is sufficient scope for substituting labour for capital in
production and the entire saving is automatically invested. Chapter 4 deals
with this controversy also. Our econometric investigation shows that so
long as the capital–labour ratio is flexible and investment is adapted to
savings, neoclassical forces may work to bring the economy towards growth
equilibrium, but the forces are so weak that a deep depression may easily
occur with a reasonable investment function, once flexibility of the capital–
labour ratio is lost or limited. A simulation of the instability process is made;
it is found that it may be comparable with the Great Depression experienced
in the thirties.

Finally, it should be noted that all conclusions drawn in Chapters 3 and 4
are based on coefficients which are subject to sampling errors.

2. *The structural model*

The model set out in this chapter is an aggregative annual model of the Keynesian type estimated by the method of two-stage-least-squares over the sample period 1902–52 (excluding 1941–5). All the series used are listed in the Appendix (pp. 68–9).[1] The variables and equations are as follows:

The endogenous variables:

Y = net national product or national income (billions of 1929 dollars)
C = consumption (billions of 1929 dollars)
D = capital consumption allowances (billions of 1929 dollars)
K = end of year capital stock (billions of 1929 dollars)
N = persons engaged (millions of persons)
p = price level (1929 base: 1)
w = wage rate (thousands of current dollars)
r = corporate bond yield (per cent per annum)
h = hours worked per person per year (thousands of hours)

The exogenous variables:

I = gross investment (billions of 1929 dollars)
B = trade balance (billions of 1929 dollars)
M = cash balances (billions of current dollars)
L = population fifteen years of age and over (millions of persons)
t = time in years (1927:0)
u = dummy variable (0 before 1941; 1 after 1946)

---

[1] The data other than the hours worked, gross investment, and depreciation series are the same as those used by L. R. Klein and R. F. Kosobud, 'Some econometrics of growth: great ratios of economics', *Quarterly Journal of Economics*, LXXV (May 1961). Most of them were estimated by S. Kuznets and J. W. Kendrick in *Capital in the American Economy: Its Formation and Financing* (Princeton University Press, 1961) and *Productivity Trends in the United States* (Princeton University Press, 1961), respectively. The hours-worked series was obtained from Kendrick, *op. cit.* pp. 305–7 and pp. 311–13, by dividing the figures in the first column of Table A-X by the corresponding figures in Table A-VI. The figures of capital consumption allowances were obtained from Kuznets, *op. cit.* pp. 555–6 and p. 499. They are column (4) minus column (5) of Table R-22, for 1901–18, and column (6) of Table R-8, for 1919–52. The gross investment series was obtained by adding the figures of capital consumption allowances to the annual increments of capital stock.

The estimated equations:

Consumption function

$$\log\frac{C_t}{L_t} = \underset{(6.5)}{0.349}\log\frac{Y_t}{L_t} + \underset{(4.4)}{0.160}\log\frac{M_t}{p_tL_t} + \underset{(5.8)}{0.460}\log\frac{C_{t-1}}{L_{t-1}} + 0.007$$

$$(2.1)$$

$$\bar{R}^2 = 0.98, \quad \delta^2/S^2 = 2.19;$$

Liquidity preference function

$$\log\frac{M_t}{p_t} = \underset{(34.2)}{1.190}\left[0.586\log Y_t + 0.414\log\frac{M_{t-1}}{p_t} + 0.295\right]$$

$$- \underset{(3.3)}{0.202}\log r_t - \underset{(2.2)}{0.048}u - 0.650 \quad (2.2)$$

$$\bar{R}^2 = 0.98, \quad \delta^2/S^2 = 1.11;$$

Production function

$$\log Y_t = 0.824\log h_tN_t + \underset{(15.4)}{0.176}\log K_{t-1} + 0.00633t$$

$$+ \underset{(3.1)}{0.052}u - 0.242655 \quad (2.3)$$

$$\bar{R}^2 = 0.93, \quad \delta^2/S^2 = 0.73;$$

Relative share equation

$$\frac{w_tN_t}{p_tY_t} = 0.824, \quad \text{or} \quad \log\frac{w_tN_t}{p_tY_t} = \underset{(3.1)}{-0.084}; \quad (2.4)$$

Wage determination equation

$$\log\frac{w_t}{h_t} = \underset{(52.4)}{1.006}\log\frac{w_{t-1}}{h_{t-1}} + \underset{(2.1)}{0.456}\left(\frac{1}{5}\log\frac{p_t}{p_{t-1}} + \frac{4}{5}\log\frac{p_{t-1}}{p_{t-2}}\right)$$

$$+ \underset{(1.1)}{0.188}\log\frac{N_t}{0.57L_t} + 0.017 \quad (2.5)$$

$$\bar{R}^2 = 0.99, \quad \delta^2/S^2 = 1.98;$$

Hours worked equation

$$\log h_t = \underset{(17.4)}{-0.282}\log\frac{w_{t-1}}{p_{t-1}h_{t-1}} + \underset{(6.1)}{0.343}\log\frac{N_t}{0.57L_t} + 0.324 \quad (2.6)$$

$$\bar{R}^2 = 0.91, \quad \delta^2/S^2 = 1.09;$$

Depreciation equation

$$\log D_t = \underset{(18.8)}{1.593}\log K_{t-1} - 2.817 \quad (2.7)$$

$$\bar{R}^2 = 0.89, \quad \delta^2/S^2 = 0.14.$$

Identities:

$$Y_t = C_t + I_t - D_t + B_t, \tag{2.8}$$

$$K_t = K_{t-1} + I_t - D_t. \tag{2.9}$$

The numbers in parentheses under the coefficients represent the so-called *t*-ratios, i.e. the estimated values of the coefficients divided by their estimated sampling errors. The measure of goodness of fit, $\bar{R}$, is adjusted for degrees of freedom, and the serial correlation statistic, δ^2/S^2, is the ratio of the mean square successive difference of residuals to the variance. For acceptance of the hypothesis of non-autocorrelation at the 5 per cent level of significance, we should have values of δ^2/S^2 in the range 1.5–2.6 for samples of the size being used. (Strictly speaking, however, this test for serial correction is not legitimate when some of the regressors are lagged dependent variables.)[1]

RATIONALE OF THE MODEL AND IMPLICATIONS OF
THE PARAMETER ESTIMATES

(1) *The consumption function*

The primary determinants of consumer expenditure are income and wealth. Consumption, income and cash balances are measured per capita and in real terms; we may, therefore, say that our equation (2.1) also takes the effects of population size and price level into account.

Economists have frequently discussed the non-linear relationship between income and consumption. Keynes pointed out that the marginal propensity to consume decreased with increases in income; the non-linearity of Engel curves has been established by many studies of family data.[2] Accordingly,

---

[1] In estimating the system (2.1)–(2.8) we used, instead of (2.8), the following log-linear expression

$$(\overline{C}/\overline{Y}) \log C_t + \{(\overline{I}+\overline{B})/\overline{Y}\} \log (I_t+B_t) - \log Y_t - (\overline{D}/\overline{Y}) \log D_t$$

$$= (\overline{C}/\overline{Y}) \log \overline{C} + \{(\overline{I}+\overline{B})/\overline{Y}\} \log (\overline{I}+\overline{B}) - \log \overline{Y} - (\overline{D}/\overline{Y}) \log \overline{D}, \quad (2.8')$$

where barred symbols represent the sample means of the respective variables. To obtain (2.8'), regard Y_t, C_t, etc. as functions of $\log Y_t$, $\log C_t$, etc., expand them into Taylor series at the point of $\log \overline{Y}$, $\log \overline{C}$, ..., respectively, and neglect terms of higher power. Independent predetermined variables of our system are $\log L_t$, $\log M_{t-1}$, $\log (I_t+B_t)$, $\log (C_{t-1}/L_{t-1})$, $\log (M_t/L_t)$, $\log (K_{t-1}/L_t)$, $\log (w_{t-1}/h_{t-1})$, $\log (w_{t-1}/p_{t-1}h_{t-1})$, $\log (p_{t-1}/p_{t-2})$, u, t, among which $\log L_t$ was not included in the list of predetermined variables used in the first stage of the two-stage-least-squares estimation procedure, because it is highly correlated with t.

[2] For example, see S. J. Prais and H. S. Houthakker, *The Analysis of Family Budgets* (Cambridge University Press, 1955).

we fitted an exponential (or a log-linear) consumption function to the observations.[1] It is seen from (2.1) that the elasticity of consumption with respect to national income is 0.349. The average propensity to consume, on the other hand, is 0.924 at the point of sample means. We find from these figures that the marginal propensity to consume is 0.322. (The average propensity to consume is simply computed as $\sum_t C_t / \sum_t Y_t$. We shall often calculate the marginal ratio from the elasticity, or the converse, by use of the average ratio at the point of sample means.) This value is lower than the figures obtained by such writers as Klein, Christ, Klein and Goldberger, and Griliches *et al.* for various sample periods. Most of them are greater than 0.5, but our estimate is comparable with Goldsmith's and Zellner's estimates of 0.36 and 0.375, respectively (see Table 1).

The value of $\partial(C/L)/\partial(M/pL)$, which measures the Pigovian effect, is computed as 0.202 at the point of sample means. The comparable findings by other economists are 0.348 by Goldsmith, 0.208 by Christ and 0.219 by Zellner. The corresponding coefficient in the Klein–Goldberger model is 0.024, a very small value which is significantly below Klein's survey estimate of 0.23.[2]

Consumers do not react immediately to changes in income and real balances; it takes a long time to achieve, say, 95 per cent of the full effects. In (2.1) the lagged consumption per capita represents the influence of the past on present consumer behaviour. Our estimate of the marginal effect of $(C/L)_{-1}$ on C/L is 0.467 at the point of sample means, which is significantly larger than those obtained by Christ, Klein and Goldberger, and Griliches *et al.*, but smaller than the estimate by Zellner. Once an estimate of the coefficient of the lagged consumption variable is given, 'short-run marginal

---

[1] Most of the other structural relations of the model also have theoretical or empirical grounds for being expressed by nonlinear functions. The relationship between the demand for money and the interest rate, the nonlinearity of which was one of the crucial points in Keynes' theory, was empirically investigated by means of the exponential function: see L. R. Klein and A. S. Goldberger, *An Econometric Model of the United States, 1929–1952* (North-Holland Publishing Co. 1955), and M. Bronfenbrenner and T. Mayer, 'Liquidity functions in the American economy', *Econometrica* (October 1960), pp. 810–34. Solow found that the results of statistical testing strongly confirmed the nonlinearity of the aggregate production function of GNP in the United States between 1919 and 1949. We assumed that each equation of the system had the log-linear form. See R. M. Solow, 'Technical change and the aggregate production function', *Review of Economics and Statistics* (August 1957), pp. 312–20.

It is well-known that Henry Moore in his *Synthetic Economics* (Macmillan, 1929) concentrated on a log-linearized general equilibrium model in order to test the Walrasian theory by means of statistical methods. Our analysis may be regarded as an application of his idea to the Keynesian system.

[2] See L. R. Klein *et al. Contributions of Survey Methods to Economics* (Columbia University Press, 1954).

propensity to consume', 'short-run Pigovian effect', and 'short-run price elasticity' are converted into the respective 'long-run' values by the familiar Klein–Goldberger method, i.e. by dividing each short-run coefficient by $(1 - \text{the coefficient of the lagged consumption variable})$. Table 1 shows that from the long-run point of view our estimates are not very different from the estimates obtained by Christ and Griliches *et al.*

We obtain from (2.1)

$$\log \frac{C_{t+q}/L_{t+q}}{C_t/L_t} = 0.349 \log \frac{Y_{t+q}/L_{t+q}}{Y_t/L_t} + 0.160 \log \frac{M_{t+q}/(p_{t+q}L_{t+q})}{M_t/(p_t L_t)}$$
$$+ 0.460 \log \frac{C_{t+q-1}/L_{t+q-1}}{C_{t-1}/L_{t-1}}, \quad (2.10)$$

i.e.

$$\log(1 + g_{C/L}) = 0.349 \log(1 + g_{Y/L}) + 0.160 \log(1 + g_{M/(pL)})$$
$$+ 0.460 \log(1 + g_{(C/L)_{-1}}),$$

where

$$\log(1 + g_{C/L}) = \frac{1}{q} \log \frac{C_{t+q}/L_{t+q}}{C_t/L_t},$$

$$\log(1 + g_{Y/L}) = \frac{1}{q} \log \frac{Y_{t+q}/L_{t+q}}{Y_t/L_t},$$

and so on; that is, $g_{C/L}$ is the average rate of growth of C_t/L_t over q years, $g_{Y/L}$ of Y_t/L_t and $g_{M/pL}$ of $M_t/p_t L_t$. As all gs are very small, we find that the following equation holds approximately:

$$g_{C/L} = 0.349 g_{Y/L} + 0.160 g_{M/pL} + 0.460 g_{(C/L)_{-1}}. \quad (2.11)$$

The average rate of growth of income is 1.33 per cent per year for the period 1902–52; those of real balances and lagged consumption are 1.95 and 1.66 per cent per year, respectively.[1] (Income, real balances and lagged consumption are measured per capita.) By use of (2.11) the rate of growth of consumption (per capita) is computed as 1.54 per cent per year, which is very close to the corresponding actual value, 1.55. We may say that

$$30[= (0.349 \times 1.33 \div 1.55) \times 100]$$

per cent of the growth of consumption in the period 1902–52 was due to the growth of income, 20 per cent to the growth of real balances, and 49 per cent to the growth of lagged consumption. As $g_{(C/L)_{-1}}$ approximates $g_{C/L}$, the contribution of the lagged consumption can be further analysed, by using the formula for computing the long-run effects, into the income and the real-

---

[1] Kuznets' concept of net national product gives a smaller figure in recent years than that of the Department of Commerce. Judgments about the growth rate of the American economy may have some Kuznets bias.

TABLE 1. *Marginal propensity to consume, the Pigovian effect, and the price elasticity of the consumption function of the United States*[a]

Investigator[b]	Period covered	Coefficients of					η_p (price elasticity)
		Y (real disposable income)	C_{-1} (real consumption lagged)	L (population)	t (time)	M/p (real balances)	
1. Goldsmith	1897–1949	0.36	—	—	—	0.348	—
2. Christ	1922–47[c]	0.512 (0.65)[f]	0.214	—	–0.21	0.208 (0.27)	–0.19 (–0.26)
3. Klein–Goldberger	1929–50[e]	[f]	0.23	0.36	—	0.024 (0.031)	—
4. Zellner	1947(I)–55(IV)[d]	0.375 (0.73)	0.489	—	—	0.219 (0.43)	–0.21 (–0.43)
5. Griliches et al.	1947(I)–60(IV)[d]	0.539 (0.73)	0.265	—	—	0.258 (0.35)	–0.21 (–0.35)
6. Valavanis-Vail	1869–1948	0.700[g] (1.02)	0.311	—	—	—	—
7. Morishima–Saito	1902–52[g]	0.322[g] (0.60)	0.467	0.427	—	0.202 (0.37)	–0.16 (–0.30)

[a] A more comprehensive summary of empirical findings is made available by Don Patinkin, *Money, Interest, and Prices* (Harper and Row, 1965), pp. 656–7. Figures in parentheses in the third and the last two columns of the table represent 'long-run marginal propensity to consume', 'long-run Pigovian effect' and 'long-run price elasticity', respectively.

[b] R. W. Goldsmith, *A Study of Saving in the United States* (Princeton University Press, 1956), vol. 3; C. Christ, 'A test of an econometric model for the United States, 1921–47', in *Conference on Business Cycles* (National Bureau of Economic Research, 1951); L. R. Klein and A. S. Goldberger, *An Econometric Model of the United States, 1929–1952* (North-Holland Publishing Co., 1955); A. Zellner, 'The short-run consumption function', *Econometrica* (October 1957); Z. Griliches, G. S. Maddala, R. Lucas and N. Wallace, 'Notes on estimated aggregate quarterly consumption function', *Econometrica* (July 1962); S. Valavanis-Vail, 'An econometric model of growth, U.S.A., 1869–1953', *American Economic Review, Papers and Proceedings* (May 1955).

[c] Excluding 1942–5.

[d] Excluding 1950(III) and 1951(I). Roman numerals in parentheses refer to quarters.

[e] Excluding 1941–5.

[f] Disposable income is decomposed into wage income, nonwage nonfarm income and farm income. Their coefficients are 0.62 (0.81), 0.46 (0.60), and 0.39 (0.51), respectively.

[g] Data refer to net national income.

balance effect. We find after this imputation that the growth of income explains 55 per cent of the entire growth of consumption per capita, while the growth of real balances explains 37 per cent.

Observations for the period 1941–6 show that real balances accumulated rapidly during the war (1941–5) and decreased in 1946–7. On the other hand, consumption per capita did not increase in the war period and grew very rapidly in 1945–6. The average rates of growth (in per cent) for 1941–6 are: $g_{C/L} = 3.60, g_{Y/L} = 2.07, g_{M/pL} = 9.55$, and $g_{(C/L)_{-1}} = 2.43$ per cent per year, on the basis of which we obtain an estimate of $g_{C/L} = 3.37$ per cent per year, which is again satisfactorily close to the actual value. We find that the second term on the right-hand side of (2.11) explains 42 per cent of the actual growth of consumption. Thus, in the war period the contribution of real balances to the growth of consumption was greater than the contribution of income (20 per cent) and the contribution of lagged consumption (31 per cent). We may say that the large amount of liquid assets which had been accumulated during the war played a very important role in the increase in consumption in 1946.[1]

One might be suspicious about taking cash balances as a proxy for wealth, as they comprise only about 10–20 per cent of total wealth. In order to defend the consumption function (2.1) from this possible criticism, we estimate an alternative consumption function of the form

$$\log\frac{C_t}{L_t} = c_1 \log\frac{Y_t}{L_t} + c_2 \log\frac{W_t}{L_t} + c_3 \log\frac{C_{t-1}}{L_{t-1}} + c_4 u + c_0,$$

where W_t represents the total national wealth (in 1929 prices, billions of dollars) in the middle of year t. The time-series data of W_t are obtained by averaging Goldsmith's two consecutive end-of-year data.[2] The result of the two-stage-least-squares estimation is

$$\log\frac{C_t}{L_t} = \underset{(4.7)}{0.340}\log\frac{Y_t}{L_t} + \underset{(1.2)}{0.162}\log\frac{W_t}{L_t}$$
$$+ \underset{(4.7)}{0.576}\log\frac{C_{t-1}}{L_{t-1}} + \underset{(1.5)}{0.022}u - \underset{(1.32)}{0.125} \quad (2.1')$$
$$\bar{R}^2 = 0.97, \quad \delta^2/S^2 = 1.71.$$

[1] For the postwar experiences of the inflationary pressures that were generated by liquid assets accumulated during the war, see A. J. Brown, *The Great Inflation: 1939–51* (Oxford University Press, 1955), Chapter x and J. G. Gurley, 'Excess liquidity and European monetary reforms, 1944–52', *American Economic Review* (March 1953).

[2] The data for total national wealth are available, for the years 1900–40, in Goldsmith, *op. cit.* Table W-3, column (1), p. 20, and, for 1945–52, in his *The National Wealth of the U.S. in the Postwar Period* (Princeton University Press, 1962), Table A-2, column (1), p. 114, in 1947–9 prices. In the conversion of the latter series into the one in 1929 prices, the ratio of the 1947–9 prices to the 1929 prices is taken as 0.573.

Comparing (2.1) and (2.1′) and neglecting errors, we have

$$\log \frac{M_t}{p_t L_t} = -0.056 \log \frac{Y_t}{L_t} + 1.013 \log \frac{W_t}{L_t} + 0.725 \log \frac{C_{t-1}}{L_{t-1}}$$
$$+ 1.375u - 0.825.$$

In this analysis we find, in view of the fact that W_t is four or six times as large as C_t, that $\log W_t/L_t$ is the dominant factor; in this sense $\log M_t/p_t L_t$ may be considered as a proxy for $\log W_t/L_t$.

(2) *The liquidity preference function*

Although production, trading, and consumption are happening every day of the year, we treat our basic period, the year, for the sake of simplicity, as if it were a kind of Hicks' Week. There is only one day in each year (say 1 January) when markets and banks are open. Plans concerning consumption and holding of money balances for the year are made at breakfast time that day and are carried out during the rest of the year in accordance with these decisions. Theoretical studies by various scholars (notably Patinkin) show that real balances may be considered as depending on price changes, the rate of interest and the sum of the real income and the real value of the total initial endowment; and consumption is related not only to income but also to the holdings of money thus determined, as (2.1) in fact confirms.

As a proxy for the real value of the total initial endowment we may take the real value of money balances in the previous period. Then we may estimate the equation

$$\log \frac{M_t}{p_t} = m_1 \log \left(Y_t + \frac{M_{t-1}}{p_t} \right) + m_2 \log r_t + m_3 \log \frac{p_t}{p_{t-1}} + m_0,$$

or

$$\log \frac{M_t}{p_t} = m_1 \left(0.586 \log Y_t + 0.414 \log \frac{M_{t-1}}{p_t} + 0.295 \right)$$
$$+ m_2 \log r_t + m_3 \log \frac{p_t}{p_{t-1}} + m_0. \quad (2.2')$$

In the latter, $\log [Y_t + (M_{t-1}/p_t)]$ is linearized around the sample means of the variables Y_t and M_{t-1}/p_t by the same method as we used to put (2.8) in the linear form (2.8′) (see note 1, p. 7).

In estimating (2.2′) we take account of the fact that during the years 1941–51 the Federal Reserve continued to maintain easy-money conditions through its pegging policy for yields on government securities. It is very likely that a quick rise in the Treasury bill rate after the war, especially after the Treasury–Federal Reserve accord, might have given a downward shift to the liquidity preference function (2.2′), in which the corporate bond yield is the sole interest-rate variable. We, therefore, introduce a dummy variable u, which takes on values of 0 before 1941 and 1 after 1946.

Many econometricians have followed A. J. Brown in including a price change variable, in addition to an interest variable, in the explanation of cash holdings.[1] The rate of interest has an effect on the choice between cash and bonds, whereas prospective price increases (which show the extent to which capital gains can be made) give rise to the purchase of capital equipment or to an increase in inventories against cash or bonds. Expectations of prospective price increases may be assumed to depend on the present level of business. However, since it was found that the coefficient of $\log p_t/p_{t-1}$ was not statistically significant, no price change variable is retained in the final form of our liquidity preference function.

In Table 2 our estimates are compared with estimates obtained by other investigators. The definitions of money and the variables used for explanation vary from study to study. From the point of view of the data used, our investigation is very close to Klein's, although he disaggregates the total money balances into M_1 (demand deposits and circulating currency) and M_2 (time deposits). Our short-run elasticity of M/p with respect to the interest rate, -0.20, is practically the same as the elasticity, -0.21, resulting from Klein's equation, whilst for the income elasticity, no such remarkable conformity is found between the two studies.

In relation to the study by Bronfenbrenner and Mayer, it is seen that our estimate is more elastic than theirs with respect to a change in income and a change in the interest rate but less elastic than theirs with respect to a change in the lagged variable M_{-1}/p. The underestimation of the effect of M_{-1}/p on M/p counteracts the overestimation of the short-run income and the short-run interest elasticity in calculating the respective long-run elasticities. It is not surprising that our study and the Bronfenbrenner–Mayer study give very close long-run income and interest elasticities in spite of the big differences in the short-run elasticities.

Finally, putting $M/p = M_{-1}/p$ in (2.2), we get

$$0.507 \log \frac{M}{p} = 0.698 \log Y - 0.202 \log r - 0.0484u - 0.299.$$

Therefore,

$$\log \frac{M}{pY} = \frac{0.191}{0.507} \log Y - \frac{0.202}{0.507} \log r - \frac{0.0484}{0.507} u - \frac{0.299}{0.507}$$

[1] See A. J. Brown, 'Interest, prices, and the demand schedule for idle money', *Oxford Economic Papers* (May, 1939); Klein and Goldberger, *op. cit.*; R. T. Selden, 'Monetary velocity in the United States', *Studies in the Quantity Theory of Money*, M. Friedman, ed. (University of Chicago Press, 1956); Bronfenbrenner and Mayer, *op. cit.*; and L. R. Klein and Y. Shinkai, 'An econometric model of Japan, 1930–59', *International Economic Review* (January 1963).

TABLE 2. *Liquidity preference functions of the United States*

Investigator[a]	Period covered	Explained variable[b]	Form of equation	Coefficients of[c]								Elasticities[d]			
												(short-run)		(long-run)	
				Y	i	i_{-1}	K	Δp	M_{-1}	Y_{-1}	t	η_Y	η_i	η_Y	η_i
Klein	1921–41[e]	M_1	linear	0.23^j	—	-0.92^m	—	—	—	0.02^j	-0.95	*	*	0.61	*
		M_2	linear	—	-1.00^m	—	—	—	0.84	—	-0.26	*	-0.21	*	-2.48
Klein–Goldberger	1929–50[e]	$M_3 - 0.14Y^h$	log-linear	—	-0.84^n	—	—	—	—	—	—	*	*	*	-1.06
		M_4	linear	0.24^k	-0.69^n	—	—	-0.27	0.64	—	—	0.45	-0.047	1.24	-0.13
Bronfenbrenner–Mayer	1919–56[f]	$M_5 - Y/4.022^i$	log-linear	—	-0.277^n	—	0.827	—	0.716	—	—	*	-0.28	*	-0.98
	1919–56	M_5	log-linear	0.344^i	-0.093^n	—	-0.116	—	0.722	—	—	0.34	-0.093	1.24	-0.33
Morishima–Saito	1902–52[g]	M/p	log-linear	0.698^l	-0.202^m	—	—	—	0.493^o	—	—	0.70	-0.20	1.38	-0.40

[a] L. R. Klein, *Economic Fluctuations in the United States, 1921–41,* (John Wiley and Sons, 1950); L. R. Klein and A. S. Goldberger, *op. cit.;* and M. Bronfenbrenner and T. Mayer, *op. cit.*

[b] M_1 = demand deposits and circulating currency, averaged during the year, measured in billions of current dollars,

M_2 = time deposits, averaged during the year, measured in billions of current dollars,

M_3 = personal holdings of currency, demand and time deposits, savings-and-loan-association shares and US Government securities, at the end of period, measured in billions of 1929 dollars,

M_4 = business holdings of currency, demand and time deposits, savings-and-loan-association shares and US Government securities, at the end of period, measured in billions of 1929 dollars,

M_5 = personal and business holdings of currency and demand deposits, at the end of year, measured in billions of 1929 dollars,

M = total deposits (demand and time) adjusted, and currency outside banks, on June 30th of each year, measured in billions of current dollars.

[c] Y = income, i = interest rate (%), K = total national net worth in 1929 dollars, p = price index, Δp = price change, M_{-1} = lagged money balances, t = time trend.

[d] η_Y = income elasticity, η_i = interest elasticity.

[e] Excluding 1942–5.

[f] Excluding 1926–27.

[g] Excluding 1941–5.

[h] Y = disposable income in current dollars.

[i] Y = private GNP in 1929 dollars.

[j] Y = NNP in current dollars.

[k] Y = wage income in 1929 dollars.

[l] Y = NNP including government in 1929 dollars.

[m] i = long-term interest rate (corporate bond yield).

[n] i = short-term interest rate (4–6 months commercial paper rate).

[o] Coefficient of M_{-1}/p.

* Not calculated.

which implies that the long-run interest elasticity of the Cambridge coefficient $k(= M/pY)$ is 0.398 ($= 0.202/0.507$). The marginal effect of a change in the interest rate on the velocity of circulation, $\partial(pY/M)/\partial r$, is then estimated at 0.132 at the point of sample means. This value is comparable with Valavanis-Vail's corresponding estimate, 0.152, for the period 1869–1953.[1]

(3) *The production function and the relative share equation*

We have followed Klein and Kosobud by adopting a Cobb–Douglas type production function which is homogeneous of degree one in labour and capital and allows for technological change with a time trend. We differ from them, however, in using a measure of manhours worked, instead of the number of workers, as a labour input measure and in using a dummy variable to represent the shift in the production function during World War II. We also follow Klein and Kosobud in accepting the finding that there is no trend in the relative share of labour.[2] Equation (2.3) is obtained on the assumption that factors are paid their marginal products.

We may be accused of implicitly supporting the neoclassical theory of growth by adopting a well-behaved production function. In a sense we are open to such a criticism. In fact, in a recent symposium, neoclassical and non-neoclassical economists confirmed that the traditional concept of the stock of capital is of little use in undertaking economic investigations dealing with the long run; that if neoclassical economists reluctantly recognize this fact and even if non-neoclassical economists reluctantly recognize the concept of capital, there is no well-behaved aggregate production function which permits substitution between labour and capital, unless a number of restrictive assumptions are satisfied, and, therefore, that the marginal productivity rule, as a theory of income distribution, should be rejected at the aggregate level.[3] Accordingly, we must be prepared to accept that we are likely to introduce certain theoretical errors as soon as we decide to assume the Cobb–Douglas function.

However, we hope that non-neoclassical economists will not condemn us to capital punishment. In estimating equations (2.1)–(2.7), we purposely treated gross investment as exogenous; investment determines savings in our system, and not vice versa, as in neoclassical growth models. No tendency to full utilization of capital, nor to full employment, is inherent in our system, although we can generate, as we shall do in Chapter 4 below,

---

[1] See Valavanis-Vail, *op. cit.* p. 210.

[2] The series on wages and labour's share include income from self-employment. This may overstate the size of labour's share and the labour exponent of the Cobb–Douglas function in comparison with the usual estimates. See Klein and Kosobud, *op. cit.* pp. 180–4.

[3] *Quarterly Journal of Economics*, November 1966. Also, see Morishima, *Theory of Economic Growth* (Oxford, 1969), Chapters V and VI.

the full-employment–full-capacity growth by assuming that gross invest-ment increases from period to period according to some particular law. Accordingly, as we shall also see in Chapter 4, the full-employment–full-capacity growth thus generated will collapse, like an avalanche, as soon as gross investment ceases to obey the neoclassical law of growth.

In Table 3 our estimate of the rate of technical progress is compared with the estimates of other authorities. It is seen, first of all, that our figure, 1.47 per cent per year, is very close to Solow's, 1.5, but significantly higher than the Klein–Kosobud estimate and lower than either the Bodkin–Klein or the Arrow–Chenery–Minhas–Solow estimate. The reason why Klein and Kosobud obtained a low figure is that they did not take into account the apparent downward trend in hours worked per person, while the reason why Bodkin and Klein, and Arrow, Chenery, Minhas and Solow obtained higher figures than ours is that they were concerned with the shift in the production function of the private, non-farm GNP, while our aggregate output includes government and farm output. It is further noticed that our estimate is com-parable with various figures which Bodkin and Klein obtained without making the assumption of constant returns to scale.

The same procedure which we followed to derive (2.11) from (2.1) is applied to (2.3) and yields

$$g_{Y/hN} = 0.0147 + 0.176 g_{K/hN},\qquad\qquad(2.12)$$

where $g_{Y/hN}$ is the average rate of growth of output per manhour, and $g_{K/hN}$ of the capital–labour ratio. The average rates of growth, $g_{Y/hN}$ and $g_{K/hN}$, for the period 1902–52, excluding 1941–5, are 1.86 and 1.21 per cent respectively. These values fulfil (2.12) with a small error.

Similarly, we have from (2.3)

$$g_{K/Y} = 0.824 g_{K/hN} - 0.0147.\qquad\qquad(2.13)$$

Putting $g_{K/hN} = 1.21$ per cent, we get $g_{K/Y} = -0.47$ per cent, which is higher than the Klein–Kosobud estimate (-0.66 per cent) obtained for the same period *including* the war period by a simple trend analysis.

(4) *The wage determination equation*

We have used a log-linear version of the Christ–Phillips type of wage determi-nation equation. There are three variables to explain the wage rate, w_t/h_t, which measures hourly earnings averaged over the year t. They are the lagged wage rate, the employment ratio, and the lagged rate of price change;[1] the

---

[1] Cf. C. Christ, *op. cit.* pp. 65–6 and 71–89. His equation (unlike ours) explicitly includes a time trend, and takes into account the influences of unemployment and price changes in terms of differences and not ratios.

TABLE 3. *Estimates of the rate of technical progress*

Investigator[a]	Period covered	Type of production function[b]	Error terms[c]	Output	Labour input	Capital input	Annual rate of technical progress (%)
Solow	1909–49	NS[d]	no	private,	manhours	utilized	1.5
	1909–29		error	nonfarm		capital	1.1
	1930–49		term	GNP			2.25
Klein–Kosobud	1900–53	CD[d]	×	NNP[g]	persons engaged	existing capital	1.08
Bodkin–Klein	1909–49	CD[d]	× +	private, nonfarm GNP	manhours	utilized capital	1.64 1.73
Morishima–Saito	1902–52[f]	CD[d]	×	NNP[g]	manhours	existing capital	1.47
Arrow–Chenery–Minhas–Solow	1909–49	CES[d]	×	private, nonfarm GNP	manhours	utilized capital	1.83
David–Klundert	1899–1960	CES[e]	×	private, domestic GNP[h]	manhours	utilized capital	1.85
Valavanis-Vail	1869–1948	CD	×	GNP[g]	manhours	existing capital and land	0.75
Bodkin–Klein	1909–49	CD CD CES CES	× + × +	private, nonfarm GNP	manhours	utilized capital	1.12 1.22 1.49 1.37

[a] R. M. Solow, *op. cit.*; L. R. Klein and R. F. Kosobud, *op. cit.*; R. G. Bodkin and L. R. Klein, 'Nonlinear estimation of aggregate production function', *Review of Economics and Statistics*, (February 1967); K. J. Arrow, H. B. Chenery, B. S. Minhas, and R. M. Solow, 'Capital labour substitution and economic efficiency', *Review of Economics and Statistics*, (August 1961); P. A. David and Th. van de Klundert, 'Biased efficiency growth and capital–labor substitution in the U.S., 1899–1960', *American Economic Review* (June 1965); S. Valavanis-Vail, *op. cit.*

[b] NS = not specified, CD = Cobb–Douglas type, CES = constant-elasticity-of-substitution type.

[c] × = multiplicative error term, + = additive error term.

[d] Constant returns to scale.

[e] Constant returns to scale + factor augmenting type of technical progress.

[f] Excluding 1941–6.

[g] Including government and farm output.

[h] Including farm output.

lagged wage variable represents an inertia effect, i.e. that the wage rate established in the previous period tends to be regarded as a standard on which wage negotiations in the current period are based. The employment ratio measures the supply–demand situation in the labour market.[1] The greater the ratio, the stronger will be the bargaining position of workers, and the wage rate will be raised. Finally, a greater price increase in the recent past will result in a greater wage increase. We assume that the wage increase, $(w_t/h_t)/(w_{t-1}/h_{t-1})$, in year t depends on the price increase, $p_{t-\theta}/p_{t-\theta-1}$. Defining $p_{t-\theta}/p_{t-\theta-1}$ as the weighted geometric average of the current price change p_t/p_{t-1} and the price change in the last year p_{t-1}/p_{t-2}, with weights $1-\theta$ and θ respectively, we find that the regression equation fits the data best when $\theta = \frac{4}{5}$ (i.e. 9.6 months).

Our wage determination equation follows from the basic hypothesis of elementary price theory that the rate of increase of the wage rate is a decreasing function of the unemployment ratio, or an increasing function of the employment ratio. In other words, we have

$$\frac{w_t/h_t}{w_t^*/h_t^*} = k\left(\frac{N_t}{0.57L_t}\right)^{\gamma} \quad (k > 0,\ \gamma > 0),$$

where w_t^*/h_t^* denotes the rate of wages from which the negotiations start in period t. Taking the inertia and the past-price effect into account, we may write

$$\frac{w_t^*}{h_t^*} = a\left(\frac{w_{t-1}}{h_{t-1}}\right)^{\alpha}, \quad k = b\left(\frac{p_{t-\frac{4}{5}}}{p_{t-1-\frac{4}{5}}}\right)^{\beta},$$

respectively. Hence we obtain

$$\frac{w_t}{h_t} = m\left(\frac{w_{t-1}}{h_{t-1}}\right)^{\alpha}\left(\frac{p_{t-\frac{4}{5}}}{p_{t-1-\frac{4}{5}}}\right)^{\beta}\left(\frac{N_t}{0.57L_t}\right)^{\gamma},$$

where $m = ab$. This is the rationale of the wage-determination equation (2.5).

Equation (2.5) can be put in the form:

$$\log\frac{w_t/h_t}{w_{t-1}/h_{t-1}} = 0.006\log\frac{w_{t-1}}{h_{t-1}} + 0.456\left(\frac{1}{5}\log\frac{p_t}{p_{t-1}} + \frac{4}{5}\log\frac{p_{t-1}}{p_{t-2}}\right)$$

$$+ 0.188\log\frac{N_t}{0.57L_t} + 0.017. \quad (2.14)$$

---

[1] We assume that the full employment level of labour is 57 per cent of 'population of fifteen years of age and over'. It is true that there is a declining tendency in the ratio of the potential labour force to the population L, but it has only a minor significance. In fact, our figures of unemployment calculated from $0.57L-N$ are very near to other statistics, e.g. S. Lebergott's estimate. See S. Lebergott, 'Annual estimates of unemployment in the United States, 1900–1950', *The Measurement and Behaviour of Unemployment* (Princeton University Press, 1957).

TABLE 4. *Wage determination equations of the United States*

Investigator[a]	Period covered	Explained variable	Form of equation	Coefficients of						
				lagged wage rate	unemployment	employ-ment ratio	price change	lagged price change	time trend	percent of wage earners unionized
Christ	1922–47[b]	w	linear	0.73	−0.011	—	0.81	—	0.005	—
Klein–Goldberger	1929–50[b]	Δw	linear	1.0	−0.75	—	—	0.56	0.56	—
Valavanis–Vail	1869–1948	Δw	linear	1.0	—	0.438	0.240	—	—	0.57
Bodkin	1914–57[c]	Δw^e	linear	1.0	−0.252 × 10⁻⁵	—	0.595 × 10⁻²f	—	0.221 × 10⁻²	—
Morishima–Saito	1902–52[d]	w	log-linear	1.006	—	0.188	—	0.456g	—	—

Elasticities with respect to

Investigator[a]	unemployment ratio	price change	lagged price change	$\Delta w/w_{-1}$ when $U = 0$,[h] and $\Delta p = \Delta p_{-1} = 0$	U^h (when $\Delta w = 0$ and $\Delta p = \Delta p_{-1} = 0$)	R^i	U^h (when $\Delta w/w_{-1} = \Delta(Y/N)/(Y/N)_{-1}$ and $\Delta p = \Delta p_{-1} = 0$)	R^i	$\Delta w/w_{-1}$
Christ	−0.495	0.878	—	0.089	8.6	0.180	7.1	0.150	0.015
Klein–Goldberger	−0.283	—	0.451	0.064	12.6	0.225	8.5	0.152	0.021
Valavanis–Vail	—	—	—	—	—	—	—	—	—
Bodkin	−0.160	0.723	—	0.049	16.0	0.308	7.9	0.152	0.025
Morishima–Saito	−0.204	0.093	0.372	0.036	8.0	0.173	4.0	0.088	0.019

[a] C. Christ, *op. cit.*; L. R. Klein and A. S. Goldberger, *op. cit.*; S. Valavanis-Vail, *op. cit.*; R. G. Bodkin, *The Wage–Price–Productivity Nexus* (University of Pennsylvania Press, 1966).
[b] Excluding 1942–5.
[c] Excluding 1934, 1945, and 1951.
[d] Excluding 1941–5.
[e] w = wage in manufacturing.
[f] Change in consumer price index.
[g] Lagged rate of price change =
$\log(p_{t-\frac{1}{2}}/p_{t-1-\frac{1}{2}}) = \frac{1}{2}\log(p_t/p_{t-1}) + \frac{4}{5}\log(p_{t-1}/p_{t-2})$.
[h] U = unemployment (millions of persons).
[i] R = rate of unemployment.

In the case of $N_t/(0.57L_t) = 1$ and $p_t/p_{t-1} = p_{t-1}/p_{t-2} = 1$, the second, third and fourth terms vanish, and (2.14) yields $(w_t/h_t)/(w_{t-1}/h_{t-1}) = 1.036$ at the point of sample means where $w_{t-1}/h_{t-1} = 0.489$. In words, when the price level remains unchanged, full employment of labour is associated with a growth rate of wages of 3.6 per cent per year. On the other hand, when $p_t/p_{t-1} = p_{t-1}/p_{t-2} = 1$, and $w_t/h_t = w_{t-1}/h_{t-1} = 0.489$, we have

$$N_t/(0.57L_t) = 0.826.$$

This implies about 8 million persons unemployed (for the sample mean of the labour force), which is comparable to Klein's estimate (6–7 million persons).[1] When the wage rate, w/h, is allowed to go up at the same rate as the productivity trend (i.e. at the rate of 1.86 per cent per year), the employment ratio associated with price stability is computed as 0.912, a figure which is still far from the goal of full employment. Table 4 compares these results with those derived from other econometric studies. Although ours are found to be the most modest, they still show that stable prices and wages will result in substantial unemployment.

Substituting for p from (2.4), the wage determination equation (2.5) can be rewritten, under the assumption that

$$(Y/hN)_t/(Y/hN)_{t-1} = (Y/hN)_{t-1}/(Y/hN)_{t-2},$$

as
$$\log\frac{w}{h} = 1.408 \log\left(\frac{w}{h}\right)_{-1} - 0.402 \log\left(\frac{w}{h}\right)_{-2}$$
$$- 0.502 \log(1 + g_{Y/hN}) + 0.207 \log\frac{N}{0.57L} + 0.019, \quad (2.15)$$

where $g_{Y/hN}$ stands for the rate of growth of the productivity of labour. When the wage rates per hour in period $t-1$ and $t-2$, $(w/h)_{-1}$ and $(w/h)_{-2}$, and the rate of increase in the productivity of labour, $g_{Y/hN}$, are given, (2.15) gives w/h as an increasing function of $N/0.57L$. We also have from (2.4)

$$\log\frac{p}{p_{-1}} = \log\frac{w/h}{(w/h)_{-1}} - \log\frac{Y/hN}{(Y/hN)_{-1}}. \quad (2.16)$$

Hence p/p_{-1} is an increasing function of $N/0.57L$; that is to say, the rate of increase in the price level, $\Delta p/p_{-1}$, is a decreasing function of the unemployment ratio, $1 - N/0.57L$.

In Figure 1, the solid curve for 1902, which is practically a straight line,

[1] See L. R. Klein, 'The empirical foundations of Keynesian economics', in *Post Keynesian Economics*, K. K. Kurihara, ed. (George Allen and Unwin, 1955), p. 308.

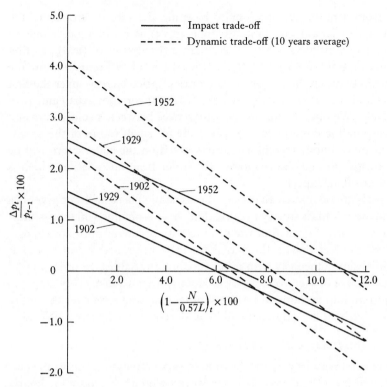

Figure 1

The estimated relationship, for 1902, 1929 and 1952, between the predicted rate of inflation and the unemployment rate.

was obtained by fixing $(w/h)_{-1}$ and $(w/h)_{-2}$ at the actual values in 1901 and 1900, respectively, and $1 + g_{Y/hN}$ at the geometric mean of the quotients, $(Y/hN)_t/(Y/hN)_{t-1}$, over the period 1902–52. Similarly, the solid curves for 1929 and 1952 were traced out on the basis of the actual values of w/h in 1928 and 1927, and in 1951 and 1950, respectively, but, as for $g_{Y/hN}$, the geometric mean of the rates of growth of the productivity of labour over the period 1930–52 was used in calculating both curves. It is clear from the figure that there is a big shift of the curve between 1929 and 1952; it shows that the dilemma between full employment and price stability is more serious in 1952 than in 1929. It is also noted that our curve for 1952 lies in a position which is comparable with the position of the corresponding curve obtained by Bodkin, but our curve is steeper than his.[1]

The relationship between unemployment of labour and price rises can be

---

[1] See R. G. Bodkin, *op. cit.*

viewed from a more dynamic angle. Keeping the rate of growth of the productivity of labour constant, we treat (2.15) as a difference equation regarding the hourly wage rate. We obtain a time series of $(w/h)_t$, so that (2.16) gives a time series of $\Delta p_t/p_{t-1}$. Dotted curves in Figure 1 show the relationship between the average of the rates of price increase over the first ten years and the rate of unemployment of labour for 1902, 1929 and 1952 respectively. We observe substantial differences between a solid curve and the corresponding dotted curve, particularly for small values of the unemployment ratio. Policy recommendations based on the static curve will be too optimistic, so that the economy will suffer from an inflation which is more serious than expected.

It must be remembered that even the dynamic curve will not give us a correct answer. This is simply because that curve is obtained on the assumption that the rate of growth of the productivity of labour does not change, in spite of the fact that in the actual world the productivity of labour is determined simultaneously with other economic variables. In order to find the correct value of the productivity of labour, we must take every equation in the system into account and make simulations extending over the entire economy. Such an investigation will be undertaken in Chapter 4 below.

(5) *Hours worked equation*

There are good reasons why the decision to vary employment of people may be separated from the decision to vary working hours. Suppose the hourly wage rate is increased in period t at the rate $d(w/h)_t/dh_t$, because the hours worked are increased by an hour. The change is positive because an increased wage is paid for overtime work. When $d(w/h)_t/dh_t$ becomes greater, entrepreneurs will save wages by increasing the number of workers employed and decreasing the hours worked per man. On the other hand, if there is an excess demand for men, they will make a given number of persons work more intensively by lengthening working hours. Let h_t^D be the demand for hours by entrepreneurs; we have

$$\log h_t^D = l\,d(w/h)_t/dh_t + m \log{(N/0.57L)_t} + n,$$

where $l < 0$, and $m > 0$; the employment ratio is used as a measure of the supply–demand relation in the market for men.

As for the supply of hours, h_t^S, by workers, we assume that it increases if $d(w/h)_t/dh_t$ increases. We also assume that it depends negatively on the real wage rate per hour. This implies that the supply curve of labour is backward-sloping; the income effect of an increase in the real wage rate on the supply of labour (or the marginal propensity to have leisure) is so strong that it dominates the substitution effect. We assume that there is a time lag of one year between an increase in the real wage rate and the corresponding decline in working hours. We have

$$\log h_t^S = a\, \mathrm{d}\left(\frac{w}{h}\right)_t \bigg/ \mathrm{d} h_t + b \log \frac{w_{t-1}}{p_{t-1}h_{t-1}} + c,$$

where $a > 0$, and $b > 0$.

Equating h_t^D with h_t^S, we obtain from these equations

$$\log h_t = \frac{-lb}{a-l}\log\frac{w_{t-1}}{p_{t-1}h_{t-1}} + \frac{am}{a-l}\log\,(N/0.57L)_t + \frac{na-cl}{a-l}.$$

Equation (2.6) is an estimate of this reduced form and fulfils the sign requirements: $-lb(a-l) < 0$ and $am/(a-l) > 0$.

Valavanis-Vail considered the decline in working hours as autonomous and found that the supply of labour is downward-sloping, in the sense that an increase in real income per capita diminishes the ratio of persons employed to the potential labour force.[1] Over a long period trade unions have undoubtedly brought great pressures to bear on entrepreneurs to shorten working hours, but they would not have succeeded in doing so if the rise in real wages had not been an incentive for the members of the trade unions to have more leisure.

(6) *The depreciation equation*

We assume that some depreciation, depending on the size of the stock of capital, occurs regardless of the degree of utilization of capital. As the coefficient of $\log K_{t-1}$ is greater than one, an increase in the stock of capital accelerates the ratio of depreciation to the stock of capital.

(7) *Investment and trade balance*

Various writers have suggested many economic forms of the investment function, usually using profits, the increment of output, the rate of interest, etc. as key explanatory variables. In this study, however, we purposely adopt the crudest assumption, regarding investment as exogenous. It is of course true that fluctuations of gross investment could be explained, to some extent, by those economic variables suggested by the usual theories of investment. But that part of investment which changes automatically due to technological innovations, or for political reasons, and so forth, is so dominant that we can hardly find an investment function which is statistically tolerably fitted to the data.

In the United States economy the trade balance is a small component of

[1] S. Valavanis-Vail, *op. cit.*

national product. (The ratio of trade balance to net national product is usually less than 2 per cent in years other than those belonging to two exceptional periods, 1915–21 and 1946–7.) Its fluctuations depend not only on economic variables, such as foreign and domestic disposable incomes and relative prices of foreign and domestic products, but also on the external politics of the United States.

(8) *The equation between savings and investment and the equation of capital accumulation*

In Kuznets' series government expenditures are allocated to either consumption or investment spending, if they are not eliminated from the net national product as intermediate expenditures. The equality between net national product and final purchases (or the equality between savings and investment) may, therefore, be written as (2.8).

The final equation (2.9) simply states that the increment of the stock of capital equals net investment, i.e. gross investment minus depreciation.

3. Short-run properties of the model

The significance of Keynesian economics from the viewpoint of economic policy lies in revealing the advantage of public investment policy over traditional monetary policy as a measure to promote full employment. Econometrically, the effectiveness of a proposal for curing unemployment is judged by the magnitude of the corresponding 'multiplier', i.e. by the rate of change in employment with respect to the strategic variable of that policy. In this chapter we shall present empirical estimates of responses in national product and employment to a unit increase in investment and to a unit increase in the quantity of money, by use of the reduced form derived from the structural equations. Our investigation supports Keynes' contention.

Keynes suggested two forms of multipliers which give the *absolute* effect of a unit increase in investment, and the proportionate effect of a given percentage change in investment, respectively.[1] Of these two, the former is constant and the latter is variable if the structural system is linear, and vice versa if it is log-linear. In our system, equations (2.1)–(2.7) are all log-linear, but (2.8) is not log-linear. We may, however, use (2.8′) (in note 1, p. 7, above) as a log-linear approximation to (2.8). The reduced form of the system consisting of (2.1)–(2.7) and (2.8′) is log-linear in predetermined (exogenous and lagged endogenous) variables. Therefore, *impact* (*one year*) *multipliers*[2] of the quantity of money or investment on national product, employment, etc. are constant in terms of elasticity, but the estimate of the multipliers depends on the values of $\bar{C}/\bar{Y}$, $(\bar{I}+\bar{B})/\bar{Y}$, and $\bar{D}/\bar{Y}$ at which (2.8) is log-linearized.

Let X_t be a column vector with components $Y_t, C_t, D_t, N_t, p_t, w_t, r_t$, and h_t, and let Z_t be a column vector with components $M_t, (I+B)_t, L_t, M_{t-1}, L_{t-1}, C_{t-1}, K_{t-1}, p_{t-1}, p_{t-2}, w_{t-1}$, and h_{t-1}. Equations (2.1)–(2.7) and (2.8′) can be written in the form:

$$A \log X_t + B \log Z_t + ct + du + e = 0, \tag{3.1}$$

[1] J. M. Keynes, *The General Theory of Employment, Interest and Money* (Macmillan, 1936). He stressed the fact that one should consider not only the absolute effect of investment on national income but also the proportionate effect when we compare the multiplier effect in a wealthy community with that in a poor community, pp. 125–8.

[2] For the definition of impact multiplier, see A. S. Goldberger, *Impact Multipliers and Dynamic Properties of the Klein–Goldberger Model* (North-Holland Publishing Co. 1959), p. 20.

where A and B are matrices of structural coefficients, and c, d, and e (column vectors) stand for the trend coefficients, the dummy coefficients and the constant terms, respectively. Solving (3.1) with respect to X_t, we have the reduced form of our model:

$$\log X_t = F \log Z_t + gt + hu + i, \tag{3.2}$$

or $$X_t = \log^{-1}(F \log Z_t + gt + hu + i), \tag{3.3}$$

where $F = -A^{-1}B$, $g = -A^{-1}c$, $h = -A^{-1}d$, and $i = -A^{-1}e$.

I. EX POST FORECASTING

Before proceeding to the business of estimating multipliers, we may examine the explanatory effectiveness of our model over the period 1902–60. In this investigation we use, instead of the log-linear approximation (2.8′), the original linear equation (2.8). We are then confronted with the original system which is non-log-linear as well as non-linear; but simple iterative computations enable us to find the values of the endogenous variables once the values of the predetermined variables are given. The so-called final method of *ex post* forecasting does not require any information other than observed values of the exogenous variables for each sample year and values of lagged endogenous variables for the first year, 1902. Values for the lagged endogenous variables in successive years are supplied by past forecasts.[1] Confronting *ex post* forecast values of the endogenous variables obtained by the final method with their observed values, we find that our model, considered as a dynamic system, is tolerably effective in explaining the growth of the American economy in the post-sample period 1953–60, as well as in the sample period 1902–52.[2] In fact, within the sample period, *ex post* forecasts of national product, consumption, hours worked, and the stock of capital are fairly close to their observed values. It is true that price, wage, and interest rate are not forecast as well as the other variables, but the computed values do follow the general drift of the actual values, if not their cyclical movements. See Figure 2.

We may alternatively investigate the explanatory effectiveness of our model over the sample period by the 'total' method in which the observed values of exogenous and lagged endogenous variables are utilized in

---

[1] See A. S. Goldberger, *op. cit.* pp. 49–51.

[2] Forecasting in the post-sample period makes a new start in 1953; the initial values of lagged endogenous variables are observed values for 1953 and not values computed by forecasting in the sample period. Many of the series for the period 1953–60 are extrapolated from US Department of Commerce data and Kendrick's preliminary estimates. We wish to express our thanks to Professor Kendrick for giving us permission to use his estimates.

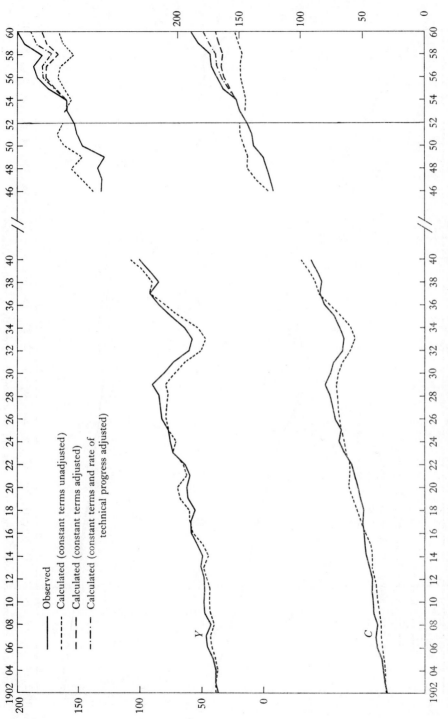

Figure 2a Comparison between the actual series and those computed from the system of equations.

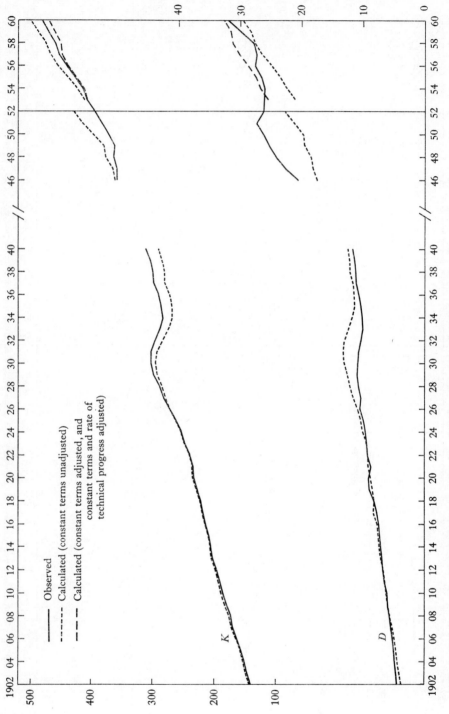

Figure 2b Comparison between the actual series and those computed from the system of equations.

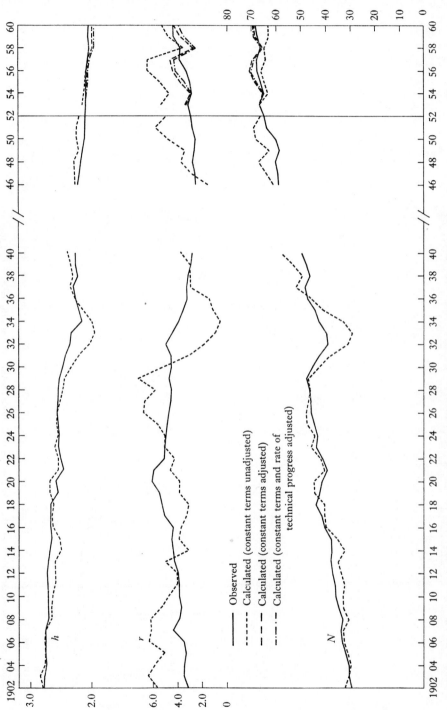

Figure 2c Comparison between the actual series and those computed from the system of equations.

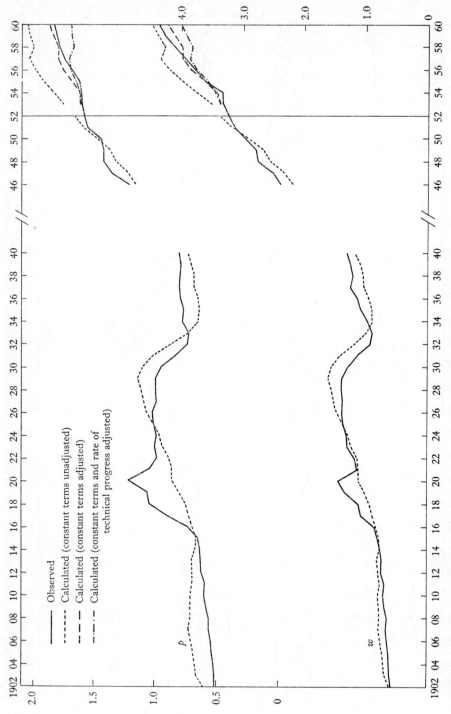

Figure 2d Comparison between the actual series and those computed from the system of equations

calculating values of the current endogenous variables. We avoid the log-linearization of (2.8) into (2.8') in order to get better forecasts and solve the non-linear system (2.1)–(2.8) with respect to X_t by the iterative method. The total forecast change in endogenous variable x_i from year $t-1$ to year t, $\hat{x}_{it} - \hat{x}_{it-1}$, thus obtained is compared with the actual change, $x_{it} - x_{it-1}$, for each of the eight variables. Out of the 44 annual observations, the direction of change of GNP was correctly forecast 39 times, that of employment 35 times, that of prices 34 times, that of wages 36 times, and that of the interest rate 28 times. The proportion of correctly forecast turning points to actually observed ones is 90 per cent for GNP, 88 per cent for employment, 50 per cent for prices, 42 per cent for wages and 72 per cent for the rate of interest. Seemingly, these results are better than the corresponding results from the Klein–Goldberger model, but it must be noticed that in our model, gross investment is regarded as exogenous, whilst the investment function is responsible for much of the failure of the Klein–Goldberger model in forecasting.

Next, forecast errors in terms of logarithms,

$$e_{it} = (\log x_{it} - \log x_{it-1}) - (\log \hat{x}_{it} - \log \hat{x}_{it-1}),$$

are calculated for the seven endogenous variables other than the capital consumption allowance, D. The variances and covariances between them over the sample period are presented, in matrix form, as

	e_Y	e_C	e_N	e_h	e_r	e_p	e_w
e_Y	1.00						
e_C	0.99	1.00					
e_N	0.46	0.38	1.00				
e_h	0.28	0.21	0.44	1.00			
e_r	0.15	0.08	0.62	0.20	1.00		
e_p	−0.28	−0.29	0.24	−0.04	0.74	1.00	
e_w	−0.31	−0.29	−0.13	−0.21	0.55	0.86	1.00

which indicates that there is a strong relation between success in forecasting GNP and success in forecasting consumption, and between success in forecasting prices and success in forecasting wages. Also, on the basis of the calculated covariances, we may conclude, as Goldberger did from a similar investigation of the Klein–Goldberger model, that the forecasts concerning real variables, C, Y, N, and h, have little relation to those for the price variables, p and w.

As for the post-sample extrapolation, we note that there is some systematic bias in the computed value of each variable (one-signed error year after year).[1] A simple device for dealing with these biases is to compute the residual for each fitted equation in the last sample year or in the first post-sample year and to adjust the constant term of each equation so that it exactly fits the observed values in that year. Figure 2 shows the results of extrapolation by the revised system of equations in which we made adjustments for the average of observed values in 1953 and 1954. The discrepancies between actual and computed values become considerably smaller, though some downward biases remain in national product and consumption.

According to Solow, there is some evidence that the rise in the rate of productivity due to technological progress is more rapid in recent years than in the early 1900s.[2] Underestimation of the scale factor of the original production function after 1954 may possibly be caused by this phenomenon. We may further conjecture that larger errors in national product and consumption in the later years of extrapolation may be closely related to the accelerated progress of technology. Thus, we might make an adjustment for the rate of technological change (as well as the level of productivity or the scale factor of the production function) by replacing 1.47 per cent of the yearly shift in the production function by 2.35 per cent, that is, by replacing $(0.00633t - 0.1907)$ by $(0.01009t - 0.2838)$ in equation (2.3).[3] This adjustment results in reasonably satisfactory extrapolations; we obtain very much improved estimates of all variables throughout the post-sample period. Estimates of national product and consumption, in particular, are very close to the actual figures, even in the later years in the extrapolation (see Figure 2).

2. THE DERIVATION OF MULTIPLIERS

The matrix F which is obtained by log-linearizing (2.8) at the point of sample means is displayed in Table 5, each element of which indicates the magnitude of the direct and indirect influence of some predetermined variable upon some current endogenous variable. For example, the percentage change in the price level induced by a unit percentage change in the wage rate in the previous year is 1.053 with all other predetermined variables held constant. We may generalize the concept of the multiplier so as to call each element of

[1] This suggests that some modifications in the conclusions will have to be made if we intend to discuss the prospects of the American economy in the light of our model. For example, the upward bias in extrapolation of the price level, together with the downward bias of employment, implies that the simple application of our model to the post-sample years is likely to exaggerate the contradictions between full employment and price stability. See Chapter 4 below. (Using the information on the autoregressive pattern of errors, our *ex post* as well as *ex ante* simulation will improve immensely.)

[2] See Solow, *op. cit.* p. 316.

[3] $-0.1907 = -0.2427 + 0.052u$. The figure 2.35 per cent is computed as an average of the rate of productivity change due to technical progress in the years 1947–54, estimated by applying the same procedure as Solow's to our data.

TABLE 5. *Impact multipliers in terms of elasticity: matrix F*

Endogenous variable	Exogenous variable				
	$\log M$	$\log M_{-1}$	$\log L$	$\log L_{-1}$	$\log(I+B)$
$\log Y$	0.200	0	0.644	−0.575	0.299
$\log C$	0.216	0	0.697	−0.622	0.084
$\log D$	0	0	0	0	0
$\log N$	0.181	0	0.838	−0.520	0.270
$\log p$	0.085	0	0.118	−0.243	0.126
$\log w$	0.104	0	−0.075	−0.298	0.155
$\log r$	−4.052	2.443	2.523	−2.599	1.352
$\log h$	0.062	0	−0.056	−0.178	0.093

Endogenous variable	Lagged endogenous variable					
	$\log K_{-1}$	$\log C_{-1}$	$\log p_{-1}$	$\log p_{-2}$	$\log w_{-1}$	$\log h_{-1}$
$\log Y$	−0.260	0.575	−0.052	0.080	−0.230	0.230
$\log C$	−0.030	0.622	−0.056	0.087	−0.249	0.249
$\log D$	1.593	0	0	0	0	0
$\log N$	−0.394	0.520	−0.257	0.073	0.002	−0.002
$\log p$	−0.379	0.243	0.236	−0.368	1.053	−1.053
$\log w$	−0.244	0.298	0.441	−0.360	0.821	−0.821
$\log r$	−1.850	2.599	0.415	−0.646	1.851	−1.851
$\log h$	−0.135	0.178	0.194	0.025	−0.281	0.281

F an 'impact multiplier in terms of elasticity' or an 'impact elasticity-multiplier'.

Table 5 implies the following estimates of multipliers. It is at once seen that the impact elasticity-multiplier of the amount of money on national product, $\partial \log Y / \partial \log M$, is 0.200,[1] that is, a 1 per cent increase in the quantity of money gives rise to a 0.200 per cent increase in national product. By use of the formula,

$$\frac{\partial \log Y}{\partial \log M} = \frac{\partial \log Y}{\partial \log (M/p)} \frac{\partial \log (M/p)}{\partial \log M} = \frac{\partial \log Y}{\partial \log (M/p)} \left(1 - \frac{\partial \log p}{\partial \log M}\right),$$

we find that the impact elasticity-multiplier of the *real* quantity of money on national product, $\partial \log Y / \partial \log (M/p)$, is 0.219. As

$$\partial \log(pY)/\log M = \partial \log p / \partial \log M + \partial \log Y / \partial \log M,$$

we also get $\partial \log(pY)/\partial \log M = 0.285$. Similarly, respective estimates of

---

[1] According to the Keynesian way of thinking, an increase in the amount of money tends to lower the rate of interest, which in turn affects investment and, therefore, national product. In our model, however, since we find no reasonable empirical results (see Klein and Goldberger, *op. cit.* pp. 67–8), the rate of interest is assumed to have no effect on investment; a creation of money raises income and employment only through the Pigovian effect of real cash balances on consumption.

employment multipliers, $\partial \log N / \partial \log M$ and $\partial \log N / \partial \log (M/p)$, are 0.181 and 0.198.

Further, we obtain the following impact investment-multipliers in terms of elasticity:

$$\frac{\partial \log Y}{\partial \log (I+B)} = 0.299, \qquad \frac{\partial \log Y}{\partial \log p(I+B)} = 0.265,$$

$$\frac{\partial \log p Y}{\partial \log p(I+B)} = 0.378, \qquad \frac{\partial \log N}{\partial \log (I+B)} = 0.270,$$

$$\frac{\partial \log N}{\partial \log p(I+B)} = 0.240, \qquad \frac{\partial \log wN}{\partial \log p(I+B)} = 0.378.$$

We can derive multipliers in absolute terms from the corresponding multipliers in terms of elasticity. The absolute multipliers depend on $Y/(I+B)$, $N/(I+B)$, etc., as the following formulas show; at the sample means of these values, the multipliers are estimated as:

$$\frac{\partial Y}{\partial (I+B)} = \frac{Y}{I+B} \frac{\partial \log Y}{\partial \log (I+B)} = 1.352,$$

$$\frac{\partial N}{\partial (I+B)} = \frac{N}{I+B} \frac{\partial \log N}{\partial \log (I+B)} = 0.705,$$

$$\frac{\partial Y}{\partial \left(\dfrac{M}{p}\right)} = \frac{pY}{M} \frac{\partial \log Y}{\partial \log \left(\dfrac{M}{p}\right)} = 0.292,$$

$$\frac{\partial p Y}{\partial M} = \frac{pY}{M} \frac{\partial \log p Y}{\partial \log M} = 0.380,$$

$$\frac{\partial N}{\partial \left(\dfrac{M}{p}\right)} = \frac{pN}{M} \frac{\partial \log N}{\partial \log \left(\dfrac{M}{p}\right)} = 0.156.$$

These absolute multipliers evidently depend on the ratios of the relevant variables and the elasticity multipliers which, in turn, depend on the structural parameters (the coefficients of equations (2.1)–(2.7)) and the three coefficients of log-linearization of the identity (2.8), $\beta_1 = \bar{C}/\bar{Y}$, $\beta_2 = (\bar{I}+\bar{B})/\bar{Y}$, and $\beta_3 = \bar{D}/\bar{Y}$. The above estimates of the multipliers are obtained by fixing β_1, β_2, and β_3 at their sample means. For the purpose of making the role of each coefficient explicit, we write (2.1)–(2.7) and (2.8′) in the following algebraic forms:

$$\log \frac{C_t}{L_t} = \alpha_{11} \log \frac{Y_t}{L_t} + \alpha_{12} \log \frac{M_t}{p_t L_t} + \alpha_{13} \log \frac{C_{t-1}}{L_{t-1}} + \alpha_{10}, \qquad (2.1^*)$$

$$\log \frac{M_t}{p_t} = \alpha_{21} \log Y_t + \alpha_{22} \log \frac{M_{t-1}}{p_t} + \alpha_{23} \log r_t + \alpha_{24} u + \alpha_{20}, \quad (2.2^*)$$

$$\log Y_t = \alpha_{31} \log h_t N_t + (1 - \alpha_{31}) \log K_{t-1} + \alpha_{32} t + \alpha_{33} u + \alpha_{30}, \quad (2.3^*)$$

$$\log \frac{w_t N_t}{p_t Y_t} = \alpha_{40}, \quad (2.4^*)$$

$$\log \frac{w_t}{h_t} = \alpha_{51} \log \frac{w_{t-1}}{h_{t-1}} + \alpha_{52} \log \frac{p_t}{p_{t-1}} + \alpha_{53} \log \frac{p_{t-1}}{p_{t-2}}$$
$$+ \alpha_{54} \log \frac{N_t}{(0.57 L_t)} + \alpha_{50}, \quad (2.5^*)$$

$$\log h_t = \alpha_{61} \log \frac{w_{t-1}}{p_{t-1} h_{t-1}} + \alpha_{62} \log \frac{N_t}{(0.57 L_t)} + \alpha_{60}, \quad (2.6^*)$$

$$\log D_t = \alpha_{71} \log K_{t-1} + \alpha_{70}, \quad (2.7^*)$$

$$\beta_1 \log C_t + \beta_2 \log (I_t + B_t) = \log Y_t + \beta_3 \log D_t + \beta_0, \quad (2.8^*)$$

where $\beta_0 = \beta_1 \log \bar{C} + \beta_2 \log (\bar{I} + \bar{B}) - \log \bar{Y} - \beta_3 \log \bar{D}$. To get more accurate yearly estimates of the multipliers, we take β_1 and β_2 as actual C/Y and $(I+B)/Y$ in each year. Then we have from (2.1^*) to (2.8^*)

$$\frac{\partial Y}{\partial (I+B)} = \frac{1}{1 - \left[\alpha_{11} - \dfrac{\alpha_{12}}{1 - \alpha_{52}} \left\{ \dfrac{1 + \alpha_{54} + \alpha_{62}}{\alpha_{31}(1 + \alpha_{62})} - 1 \right\} \right] \beta_1} = \frac{1}{1 - 0.282 \beta_1}, \quad (3.4)$$

$$\frac{\partial N}{\partial (I+B)} = \frac{N}{I+B} \cdot \frac{1}{\alpha_{31}(1 + \alpha_{62})}$$
$$\times \frac{\beta_2}{1 - \left[\alpha_{11} - \dfrac{\alpha_{12}}{1 - \alpha_{52}} \left\{ \dfrac{1 + \alpha_{54} + \alpha_{62}}{\alpha_{31}(1 + \alpha_{62})} - 1 \right\} \right] \beta_1} = \frac{N}{Y} \cdot \frac{1}{1.107 - 0.312 \beta_1}, \quad (3.5)$$

$$\frac{\partial Y}{\partial \left(\dfrac{M}{p} \right)} = \frac{pY}{M} \cdot \frac{\alpha_{12} \beta_1}{1 - \alpha_{11} \beta_1} = \frac{pY}{M} \cdot \frac{0.160 \beta_1}{1 - 0.349 \beta_1}, \quad (3.6)$$

$$\frac{\partial N}{\partial \left(\dfrac{M}{p} \right)} = \frac{N}{Y} \cdot \frac{pY}{M} \cdot \frac{\alpha_{12} \beta_1}{\alpha_{31}(1 + \alpha_{62})(1 - \alpha_{11} \beta_1)}$$
$$= \frac{N}{Y} \cdot \frac{pY}{M} \cdot \frac{0.160 \beta_1}{1.107 - 0.386 \beta_1}. \quad (3.7)$$

Contingent on $\beta_1, \beta_2, Y, I+B, M, N$, and p, these multipliers vary from year to year. For example, the value of the investment multiplier (3.4) is estimated to be 1.31 in 1902, 1.34 in 1929, and 1.46 in 1933. Fluctuations of the multipliers from year to year will be discussed in detail in the next section.

Let us now consider a subsystem consisting of equations (2.1*), (2.3*), (2.6*), and (2.8*), and regard p and w as constant. Such a system is called the real economy, whose only endogenous variables are income, consumption, employment, and the hours worked per man per year. In the real economy, the investment multipliers are

$$\frac{\partial Y}{\partial (I+B)} = \frac{1}{1-\alpha_{11}\beta_1}$$

and
$$\frac{\partial N}{\partial (I+B)} = \frac{N}{(I+B)} \cdot \frac{\beta_2}{\alpha_{31}(1+\alpha_{62})(1-\alpha_{11}\beta_1)},$$

but the monetary multipliers, $\partial Y/\partial(M/p)$ and $\partial N/\partial(M/p)$, are the same as those in the complete system.[1] At the point of sample means, the investment multipliers are estimated at 1.48 on income and 0.77 on employment, both of which are greater than the corresponding multipliers in the complete system by 10 per cent.

One may compare our estimate of the multiplier, $\partial Y/\partial(I+B) = 1.35$, with Goldberger's impact multiplier of government expenditure on GNP, which was estimated at 1.386 in the predetermined tax yield case and at 1.229 in the endogenous tax yield case. He also estimated the impact multiplier of government expenditure on total civilian employment at 0.611 and 0.542, in the predetermined and endogenous tax yield cases respectively.[2] These values may be compared with our estimate of $\partial N/\partial(I+B)$, 0.71.

There are, however, the following differences between Goldberger's analysis and ours. (i) Our model with no tax variable may be interpreted as a system which is obtained when tax variables are eliminated by substitution, so that our multipliers should be compared with Goldberger's multipliers in the case of endogenous tax yields. (ii) Klein and Goldberger regard the hours worked as exogenous. Therefore, Goldberger's multipliers are comparable with those of our multipliers which are derived from equations (2.1*)–(2.5*) and (2.8*) by treating the hours worked as constant. (iii) In our model the depreciation equation plays no part in the calculation of impact multipliers, while in the Klein–Goldberger model depreciation makes some (but very small) contributions to impact multipliers. For rigorous comparison, the contributions of depreciation must be deducted from Goldberger's multipliers. (iv) Klein and Goldberger take 1929–52, excluding 1942–5, as the sample period for estimating their equations. Our multipliers

---

[1] Of course, the multiplier, $\partial p Y/\partial M$, in the real economy is different from that in the complete economy. They are estimated at 0.29 and 0.38, respectively, at the point of sample means.

[2] See Goldberger, *op. cit.* p. 25 and p. 40.

are made comparable with theirs by re-estimating them at the point of means of the series C/Y and N/Y over 1929–52 (excluding 1941–5).

Making the adjustments which are suggested in (ii), (iii), and (iv) above, we obtain $\partial Y/\partial(I+B) = 1.351$ and $\partial N/\partial(I+B) = 0.817$ from our model and $\partial Q/\partial G = 1.2367$ and $\partial N_w/\partial G = 0.5438$, where G represents government expenditures and exports, Q gross national product and N_w the number of employees, from the Klein–Goldberger model. It is noted that in an exogenous depreciation system there is no discrepancy between the effects on gross and net national product, Q and Y. It is also noted that our N denotes the total number of persons engaged, so that it includes not only the number of wage and salary earners, N_w, but also the number of non-farm entrepreneurs and farm operators; this difference in the measure of employment would partly explain the large difference which is found between our estimate of the investment multiplier on employment and Goldberger's.

Table 6 compares our estimates of the multipliers for income and consumption with those made by other writers. It is true that the multipliers, $\partial \log pC/\partial \log pI$ and $\partial \log pC/\partial \log M$, obtained for the United Kingdom by Barrett and Walters are considerably higher than our corresponding estimates, and that Goldberger's monetary multipliers are less than half our estimates. But we still find a substantial degree of conformity between the figures listed in Table 6.

3. MONETARY POLICY VERSUS PUBLIC INVESTMENT POLICY

In this section, we examine how the impact multipliers will adapt themselves to the changing phases of the economy and discuss whether monetary or public investment policy is more advantageous in a slump year. The discussion below will lead to a confirmation of the importance of Keynes' analysis.

As the formula (3.4) shows, the investment multiplier for income depends on the average propensity to consume, $\beta_1 = C/Y$. We may anticipate that C/Y rises in depression and declines in prosperity, because an income-elasticity of consumption less than one implies an average propensity to consume which decreases when income increases, *ceteris paribus*. In fact, if we take $N/0.57L$ as an indicator of economic activity and make a scatter diagram of C/Y on it, we find that there is a strong negative relationship between C/Y and $N/0.57L$ which shifts downwards in the thirties and upwards after World War II. Computing the multiplier for each year by use of the formula (3.4), we get a scatter diagram between $\partial Y/\partial(I+B)$ and

TABLE 6. *Impact multipliers on income and consumption of the United States and the United Kingdom*

Investment multipliers

Investigator[a]	Period covered	$\dfrac{\partial \log Y}{\partial \log I}$	$\dfrac{\partial Y}{\partial I}$	$\dfrac{\partial \log pY}{\partial \log pI}$	$\dfrac{\partial pY}{\partial pI}$	$\dfrac{\partial \log C}{\partial \log I}$	$\dfrac{\partial C}{\partial I}$	$\dfrac{\partial \log pC}{\partial \log pI}$	$\dfrac{\partial pC}{\partial pI}$
Ando–Modigliani[b]	1929–58[g]	—	—	—	—	—	—	—	0.62
Goldberger[c]	1929–52[h]	—	1.386[l] 1.229[m]	—	—	—	—	—	—
Barret–Walters[d]	1878–1963[i]	—	—	—	—	—	—	0.328	—
	1878–1914	—	—	—	—	—	—	0.181	—
	1921–1938	—	—	—	—	—	—	0.232	—
	1948–1963	—	—	—	—	—	—	0.523	—
Evans–Klein[e]	1948(I)–64(IV)	—	1.98	—	—	—	—	—	—
Evans[e]	1948(I)–64(IV)	—	1.45	—	—	—	—	—	—
Morishima–Saito[f]	1902–52[j]	0.299	1.352	0.377	1.681	0.084	0.351	0.187	0.773
	1929–52[k]	0.272	1.369	0.347	1.649	0.077	0.371	0.172	0.779

Monetary multipliers

Investigator[a]	Period covered	$\dfrac{\partial \log Y}{\partial \log (M/p)}$	$\dfrac{\partial Y}{\partial (M/p)}$	$\dfrac{\partial \log pY}{\partial \log M}$	$\dfrac{\partial pY}{\partial M}$	$\dfrac{\partial \log C}{\partial \log (M/p)}$	$\dfrac{\partial C}{\partial (M/p)}$	$\dfrac{\partial \log pC}{\partial \log M}$	$\dfrac{\partial pC}{\partial M}$
Ando–Modigliani[b]	1929–58[g]	—	—	—	—	—	—	—	0.21
Goldberger[c]	1929–52[h]	—	0.0998[l,n] 0.1921[l,o] 0.0885[m,n] 0.1711[m,o]	—	—	—	0.1007[l,n] 0.0538[l,o] 0.0891[m,n] 0.0323[m,o]	—	—
Barret–Walters[d]	1878–1963[i]	—	—	—	—	—	—	0.486	—
	1878–1914	—	—	—	—	—	—	0.595	—
	1921–1938	—	—	—	—	—	—	0.163	—
	1948–1963	—	—	—	—	—	—	0.763	—
Evans–Klein[e]	1948(I)–64(IV)	—	—	—	—	—	—	—	—
Evans[e]	1948(I)–64(IV)	—	—	—	—	—	—	—	—
Morishima–Saito[f]	1902–52[j]	0.218	0.292	0.285	0.380	0.236	0.292	0.301	0.373
	1929–52[k]	0.230	0.273	0.299	0.355	0.240	0.272	0.308	0.349

[a] A. Ando and F. Modigliani, 'The relative stability of monetary velocity and the investment multiplier', *American Economic Review*, (September, 1965); A. S. Goldberger, *Impact Multipliers and Dynamic Properties of the Klein–Goldberger Model* (North-Holland Publishing Co, 1959); C. R. Barrett and A. A. Walters, 'The stability of Keynesian and monetary multipliers in the United Kingdom', *Review of Economics and Statistics*, (November, 1966); M. K. Evans and L. R. Klein, *The Wharton Econometric Forecasting Model*, Studies in Quantitative Economics, No. 2, University of Pennsylvania, 1968; M. K. Evans, 'Computer simulations of non-linear econometric models', Discussion Paper No. 97, University of Pennsylvania.

[b] Multipliers for the USA. pC = consumption expenditure+net change in inventory−imports; pI = net investment+government expenditure+exports; M = the estimated maximum amount of money that could be created by the banking system on the basis of the reserves supplied by the monetary authority; all in current prices.

[c] Multipliers for the USA. Y = gross national product; I = government expenditure; M/p = liquid assets held at the end of the last year; all in 1939 constant prices.

[d] Multipliers for the UK. pC = consumer's expenditures; pI = gross private domestic investment+government expenditure+exports−imports; M = cash balances at the end of the last year; all in current prices.

[e] Multipliers for the USA. Y = gross national product; I = government purchases (government wage bill, government output originating and government employment are also adjusted); all in 1958 dollars.

[f] Multipliers for the USA. Y = net national product; I = gross private plus government investment+trade balance; M = cash balances on June 30 of each year. Y and I are in 1929 dollars and M is in current dollars. p = NNP deflator.

[g] Excluding 1942–6.

[h] Excluding 1942–5.

[i] Excluding 1915–19 and 1939–47.

[j] Excluding 1941–5.

[k] The structural equations are estimated on the data from 1902 to 1952 (excluding 1941–5), but the multipliers are calculated for 1929–52 (excluding 1941–5).

[l] Tax yields are exogenous.

[m] Tax yields are endogenous.

[n] With respect to household liquid assets.

[o] With respect to business liquid assets.

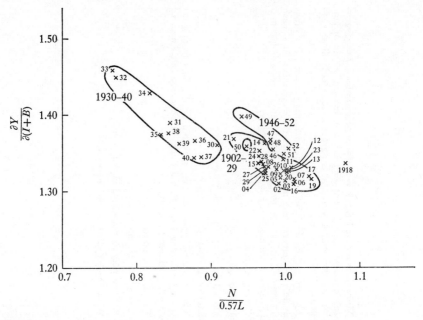

Figure 3
Scatter diagram of $\partial Y/\partial(I+B)$ on $N/0.57L$, 1902–52 excluding 1941–5.

$N/0.57L$, such as that shown in Figure 3, which indicates the following things.

First, the whole period may be grouped into three subperiods, 1902–29 (excluding 1918), 1930–40, and 1946–52,[1] so that within each subperiod an increase in the employment ratio $N/0.57L$ gives rise to a decrease in the multiplier. The full-employment multiplier is thus smaller than the multiplier with under-employment, as was expected by Keynes and other writers. Secondly, although the values of the multiplier for the thirties are high, they would be smaller than those for 1902–29 if the employment ratio were adjusted to the same level. This is probably one of the reasons for the fact that it took a very long time to recover from the Great Depression. It is also seen from Figure 3 that if the employment ratio is adjusted, the multiplier for the postwar period exceeds that for the prewar period, although this should be discounted to some extent, because more built-in stabilizers not included in our model are available in the postwar period. This suggests one reason for the prosperity of the postwar period.

[1] The year 1918 is excluded because the employment ratio for this year is exceptionally high, while the corresponding national product figure fails to reflect the large-scale production of munitions.

It is clear from (3.5) that the multiplier effect of investment on employment depends not only on the average propensity to consume, C/Y, but also on the productivity of labour, Y/N. The latter is apparently on an upward trend in the long run, tracing out short-run fluctuations (that is, rising in periods of prosperity and declining in periods of depression).[1] It is seen that cyclic fluctuations in the productivity of labour, together with the fact that the propensity to consume declines as we approach full employment, produce a strong tendency for the employment multiplier, $\partial N/\partial(I+B)$, to become smaller as the employment ratio is greater; and 'it will become more and more troublesome to secure a further given increase of employment by further increasing investment', as Keynes stated.[2] Figure 4 also shows that the strong upward trend in Y/N makes the relationship between $\partial N/(\partial I+B)$ and $N/0.57L$ shift downwards. That is, the period 1902–29, excluding 1918, is now clearly separated into two subperiods, 1902–20 (excluding 1918) and 1921–9, whereas no distinction has been found between them in the relationship of $\partial Y/\partial(I+B)$ to $N/0.57L$. It is also worth noticing that in Figure 4 the points for 1946–52 lie below those for 1902–9, while the reverse is the case in Figure 3.

The long-run falling tendency of the employment multiplier implies that the amount of government investment required to bring about full employment was small in the period 1902–29 but became very large in the thirties. This explains why the USA suffered from severe unemployment in the thirties, although full employment had, in effect, been maintained until 1929.

Let us now pass on to consider the effects of an increase in real cash balances on income and employment. It is at once seen from (3.6) that the multiplier $\partial Y/\partial(M/p)$ is a decreasing function of the Cambridge k, i.e. M/pY and an increasing function of the average propensity to consume C/Y. If we fix C/Y at 0.924, the average of C/Y over the sample period, and confine ourselves to examining the effects of changes in M/pY, on $\partial Y/\partial(M/p)$, then we observe the following two tendencies, long-run and short-run. As M/pY tends upwards in the long run, there is a noticeable downward trend in $\partial Y/\partial(M/p)$. In the short run, however, M/pY falls during business expansion and rises during contractions, so that the multiplier $\partial Y/\partial(M/p)$ is greater as the employment ratio is greater.[3] Thus we get, under the assumption that C/Y is fixed, a positive relationship between the monetary multiplier on

[1] For the behaviour of productivity in the United States, 1889–1953, see the summary of Kendrick's work by S. Fabricant, *Basic Facts on Productivity Change*, Occasional Paper 63 (National Bureau of Economic Research, 1959), pp. 10–17.

[2] See J. M. Keynes, *op. cit.* p. 127.

[3] See R. T. Selden *op. cit.* p. 188 and pp. 192–5; and M. Friedman, *A Theory of Consumption Function* (Princeton University Press, 1957).

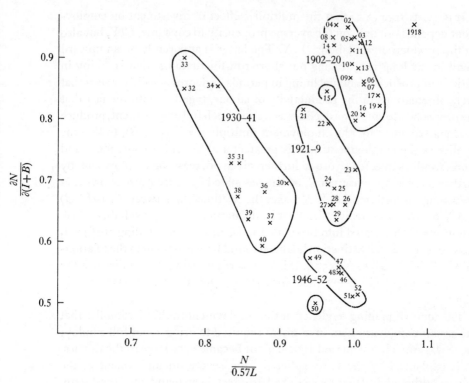

Figure 4
Scatter diagram of $\partial N/\partial(I+B)$ on $N/0.57L$, 1902–52 excluding 1941–5.

income and the employment ratio which shifts downwards as time goes on.
(See Figure 5.[1])

Regarding the effects of the average consumption ratio on the monetary
multiplier, it can be seen that C/Y has the same short-run and long-run
tendencies as M/pY. It declines in boom and increases in slump, with a
long-run upward tendency. Therefore, it affects the monetary multiplier so
as to over- or under-compensate for the effects of M/pY and C/Y, to the
effect that the monetary multiplier is not correlated with the unemployment
ratio.

From formula (3.7), we find that the monetary multiplier on employment,
$\partial N/\partial(M/p)$, is a decreasing function of M/pY and Y/N, and an increasing
function of C/Y. If we tentatively disregard the last factor, we find that there
is a remarkable trend in the multiplier which results from the long-run
upward trends in the first two. In the short run, however, M/pY and Y/N

---

[1] Immediately after World War II there was an enormous stock of liquid assets which had
been accumulated during the war. Thus, 1946 is to be treated as an exceptional year.

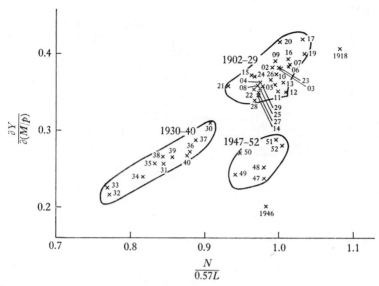

Figure 5
Scatter diagram of $\partial Y/\partial(M/p)$ at $C/Y = 0.924$ on $N/0.57L$, 1902–52, excluding 1941–5.

move in opposite directions, and as a result the product (Y/N) (M/pY) remains almost constant. Therefore, as Figure 6 shows, the relationship between the monetary multiplier on employment and the employment ratio is horizontal within each subperiod. However, if we take the average consumption ratio into account, the strong long-run downward tendency in the multiplier is neutralized to the extent that there remains only a slight tendency to fall; and we do not observe any clear short-run correlation between the actual value of the monetary multiplier on employment and the employment ratio.

Our investigations into short-run multiplier effects lead us to the following conclusion, which supports Keynesian public investment policy *vis-à-vis* monetary policy. The relative effectiveness of these policies may be measured by the ratio γ of $\partial N/\partial(I+B)$ to $\partial N/\partial(M/p)$,[1] which may be called the *marginal rate of substitution of monetary policy for public investment policy*. It gives the amount of real cash balances which is required in order to maintain the level of employment, in spite of a marginal decrease in investment. It is clear from our finding on $\partial N/\partial(I+B)$ and $\partial N/\partial(M/p)$ that there are short-run fluctuations and a long-run trend in the ratio γ. Table 7 shows how γ depends on the employment ratio and shifts from period to period. (The figure in each

[1] It is easily shown, by use of the formulas (3.4)–(3.7), that γ equals the ratio of $\partial Y/\partial(I+B)$ to $\partial Y/\partial(M/p)$. Note that in calculating $\partial N/\partial(M/p)$ we fixed the consumption ratio at 0.924, the mean of the ratios over the sample period.

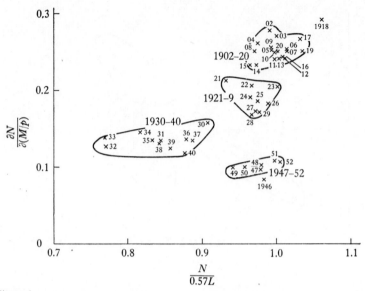

Figure 6
Scatter diagram of $\partial N/\partial(M/p)$ at $C/Y = 0.924$ on $N/0.57L$, 1902–52, excluding 1941–5.

cell is the average of those γs which are classified in that cell.) Reading the table vertically, we find that, as a measure to cure unemployment, public investment policy becomes more important at a time when there is severe unemployment than when full employment is approached. On the other hand, reading the table horizontally, we find that although both policies become less effective in promoting employment as time goes on, public investment policy tends to be relatively more effective.[1] It seems that there is a noticeable break in the time series of the marginal rate of substitution between the two employment policies at about 1930, when the effect of serious unemployment was superimposed on the historical trend.

Before we conclude this policy recommendation section, it must be noted that we are not advocating public investment policy as opposed to monetary policy, but simply comparing the relative effectiveness of both policies in one state of affairs (or in one period) with that in another situation (or in another period). In fact, a dollar's increment in I should not be compared with a dollar's increment in M/p. In the first place, one is a flow, and the other is a stock. Secondly, a fractional reserve banking system exists in the USA, so that relatively small open-market operations – central bank buying

[1] If $\partial N/\partial(I+B)$ were compared with the multiplier $\partial N/\partial(M/p)$ calculated on the basis of the actual consumption ratios, instead of the multiplier $\partial N/\partial(M/p)$ based on the average consumption ratio, the vertical tendency of the figures in Table 7 would be unclear, but we would still observe substantially the same horizontal tendency that Table 7 reveals.

TABLE 7. *Marginal rate of substitution of public investment policy for monetary policy*

Employment ratio in %	Period				
	1902–9	1910–20[a]	1921–9	1930–40	1947–52
75.0–77.4	—	—	—	6.59	—
77.5–79.9	—	—	—	—	—
80.0–82.4	—	—	—	5.97	—
82.5–84.9	—	—	—	5.31	—
85.0–87.4	—	—	—	5.14	—
87.5–89.9	—	—	—	4.92	—
90.0–92.4	—	—	—	4.39	—
92.5–94.9	—	—	3.82	—	5.40
95.0–97.4	3.69	3.77	3.80	—	—
97.5–99.9	3.49	3.68	3.69	—	5.29
100.0–102.4	3.42	3.48	3.49	—	4.82
102.5–104.9	—	3.21	—	—	—

[a] Excluding 1918.

and selling of government securities to cover treasury operations – can generate larger changes in money stock. What is important is not the value of γ in each cell of Table 7 but changes in γ from cell to cell.

4. INTERMEDIATE-RUN MULTIPLIERS

We have so far been concerned only with impact (one-year) multipliers. Since their introduction into economic analysis, however, multipliers have always been regarded as being intrinsically dynamic in character. In fact, an impact multiplier is no more than the first term of a sequence of dynamic (t-year) multipliers ($t = 1, 2, 3, ...$).

Dynamic multipliers are obtained by the following procedure. Consider two states, 0 and 1, where I is fixed, respectively, at its 1929 value, 20.32, and at a higher value, say 22.35, all the other exogenous variables (including t, which is a parameter representing technological improvements) being kept constant at their observed values in 1929. These two sets of exogenous variables generate two time paths (Y_τ^0, N_τ^0) and (Y_τ^1, N_τ^1), where Y_τ and N_τ are income and employment in the τth year. (These paths are obtained by solving non-linear equations (2.1)–(2.9) successively by the same method that we used for *ex post* forecasting.) Then the τth year multipliers are computed as:

$$\frac{\Delta Y_\tau}{\Delta I_\tau} = \frac{Y_\tau^1 - Y_\tau^0}{22.35 - 20.32} \quad \text{and} \quad \frac{\Delta N_\tau}{\Delta I_\tau} = \frac{N_\tau^1 - N_\tau^0}{22.35 - 20.32}.$$

TABLE 8. *Intermediate-run multipliers*

	Investigator	Year τ							
		1	2	3	4	5	6	7	8
$\dfrac{\Delta Y_\tau}{\Delta I_\tau}$	Morishima–Saito I	1.341	1.373	1.284	1.133	0.962	0.788	0.624	0.477
	Morishima–Saito II	1.460	1.656	1.747	1.761	1.724	1.660	1.579	1.488
	Goldberger[a]	1.177	1.851	2.065	2.084	2.045	1.992	1.936	1.882
$\dfrac{\Delta N_\tau}{\Delta I_\tau}$	Morishima–Saito I	0.704	0.662	0.600	0.511	0.416	0.322	0.233	0.155
	Morishima–Saito II	1.034	1.129	1.154	1.128	1.074	1.004	0.926	0.846
	Goldberger	0.542	0.849	0.939	0.939	0.914	0.883	0.852	0.823

[a] Obtained as his government-expenditure multiplier on GNP minus his government-expenditure multiplier on depreciation.

Our dynamic multipliers, $\Delta Y_\tau/\Delta I_\tau$ and $\Delta N_\tau/\Delta I_\tau$, thus obtained are referred to as series I in Table 8. Unlike Goldberger's multipliers, they hardly rise at all. They begin to decline almost as soon as they start, and decrease to very low figures after seven years. And we find that such low values of the investment multipliers result from price and wage increases induced by the assumed increase in investment. A dichotomization into the real and the price sector is suggested in order to cut off strong feedbacks from the price sector to the real sector. A second series of dynamic multipliers (series II) is computed for the real sector, consisting of equations (2.1), (2.3), (2.6) and (2.8), on the assumption that p and w are held constant. Table 8 shows that the new figures are comparable with Goldberger's figures computed for the endogenous tax yield case. Both series reach their respective peaks in the same year (i.e. the fourth year in the case of the multiplier on income and the third year in the case of the multiplier on employment). It is not surprising to find that our series are more stationary than Goldberger's; we would have more dynamic series if we regarded investment as endogenous as Klein and Goldberger did.

4. Long-run properties of the model

It is no exaggeration to say that the recent development of the theory of economic growth has pivoted around the controversy on the stability of growth equilibrium. Neoclassical economists such as Meade, Solow and Uzawa have demonstrated, in a number of abstract models, a long-run tendency for the full-employment–full-capacity growth path, starting from an arbitrarily (or historically) given capital–labour endowment, to approach a state of growth equilibrium where the 'warranted' rate of growth equals the 'natural' rate. On the other hand, Harrod has insisted that centrifugal forces would prevail around the 'warranted-growth' path, so that a given discrepancy between the warranted and the natural rate of growth would in any case generate a divergence of the actual rate of growth from the warranted rate. In fact, history provides instances of both stabilizing and destabilizing processes; for example, we all remember that some major capitalist countries suddenly fell off the wall, like Humpty Dumpty, as soon as the Golden Twenties were over. In this chapter we apply the method of simulation in order to test the ability of our econometric model to generate both of these extremes.

I. FULL-EMPLOYMENT–FULL-CAPACITY GROWTH

There are two idealized states of affairs which have recently been studied intensively by various economists, i.e. the state of long-run growth maintaining perpetually full employment of labour and capital, and the state of balanced growth in which prices remain constant over time. The former is the main concern of neoclassical economists, whilst attention is paid to the latter by a broad group, including J. von Neumann and Joan Robinson. If the supply of labour is assumed to be inelastic with respect to wages and to grow at a constant rate in proportion to population, we may argue (since the neoclassical aggregate production function is assumed) that price stability and full-employment growth are compatible with each other; the path that real income and the stock of capital must take if neither unemployment nor excess capacity are to appear will eventually approach a state of balanced growth with constant prices, provided that there is no technical progress. In our model, however, the simple supply function of labour is replaced by the empirical equation of wage determination (2.5). We shall therefore arrive at the pessimistic conclusion that we cannot simultaneously achieve full employment growth and price stability; it will be shown that, unless there is very rapid technical progress, severe unemployment is necessary for the establishment of stable prices, while the maintenance of full employment produces a marked rate of increase in prices.[1]

We begin with the case of no technical progress. It is assumed that the production function for 1902, i.e. (2.3) for $t = -25$, fits for any t. We shall first examine the conditions to be fulfilled if a growing economy is to maintain full employment or any other constant high rate of employment. It is true that it is difficult to ensure such a state of affairs in any actual economy, but it was actually sustained throughout the first half of our sample period, that is, until 1929. In fact, with only a few exceptions, all the 1900–29 figures for the employment ratio lie between 0.96 and 1.03, the average being 0.99. Throughout the following analysis we fix the employment ratio, the ratio of cash balances to income and the ratio of trade balances to income at the means of the respective figures;[2] we therefore have

$$N/0.57L = 0.99, \quad M/pY = 0.604, \quad B/Y = 0.007.$$

It will be shown that our model (2.1)–(2.9) possesses an *almost-full-employment growth equilibrium*, by which we mean a state of affairs fulfilling the following requirements: (1) 99 per cent of the potential workers are employed at any point of time; (2) output, consumption, net investment and capital stock grow at the same rate as the labour force, while the standard hours worked remain unchanged; (3) the supply of money is adjusted so as to keep the Cambridge coefficient at 0.604; and (4) there is no influence from outside the economy, that is, the ratio of trade balances to income is fixed at 0.007. We write

$$y_t = Y_t/L_t, \quad c_t = C_t/L_t, \quad k_{t-1} = K_{t-1}/L_t, \quad b_t = B_t/L_t,$$
$$i_t = (I_t - D_t)/L_t, \quad \alpha_t = (I_t - D_t)/Y_t.$$

In the state of almost-full-employment growth equilibrium our new variables, y, c, k, b, i, α, as well as h, remain constant over time, while p, w, r,

[1] Using American data, Samuelson and Solow have tentatively estimated that price stability may yield unemployment of about 5.5 per cent per year, whereas unemployment of 3 per cent per year may accompany a price rise of about 4.5 per cent per year. See P. A. Samuelson and R. M. Solow, 'Analytical aspects of anti-inflation policy', *American Economic Review* (May 1960), pp. 192–3.

[2] In calculating the mean of M/pY we omitted the figures for 1916–20 because they are exceptionally low; similarly, the figures of B/Y for 1900 and 1915–21 were excluded in calculating its mean since its value for 1900 is unavailable and those for 1915–21 are exceptionally high. Throughout the following the ratio B/Y is assumed to be an exogenous variable.

and L are subject to changes. We may, therefore, put equations (2.1)–(2.6) and (2.8) into the form[1]

$$\log c = 0.943 \log y + 0.297 \log 0.604 + 0.013, \tag{4.1}$$

$$0.507 \log 0.604 = 0.190 \log y - 0.493 \log (p_t/p_{t-1}) - 0.302 \log L_t$$
$$+ 0.493 \log L_{t-1} - 0.202 \log r_t - 0.299, \tag{4.2}$$

$$\log y = 0.824 \log h + 0.824 \log 0.99 + 0.176 \log k - 0.6021, \tag{4.3}$$

$$\log (0.99 w_t/p_t y) = 0.160, \tag{4.4}$$

$$\log w_t = 1.006 \log w_{t-1} - 0.006 \log h + 0.456(\tfrac{1}{5}\log (p_t/p_{t-1})$$
$$+ \tfrac{4}{5}\log (p_{t-1}/p_{t-2})) + 0.188 \log 0.99 + 0.017, \tag{4.5}$$

$$0.718 \log h = -0.282 \log (w_t/p_t) + 0.343 \log 0.99 + 0.324, \tag{4.6}$$

$$i = \alpha y, \tag{4.7}$$

$$b = 0.007 y, \tag{4.8}$$

$$\log c/y = \log (1 - \alpha - 0.007). \tag{4.9}$$

As the stock of capital grows in step with the labour force, we have from (2.9)

$$(1 + l_t) K_{t-1} = K_{t-1} + I_t - D_t,$$

l_t being the rate of growth of the labour force in period t; in the following discussion it is fixed at 1.87 per cent per year, which is the average rate of growth of the population aged fifteen years and over for the period 1900–29. This equation, in view of the definition of l_t, yields

$$k = \frac{\alpha}{0.0187} y. \tag{4.10}$$

Our growth model (4.1)–(4.10), which is based on the assumption that the Cambridge coefficient is constant, may be decomposed into three subsystems determining (1) output per man, capital per man, consumption per man, investment per man, the real wage rate and hours worked, (2) the price level and the money wage rate, and (3) the rate of interest, respectively. The first subsystem consisting of all the equations other than (4.2) and (4.5) works as follows. At any moment of time, the rate of capital accumulation $\Delta K/K$ is identically equal to the ratio of net investment to income $\Delta K/Y$ divided by the capital coefficient K/Y. We find, therefore, that in order to establish the state of almost-full-employment growth equilibrium where capital and labour increase at a common rate, the capital coefficient should

---

[1] In the following, the argument proceeds in terms of net investment, so that the depreciation equation (2.7) is left out.

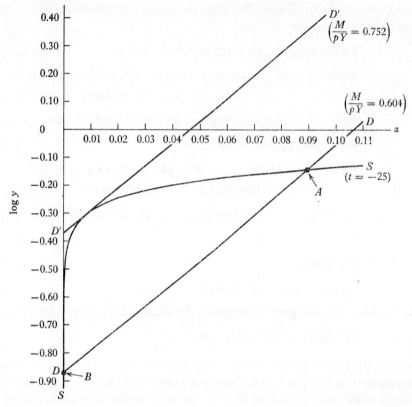

Figure 7

equal the ratio of investment to income divided by the rate of population growth. This situation is described by equation (4.10). Secondly, as the production function is of the Cobb–Douglas type, the marginal productivity condition (4.4) implies that the real wage rate is proportional to the productivity of labour, i.e. the output per man divided by the employment ratio, the latter being fixed at 0.99. Thirdly, it follows from (4.6) that an increase in the real wage rate results in a decrease in the standard hours worked. Combining (4.4) and (4.6), we find that the hours worked depend on output per man. Substituting for h from this relationship and for k from (4.10), equation (4.3) can finally be written as

$$\log y = 0.1538 \log \alpha + 0.015. \qquad (4.11)$$

On the other hand, we obtain from (4.1) and (4.9)

$$\log y = -17.693 \log (1 - \alpha - 0.007) - 0.9239. \qquad (4.12)$$

Equations (4.11) and (4.12) can now determine those values of α and y that establish the state of almost-full-employment growth equilibrium; we have

$$\alpha = 0.0892, \quad y = 0.713.$$

The values of k and h corresponding to these values of α and y are

$$k = 3.403, \quad h = 2.773.$$

The capital coefficient is calculated at 4.77, which is higher than the figure for 1914, the highest in the 1900–29 series, but lower than the corresponding figure for 1933. The equilibrium output per man, 0.713, and the equilibrium hours worked, 2.773, are very close to the respective figures actually observed in 1902.

A few remarks on the existence and meaningfulness of the almost-full-employment growth equilibrium would provide more information about the structure of our model. Equations (4.11) and (4.12) can more generally be written as

$$\log y = 0.154 \log \alpha + 0.0055t - 0.154 \log l - 0.1129, \tag{4.11'}$$

$$\log y = -17.693 \log(1 - \alpha - B/Y) + 5.250 \log(M/pY) + 0.2257. \tag{4.12'}$$

$M/pY, B/Y, l$, and t are fixed at 0.604, 0.007, 0.0187, and -25, respectively; then (4.11') and (4.12') are graphed, in the α-$\log y$ plane, as the curves SS and DD of Figure 7, respectively. It is then seen that they have two intersections, one of which, namely A in the figure, gives the solution we referred to above as the almost-full-employment growth equilibrium, while the other, B, gives a meaningless solution whose y (calculated at 0.135) is less than one-fifth of the actual income per man in 1902, so that it would be far below the subsistence level. (The point B is probably unstable.)

In Figure 7, an increase in the value of the parameter t (i.e. technical progress) shifts the SS curve upwards, so that, other things being equal, it results in an increase in the meaningful long-run equilibrium value of output per man. A decrease in the rate of growth of the population, l, has a similar effect. On the other hand, an increase in M/pY or B/Y shifts the DD curve upwards; therefore it lowers the meaningful long-run equilibrium. It is obvious from the figure that when the combination of the values of the relevant parameters is not adequate, the SS and the DD curve may have no intersection. For example, if M/pY is greater than 0.752 while $B/Y, l$, and t continue to take on the same values as before, there is no almost-full-employment growth equilibrium at all.

Let us next establish the stability of the meaningful (upper) almost-full-employment growth equilibrium by showing that eventually it will be approached by any growth path retaining the employment ratio of 0.99 and starting with an arbitrary initial composition of capital and labour.[1] When the initial capital per man does not equal the equilibrium value, $k = 3.403$, then fluctuation in the capital–labour ratio will arise; that is, the stock of capital does not grow at the same rate as the labour force. Let g_t be the rate of capital accumulation in period t, i.e.

$$K_t = (1+g_t)K_{t-1}.$$

We also have

$$g_t K_{t-1} = I_t - D_t.$$

Dividing these two equations by L_t and remembering $L_{t+1} = 1.0187 L_t$, we have

$$1.0187 k_t = (1+g_t)k_{t-1}, \tag{4.13}$$

$$g_t k_{t-1} = \alpha_t y_t, \tag{4.14}$$

respectively. It is obvious that α_t in the last equation must satisfy

$$\log(c_t/y_t) = \log(1 - \alpha_t - 0.007). \tag{4.15}$$

On the other hand, output per man, consumption per man, and the hours worked may now change from period to period. Eliminating the real wage rate from the hours worked equation by use of the relative share equation, we have

$$\log h_t = -0.282 \log y_{t-1} + 0.282 \log h_{t-1} + 0.2767. \tag{4.16}$$

This enables us to eliminate h_t from the production function, so that

$$\log y_t = -0.2324 \log y_{t-1} + 0.2324 \log h_{t-1}$$
$$+0.176 \log k_{t-1} - 0.3773, \tag{4.17}$$

which, in turn, is substituted into the consumption function; we then obtain

$$\log c_t = -0.1183 \log y_{t-1} + 0.1183 \log h_{t-1} + 0.460 \log c_{t-1}$$
$$+0.0898 \log k_{t-1} - 0.2203. \tag{4.18}$$

The whole system (4.13)–(4.18) may be decomposed into two subsystems. The first, (4.13)–(4.15), determines k_t, g_t and α_t in terms of y_t, c_t and k_{t-1}; and the second, (4.16)–(4.18), determines y_t, c_t, and h_t in terms of k_{-1}, $k_0, ..., k_{t-1}$ and the initial values of y, c, and h. These relationships enable us to eliminate y_t and c_t from the parametric expression of k_t obtained as the solution of the first subsystem; we thus have

$$k_t = F(k_{-1}, k_0, ..., k_{t-1}, y_0, c_0, h_0). \tag{4.19}$$

[1] In the following analysis, we fix M/pY and B/Y at 0.604 and 0.007, respectively. We also assume the absence of technical progress and accept the state of technology in 1902.

Once the time path of k is determined, it is not difficult to obtain the paths of the other variables.

It is, however, not easy to see whether the solution k_t of equation (4.19) will approach the equilibrium value, $k = 3.403$, when t tends to infinity. We therefore give up the direct and frontal attack and introduce an auxiliary system to show that the time path of k calculated from the auxiliary system closely approximates the true path of k and converges to the point of the almost-full-employment growth equilibrium. For this purpose we neglect time-lags between $(\log y_t, \log c_t, \log h_t)$ and $(\log y_{t-1}, \log c_{t-1}, \log h_{t-1})$ in the second subsystem. We then obtain from (4.16)–(4.18)

$$\log y_t = 0.1333 \log k_{t-1} - 0.2173, \qquad (4.16^*)$$

$$\log c_t = 0.1257 \log k_{t-1} - 0.2573, \qquad (4.17^*)$$

$$\log h_t = -0.0524 \log k_{t-1} + 0.4708. \qquad (4.18^*)$$

Once k_{t-1} takes on a definite value, the corresponding y_t and c_t are obtained from (4.16*) and (4.17*), respectively. Therefore, α_t is determined by (4.15), g_t by (4.14), and k_t by (4.13). The curve $k_t = f^*(k_{t-1})$ in Figure 8 traces out the k_t corresponding to every possible value of k_{t-1}. Its intersection $\bar{k}$ with the 45° line represents the equilibrium value of k. As Figure 8 illustrates, any path starting from a reasonable initial point k_0 eventually reaches the point of equilibrium $\bar{k}$. This shows that the almost-full-employment growth equilibrium is practically globally stable, if time lags between (y_t, c_t, h_t) and $(y_{t-1}, c_{t-1}, h_{t-1})$ are abstracted from (4.16)–(4.18).

Let us compare the values of y_t, c_t, h_t, and α_t calculated from the true system (4.13)–(4.18) with the approximate solutions obtained from the 'time-lagless' system (4.13)–(4.18*). We start with the actual values of y, c, h and k_{-1} in 1901. It is seen from Figure 9 that the true paths of y_t, c_t, h_t and α_t (plotted by dots) rapidly and smoothly converge to the paths (straight lines) which the time-lagless system generates. After two periods from the start, the true $\log y_t$ and $\log h_t$ have already joined the respective straight lines, although it takes six or seven periods for $\log c_t$ and α_t to do so. By a number of experiments we have confirmed that similar results are obtained for different initial points. We may, therefore, safely conclude that the neglect of time-lags has no crucial effect on the stability of the growth equilibrium.[1]

[1] However, it is to be remembered that the stability assured is very weak indeed. It is shown that it takes about 150 years for the US economy to reach a point which is within one-tenth of the initial displacement from the growth equilibrium. Thus, the neoclassical harmonizing forces, even if they are at work, are not to be relied upon in practice. Cf. R. Sato, 'Fiscal policy in a neo-classical growth model: an analysis of time required for equilibrating adjustment', *Review of Economic Studies* (February 1963).

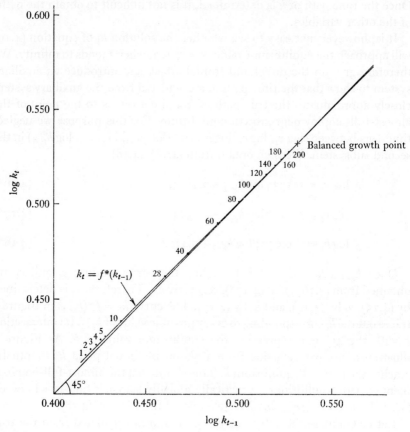

Figure 8
$k_t = f^*(k_{t-1})$.

Let us now turn to the determination of the money wage rate. As it follows from the relative share equation that

$$\log p_t = \log w_t - \log y_t - 0.160 + \log 0.99$$

for all t, we have

$$\log p_t - \log p_{t-1} = (\log w_t - \log w_{t-1}) - (\log y_t - \log y_{t-1}).$$

By substitution into the wage determination equation we have

$$\log w_t = 1.408 \log w_{t-1} - 0.402 \log w_{t-2} + 1.100 \log h_t$$
$$- 1.107 \log h_{t-1} - 0.100 (\log y_t - \log y_{t-1})$$
$$- 0.402(\log y_{t-1} - \log y_{t-2}) + 0.0183. \qquad (4.20)$$

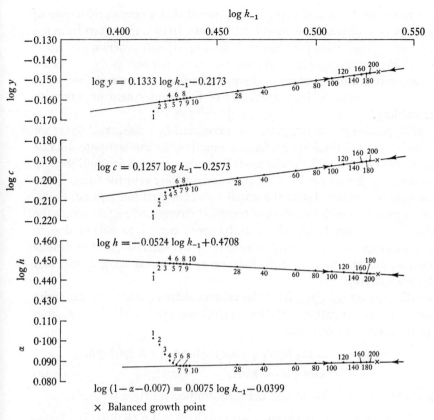

log (1 − α − 0.007) = 0.0075 log k_{-1} − 0.0399

× Balanced growth point

Figure 9

Substituting for log y and log h from (4.16*) and (4.18*), this can further be expressed in the form,

$$\log w_t = 1.408 \log w_{t-1} - 0.402 \log w_{t-2}$$
$$- 0.071(\log k_{t-1} - \log k_{t-2}) - 0.054(\log k_{t-2} - \log k_{t-3})$$
$$+ 0.00037(\log k_{t-2} - 0.5319) + 0.0154, \qquad (4.20^*)$$

where 0.5319 is the growth equilibrium value of capital per man. As log k_t changes very slowly and the coefficient applied to (log k_{t-2} − 0.5319) is very small, (4.20*) may safely be approximated by

$$\log w_t = 1.408 \log w_{t-1} - 0.402 \log w_{t-2} + 0.0154, \qquad (4.21)$$

which has a stationary solution, log w = −2.36; this is, however, too low to be economically meaningful. The characteristic equation of (4.21) is

$$\mu^2 - 1.408\mu + 0.402 = 0,$$

whose roots are 1.011 and 0.40. It is apparent that a considerable rate of wage increase is obtained for most initial points. In fact, if we start from the actual money wage rates for 1900 and 1901, (4.21) will generate persistent increases in money wages at an average rate of 6.3 per cent per year. As the real wage rate is almost constant, the price level also increases at the same rate.[1] This suggests the incompatibility of full employment growth with price stability.

Finally, putting $y = 0.713$, $p_t/p_{t-1} = 1.063$, and $L_t =$ the actual figure for L in period t in the liquidity preference function, we can compute the rate of interest associated with the almost-full-employment growth equilibrium. It is estimated at 2.95 per cent for 1902 and 4.69 per cent for 1929. These values may be compared with the actual figures of 3.16 and 4.73 per cent.

Let us now deal with the effect of technical changes. We again utilize the production function (2.3), which shifts from period to period due to technical changes, but, as before, we fix the employment ratio, the Cambridge coefficient, and the ratio of trade balance to income at 0.99, 0.604, and 0.007, respectively.

Substituting for w_{t-1}/p_{t-1} from the relative share equation, we can write the hours worked equation in the form (4.16) and use it to eliminate h_t from the production function; then

$$\log y_t = -0.2324 \log y_{t-1} + 0.2324 \log h_{t-1} + 0.176 \log k_{t-1}$$
$$+ 0.00633t - 0.2191, \tag{4.22}$$

which is further substituted into the consumption function to obtain

$$\log c_t = -0.1183 \log y_{t-1} + 0.1183 \log h_{t-1} + 0.0898 \log k_{t-1}$$
$$+ 0.460 \log c_{t-1} + 0.0032t - 0.1397. \tag{4.23}$$

In view of (4.22) and (4.23), the savings–investment identity,

$$\log(1 - \alpha_t - 0.007) = \log(c_t/y_t),$$

may be written as

$$\log(1 - \alpha_t - 0.007) = 0.1141 \log y_{t-1} - 0.1141 \log h_{t-1}$$
$$- 0.0866 \log k_{t-1} + 0.460 \log c_{t-1}$$
$$- 0.0031t + 0.0793. \tag{4.24}$$

We also have from (4.13) and (4.14)

$$\log k_t = \log(k_{t-1} + \alpha_t y_t) - 0.008. \tag{4.25}$$

[1] For the period 1902–29, the actual price rise is an average of 2.5 per cent per year, and the actual rise in wages is 3.4 per cent. It is not surprising that there are big differences between our estimates and the actual figures. There are technical changes in the actual economy, which mitigate the price increases and raise the real wage rate.

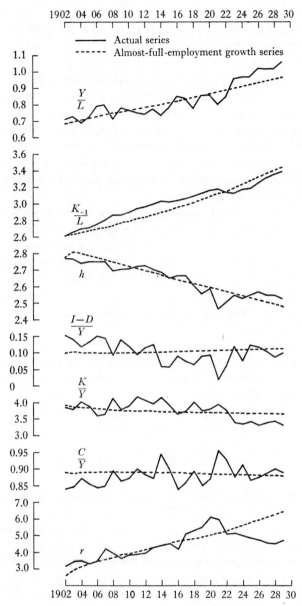

Figure 10
Comparison between the actual and the almost-full-employment series, 1902–29.

The system of equations, (4.16), (4.22)–(4.25), determines h_t, y_t, c_t and k_t once h_{t-1}, y_{t-1}, c_{t-1} and k_{t-1} are given. It is seen that the path (h_t, y_t, k_t) starting from the almost-full-employment equilibrium that would be established eventually if there were no technical progress ever after 1902 is dynamic by virtue of technical changes; a simulation shows that it is approached by the path starting from the actual 1902 state. Figure 10 compares the almost-full-employment growth path of h, y, k, and so on (all of them starting from the 1902 state) with the corresponding actual series. It is interesting to note that the almost-full-employment capital–output ratio shows a declining trend, while the almost-full-employment path of the consumption–income ratio, as well as that of the ratio of investment to income, has practically no trend.

It is obvious that (4.20) holds although technical improvements occur. As the time paths of h_t and y_t are known, (4.20) gives the behaviour of the wage rate; we find that it increases at an average rate of 4.2 per cent per year and is accompanied by a price rise of 2.9 per cent per year. These figures are less than the corresponding ones obtained in the absence of technical progress, because it is clear from (4.20) that a decrease in the hours worked and an increase in output per man caused by technical improvements have stabilizing effects on wage determination.

Once y_t, y_{t-1}, and p_t/p_{t-1} are known, we may solve the liquidity preference equation with respect to the rate of interest, because M/pY is fixed at 0.604, and Y_t equals $y_t L_t$ by definition. Figure 10 also compares the computed interest rates with the actual series.

As the employment ratio is kept constant along the almost-full-employment growth path, we obtain from the production function (2.3)

$$\log \frac{y_t/h_t}{y_{t-1}/h_{t-1}} = 0.176 \log \frac{k_{t-1}/h_t}{k_{t-2}/h_{t-1}} + 0.00633.$$

Since $0.00633 = \log 1.0147$, we find that in the absence of capital accumulation the upward shift in the production function would give rise to an increase of 1.47 per cent per year in output per man hour, y_t/h_t. It is also seen that capital per manhour, k_{t-1}/h_t, increases at an average rate of 1.36 per cent per year and hence generates an increase in the output per manhour at a rate of 0.24 per cent per year. Therefore, about 86 per cent of the increase in output per manhour can be attributed to technical change and the remaining 14 per cent to increased use of capital.[1]

---

[1] Similar figures which are very close to ours have been obtained by Solow for the period 1909–49. See his 'Technical change and the aggregate production function', p. 320.

2. PRICE STABILITY

So far we have been concerned with a growing economy which maintains a prescribed rate of employment. What happens if this is not so – if prices are pegged, say, at the 1902 level? We shall show that severe unemployment will accompany the state of balanced growth, provided that the wage rate and hours worked also remain constant over time.

Let us fix the Cambridge coefficient of cash balances and the ratio of trade balance to income at 0.604 and 0.007 as before, and the price p at the 1902 level, 0.511. We begin with the case of no technical progress and assume that the production function for 1902 is valid for the entire period. We have from the relative share equation

$$\log w = \log y - \log n + \log 0.511 + 0.160, \tag{4.26}$$

where n represents the employment ratio, $N/0.57L$. If we assume that h and w do not change, i.e. $h_t = h_{t-1}$ and $w_t = w_{t-1}$, we can eliminate w from the relative share equation (4.26), the wage determination equation and the hours worked equation; we get

$$\log n = -0.0467 \log y - 0.0806, \tag{4.27}$$

and $\qquad \log h = -0.4337 \log y + 0.3186. \tag{4.28}$

By substitution for n from (4.27), for h from (4.28), and for k from (4.10), the production function may be written after reformulation as:

$$\log y = 0.1447 \log \alpha - 0.0828.$$

This, together with (4.12), which should also be satisfied when prices and wages are held constant, gives the equilibrium values of α and y; we have

$$\alpha = 0.0778, \quad y = 0.572,$$

to which correspond the following values of n, h, and w:

$$n = 0.853, \quad h = 2.655, \quad w = 0.495.$$

It is seen that the investment–income ratio of 0.0778 implies a capital coefficient of 4.16, which is comparable with the figure for 1914, the highest in the 1900–29 series. The output per man of 0.572 amounts to 80 per cent of the output per man in the state of almost-full-employment growth equilibrium, while we can find no significant difference in the hours worked. It should be noted that the wage rate of 0.495 is only 87 per cent of the 1902 rate. It is also worth noticing that the employment ratio of 0.853 is slightly greater than the average of the figures in the Great Depression, which is 0.84. The rate of interest computed from the liquidity preference equation depends on L_t; it is estimated at 3.42 per cent for 1902 and 5.44 per cent for 1929. These figures are greater than the corresponding figures associated with the almost-full-employment growth equilibrium. This is not surprising, because price stability, on the one hand, induces severe unemployment (which further induces a decrease in income per capita) and, on the other hand, has favourable effects on the demand for money; clearly, the former is a cause of an excess supply of cash balances, while the latter, *ceteris paribus*, gives rise to an excess demand for them. Thus, two counteracting forces are at work; the positive force dominates the negative one in 1902 and 1929, so that the rate of interest required for price stability is higher than the almost-full-employment growth equilibrium rate of interest in these years.

Next, we shall be concerned with the case of technical progress; as before, p is pegged at the 1902 level, 0.511. From the production function, the relative share equation, the wage determination equation and the hours worked equation, we have

$$\log y_t = -2.7204 \log \frac{w_{t-1}}{h_{t-1}} + 0.6355 \log k_{t-1} + 0.0228t - 1.8981,$$

$$\log \frac{w_t}{h_t} = 0.5828 \log \frac{w_{t-1}}{h_{t-1}} + 0.0781 \log k_{t-1} + 0.0028t - 0.2639.$$

We also have from the consumption function and the equality between savings and investment

$$\log c_t = 0.5092 \log y_t + 0.460 \log c_{t-1} - 0.0282,$$

$$\log (1 - \alpha_t - 0.007) = -0.4908 \log y_t + 0.460 \log c_{t-1} - 0.0282,$$

where the Cambridge coefficient and the ratio of trade balance to income are fixed at 0.604 and 0.007, respectively. The last four equations, together with (4.25), constitute a closed system of difference equations; we can determine y_t, c_t, w_t/h_t, and k_t once their values in the previous period are known.

It is seen that in the absence of technical change we obtain a stationary time path if w/h, c, and k are initially set at 0.186, 0.523 and 2.378, respectively, and 14.7 per cent of the labour force will at all times be unemployed. In the presence of technical change, however, a dynamic path is generated from the same initial position; output per man, capital per man, and the money wage rate per hour worked will increase, but the capital–output ratio will decline. It is also seen that, along this path, unemployment at an average rate of 8.0 per cent is required to ensure price stability. This, together with our previous finding that technical progress reduces the price increase associated with almost-full-employment growth, leads to the following

TABLE 9. *Comparison of full employment and price stability simulations*

		Full employment simulation		Price stability simulation	
	Observed (1)	No technical progress (2)	Technical progress (3)	No technical progress (4)	Technical progress (5)
Average rate of wage rise, %	2.1 (3.4)	7.1 (6.3)	5.2[a] (4.2)	0 (0)	1.6[b] (1.3)
Average rate of price rise, %	0.6 (2.5)	7.1 (6.3)	3.8[a] (2.9)	0 (0)	0 (0)
Average unemployment ratio, %	10.3 (1.0)	1.0 (1.0)	1.0 (1.0)	17.0[b] (14.7)	11.6[b] (8.0)

[a] The average of the results of the simulation for 1930–40 and the results of the simulation for 1947–52. The year 1946 was excluded, because the values of the lagged endogenous variable for that year were found to be abnormal.
[b] The average of the results of the simulation for 1930–40 and the results of the simulation for 1946–52. In these simulations the price level was pegged at the 1930 and the 1946 level, respectively.

conclusion: the contradiction between price stability and full employment will be mitigated by technical progress.

A similar analysis can be made for the last half of our sample period, 1930–52 (excluding the war period, 1941–5), by fixing the Cambridge coefficient at the mean of the 1930–52 (excluding 1931–5 and 1941–9) series, the ratio of trade balance to income at the mean of the 1930–52 (excluding 1931–5 and 1941–7) series, and the growth rate of the population fifteen years of age and over at the mean of the 1930–52 series. Table 9 summarizes the results of the simulations. For convenience of comparison, the corresponding figures obtained by the simulations for the period 1902–29 are given in parentheses. It is interesting to find that the basic contradiction between price stability and full employment was more severe in the period 1930–52, excluding the war period, than in 1902–29. It is also worth noting that the figures actually observed in 1930–52, excluding 1941–5, are very near to the results of the price stability simulation for the same period (see the figures without parentheses in column 5 of the table), whereas the actual figures in 1902–29 are very near to the results of the full-employment simulation for that period (see the figures in parentheses in column 3). We may, therefore, conjecture that a drastic change in the dynamic mechanism occurred at the end of the Golden Twenties.

3. A SORT OF HARRODIAN INSTABILITY –
A SIMULATION OF THE GREAT DEPRESSION

It is absurd to derive from this the conclusion that price-stability policy was effective in the thirties. It is no more than a topsy-turvy logic; in fact, we may merely conclude that a policy aiming purely at price stability has such an adverse effect on unemployment as to bring about unemployment on such a scale as that actually experienced during the gloomy thirties. The interesting problem of discovering the true causes of the Great Depression is still unsolved. In this section we shall present the results of a simulation, in order to show that the neoclassical growth equilibrium established in Section 1 above could easily fall into a bottomless depression comparable with the Great Depression, if we assume some hypothetical yet plausible investment function.

Throughout the following discussion let us assume, as before, that there prevail the technology that existed in 1902 and the ratio of trade balance to income that was experienced, on the average, during the period 1901–29 (excluding the exceptional years 1915–21). On the other hand, the present model differs from the model used for the neoclassical simulation in assuming that the savings–income ratio and the capital–labour (manhour) ratio remain constant, while the Cambridge coefficient is adapted so as to keep the savings–income ratio at the prescribed value. We abandon the neoclassical preference for capitalism, which assumes that the employment ratio always automatically attains such a high figure as 99 per cent. Instead, we now explicitly introduce into the system an independent investment function of the Adaptable-Acceleration-Principle type.

We begin with the state of 'almost-full-employment' balanced growth equilibrium which would be obtained if the Cambridge coefficient for cash balances and the rate of growth of the labour force took on the values of 0.604 and 1.87 per cent per year, respectively. Then the initial values of capital per man, income per man, the employment ratio, the real wage rate, the hours worked and the investment–income ratio are:

$$k = 3.403, \quad y = 0.713, \quad N/0.57L = 0.99, \quad w/p = 1.041,$$

$$h = 2.773, \quad \alpha = 0.0892,$$

respectively. These imply that the savings–income ratio, the capital–labour (manhour) ratio, and the capital–output ratio have the values, 0.0892, 2.175 and 4.77, respectively. Throughout the following, we fix the savings–income ratio and the capital–labour (manhour) ratio at these values and regard a capital–output ratio of 4.77 as 'optimal', so that firms are assumed to aim at keeping that value of the capital–output ratio in making their investment decisions.

The natural rate of growth (or the rate of growth of the labour force) is 1.87 per cent per year, and the warranted rate of growth, that is the 'optimal' capital–output ratio divided by the savings–income ratio, also takes on the same value. Thus, the Harrodian equilibrium condition that the natural and the warranted rates of growth are equal to each other is satisfied. Since the economy is assumed to be already on the equilibrium growth path, income, consumption, employment and the stock of capital continue to grow at the common rate of 1.87 per cent per year, while the real wage rate and the hours worked remain unchanged; there is no contradiction to be found in this economy.

Let us now suppose that the natural rate of growth is reduced to 1.80 per cent per year for some reason or other, so that the warranted rate exceeds the natural rate. Then, as the stock of capital expands more rapidly than the labour force, some of it will become redundant. Labour will be the limiting factor of production, so that the actual rate of growth of output will at most be as high as the natural rate. Once excess capacity appears and the actual rate of growth does not reach the warranted rate, a further (and more serious) decline in the actual rate will be generated; and the slump which emerges in this way will become deeper and deeper as time goes on.

This avalanche from the Harrodian ridge may be explained by introducing an investment function of the Adaptable-Acceleration-Principle type. As the optimal capital coefficient is assumed to be 4.77, the desired stock of capital in period t is given by $4.77 Y_t$. If the existing stock of capital K_{t-1} equals the desired stock, $4.77 Y_t$, entrepreneurs will be satisfied with the existing stock which has resulted from investment in period $t-1$ and will be prepared to invest again in period t at the same rate of net investment per capita as they did in period $t-1$, so that

$$(I_t - D_t)/K_{t-1} = (I_{t-1} - D_{t-1})/K_{t-2}.$$

On the other hand, if the desired stock of capital exceeds or falls short of the existing stock, K_{t-1}, entrepreneurs have to adjust upwards or downwards, and the ratio $(I_t - D_t)/K_{t-1}$ is greater or smaller than $(I_{t-1} - D_{t-1})/K_{t-2}$ accordingly. Such an attitude towards investment was assumed by Harrod when he established the instability of the growth equilibrium in his now classic work;[1] it fits in with the other equations of our model if it is formulated as

$$g_t/g_{t-1} = (4.77 Y_t/K_{t-1})^a, \tag{4.29}$$

where $g_t = (I_t - D_t)/K_{t-1}$, and a is a positive constant.

[1] R. F. Harrod, *Towards a Dynamic Economics* (Macmillan, 1948), lecture three.

The equation between savings and investment can now be written as

$$0.0892 Y_t = g_t K_{t-1}, \tag{4.30}$$

which enables us to eliminate Y_t/K_{t-1} from (4.29). We obtain

$$g_t/g_{t-1} = (g_t/0.0187)^a. \tag{4.31}$$

It is shown that when a is less than 2, the actual rate of growth of the capital stock, g_t, obeying the formula (4.31), diverges through time farther and farther from the warranted rate, whereas when a is greater than 2, the actual rate traces damped oscillations around the warranted rate. Throughout the rest of this section, we set a at 0.5 as an experiment, so that (4.31) can be put in the following log-linear form:

$$\log g_t = 2 \log g_{t-1} - \log 0.0187. \tag{4.32}$$

Let us now suppose that the decrease in the rate of growth of the labour force from 1.87 to 1.80 per cent per year gives rise to the same decrease in the actual rate of growth of the capital stock. It is a reasonable assumption, because, as we have already accepted the assumption that the capital–labour (manhour) ratio is inflexible, the stock of capital must grow at the same rate as the labour force unless there is a change in the working hours. When the value of g in period 0 is thus given at 1.80 per cent per year, (4.32) is solved as $g_t = 0.0187(1.80/1.87)^{2^t}$. As soon as the value of the actual growth rate g_t in each period is known, the formula,

$$k_t = \frac{1+g_t}{1.0180} k_{t-1},$$

which directly follows from $K_t = (1+g_t)K_{t-1}$ and $K_{t+1} = 1.0180 L_t$, gives the value of the capital per man in each period, since the initial capital per man is given as 3.403. As we know the values of g_t and k_{t-1} for each period, we can calculate the values of income per man, y_t, by use of the formula,

$$0.0892 y_t = g_t k_{t-1},$$

which is obtained by dividing (4.30) by L_t.

Because the production function (2.3) is homogeneous of degree one with respect to N_t, K_{t-1}, and h_t, it can be written as

$$\log \frac{y_t}{h_t} \frac{L_t}{N_t} = 0.176 \log \frac{K_{t-1}}{h_t N_t} + 0.00633t + 0.519u - 0.242655. \tag{4.33}$$

Since we assume the inflexibility of the capital–labour (manhour) ratio and fix it at 2.175, and since we assume that the technology of 1902 continues to prevail throughout the period, the right-hand side of (4.33) takes on a

TABLE 10. *The results of an experiment on the Harrodian avalanche*

Period	g_t (%)	k_t	y_t	c_t
-1		3.403		
0	1.80	3.403	0.687	0.621
1	1.73	3.401	0.660	0.596
2	1.60	3.394	0.610	0.551
3	1.38	3.380	0.525	0.475
4	1.02	3.354	0.386	0.349

	$\dfrac{N_t}{0.57L_t}$ (%)	h_t	w_t	p_t
0	96.4	2.75	0.504	0.489
1	93.5	2.72	0.490	0.480
2	88.2	2.66	0.464	0.464
3	78.9	2.56	0.419	0.435
4	62.8	2.37	0.342	0.384

constant value. Combining (4.33) with the relative share equation (2.4) we obtain

$$\log \frac{w_t}{p_t h_t} = -0.425812. \tag{4.34}$$

Substituting for w/ph from this, the hours worked equation (2.6) can be written as

$$\log h_t = 0.343 \log (N_t/0.57L_t) + 0.4441, \tag{4.35}$$

which, in turn, is substituted into (4.33) to obtain finally

$$\log (N_t/0.57L_t) = 0.7446 \log y_t + 0.1054. \tag{4.36}$$

As the value of y_t is determined for each t, (4.36) determines the employment ratio, $N_t/0.57L_t$; then (4.35) determines the hours worked, h_t, and (4.34) the real-wage rate, w_t/p_t. Given the values of the employment ratio, the hours worked, the real-wage rate and the price levels in periods $t-1$ and $t-2$, the wage determination equation (2.5) gives the money wage rate or the price level in period t. The remaining variables to be determined are the real cash balances per capita and the rate of interest. They are determined by the consumption function (2.1) and the liquidity preference equation (2.2) respectively.

The results of the simulation are listed in Table 10. However, in order to judge the magnitude of the crisis thus generated and compare it with an actual one (say, the magnitude of the Great Depression), the figures in the table and the corresponding actual figures must be translated into an equivalent basis. For this purpose, we first estimate from the production

3

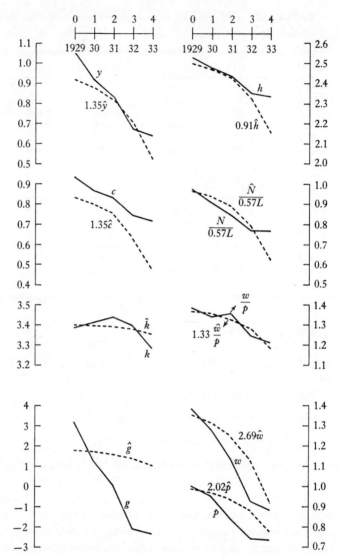

Figure 11
The results of the simulation compared with the Great Depression.

function in 1902 the value of productivity Y/hN in a state of almost-full-employment growth equilibrium and from the production function in 1929 the value of Y/hN corresponding to the actual capital per manhour, K_{-1}/hN, in 1929. It is found that the latter is 1.5 times as high as the former. Next, the actual figure of hours worked, h, in 1929 is nine-tenths of the almost-full-employment growth equilibrium value of h resulting from the same conditions as the simulation assumes. We therefore multiply the figures for income per man and consumption per man obtained by the simulation, by

$$1.35 \ (= 1.5 \times 0.9)$$

and the hours worked by 0.9, but the figures of capital per man are compared with each other on a one-to-one basis. Finally, the price level in 1928 is 2.02 times as high as the price level in 1901, while the real-wage rate in 1929 is 1.33 times as high as the almost-full-employment growth equilibrium real-wage rate. Consequently, the results of the simulation concerning the price and wage levels are multiplied by 2.02 and 2.69 respectively. The graphs in Figure 11 are drawn after such adjustments, from which the reader will clearly find that the slump generated by our simulation is of a similar magnitude as was the Great Depression. (Concerning the consumption per man, it is seen that the results of the simulation differ from the actual figures in the Great Depression rather significantly. This is, however, mainly due to our assumption in the simulation that the consumption–income ratio remains constant, which evidently is not consistent with the obvious fact that the propensity to consume increases in times of depression.) It is recognized that it is the form of the investment function rather than the other assumptions, such as the fixed capital–labour (manhour) ratio and the fixed savings–income ratio, that is crucial in generating instability. Then we may conclude our investigation by saying that the choice between neo-classical tranquillity and Harrodian instability is in the hands of entrepreneurs, whose attitudes towards investment determine everything.[1]

[1] An extension of the simulation of the Great Depression beyond four years generates higher levels of unemployment than those which were in fact observed after 1934. This suggests that there was a drastic, favourable change in the investment function in 1933 and 1934.

Year	Y	C	K	M	D	I^a	B^b
1900	33.0	27.8	131.57	8.9	—	—	—
1901	36.3	30.5	136.71	10.0	4.28	9.42	0.66
1902	36.8	30.9	142.27	10.8	4.44	10.00	0.34
1903	38.8	32.9	147.72	11.5	4.61	10.06	0.45
1904	38.1	33.3	152.20	12.0	4.80	9.28	0.32
1905	40.7	34.9	157.65	13.2	4.94	10.39	0.35
1906	45.4	38.3	164.50	14.1	5.18	12.03	0.25
1907	46.7	39.7	171.25	15.1	5.54	12.29	0.25
1908	42.6	38.1	175.31	14.7	5.72	9.78	0.44
1909	47.8	41.4	182.05	15.8	5.94	12.68	−0.34
1910	48.2	42.1	187.86	17.0	6.13	11.94	0.29
1911	47.9	43.2	192.45	17.8	6.43	11.02	0.11
1912	48.5	42.8	198.04	18.9	6.64	12.23	0.11
1913	51.3	44.7	204.38	19.4	6.89	13.23	0.26
1914	49.8	47.1	207.28	20.0	7.12	10.02	−0.20
1915	53.7	48.2	210.36	20.7	7.35	10.43	2.42
1916	58.8	49.4	215.70	24.2	7.54	12.88	4.06
1917	59.0	50.8	220.26	28.2	7.84	12.40	3.64
1918	55.4	49.6	223.94	31.4	8.37	12.05	2.12
1919	61.1	52.2	229.37	35.6	9.14	14.57	3.47
1920	62.2	54.2	235.13	39.9	9.18	14.94	2.24
1921	59.6	57.0	236.19	37.8	8.79	9.85	1.54
1922	63.9	59.2	240.15	39.0	9.29	13.25	0.74
1923	73.5	64.3	248.87	42.7	9.53	18.25	0.48
1924	75.6	69.0	254.47	44.5	9.66	15.26	1.00
1925	77.3	67.1	264.08	48.3	10.0	19.61	0.59
1926	82.8	72.5	273.94	50.6	10.6	20.46	0.44
1927	83.6	74.2	282.61	52.2	10.5	19.17	0.73
1928	84.9	76.3	290.20	54.7	10.8	18.39	1.01
1929	90.3	80.3	299.42	55.2	11.1	20.32	0.78
1930	80.5	75.9	303.30	54.4	11.0	14.88	0.72
1931	73.5	73.2	303.42	52.9	10.8	10.92	0.18
1932	60.3	66.4	297.12	45.4	10.4	4.10	0.20
1933	58.2	65.0	290.12	41.7	10.1	3.10	0.20
1934	64.4	68.6	285.43	46.0	10.2	5.51	0.49
1935	75.4	73.1	287.78	49.9	10.4	12.75	−0.05
1936	85.0	80.8	292.11	55.1	10.8	15.13	−0.13
1937	92.7	84.4	300.33	57.3	11.2	19.42	0.08
1938	85.4	83.0	301.38	56.6	11.3	12.35	1.35
1939	92.3	87.0	305.58	60.9	11.5	15.70	1.10
1940	101.2	91.7	313.32	67.0	11.8	19.54	1.76
1941	113.3	97.9	327.41	74.2	12.9	26.99	1.31
1942	107.8	96.2	338.98	82.0	14.8	26.37	0.03
1943	105.2	98.8	347.08	110.2	16.7	24.80	−1.70
1944	107.1	102.2	353.46	136.2	19.6	25.98	−1.48
1945	108.8	109.1	354.13	162.8	21.4	22.07	−0.97
1946	131.4	122.3	359.43	171.2	20.5	25.80	3.80
1947	130.9	124.9	359.30	165.5	22.6	22.47	6.13
1948	134.7	127.5	365.19	167.9	24.1	24.99	1.31
1949	129.1	130.7	363.21	167.9	25.3	23.32	0.38
1950	147.8	138.7	373.73	173.8	26.2	36.72	−1.42
1951	152.1	139.8	385.95	181.0	27.4	39.62	0.08
1952	154.3	143.9	396.47	191.0	26.2	36.72	−0.12

^{a} Computed by the formula: $I_t = K_t - K_{t-1} + D_t$
^{b} Computed by the formula: $B_t = Y_t - C_t - I_t + D_t$

Year	L	N	h	p^c	w^d	r
1900	49.948	27.295	2.766	0.497	0.546	2.92
1901	51.088	28.425	2.771	0.496	0.556	2.95
1902	52.301	29.647	2.770	0.511	0.568	3.16
1903	53.463	30.525	2.769	0.515	0.587	3.49
1904	54.679	30.419	2.740	0.522	0.602	3.45
1905	55.988	31.814	2.749	0.533	0.613	3.31
1906	57.281	33.071	2.749	0.546	0.634	3.51
1907	58.543	33.848	2.747	0.567	0.654	4.18
1908	59.905	33.086	2.696	0.566	0.637	3.86
1909	61.315	34.785	2.704	0.588	0.678	3.69
1910	62.787	35.708	2.705	0.602	0.697	3.90
1911	63.859	36.274	2.715	0.597	0.680	3.90
1912	64.912	37.341	2.722	0.623	0.729	3.99
1913	66.243	37.896	2.704	0.626	0.736	4.29
1914	67.556	37.475	2.688	0.635	0.755	4.42
1915	68.544	37.669	2.654	0.655	0.798	4.51
1916	69.514	40.126	2.668	0.740	0.855	4.22
1917	70.517	41.531	2.665	0.914	1.072	5.10
1918	71.213	43.998	2.611	1.051	1.125	5.29
1919	71.677	42.313	2.551	1.067	1.336	5.49
1920	72.677	41.497	2.584	1.217	1.436	6.12
1921	74.146	39.361	2.461	1.037	1.127	5.97
1922	75.233	41.383	2.508	0.986	1.176	5.10
1923	76.743	43.938	2.544	1.008	1.298	5.12
1924	78.486	43.315	2.527	0.995	1.307	5.00
1925	79.906	44.512	2.549	1.017	1.366	4.88
1926	81.302	45.795	2.563	1.022	1.380	4.73
1927	82.775	45.900	2.547	0.994	1.373	4.57
1928	84.207	46.382	2.545	1.001	1.392	4.55
1929	85.565	47.611	2.528	1.000	1.384	4.73
1930	87.738	45.465	2.477	0.955	1.281	4.55
1931	88.231	42.607	2.435	0.839	1.136	4.58
1932	89.323	39.274	2.352	0.743	0.926	5.01
1933	90.435	39.615	2.336	0.732	0.886	4.49
1934	91.641	42.739	2.167	0.781	0.967	4.00
1935	92.867	44.224	2.210	0.772	1.079	3.60
1936	94.067	47.078	2.269	0.804	1.134	3.24
1937	95.252	48.233	2.311	0.810	1.257	3.26
1938	96.503	46.379	2.238	0.806	1.209	3.19
1939	97.761	47.769	2.272	0.800	1.249	3.01
1940	99.017	49.606	2.278	0.808	1.313	2.84
1941	100.194	54.097	2.296	0.874	1.512	2.77
1942	101.384	59.056	2.342	0.988	1.800	2.83
1943	102.508	64.864	2.410	1.076	1.905	2.73
1944	103.525	66.020	2.424	1.108	2.061	2.72
1945	104.454	64.363	2.331	1.142	2.134	2.62
1946	104.861	58.917	2.232	1.221	2.389	2.53
1947	106.259	59.264	2.199	1.367	2.507	2.61
1948	107.883	60.216	2.176	1.431	2.763	2.82
1949	109.497	58.702	2.153	1.439	2.797	2.66
1950	110.922	60.041	2.131	1.455	2.964	2.62
1951	112.091	63.759	2.117	1.565	3.149	2.86
1952	113.144	64.894	2.113	1.592	3.248	2.96

[c] Obtained by dividing the Kuznets net national product estimates in current dollars by the Kuznets net national product estimates, *Y*, in 1929 dollars.

[d] Obtained by dividing the earned income estimates (used by Klein and Kosobud, *op. cit.* pp. 183–4) by the number of persons engaged, *N*. From 1941 we made the same adjustment as Klein and Kosobud to the earned income series. See *op. cit.* p. 182, footnote 2.

PART II

Input–output analysis of the effectiveness
of fiscal policies for the United Kingdom, 1954

by M. Morishima and T. Nosse

1. *Introduction*

A 'multiplier' measures the marginal effect of a unit increase of government expenditure upon one of various measures of national income, such as national income at factor cost, national income at market prices, and disposable income. Since Keynes (or since Kahn) they have been discussed in a non-numerical way by many economists, but, apart from that pioneering work of Richard and W. M. Stone, it was Arthur S. Goldberger who first estimated the values of multipliers econometrically.[1] Estimations so far made have usually been for macroeconometric models. Although they consist of a number of structural equations and identities (for example, the Klein–Goldberger model is a system of twenty-one behavioural, technological and definitional equations) most of them do not disaggregate the government sector, so that the multipliers derived from these models are independent of the sectors to which the increase in government expenditure is directed.[2] In contrast, our mixed Keynes–Leontief model, developed in Chapter 2 below, treats the government sector as an industry, which produces the services of 'public administration, etc.' and buys goods from other industries and households. This enables us to analyse fiscal policy problems on a more disaggregated level. In fact, in this model the effects of changes in government expenditure upon outputs of industries are given by the Leontief inverse of the matrix of total transaction coefficients. The multipliers differ from output to output and their values depend on where the initial impulse is directed. The effect of an increase in government expenditure on the national income at factor cost, for instance, is an aggregation of effects on outputs, which also varies according to the channel via which the government expenditure is injected.

The choice of industries to which to allocate government expenditure is thus an important choice for the public authorities. In Chapter 3 it is shown that the criteria for optimal marginal expenditure are different from the

---

[1] R. and W. M. Stone, 'The marginal propensity to consume and the multiplier: a statistical investigation', *Review of Economic Studies* (October 1938). A. S. Goldberger, *Impact Multipliers and Dynamic Properties of the Klein–Goldberger Model* (North-Holland Publishing, Co. 1959).

[2] One of the exceptions is the Brookings model. It is highly disaggregated in the government sectors as well as in the industrial sectors. See *The Brookings Quarterly Econometric Model of the United States*, ed. by J. S. Duesenberry, G. Fromm, L. R. Klein and E. Kuh (North-Holland Publishing Co. 1965).

criteria for the global optimum allocation of total government expenditure. It is also seen that Samuelson's LeChatelier principle is related to this problem.[1] In fact, the former criteria are given in terms of the impact multipliers obtained when outputs of all industries are flexible, whilst the latter are given in terms of the most restrictive multipliers, which assume that the output of only one industry is flexible and all others are set at some fixed amounts. They are respectively the last and the first of the Samuelson–LeChatelier sequences of multiplier effects. Thus, according to these criteria, an actual budget, i.e. the 1954 budget of the United Kingdom in our case, may be examined for efficiency from both the global and the local points of view. We calculate interindustrial impact multipliers of various orders, on the basis of which we decide whether a given budget fully or tolerably maximizes the income-generating power of government expenditure.

Chapter 4 is devoted to an analysis of the catalytic action of a tax increase, which leads to an extension of the theory of the balanced-budget multiplier due to T. Haavelmo.[2] It begins by pointing out the negative effects of a tax increase on national income, and then shows that a tax increase is transmuted into a positive income-generator when it is combined with an increase in the government expenditure. The multiplier effect of a balanced budget is no more than the catalytic effect of a tax increase in the extreme case. In fact, in the case where a balanced budget is strictly required, marginally or globally, it is impossible to have a policy relying on public expenditure, because it always results in a deficit, marginal or global; a deficit can be avoided only if the expenditure policy is combined with a tax increase plan. Similarly, in the more general case of a given size of deficit, ζ, being allowed to the public authorities, a pure expenditure policy is feasible only to a limited extent, so that it cannot have much effect on national income. However, with the same limitation of the deficit, an expenditure policy is possible to a greater extent if it is combined with a policy of increased taxation in appropriate proportions. An increase in the multiplier effect brought about in this way may be attributed to the catalytic effect of the tax increase policy.

The rest of Chapter 4 deals with the built-in flexibilities of personal and/or excise taxes, both short- and longer-term. In spite of general recognition of the importance of the problem, we have so far been provided only with rather poor estimates of the effectiveness of built-in flexibility. The most elaborate estimates are still Goldberger's, based on the Klein–Goldberger macroeconometric model. As far as the authors know, there is no estimate

[1] P. A. Samuelson, 'An extension of the LeChatelier principle', *Econometrica* (April 1960).
[2] T. Haavelmo, 'Multiplier effects of a balanced budget', *Econometrica* (October 1945).

based on input–output tables. We compare our figures with Goldberger's and other authors', with the hope that more elaborate investigations will be undertaken in the future, and will, in particular, take explicit account of the non-linearity of the tax functions.

Finally, in the following econometric investigation we use the *Input–Output Tables for the United Kingdom, 1954, Blue Books* and *Family Expenditure Survey Reports* as the main source of data. The parameters of the model outlined in the first half of Chapter 2 are estimated in its second half. The new *Input–Output Tables for the United Kingdom, 1963*[1] became available only after completion of the work for the UK for 1954. We have repeated the exercise for 1963. Although we report below only on the work for 1954, most of our main conclusions are confirmed by our work for 1963.

[1] London: HMSO, 1970.

2. An interindustrial model with endogenous consumption

1. A MIXED LEONTIEF–KEYNES MODEL

In the usual static, open model of interindustrial relations, the economy is divided into a number of industries, and the final demands for outputs (comprising demands for the future (investment) as well as demands from persons, public authorities and foreign countries) are all treated as exogenous. If we assume constant input coefficients, the model can be solved for the outputs necessary to fill the given array of final demands. It can also compute the effects of an autonomous change in the final demand for a good on the outputs of various industries.

This view of economic repercussions, which is due to Leontief, is contrasted with Keynes' view. Keynes completely ignored interindustrial phenomena and treated consumption as a generator of the income propagation process. But both views should be synthesized because, on the one hand, the Leontief process only gives partial streams of outputs, obtained by damming up the back flows through the channel of consumption and, on the other, Keynes' theory of the multiplier can be valid only if it is supplemented by accurate information about the structure of industrial outputs. In fact, if the tax rate on employment income is different from the tax rate on profits, as is usually the case, the exact value of the multiplier cannot be computed – even if we accept Keynes' consumption function, which neglects the difference in the propensity to consume between workers and capitalists – unless we know the proportion of wages to profits, which depends on the industrial distribution of outputs.

With the intention of building a pair of semi-detached houses for Keynes and Leontief, a connection is made between the national income accounting system and the input–output table.[1] In Table 1, Y_{ij} and M_j represent the quantity of industry i's output and the quantity of imported goods bought by industry j for the purpose of current production. After subtracting the material input, $\sum\limits_{i} Y_{ij} + M_j$, wages, W_j, and taxes, T_j, from the total output of industry j, Y_j, and adding subsidies, S_j, which are granted to industry j

[1] This idea was first developed by Kenichi Miyazawa, 'Foreign trade multiplier, input–output analysis and the consumption function', *Quarterly Journal of Economics*, vol. 74, no. 1, 1960, pp. 53–64. But he did not investigate the tax problem. See also K. Miyazawa and S. Masegi 'Interindustry analysis and the structure of income-distribution', *Metroeconomica*, vol. xv, 1963, pp. 89–103.

TABLE I. *The basic accounting system*

		Consuming industries				Persons	Public authorities	Gross domestic capital formation	Exports	Stock appreciation	Row sum
		1	2	...	n						
Producing industries	1	Y_{11}	Y_{12}	...	Y_{1n}	C_1	G_1	I_1	E_1	D_1	Y_1
	2	Y_{21}	Y_{22}	...	Y_{2n}	C_2	G_2	I_2	E_2	D_2	Y_2
		⋮	⋮		⋮	⋮	⋮	⋮	⋮	⋮	⋮
	n	Y_{n1}	Y_{n2}	...	Y_{nn}	C_n	G_n	I_n	E_n	D_n	Y_n
Imports		M_1	M_2	...	M_n	C_M	G_M	I_M	E_M	D_M	M
Taxes on expenditure (less) subsidies		T_1 $-S_1$	T_2 $-S_2$	...	T_n $-S_n$	T_C $-S_C$	T_G $-S_G$	T_I $-S_I$	—	—	T $-S$
Income from employment		W_1	W_2	...	W_n	—	—	—	—	—	W
Gross profits and other trading income		P_1	P_2	...	P_n	—	—	—	—	—	P
Column sum		Y_1	Y_2	...	Y_n	C	G	I	E	D	$Y = \Sigma Y_i$

by the public authorities, we obtain an amount which accrues to the industrialists as gross profits, P_j. This is the cost–profit identity which must hold for each industry. On the other hand, a horizontal reading of Table I enables us to find a set of demand–supply equations, a typical one of which states that the total output of industry i, Y_i, must be equated, after a suitable adjustment to stock, D_i, with the sum of consumption, C_i, government expenditure, G_i, investment, I_i, exports, E_i, and intermediate demands $Y_{i1}, ..., Y_{in}$, by industries. We thus have two sets of equations which can be written as

$$Y_j = \sum_i a_{ij} Y_j + a_{Mj} Y_j + T_j - S_j + W_j + P_j \quad (j = 1, ..., n), \qquad (2.1)$$

and

$$Y_i = \sum_j a_{ij} Y_j + C_i + G_i + I_i + E_i + D_i \quad (i = 1, ..., n), \qquad (2.2)$$

respectively, with input coefficients, $a_{ij} = Y_{ij}/Y_j$ and $a_{Mj} = M_j/Y_j$, which are assumed constant throughout the following analysis.[1]

[1] Two different rationalizations of the assumption of constant input coefficients have been offered by Samuelson and Klein. See P. A. Samuelson, 'Abstract of a theorem concerning substitutability in open Leontief models', *Activity Analysis of Production and Allocation*, ed. T. C. Koopmans (John Wiley and Sons, Inc. 1951), pp. 142–6, and L. R. Klein, 'On the interpretation of Professor Leontief's system', *Review of Economic Studies* (1952–3). But they neglect excise taxes. Our assumption may be justified if we assume a linear

Two concepts of national income are now defined, in terms of the inter-industrial flows of goods and services. To establish them the domestic net output Y^* is first defined as the part of the total output Y which remains after the part consumed by industries for current production, $\sum_i \sum_j Y_{ij} + \sum_i M_i$, has been deduced. From (2.2) we have

$$Y^* = C^* + G^* + I^* + (E^* - M) + D^*,$$

where C^* is the total personal consumption of goods (including imported goods) and services, i.e. $C^* = \sum_i C_i + C_M$; and similarly for G^*, etc. Y^* includes outlay taxes on industrial transactions (less subsidies to industries) so that the gross domestic income at factor cost Y_f is obtained by deducting $\sum_{i=1}^{n}(T_i - S_i)$ from Y^*. We get from (2.1)

$$Y_f = W + P = C^* + G^* + I^* + (E^* - M) + D^* - \sum_{i=1}^{n}(T_i - S_i).$$

On the other hand, Y^* does not include outlay taxes on final expenditures (less subsidies to final buyers). Therefore, to obtain the domestic gross income at market prices, Y_m, the amount, $\sum_{i=C,G,I}(T_i - S_i)$, must be added:

$$Y_m = C^* + G^* + I^* + (E^* - M) + D^* + \sum_{i=C,G,I}(T_i - S_i).$$

As in our notation C, G, etc. symbolize the respective final demands at market prices (note that $D^* = D$), we can derive the well-known national income accounting formulas:

$$Y_f = C + G + I + (E - M) + D - (T - S), \tag{2.3}$$

$$Y_m = C + G + I + (E - M) + D. \tag{2.4}$$

Let us now specify the personal consumption function which plays the pivotal role in the multi-sectoral analysis of income propagation. First, let t_{ci} be the outlay tax rate levied on personal expenditure on good i ($i = 1, ..., n, M$). We then have

$$T_C = \sum_{i=1}^{n} t_{ci} C_i + t_{cM} C_M, \tag{2.5}$$

production function for each industry and independence of prices from the excise tax rates. In the case of production functions being of the Cobb–Douglas form, we may derive, under the assumptions that perfect competition prevails and that each industry maximizes its gross profits, the marginal conditions:

$$Y_{ij}/Y_j = \alpha_{ij}/(1 + t_{ei}) \quad (i, j = 1, ..., n),$$

were α_{ij} is an exponent of the Cobb–Douglas production function of industry j and t_{ei} the excise tax rate on industrial outlay on good i. In this case (a variant of which will be discussed in Part III below), a reduction of t_{ei} gives rise to an increase in input coefficients.

so that the column summation of personal expenditures in Table 1 implies

$$C + S_C = \sum_{i}^{n} (1 + t_{ci}) C_i + (1 + t_{cM}) C_M. \tag{2.6}$$

Bearing in mind that the personal demands, $C_1, ..., C_n$ and C_M, comprise demands not only from recipients of wages and distributed profits (denoted by $C_1', ..., C_n', C_M'$) but also people receiving subsidies (denoted by $C_1'', ..., C_n'', C_M''$), (2.6) can be written as

$$C + S_C = \left[\sum_{i=1}^{n} (1 + t_{ci}) C_i' + (1 + t_{cM}) C_M' \right] + \left[\sum_{i=1}^{n} (1 + t_{ci}) C_i'' + (1 + t_{cM}) C_M'' \right]. \tag{2.7}$$

Since it is very natural to assume that there are no savings from subsidies, (2.7) can be split into two equations,

$$S_C = \sum_{i=1}^{n} (1 + t_{ci}) C_i'' + (1 + t_{cM}) C_M'' \tag{2.8}$$

and

$$C = \sum_{i=1}^{n} (1 + t_{ci}) C_i' + (1 + t_{cM}) C_M'. \tag{2.9}$$

Next we assume that each person (including those subsidized) has the same utility function, of the log-linear (Cobb–Douglas) form. Then we can establish:[1]

$$\frac{C_i'}{C} = \frac{C_i''}{S_C} = \beta_i, \tag{2.10}$$

where

$$(1 + t_{ci}) \beta_i = \frac{\gamma_i}{\sum_{j} \gamma_j + \gamma_M} \quad (i = 1, ..., n, M), \tag{2.11}$$

where $\gamma_1, ..., \gamma_n, \gamma_M$ are the Cobb–Douglas indices of the utility function. Hence

$$C_i = \beta_i (C + S_C) \quad (i = 1, ..., n, M). \tag{2.12}$$

[1] Let x_i be the quantity of good i bought by a particular person and p_i the price of good i. Let

$$U = k x_1^{\gamma_1} ... x_n^{\gamma_n} x_M^{\gamma_M}$$

be his ultility function. Maximize U subject to

$$c = \sum_{i=1}^{n} (1 + t_{ci}) p_i x_i + (1 + t_{cM}) p_M x_M.$$

We easily find that the budget equation and the marginal conditions imply

$$\frac{p_i x_i}{c} = \frac{1}{1 + t_{ci}} \frac{\gamma_i}{\sum_{j=1}^{n} \gamma_j + \gamma_M} = \beta_i \quad (i = 1, ..., n, M).$$

Therefore, (2.5) can be written as

$$T_C = t_c \left(\sum_{i=1}^{n} \beta_i + \beta_M \right)(C + S_C), \tag{2.13}$$

where t_c is the average outlay tax rate on personal expenditures defined by

$$t_c = \frac{\sum_{i=1}^{n} t_{ci}\beta_i + t_{cM}\beta_M}{\sum_{i=1}^{n} \beta_i + \beta_M}.$$

Evidently, t_c is constant so long as $t_{c1}, \ldots, t_{cn}$ and t_{cM} remain constant.

As we have assumed that the propensity to consume of subsidized persons is unity, consumption from subsidies and the taxes on them are cancelled by subsidies in the calculation of total consumption at market prices C, so that the latter must equal total consumption (after tax) from wages and distributed profits, as equation (2.9) shows. We may, therefore, assume that real consumption per capita, $C/p_c N$, deflated by the consumers' price index, p_c, and the total population, N, depends on total disposable personal real income per capita, $Y_d/p_c N$, and the lagged real consumption per capita, $(C/p_c N)_{-1}$, where the subscript -1 indicates that the value shown is for the previous year. Obviously the second variable represents the so-called Duesenberry–Modigliani effect. As for the first variable we have to note that total disposable personal income is exclusive of subsidies, so that it equals wages *plus* distributed profits *minus* taxes on both. In linear form the aggregate consumption function can be written as

$$\frac{C}{p_c N} = a_1 \frac{Y_d}{p_c N} + a_2 \left(\frac{C}{p_c N} \right)_{-1} + a_0. \tag{2.14}$$

Finally, we have to express Y_d in terms of the coefficients of the input–output analysis. Let l_i be the labour–input coefficient of industry i defined as $l_i = W_i/Y_i$. Let t_{ei} be the excise tax rate on industrial outlay on good i. The average excise tax rate for industry j is given by

$$t_j = \frac{\sum_{i=1}^{n} t_{ei}a_{ij} + t_{eM}a_{Mj}}{\sum_{i=1}^{n} a_{ij} + a_{Mj}}. \tag{2.15}$$

Because of (2.1) the profits of industry j can then be written as

$$P_j = \left[1 - (1 + t_j)\left(\sum_{i=1}^{n} a_{ij} + a_{Mj} \right) - l_j \right] Y_j + S_j. \tag{2.16}$$

Next, we assume that a constant fraction of total profits is distributed to persons (capitalists). Then total personal income from profits amounts to

$$\Pi = b \sum_{j=1}^{n} P_j. \tag{2.17}$$

Since employment income and personal income from profits are taxed at the rates t_w and t_π respectively, we can finally calculate the disposable income, Y_d, as

$$Y_d = (1 - t_w) \sum_{j=1}^{n} W_j + (1 - t_\pi) \Pi. \tag{2.18}$$

It is now easy to derive the fundamental equations of the input–output model with endogenous consumption. On substituting (2.12), (2.14), (2.16), (2.17), and (2.18), equations (2.2) become:

$$Y_i = \sum_{j=1}^{n} A_{ij} Y_j + F_i + H_i \quad (i = 1, ..., n), \tag{2.19}$$

where

$$F_i = a_1 b (1 - t_\pi) \beta_i \sum_{j=1}^{n} S_j + \beta_i S_C + G_i + I_i + E_i + D_i \tag{2.20}$$

and

$$H_i = p_c N \beta_i \left(a_2 \left(\frac{C}{p_c N} \right)_{-1} + a_0 \right). \tag{2.21}$$

A_{ij} is the sum of input coefficient a_{ij} and the consumption coefficient,

$$c_{ij} = a_1 (1 - t_w) \beta_i l_j + a_1 b (1 - t_\pi) \beta_i$$
$$\times \left[1 - (1 + t_j) \left(\sum_{k=1}^{n} a_{kj} + a_{Mj} \right) - l_j \right] \tag{2.22}$$

and is called the total transaction coefficient. As we assume (i) that input coefficients, including labour–input coefficients, are all constant, (ii) that the marginal propensity to consume, a_1, and the ratio of personal income from profits to total profits, b, are constant, and (iii) that the consumption quotas, β_i, are constant provided the outlay tax rates on personal expenditures do not change, so the total transaction coefficients depend only on various tax rates. So long as we confine ourselves to the comparative statics analysis, the assumption of constant tax rates is harmless for outlay taxes, but not for income taxes because they are heavily graduated. If, however, we decide as a first approximation to regard income tax rates t_w and t_π as being independent of the respective income levels, we can take advantage of the linearity of equations (2.19). We can easily calculate the Leontief inverse of the matrix of the total transaction coefficients

$$L \equiv (L_{ij}) \equiv \begin{bmatrix} 1 - A_{11} & -A_{12} & \cdots & -A_{1n} \\ -A_{21} & 1 - A_{22} & \cdots & -A_{2n} \\ \cdot & \cdot & \cdots & \cdot \\ -A_{n1} & -A_{n2} & \cdots & 1 - A_{nn} \end{bmatrix}^{-1} \tag{2.23}$$

and can solve (2.19) with respect to outputs, $Y_1, ..., Y_n$:

$$
\begin{pmatrix} Y_1 \\ Y_2 \\ \vdots \\ Y_n \end{pmatrix} = L \left\{ \begin{pmatrix} \beta_1 a_2 C_{-1} \dfrac{p_c N}{(p_c N)_{-1}} + \beta_1 a_0 p_c N \\ \vdots \\ \beta_n a_2 C_{-1} \dfrac{p_c N}{(p_c N)_{-1}} + \beta_n a_0 p_c N \end{pmatrix} \right.
$$

$$
\left. + \begin{pmatrix} a_1 b(1 - t_\pi) \beta_1 \sum\limits_{j=1}^{n} S_j + \beta_1 S_C + G_1 + I_1 + E_1 + D_1 \\ \vdots \\ a_1 b(1 - t_\pi) \beta_n \sum\limits_{j=1}^{n} S_j + \beta_n S_C + G_n + I_n + E_n + D_n \end{pmatrix} \right\}. \qquad (2.24)
$$

In (2.24) the elements in the second pair of round parentheses may deliberately be treated as constant in the analysis of the income propagation process. On the other hand, those in the first pair of round parentheses are given from the viewpoint of the current period, although they will, of course, fluctuate through time.

2. ESTIMATION OF THE PARAMETERS

In our study the data used in the computation of the total transaction coefficients were taken from published sources, primarily from *Input–Output Tables for the United Kingdom 1954*[1] and *Inland Revenue Annual Reports*. The major input–output tables contain 46 industrial sectors, so that a detailed investigation would be possible if the final buyers were disaggregated into households, the government sector and the sector of gross fixed capital formation. We have saved labour by not making such an attempt and deciding instead to use the summary table with 12 industrial sectors[2] and personal consumption clearly distinguished from other sectors of final demand.

However, the table deviates in two ways from the theoretical scheme explained in the preceding section. First, it contains, in addition to the twelve industries and the imports sector, the sector of 'sales by final buyers to one another', which was ignored in the theoretical discussion for the sake of simplicity. If these sales were entirely confined to final buyers, there would

[1] Studies in Official Statistics, no. 8, Board of Trade and Central Statistical Office (London: HMSO) 1961.

[2] They are (1) agriculture, forestry and fishing, (2) mining and quarrying, (3) food, drink and tobacco, (4) chemicals and allied industries, (5) metal manufacture, (6) engineering and allied industries, (7) textile, leather and clothing, (8) other manufacturing, (9) construction, (10) gas, electricity and water, (11) services, and (12) public administration, etc.

be no effect on industries. But the fact is that some of the sales are made to industries, so that they are included in the primary inputs of the respective outputs. We assume that the ratio of 'sales by final buyers to an industry' to the output of that industry is constant. Similarly, we assume that sales by final buyers to persons are a constant fraction of total consumption plus subsidies to persons, $C + S_C$. In addition to these assumptions, however, it is also assumed that the demands induced in such ways are easily and quickly absorbed within the sector of final buyers. Therefore they do not give rise to any repercussions among the industries.

Next, the input–output table does not provide figures for taxes on expenditure and subsidies separately, but only the differences between them. In order to meet the theoretical requirements, we have to obtain figures for industrial subsidies by industry group and income subsidies to persons from other sources. The *Civil Estimates 1954–55*[1] provide data on subsidies, which were added to taxes on expenditure *less* subsidies in the summary input–output table, in estimating outlay tax liability by sector. Investigation of the *Civil Estimates* shows the following subsidies

		£ thousand
Class VI	Trade, labour, materials and supply	9,932
Class VIII	Agriculture and food	319,320
Class IX	Transport, fuel, power and research	76,227
	Total	405,479

As total outlay taxes less subsidies in the input–output table amount to £2,061 million, the total of taxes on expenditures was estimated as £2,466 million ($= 2,061 + 405$),[2] which was further allocated according to the industries where the expenditure was made, in order to estimate the allocation of total outlay taxes to the sectors. The results enabled us to rearrange the interindustry flow figures of the summary table for the UK (1954) in the form of Table 2, which is completely consistent with our theoretical structure.

As usual, the amount of output i bought by industry j is divided by the output of industry j. The input coefficient is calculated not only for goods coming from other industries but also for goods from foreign countries (imports) and goods from final buyers (when non-zero). Similarly, the

[1] London: HMSO, 1954.

[2] On the other hand, actual data in the *1963 Blue Book* show that the total subsidies (i.e. subsidies by central government *plus* subsidies by local authorities) were £424 million, while the total outlay taxes (i.e. taxes on expenditure *plus* local rates) were £2,503 million. Therefore, the rate of error in our estimate was 4.5 per cent for subsidies and 1.5 per cent for outlay taxes.

TABLE 2. *Input–output table for UK 1954*[a]

| Producing industries | Consuming industries | | | | | | | | | | | | Final buyers | | | | | |
	1	2	3	4	5	6	7	8	9	10	11	12	Persons	Government	Capital formation	Exports	Stock appreciation	Total gross output
1	—	—	585	—	—	—	14	10	—	—	—	—	679	8	9	22	12	1,339
2	9	—	14	112	34	19	19	75	31	191	96	—	141	15	4	53	3	816
3	232	—	—	18	—	100	2	2	—	—	43	—	2,678	22	-10	143	5	3,135
4	110	17	100	—	97	—	54	95	116	17	117	—	196	95	29	290	-5	1,384
5	1	25	7	23	—	772	5	16	121	18	18	—	15	10	30	175	5	1,236
6	60	43	63	55	95	—	61	78	6	43	280	—	356	620	1,008	1,180	35	4,098
7	8	6	14	10	19	48	—	94	72	14	47	—	987	50	60	453	—	1,787
8	14	30	84	51	6	204	39	—	272	2	378	—	477	80	65	198	5	1,930
9	35	25	8	6	29	19	12	9	—	6	103	—	236	195	1,070	—	15	1,741
10	13	16	16	29	—	55	19	31	6	—	153	—	309	41	67	4	—	788
11	164	82	327	237	228	419	265	296	148	95	—	—	3,608	482	264	882	10	7,507
12	—	—	—	—	—	—	—	—	—	—	—	—	701	1,494	—	—	—	2,195
Imports	96	12	486	348	210	116	449	293	54	9	303	—	993	101	32	140	-10	3,652
Sales by final buyers to one another	—	—	—	—	30	—	8	1	—	—	—	—	76	-134	-60	79	—	—
Taxes on expenditure	150	8	850	23	3	23	10	18	33	32	523	—	658	60	70	—	—	2,061
less subsidies	-319	-1	—	—	—	-2	—	—	-20	-1	-3	—	-54	—	—	—	—	—
Income from employment	304	489	276	229	297	1,566	574	636	708	199	3,313	1,662	—	—	—	—	—	10,253
Gross profits and other trading income	462	64	305	243	185	709	256	306	194	168	2,136	533	—	—	—	—	—	5,561
Total input	1,339	816	3,135	1,384	1,236	4,098	1,787	1,930	1,741	788	7,507	2,195	12,056	3,139	2,638	3,619	75	49,483

[a] See note 2, p. 82, for the classification of industries.

TABLE 3. *Material and labour input coefficients, consumption quotas and outlay tax rates, UK 1954*[a]

	j												
i	1	2	3	4	5	6	7	8	9	10	11	12	β_i
a_{ij}													
1	—	—	0.1866	0.0809	—	0.0046	0.0078	0.0052	0.0178	0.2424	—	—	0.0561
2	0.0067	—	0.0045	0.0130	0.0275	—	0.0106	0.0389	—	—	0.0128	—	0.0116
3	0.1733	—	—	—	0.0785	—	0.0011	0.0010	—	—	0.0057	—	0.2211
4	0.0822	0.0208	0.0319	—	—	0.0244	0.0302	0.0492	0.0414	0.0216	0.0156	—	0.0162
5	0.0007	0.0306	0.0022	0.0166	—	0.1884	0.0028	0.0083	0.0666	0.0228	0.0024	—	0.0012
6	0.0448	0.0527	0.0201	0.0397	0.0769	—	0.0341	0.0404	0.0695	0.0546	0.0373	—	0.0294
7	0.0060	0.0074	0.0045	0.0072	0.0024	0.0117	—	0.0487	0.0034	0.0013	0.0063	—	0.0815
8	0.0105	0.0368	0.0268	0.0368	0.0154	0.0498	0.0218	—	0.1562	0.0178	0.0504	—	0.0394
9	0.0261	0.0306	0.0026	0.0043	0.0049	0.0046	0.0067	0.0047	—	0.0025	0.0137	—	0.0195
10	0.0097	0.0196	0.0051	0.0210	0.0235	0.0134	0.0106	0.0161	0.0034	—	0.0204	—	0.0255
11	0.1225	0.1005	0.1043	0.1712	0.1845	0.1022	0.1483	0.1534	0.0850	0.1206	—	—	0.2979
12	—	—	—	—	—	—	—	—	—	—	—	—	0.0579
13	0.0717	0.0147	0.1550	0.2514	0.1699	0.0405	0.2153	0.1363	0.0310	0.0114	0.0404	—	0.0820
14	—	—	—	—	0.0231	—	0.0045	0.0039	—	—	—	—	0.0063
t_j	0.2022	0.0313	0.4988	0.0259	0.0040	0.0128	0.0106	0.0186	0.0400	0.0821	0.3401	—	0.0575
l_j	0.2270	0.5993	0.0880	0.1655	0.2403	0.3821	0.3212	0.3295	0.4067	0.2525	0.4413	0.7572	—

[a] See note 2, p. 82 for the classification of industries. Sectors 13 and 14 refer to imports and sales by final buyers to one another respectively.

labour–input coefficients are obtained by dividing wages by the corresponding outputs, while personal consumption of goods and services (including inter-personal sales) are divided by total consumption *plus* subsidies to persons, to give the consumption quotas. All the results are listed in Table 3.

Next, the average outlay tax rates of industrial transactions and personal expenditure, t_j and t_c, were computed by dividing the outlay tax liability of each sector (estimated above) by its total expenditure on goods and services as the actual tax base. These are also listed in Table 3. The effective income tax rate on employment, t_w, was computed by dividing the income tax revenue under Schedule E in the *Ninety-Ninth Report of the Commissioners of Her Majesty's Inland Revenue for the Year ended 31st March 1956*[1] by the total employment income in the year 1954. The tax revenue in the 1954 calendar year was obtained from the figure for the 1954 fiscal year by carrying in an averaged quarterly amount from the 1953 fiscal year and carrying out a corresponding amount to the 1955 calendar year. The rate was 5.94 per cent for 1954. The effective income and surtax rate on other personal income, t_π, was computed, after adjusting the tax revenue for the calendar year, according to the following formula:

$$t_\pi = \frac{\text{total taxes on personal income} - \text{income tax on employment income}}{\text{other personal income}}.$$

A rate of 21.82 per cent was obtained for 1954.[2]

As for the ratio of personal income from profits to total gross profits, b, it was estimated by dividing the total of self-employment income, dividends and rent (taken from the *1964 Blue Book*) by the total gross profits before providing for depreciation and stock appreciation (available in the summary input–output table). The result was 0.54 for 1954. On the basis of the data from the *1964 Blue Book*, similar calculations were made for a number of years adjacent to our sample year.[3] From the results which are shown in

[1] London: HMSO, 1957, p. 63.

[2] For reference, time series estimates of t_w and t_π from the 101st to the 105th reports of the *Inland Revenue Reports* were as follows:

Year	1952	1953	1954	1955	1956	1957	1958	1959
t_w	5.8	5.6	5.9	6.0	6.5	6.9	7.3	7.1
t_π	22.9	20.9	21.8	21.5	20.4	20.0	20.5	19.7

The figures are all in percentage terms.

[3] Note that the gross profits *plus* the residual error were taken as the denominator of the calculation.

TABLE 4. *The ratio of personal income from profits to total gross profits*

Year	1953	1954	1955	1956	1957	1958	1959
The ratio	0.57	0.55	0.56	0.54	0.53	0.55	0.56

Table 4 it is seen that the ratio seems fairly stable and the assumption of constancy of the ratio will be supported at least as a first approximation to reality as far as this period is concerned.

Our final problem is to estimate the marginal propensity to consume, a_1, and the Duesenberry–Modigliani inertia coefficient, a_2. For this purpose we used annual time series data mostly taken from the new series in the *1963 Blue Book*,[1] in addition to cross-section data derived from the *Family Expenditure Surveys* for five years (1953 and the four years from 1959 to 1962).[2] Since the data were published at current market prices, they were normalized by using the consumers' price index[3] (with the base 1954 = 100) in compiling their real values.

To obtain the cross-section data on disposable income and consumption, the households were separated, according to their gross income, into eight classes. A series of disposable income was computed by deducting the compulsory payments from the mean value of gross income for each class. Since the *Family Expenditure Surveys* define gross income of households as the actually received weekly income before deducting the compulsory payments (income tax, surtax and National Insurance contributions), but excluding interpersonal payments and free goods or grants, we multiplied the mean values of gross income by 52 (weeks) and deducted from them the compulsory payments which are given in separate codes. Thus annual disposable incomes analysed by gross income size were computed for five years, giving 40 samples. As for consumption, the grand total of average weekly expenditure of the households was taken as consumers' expenditures, which were grouped according to the gross income of the households; recorded bets were added. These totals include expenditure on housing,

---

[1] Where there is a discontinuity between the old and new series, the value was estimated on the basis of the new series.

[2] They are *Report of an Enquiry into Household Expenditure in 1953–54*, Ministry of Labour and National Service (London: HMSO) 1957; *Family Expenditure Survey, Report for 1957–59*, Ministry of Labour (London: HMSO) 1961; *Family Expenditure Survey, Report for 1960 and 1961*, Ministry of Labour (London: HMSO) 1962; and *Family Expenditure Survey, Report for 1962*, Ministry of Labour (London: HMSO) 1963. For convenience, we shall call these surveys for the five years simply *Family Expenditure Surveys* hereafter.

[3] Mainly taken from the *1963 Blue Book*, p. 15. The 1956 edition (p. 23) and 1962 edition (p. 15) were also used. Some adjustments were made to the values in the old series.

clothing and footwear, durable goods, other goods, transport and vehicles, fuel, light and power, services and miscellaneous items. This definition of consumption is intended to be the same as that in the *Blue Books*.

To obtain the time series data, the value of personal income before tax *minus* taxes on income *minus* additions to tax reserves *minus* National Insurance and health contributions was computed, for each year, from the data in the *1963 Blue Book*. Personal income before tax includes income from employment, income from self-employment, rent, dividends and interest, National Insurance benefits and other current grants from public authorities. On the other hand, the series of personal consumers' expenditure is available directly from the *1963 Blue Book*. The 1954 figure in this series should coincide with the value of personal consumption in the *Input–Output Tables*, and, as was mentioned above, there is no substantial difference in the definition of consumption between the time series and cross-section data.[1]

These data were then translated into figures per capita. The cross-section data were divided by the respective numbers of persons per household, which are available in the *Surveys*. The per capita figures for the time series data were derived, of course, by dividing the figures in year t by the total population in the same year. However, we have reliable population figures only for 1951 and 1961.[2] The total populations in other years were estimated, on the basis of the actual figures for 1951 and 1961, by the use of the formula of geometrical progression.

In Table 5*a*, the cross-section data are grouped according to the gross

---

[1] The codes in the *Family Expenditure Surveys* are the same as those in the *Blue Books*. The basic problem is that the classification in the *Blue Books* is different from that in the *Input–Output Tables*. The former is made from the viewpoint of the final consumer goods, while the latter is made in terms of the old Standard Industrial Classification, 1948, from the point of view of consumer goods produced in different industries. However, the differences between them are not serious. In fact, according to the *1963 Blue Book*, the components of consumption in 1954 are

	£ million
Consumers' expenditure by the British and by foreign tourists	11,993
Consumers' expenditure abroad by the British	185
Expenditure by foreign tourists in UK	−123
Total consumers' expenditure	£12,055

at current market prices, while the *Input–Output Table* for 1954 shows:

Purchases of goods and services by persons	11,452
Taxes on expenditures *less* subsidies on persons	604
Total consumption by persons	£12,056

[2] *Census 1951, England and Wales* (General Report, General Register Office, London: HMSO, 1958, p. 74), *Census 1951, Scotland* (vol. III, General Volume, General Registry Office, Edinburgh: HMSO, 1954, p. v), *Census 1961, England and Wales* (Preliminary Report, General Register Office, London: HMSO, 1961, p. 75) and *Preliminary Report of the Sixteenth Census of Scotland 1961* (General Registry Office, Edinburgh: HMSO, 1961, p. 47).

TABLE 5. Data for estimating the consumption function

(a) Cross-section data

Income group	Year	I (under £3)	II (£3–£6)	III (£6–£8)	IV (£8–£10)	V (£10–£14)	VI (£14–£20)	VII (£20–£30)	VIII (£30–£50)
Number of samples	1953	747	1,279	1,437	2,031	3,425	2,578	1,065	271
	1959	87	354	152	206	549	808	628	239
		(under £4)	(£4–£6)	(£6–£10)	(£10–£14)	(£14–£20)	(£20–£25)	(£25–£30)	(£30–£40)
	1960	60	379	168	208	594	927	838	296
					(£10–£15)	(£15–£20)			
	1961	151	195	338	532	867	567	337	288
	1962	141	213	326	651	751	534	384	371
Disposable income per capita (£1)	1953	136.8	116.5	130.5	145.0	177.3	225.1	289.0	443.1
	1959	99.0	131.4	145.5	152.6	162.3	209.9	284.4	396.8
	1960	130.4	143.4	153.9	153.4	166.2	210.3	281.2	408.9
	1961	164.5	151.3	164.5	170.5	205.9	251.7	293.2	338.1
	1962	157.9	153.9	166.5	171.4	202.6	251.1	293.5	336.6
Consumption per capita (£1)	1953	155.9	148.4	157.2	167.1	187.6	221.1	263.9	340.5
	1959	172.8	177.5	191.5	182.2	177.0	208.7	260.2	323.1
	1960	173.6	167.6	187.2	176.4	183.4	212.8	263.0	348.6
	1961	184.5	195.3	189.3	193.7	213.5	245.3	279.8	311.8
	1962	182.0	180.0	206.0	187.4	205.0	223.6	277.4	304.1

(b) Time-series data

Year	1948	1949	1950	1951	1952	1953	1954	1955	1956	1957	1958	1959	1960	1961	1962
Disposable income per capita (£1)	220.4	224.6	229.4	224.4	227.1	238.3	244.9	257.4	263.3	268.7	270.0	285.0	297.7	307.2	309.2
Consumption per capita (£1)	219.3	221.0	226.8	222.1	218.7	228.4	236.6	246.2	246.8	251.8	254.0	268.2	274.5	277.4	283.5

weekly income of the households recorded in the *Family Expenditure Surveys*. The grouping has been altered in 1960 and 1961. The new income ranges, which are shown in parentheses above the data for the sample numbers of households for 1960 and 1961, are effective for the figures in the later years. We do not repeat similar notes for other variables, disposable income and consumption. Table 5*b* contains the time-series data on disposable income per capita and consumption per capita.

In Table 5*a* it should be noticed that for those persons belonging to the three or four lowest income groups real consumption per capita is comparatively stable from year to year, showing that the consumption per capita does not increase till the disposable income per capita reaches subsistence level. We took the average of the real consumption per capita for the three lowest income groups (weighted by the numbers of samples) as the subsistence level of real consumption and calculated it for the years 1953, 1959, 1960, 1961, and 1962, at 153.7, 180.4, 173.6, 189.9, and 192.9, respectively. The subsistence level of disposable income is defined as the income level which is just enough to pay for consumption at the subsistence level. It is seen from Table 5*a* that persons in income group IV received, in each of the five sample years, an income which was below the subsistence level, while those of group V received income exceeding the subsistence level in 1953, 1961 and 1962, but not in 1959 and 1960.

On the assumption that a previously higher level of real consumption per capita $(C/p_cN)_{-1}$ pushes up the subsistence level of consumption, $\bar{C}/p_cN$, the relationship

$$\frac{\bar{C}}{p_cN} = \alpha_0 + \alpha_1 \left(\frac{C}{p_cN}\right)_{-1}$$

was fitted to the time series of $\bar{C}/p_cN$ just obtained and the time series of $(C/p_cN)_{-1}$ in Table 5*b*. With the addition of a disturbance term, assumed to possess the properties appropriate for least-squares estimation, the above equation was estimated, by the method of least squares, as

$$\frac{\bar{C}}{p_cN} = 20.41 + \underset{(4.4)}{0.61} \left(\frac{C}{p_cN}\right)_{-1} \quad (R^2 = 0.99), \tag{2.25}$$

where the figure appearing in parentheses below the regression coefficient, α_1, is the value of the t-statistic of α_1; this value of the t-statistic shows that α_1 is significantly positive with the confidence interval of the 95 per cent level of probability. (There are three degrees of freedom in the present case.)

By the use of (2.25) we can estimate the subsistence level of real consumption per capita, $\hat{\bar{C}}/p_cN$, for each of the five sample years, which is equal to the subsistence level of disposable income for the same year, $\bar{Y}_d/p_cN$, by

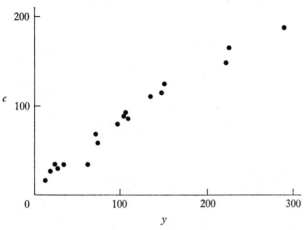

Figure 1
The Engel relationship between excess consumption, c, and excess income, y.

definition. Comparing the disposable incomes listed in Table 5a with the subsistence levels thus obtained, we find that all samples belonging to classes I–IV, and two samples belonging to class V, have disposable incomes which fall short of the corresponding subsistence levels. For each of the remaining eighteen samples we calculate the difference between the actual income per capita Y_d/p_cN and the subsistence level of income, $\overline{Y}_d/p_cN$, and the difference between actual consumption per capita, C/p_cN, and the subsistence level of consumption $\hat{\overline{C}}/p_cN$. We then have the scatter diagram, Figure 1, which shows that between consumption and disposable income there is a kind of Engel relationship, $c = \theta y^\rho$, where

$$c = (C/p_cN)-(\hat{\overline{C}}/p_cN) \quad \text{and} \quad y = (Y_d/p_cN)-(\overline{Y}_d/p_cN).$$

Instead of estimating this log-linear relationship, we estimated, for the sake of simplicity, its linear version, and obtained

$$\frac{C}{p_cN} - \frac{\hat{\overline{C}}}{p_cN} = \underset{(4.3)}{15.445} + \underset{(23)}{0.638}\left[\frac{Y_d}{p_cN} - \frac{\overline{Y}_d}{p_cN}\right] \quad (R^2 = 0.99). \quad (2.26)$$

Substituting (2.25) into (2.26) and considering $\hat{\overline{C}}/p_cN = \overline{Y}_d/p_cN$, we finally have

$$\frac{C}{p_cN} = 22.831 + 0.638\left(\frac{Y_d}{p_cN}\right) + 0.220\left(\frac{C}{p_cN}\right)_{-1}. \quad (2.27)$$

The goodness of fit of the equation may be measured by the correlation co-efficient between the actual values, C/p_cN, and the regression values, $\hat{C}/p_eN$, given by the equation (2.27). It is as high as 0.97 for the cross-section data which were used for estimating the equation. In the case of the time-series

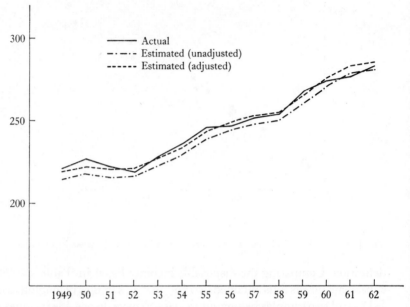

Figure 2
Estimates of the real consumption per capita and time series data.

data (Table 5*b*), however, it is not so high, as might be expected from the fact that only a few of the observations were utilized in estimating the subsistence levels of real consumption per capita. Nevertheless, it is seen from Figure 2 that an adjustment in the height of the line (2.27), with no change in the slope coefficients, greatly improves the fitting of the line to the time series data.[1] This implies that our estimates of the marginal propensity to consume and the Duesenberry–Modigliani coefficient are highly reliable, and the consumption coefficients (2.22) were therefore calculated on the basis of them.

Although different data have been analysed by different methods under different assumptions, it is interesting to compare our results with those of others. Utilizing time-series data over the period 1950–60, Ball and Drake estimated the aggregate consumption function for the UK economy.[2] Their result was

$$C = 0.45\,Y + 0.54C_{-1},$$

where Y and C represent aggregate personal disposable income and aggregate

[1] After the adjustment, the correlation coefficient between the time series data $C/p_c N$, and the estimates, $\hat{C}/p_c N$, attains a value of 0.98.

[2] R. J. Ball and P. S. Drake, 'The relationship between aggregate consumption and wealth', *International Economic Review*, vol. 5, no. 1 (January 1964), pp. 63–81.

consumption respectively. Obviously our estimate of the marginal propensity to consume, 0.638, is larger than their estimate, 0.45;[1] while our estimate of the Duesenberry–Modigliani coefficient, 0.220, is significantly smaller than theirs, 0.54. As for the long-run propensity to consume derived on the condition that $C = C_{-1}$, we obtain 0.98 from the above equation by Ball and Drake, whereas the corresponding figure from our equation (2.27) is only 0.81.[2]

Another comparison can be made with Stone's findings. He estimated the private saving equation in Britain for the period 1948–62.[3] Transforming saving into consumption, his result can be written as

$$C = 0.561\,Y_d + 0.222C_{-1} + 0.057W - 6.93\Delta V_{-1},$$

where Y_d denotes personal disposable income, W the wealth of personal net worth, and V government measures to discourage spending. It is seen that our estimate of the marginal propensity to consume is higher than Stone's, while there is no difference in the value of the Duesenberry–Modigliani coefficient between the studies. Furthermore, taking the wealth effect of the Stone consumption function into consideration, we may say that the difference between the two estimates of the marginal propensity to consume is reasonable, although it might be suspected of being significant at first sight.

We can now easily calculate the 12×12 consumption coefficients according to the formula (2.21). They are added to the input coefficients in Table 2. The total transaction coefficients are then determined, so that the Leontief inverse of the matrix of total transaction coefficients can be computed. The figures obtained are listed in Tables 6 and 7.

---

[1] We have to note that our estimate might be lower if we could take the cross-section samples in the highest income group into account. It was impossible to do so because only the lower limit of the gross income was recorded for the highest income group, so that the mean value of the income range could not be determined. Although the omission of these samples would not seriously affect the result, there is a possibility that the propensity to consume may have been somewhat overestimated.

[2] Derived on the condition that $C/p_c N = (C/p_c N)_{-1}$.

[3] R. Stone, 'Private savings in Britain, past, present and future', *The Manchester School of Economics and Social Studies*, vol. XXXII, no. 2 (May 1964), pp. 79–112.

TABLE 6. *The total transaction coefficients, A_{ij}, for UK 1954: the case of endogenous taxes*[a]

i \ j	1	2	3	4	5	6	7	8	9	10	11	12
1	0.9908	−0.0213	−0.1910	−0.0082	−0.0103	−0.0155	−0.0208	−0.0187	−0.0152	−0.0117	−0.0191	−0.0291
2	−0.0086	0.9956	−0.0054	−0.0826	−0.0206	−0.0078	−0.0133	−0.0417	−0.0209	−0.2448	−0.0168	−0.0060
3	−0.2097	−0.0841	0.9826	−0.0454	−0.0407	−0.0609	−0.0522	−0.0541	−0.0599	−0.0460	−0.0811	−0.1148
4	−0.0849	−0.0270	−0.0332	0.9976	−0.0815	−0.0289	−0.0339	−0.0531	−0.0458	−0.0250	−0.0211	−0.0084
5	−0.0009	−0.0311	−0.0023	−0.0168	0.9998	−0.1887	−0.0031	−0.0086	−0.0669	−0.0230	−0.0028	−0.0006
6	−0.0496	−0.0639	−0.0224	−0.0440	−0.0823	0.9919	−0.0409	−0.0475	−0.0775	−0.0607	−0.0473	−0.0153
7	−0.0194	−0.0384	−0.0109	−0.0191	−0.0174	−0.0342	0.9812	−0.0683	−0.0255	−0.0183	−0.0341	−0.0423
8	−0.0170	−0.0518	−0.0299	−0.0426	−0.0227	−0.0607	−0.0309	0.9905	−0.1669	−0.0260	−0.0638	−0.0205
9	−0.0293	−0.0380	−0.0041	−0.0072	−0.0085	−0.0100	−0.0112	−0.0094	0.9947	−0.0066	−0.0203	−0.0101
10	−0.0139	−0.0293	−0.0071	−0.0247	−0.0282	−0.0204	−0.0165	−0.0222	−0.0103	0.9947	−0.0291	−0.0132
11	−0.1716	−0.2138	−0.1278	−0.2148	−0.2394	−0.1843	−0.2171	−0.2249	−0.1657	−0.1826	0.8984	−0.1547
12	−0.0095	−0.0220	−0.0046	−0.0085	−0.0107	−0.0160	−0.0134	−0.0139	−0.0157	−0.0121	−0.0197	0.9699

[a] See note 2 on p. 82 for the classification of industries.

TABLE 7. The Leontief inverse, L_{ij}, of the total transaction coefficient matrix[a]

i \ j	1	2	3	4	5	6	7	8	9	10	11	12
1	1.081	0.074	0.225	0.049	0.052	0.063	0.059	0.063	0.066	0.063	0.061	0.076
2	0.044	1.043	0.031	0.113	0.068	0.049	0.041	0.076	0.063	0.278	0.047	0.029
3	0.293	0.175	1.111	0.122	0.124	0.149	0.122	0.138	0.156	0.149	0.148	0.180
4	0.126	0.071	0.074	1.038	0.117	0.080	0.065	0.090	0.097	0.071	0.054	0.039
5	0.030	0.064	0.021	0.044	1.035	0.211	0.026	0.037	0.103	0.062	0.027	0.016
6	0.102	0.121	0.065	0.093	0.133	1.073	0.083	0.099	0.140	0.127	0.088	0.052
7	0.054	0.078	0.039	0.054	0.054	0.073	1.049	0.103	0.073	0.064	0.064	0.068
8	0.077	0.115	0.071	0.094	0.081	0.118	0.078	1.066	0.227	0.095	0.107	0.061
9	0.046	0.056	0.021	0.025	0.027	0.029	0.026	0.028	1.025	0.033	0.034	0.023
10	0.039	0.056	0.027	0.049	0.055	0.050	0.038	0.048	0.041	1.038	0.048	0.031
11	0.371	0.423	0.284	0.388	0.429	0.409	0.368	0.413	0.408	0.421	1.259	0.293
12	0.027	0.042	0.018	0.026	0.029	0.035	0.028	0.032	0.037	0.035	0.034	1.043

[a] See note 2 on p. 82 for the classification of industries.

3. Impact multipliers and efficient budget of the government

I. THE THREE HICKSIAN LAWS AND THE SAMUELSON–LECHATELIER PRINCIPLE

In the following discussion the most important role is played by the Leontie inverse of the total-transaction-coefficient matrix, so its general properties are first examined. The matrix of total transaction coefficients is a non-negative matrix whose typical element A_{ij} is the sum of the corresponding input coefficient a_{ij} and consumption coefficient c_{ij}.[1] Each column sum of the elements of the matrix is less than unity because the total input (after outlay taxes) per unit of output, the sum of the consumption quotes, $\Sigma \beta_i$, the marginal propensity to consume, and the ratio of personal income from profits to total profits are all less than unity.

Let us define the *exogenous* demand for good j as the sum of public authorities' current expenditure on good j and total gross capital formation and exports of good j. It is less than the *final* demand for good j by the amount of consumers' expenditure on it, since consumers' expenditures are regarded as endogenous variables. Given the above properties, it is shown that the transaction matrix is convergent and therefore the model obeys the following rules of comparative statics.[2] Given an increase in the exogenous demand for good j, with the exogenous demand for all other goods held constant, then the output of industry j increases (Hicks law I), the output of every other industry must increase too (Hicks law II), and the output of industry j will increase by the largest percentage (Hicks law III).[3] Next, the elasticity of the output of industry j with respect to the exogenous demand for good j does not exceed unity and therefore the output of all other industries will increase, with elasticities of less than unity (the elasticity law). Furthermore, since all the column sums of the total transaction coefficient matrix are less than unity, it fulfils the conditions for Metzler's theorem, so that the diagonal elements of the Leontief inverse $(I-A)^{-1}$ are greater than the off-diagonal elements of the corresponding

---

[1] For the definition of the consumption coefficient, see formula (2.22) in the last chapter.

[2] In the following discussion we assume that the transaction coefficient matrix is 'indecomposable'; that is to say, all industries are directly or indirectly related to each other through the transaction relationship, as in our model.

[3] J. R. Hicks, *Value and Capital*, (Oxford University Press, 1939), pp. 72–5. Hicks himself has derived these laws not for outputs but for prices.

rows.[1] This mathematical property implies that the output of any industry j is (algebraically) more affected by the exogenous demand for itself than the exogenous demand for the output of any other industry (the Metzler law). Finally, we can show that an increase in output of any commodity resulting from an increase in the exogenous demand for the same or some other commodity is less if outputs of a number of commodities are kept constant than it will be if some of them are permitted to vary (the Samuelson–LeChatelier law).

These mathematical properties have been discussed by many writers.[2] But for the convenience of the reader simple and elementary proofs are given below, although they, particularly Theorem 1, are familiar to economic students.

THEOREM 1. *If all column sums of a non-negative matrix A are less than 1 i.e. if*

$$\sum_i A_{ij} < 1 \quad for \ all \ j = 1, ..., n, \tag{3.1}$$

then A is convergent so that $\lim_{t \to \infty} A^t = 0$. *Moreover,* $(I - A)^{-1} > 0$ *if A is indecomposable.*

PROOF. From (3.1), it is obvious that there is a λ, with $0 < \lambda < 1$, such that

$$eA < \lambda e, \tag{3.2}$$

where e is an n-dimensional row vector whose elements are all unity.

As A is a non-negative matrix, we have from (3.2)

$$eA^2 < \lambda eA < \lambda^2 e.$$

Similarly, $eA^t < \lambda^t e$ for any integer t. Bearing $0 < \lambda < 1$ in mind, we obtain $\lim_{t \to \infty} eA^t = 0$, which establishes $\lim_{t \to \infty} A^t = 0$ because $A \geqslant 0$.

Thus A is convergent, so that

$$I + A + A^2 + ... = (I - A)^{-1}.$$

On the other hand, the non-negativeness and indecomposability of A implies $A + A^2 + ... + A^n > 0$, so that $(I - A)^{-1} > 0$, from which Hicks laws I and II immediately follow since $dY_i/dQ_j = L_{ij}$, where Y_i is the output of commodity i, Q_j the exogenous demand for good j and L_{ij} the (i, j) element of the Leontief inverse, $(I - A)^{-1}$.

Metzler's theorem can easily be proved. From $(I - A)^{-1}(I - A) = I$, we have $\quad -A_{12}L_{11} + (1 - A_{22})L_{12} - ... - A_{n2}L_{1n} = 0$.

[1] L. A. Metzler, 'A multiple-country theory of income transfers', *Journal of Political Economy*, (February 1951).

[2] See, for example, M. Morishima, *Equilibrium, Stability and Growth* (Oxford: Clarendon Press, 1964), pp. 14–20.

Hence,

$$A_{12}\frac{L_{11}}{L_{12}}+A_{22}\frac{L_{12}}{L_{12}}+\ldots+A_{n2}\frac{L_{1n}}{L_{12}}=\text{1}. \qquad (3.3)$$

Suppose now the contrary; then the Leontief inverse has an off-diagonal element, which is not less than any other element of the same row. Let L_{12} be such an element of the first row. Since all L_{1i}/L_{12}, $i=\text{1},\ldots,n$, are positive and not greater than one and, by hypothesis, ΣA_{i2} is less than one, then the left-hand side of (3.3) must be less than one, so that (3.3) is self-contradictory. Hence any off-diagonal element cannot be the greatest member; we thus obtain Metzler's property.

Next we prove an important theorem, from which the remaining laws of comparative statics all follow.

THEOREM 2. *Let A be an indecomposable non-negative matrix which is convergent. Then its Leontief inverse satisfies, with arbitrary positive numbers $z_1, z_2, \ldots, z_n$, the following inequalities:*

$$L_{ii}/(\sum_k L_{ik}z_k) > L_{ji}/(\sum_k L_{jk}z_k) \quad \text{for all pairs } (i,j), \quad i \neq j. \qquad (3.4)$$

PROOF. Suppose the contrary. Then there is a j ($\neq i$) such that for some $z_1, \ldots, z_n$

$$L_{ji}/(\sum_k L_{jk}z_k) \geqq L_{hi}/(\sum_k L_{hk}z_k) \quad (h=\text{1},\ldots,j-\text{1},j+\text{1},\ldots,n). \qquad (3.5)$$

We have, from $(I-A)(I-A)^{-1}=I$,

$$L_{ji}=\sum_h A_{jh}L_{hi} \quad (j \neq i), \qquad (3.6)$$

$$L_{jj}=\sum_h A_{jh}L_{hj}+\text{1}. \qquad (3.7)$$

Since $j \neq i$,

$$\frac{L_{ji}}{\sum_k L_{jk}z_k}(\sum_k L_{jk}z_k) = \sum_h A_{jh}\frac{L_{hi}}{\sum_k L_{hk}z_k}(\sum_k L_{hk}z_k).$$

Hence,

$$\sum_k L_{jk}z_k = \sum_h A_{jh}\left[\frac{L_{hi}/\sum_k L_{hk}z_k}{L_{ji}/\sum_k L_{jk}z_k}\right](\sum_k L_{hk}z_k). \qquad (3.8)$$

On the other hand, by Theorem 1, all elements of the Leontief inverse are positive, since A is indecomposable. Consequently, it follows from (3.5) that, for each h, the part in the square brackets on the right-hand side of (3.8) does not exceed unity. Therefore,

$$\sum_k L_{jk}z_k \leqq \sum_k \sum_h A_{jh}L_{hk}z_k. \qquad (3.9)$$

Viewing (3.6) and (3.7), we find that the right-hand side of (3.9) equals $\sum\limits_{k} L_{jk} z_k - z_j$. As $z_j > 0$, (3.9) amounts to asserting a contradictory proposition that $\sum\limits_{k} L_{jk} z_k$ is less than itself.

From Theorem 2 the following laws are derived. First, by solving the transaction equations, $Y = AY + Q$, we get $Y_h = \sum\limits_{k} L_{hk} Q_k$, $h = 1, ..., n$. Therefore, taking z_k in (3.4) as Q_k, (3.4) can be put, after multiplying it by Q_i, in the form

$$\frac{Q_i}{Y_i} \frac{dY_i}{dQ_i} > \frac{Q_i}{Y_j} \frac{dY_j}{dQ_i}$$

which is Hicks law III. Moreover, it is evident that

$$\frac{Q_i}{Y_i} \frac{dY_i}{dQ_i} = \frac{L_{ii} Q_i}{\sum\limits_{k} L_{ik} Q_k}$$

is less than unity, because the numerator on the right-hand side is less than the denominator. This, together with Hicks law III, yields the elasticity law.

Finally, let us prove the Samuelson–LeChatelier law. We have so far regarded all Q_ks as parameters and all Y_hs as unknowns to be determined by the transaction equations. The effect of an increase in Q_j on Y_i in such a system is now compared with the similar effect in a system where $Y_1, Q_2, ..., Q_n$ are taken as parameters and $Q_1, Y_2, ..., Y_n$ as variables.

In the original system, an increase in Q_j affects not only $Y_2, ..., Y_n$, but also Y_1. In the second system, however, Y_1 is taken as given, while Q_1 is flexible. Therefore, the effect upon Y_i of an increase in Q_j in the second system, *ceteris paribus*, can be regarded as the effect upon Y_i, in the original system, of an increase in Q_j combined with such a change in Q_1 as would leave Y_1 unaffected. As

$$dY_1 = L_{11} dQ_1 + L_{1j} dQ_j,$$

Y_1 would be kept constant if $dQ_1 = -(L_{1j}/L_{11}) dQ_j$. Consequently, the effect on Y_i of dQ_j in the second system would be

$$dY_i = L_{i1} dQ_1 + L_{ij} dQ_j = (L_{ij} - L_{i1} L_{1j}/L_{11}) dQ_j. \tag{3.10}$$

Because of Theorem 2 we have, on the other hand,

$$\frac{L_{11}}{\sum\limits_{k} L_{1k} z_k} > \frac{L_{i1}}{\sum\limits_{k} L_{ik} z_k}.$$

TABLE 8. *Elasticities of outputs with respect to exogenous demand for goods: estimated on the basis of the actual 1954 outputs and exogenous demands*[a]

Outputs	Exogenous demands											
	1	2	3	4	5	6	7	8	9	10	11	12
1	0.247	0.007	0.234	0.017	0.009	0.139	0.042	0.025	0.067	0.013	0.137	0.099
2	0.016	0.163	0.051	0.067	0.019	0.177	0.047	0.049	0.106	0.092	0.170	0.060
3	0.028	0.007	0.493	0.018	0.009	0.141	0.037	0.023	0.068	0.013	0.141	0.102
4	0.028	0.007	0.075	0.361	0.019	0.173	0.044	0.034	0.096	0.014	0.115	0.048
5	0.008	0.007	0.024	0.017	0.190	0.509	0.019	0.016	0.114	0.014	0.065	0.023
6	0.008	0.004	0.022	0.011	0.007	0.779	0.019	0.013	0.047	0.008	0.064	0.023
7	0.009	0.006	0.030	0.015	0.007	0.122	0.546	0.030	0.056	0.010	0.107	0.066
8	0.012	0.008	0.051	0.024	0.010	0.180	0.038	0.290	0.161	0.013	0.166	0.055
9	0.008	0.004	0.017	0.007	0.003	0.048	0.014	0.008	0.806	0.005	0.058	0.023
10	0.015	0.009	0.047	0.030	0.016	0.189	0.045	0.032	0.073	0.354	0.184	0.068
11	0.015	0.007	0.053	0.025	0.013	0.162	0.046	0.029	0.074	0.015	0.501	0.067
12	0.004	0.002	0.011	0.006	0.003	0.048	0.012	0.008	0.023	0.004	0.046	0.834

[a] See note 2 on p. 82 for the classification of industries.

TABLE 9. *The Leontief inverse of the total transaction coefficient matrix when the output of the industry, 'public administration, etc.', is kept constant*[a]

i \ j	1	2	3	4	5	6	7	8	9	10	11
1	1.080	0.071	0.224	0.047	0.050	0.061	0.057	0.061	0.064	0.061	0.059
2	0.043	1.042	0.030	0.112	0.068	0.048	0.041	0.075	0.062	0.277	0.046
3	0.290	0.169	1.108	0.119	0.119	0.144	0.118	0.133	0.150	0.144	0.143
4	0.125	0.070	0.073	1.037	0.116	0.079	0.064	0.089	0.096	0.069	0.053
5	0.030	0.064	0.021	0.043	1.035	0.211	0.026	0.036	0.103	0.062	0.027
6	0.101	0.119	0.065	0.092	0.132	1.071	0.081	0.097	0.139	0.125	0.087
7	0.053	0.076	0.038	0.052	0.052	0.071	1.047	0.101	0.071	0.062	0.062
8	0.076	0.113	0.070	0.093	0.079	0.116	0.076	1.064	0.226	0.093	0.105
9	0.046	0.056	0.021	0.025	0.026	0.028	0.025	0.027	1.025	0.032	0.033
10	0.039	0.055	0.026	0.048	0.054	0.049	0.037	0.047	0.040	1.037	0.047
11	0.365	0.413	0.280	0.382	0.422	0.400	0.361	0.406	0.399	0.413	1.251

[a] See note 2 on p. 82 for the classification of industries.

By taking all z_k other than z_1 and z_j sufficiently small, this is reduced to

$$\frac{L_{11}}{L_{11}z_1 + L_{1j}z_j} \geq \frac{L_{i1}}{L_{i1}z_1 + L_{ij}z_j} \quad \text{for } z_1 \text{ and } z_j > 0,$$

from which we have $L_{ij}L_{11} - L_{i1}L_{1j} \geq 0$. Hence, from (3.10) it follows that the effect of a rise in Q_j upon Y_i is non-negative in the second system. Comparing this effect with the corresponding effect, $dY_i = L_{ij}dQ_j$, in the first system, we find that the former is algebraically smaller than the latter because L_{i1}, L_{1j} and L_{11} are all positive. Thus we have proved the Samuelson–LeChatelier law for the simplest case where only one Y_h, say Y_1, is fixed and the corresponding Q_1 is made flexible. Exactly the same proof is applicable to the more general case of two or more Y_hs being kept constant.

The abstract properties established above are numerically confirmed in our model. Table 7 shows that each element of the Leontief inverse of the total transaction coefficient matrix is positive, that all elements on the diagonal are greater than unity, but that there are no off-diagonal elements which are greater than unity. Clearly, the former finding confirms Hicks laws I and II, while the latter confirms Metzler's theorem. Multiplying the i, j element of the Leontief inverse by Q_j / Y_i, we obtain the elasticity of the output of industry i with respect to the exogenous demand for j. All such elasticities (direct and cross) are listed in Table 8. Cross elasticities are less than the corresponding direct elasticities which, in turn, are less than unity (the maximal one is 0.83), and Hicks law III therefore operates.

Table 9 gives the lower Leontief inverse which is obtained when the final demand for industry, 'public administration, etc.', is adjusted so as to keep its output constant. Comparing its elements with the corresponding elements of the original Leontief inverse in Table 7, we find that the Samuelson–LeChatelier effects are not of great numerical significance, as far as elemental effects are concerned. In fact, they are generally less than 0.006, with the exception of the effects on the elements on the eleventh row, and even these only reach a magnitude of 0.01 at most. Nevertheless, this finding will not lessen the econometric importance of the Samuelson–LeChatelier analysis, because, as we shall observe in the next section, the similar effects on macro-variables, such as aggregate output, national income and consumption, are not so negligible as the effects on outputs of individual industries.

2. IMPACT MULTIPLIERS IN THE ENDOGENOUS TAX REVENUE CASE

In our mixed Leontief–Keynes economy, outputs of various industries depend on final demands for them. Among the components of final demand parts of personal consumption vary in proportion to the total personal real consumption, whose per capita value in turn depends on the real consumption per capita in the previous period, as well as the total current disposable personal real income per capita. It is obvious that the multiplier process in such an economy propagates itself through time. An increase in exogenous demand gives rise to an expansion of the output of every industry, which is accompanied by an increase in real income per capita and the real consumption per capita, so that real consumption per capita in the next period will be increased via the channel of the Duesenberry–Modigliani effect, which is assumed to be brought about with a time lag of one period. Leaving the dynamic analysis of the propagation process to a later chapter, we confine ourselves in this chapter to the analysis of 'impact' multipliers, so that instantaneous responses of endogenous variables to changes in predetermined variables are the only effects which are taken into account.

Let us take a unit of government expenditure, which is directed exclusively to industry k, as an exogenous impulse. It induces an increase in the gross domestic income at factor cost of the amount,

$$\Delta Y_f = \sum_j^n (l_j + \pi_j) \Delta Y_j,$$

because Y_f is defined as

$$Y_f = \sum_j (W_j + P_j) = \sum_j l_j Y_j + \sum_j (\pi_j Y_j + S_j), \tag{3.11}$$

where W_j and P_j represent wages and profits of industry j, while S_j denotes subsidies which are granted to industry j and is regarded as constant throughout the process of repercussions; l_j stands for the labour-input coefficient, W_j / Y_j, and π_j for the marginal profit coefficient of industry j defined as

$$\pi_j = 1 - (1 + t_j) \left(\sum_i^n a_{ij} + a_{Mj} \right) - l_j. \tag{see (2.16)}$$

Since the effect of an additional unit of government spending in industry k on the output of industry j is given by the (j, k) element of the Leontief inverse of the total transaction coefficient matrix, we have $\Delta Y_j = L_{jk}$, so that

$$\Delta Y_f = \sum_j f_j L_{jk}, \tag{3.12}$$

where $f_j = l_j + \pi_j$.

The multiplier effect which is obtained when the government expenditure is concentrated in a specific industry may be called the partial multiplier effect. It is contrasted with the general, or total, multiplier effect resulting from a unit increase of government expenditure which is distributed to all industries according to the pattern observed in the actual budget. Let g_i be the fraction of total government expenditure which is directed to industry i. The ratios, g_i $(i = 1, ..., n)$, can at once be derived from the data compiled in the input–output table. On the assumption that an additional increment in government expenditure is also distributed among industries in the same proportions as g_is, then the general multiplier effect is given as the average of the partial effects (3.12) with weights $g_1, ..., g_n$. We thus have

$$\Delta Y_f = \sum_k^n \left(\sum_j^n f_j L_{jk} \right) g_k, \tag{3.13}$$

where it must be noted that the sum of g_is is unity.

Similarly, partial and general multiplier effects on the gross national income at market prices, Y_m, can be calculated. From the definitional formulas for Y_f and Y_m, we have

$$Y_m = Y_f + \sum_j^n (T_j - S_j) + \sum_{i=C,G,I} (T_i - S_i). \tag{3.14}$$

In this equation, all S_is and T_G and T_I are kept constant in the calculation of multipliers. As for outlay taxes paid by industries and persons, we have

$$T_j = t_j \left(\sum_i^n a_{ij} + a_{Mj} \right) Y_j \quad (j = 1, ..., n), \tag{3.15}$$

and

$$T_c = t_c (\sum_i \beta_i + \beta_M)(C + S_c), \tag{3.16}$$

respectively, where t_j is the average outlay tax rate for industry j, t_c the similar tax rate on personal expenditures, a_{ij}s input coefficients, a_{Mj}s import coefficients, and β_is consumption quotas. Total consumption C depends on the disposable personal income Y_d with the marginal propensity to consume a_1, while Y_d is connected with outputs of industries by the formula,

$$Y_d = (1 - t_w) \sum_j l_j Y_j + (1 - t_\pi) b \sum_j (\pi_j Y_j + S_j), \tag{3.17}$$

which is obtained from (2.17) and (2.18)[1] .The subsidies, S_c, granted to persons, like subsidies to industries, are kept unchanged throughout the following discussion.

---

[1] Note that t_w and t_π are personal income tax rates applied to wages and personal income from profits, and b is the ratio of personal income from profits to total profits.

TABLE 10. *Impact multipliers due to a unit change in government expenditure: the endogenous tax revenue case*

Industry where the additional government expenditure is made	Multiplier effects on			The government expenditure ratio in the actual 1954 budget: g_i (in %)
	Y_f	Y_m	Y_d	
1. Agriculture, forestry and fishing	0.96	1.22	0.72	0.26
2. Mining and quarrying	1.38	1.52	1.12	0.48
3. Food, drink and tobacco	0.68	1.05	0.49	0.71
4. Chemicals and allied industries	0.95	1.07	0.70	3.05
5. Metal manufacture	1.05	1.16	0.78	0.32
6. Engineering and allied industries	1.25	1.37	0.95	19.92
7. Textiles, leather and clothing	1.00	1.11	0.76	1.61
8. Other manufacturing	1.13	1.26	0.86	2.57
9. Construction	1.26	1.40	1.00	6.27
10. Gas, electricity and water	1.27	1.43	0.95	1.32
11. Services	1.23	1.41	0.91	15.49
12. Public administration, etc.	1.47	1.60	1.17	48.01
When the additional government expenditure is distributed among industries in the actual 1954 proportions	1.33	1.47	1.04	100.00

Substituting T_j and T_c from (3.15) and (3.16) and bearing (3.11) and (3.17) in mind, we can write (3.14) as

$$Y_m = \sum_j m_j Y_j + \text{constant},$$

where

$$m_j = f_j + t_j (\sum_i a_{ij} + a_{Mj}) + a_1 t_c (\sum_i \beta_i + \beta_M)[(1-t_w)l_j + (1-t_\pi)b\pi_j].$$

Since all coefficients appearing in this expression are given, m_js are regarded as constant, so that we have, as the formula of the partial multiplier effect of an additional unit of government expenditure in industry k upon gross national income at market prices,

$$\Delta Y_m = \sum_j^n m_j L_{jk}. \tag{3.18}$$

It is evident that the corresponding general multiplier effect on gross national income at market prices is obtained by averaging these partial effects with weights $g_1, ..., g_n$:

$$\Delta Y_m = \sum_k^n \left(\sum_j^n m_j L_{jk} \right) g_k. \tag{3.19}$$

Finally, we can derive immediately from (3.17) the formulas for partial and general multiplier effects on disposable personal income, which are written, respectively, as

$$\Delta Y_d = \sum_j^n d_j L_{jk},\tag{3.20}$$

$$\Delta Y_d = \sum_k^n \left(\sum_j^n d_j L_{jk} \right) g_k,\tag{3.21}$$

with $d_j = (1 - t_w) l_j + (1 - t_\pi) b \pi_j$.

Let us now estimate partial and general multipliers on the basis of the data collected in the previous chapter. The Leontief inverse of the total transaction coefficient matrix has already been calculated, and the same data provide the figures for the coefficients of f_j, m_j, d_j for the United Kingdom, 1954. The partial multipliers of gross national income at factor cost and at market prices and of disposable personal income can easily be calculated according to the formulas (3.12), (3.18) and (3.20) respectively. From the results which are listed in Table 10 it is seen that there are large differences in partial multipliers, so that it is of great policy importance to choose among industries when public authorities decide to increase their expenditure. When the objective of the public spending policy is to maximize the gross national income, Table 10 suggests that industries 2, 6, 9, 10, 11, and 12 may be recommended as recipients of government expenditure.

The last row of Table 10 gives the figures for the general multipliers. These are calculated, on the basis of the actual 1954 government expenditure ratios (displayed in the last column), by formulas (3.13), (3.19), and (3.21) respectively. A comparison of our results with earlier works will be useful and desirable, although they are different in sample years and sample countries, because our input–output investigation is methodologically distinct from the others, which are mostly based on macroeconometric models of the Tinbergen–Klein type.

An elaborate and very well-known study on the issue is that of A. S. Goldberger.[1] His computation rests on a linearized version of the reduced form derived from the Klein–Goldberger model of the United States, 1929–52.[2] Taking a unit increase of government expenditure, Goldberger has estimated the multiplier of GNP at market prices at 1.2294 in the endogenous tax revenue case. But, as he has pointed out, this figure is too low to be reckoned a realistic appraisal of the impact multiplier. The kind of increase in government expenditure considered here is directed exclusively

[1] A. S. Goldberger, *op. cit.*
[2] L. R. Klein and A. S. Goldberger, *op. cit.*

to purchasing privately produced goods, and is therefore different from the actual increase of government expenditure, of which 50 per cent was, in 1952, paid as part of the government wage bill. Also, 64 per cent of the increase in government payrolls in 1952 was devoted to expanding government employment. We must, therefore, take into account the effects upon GNP of a transfer of government expenditure from purchases of privately produced goods to government payrolls. Goldberger has estimated that GNP increases by 0.3433 when there is a unit transfer of government expenditure from purchases of privately produced goods to government produced services, and decreases by 0.0079 when there is a unit expansion of government employment. Therefore, the total effect, after these additional effects have been taken into account, will be given by the sum of the separate effects:

$$\Delta Y_f = 1.2294 \times 1.00 + 0.3433 \times 0.50 - 0.0079 \times 0.50 \times 0.64$$
$$= 1.3985.[1]$$

This is the Goldberger estimate of the impact multiplier of GNP which is obtained under the 1952 package specification of a unit increase in the government budget. Of course no direct comparison of our result of 1.47 with Goldberger's 1.3985 is possible, and a hasty comparison is dangerous, because they are concerned with different countries in different periods. However, the following considerations seem relevant. (i) The marginal propensity to consume in our model is different to that in the Klein–Goldberger model, which makes the multiplier higher in the system with a higher marginal propensity to consume. It is not surprising to see that our estimate, 0.638, of the marginal propensity to consume (which might be too high, as has been mentioned, because of the omission of the highest income group from the cross-section sample) produces, other things being equal, a multiplier which is higher than the estimate by Goldberger, who has estimated the marginal propensity to consume at 0.55 for wage income, 0.41 for nonwage, nonfarm income, and 0.34 for farm income. (ii) More significant differences are found in effective tax rates. In the Klein–Goldberger model, the employment income tax rate, 0.150, is nearly three times as large as our estimate for the UK, 0.055, while the other personal income tax rate, 0.300, is about 50 per cent higher than ours, 0.218. Obviously, a high tax rate will stabilize the flexible change in GNP, due to a high leakage of income through taxation. Furthermore, as we are considering impact multipliers for a one-year period at present, there is no

[1] This formula is exactly the same as the one Goldberger uses for calculating the corresponding multiplier in the predetermined tax yield case. See Goldberger, *op. cit.* pp. 34–5.

induced investment, so that the repercussions via personal consumption of goods and services are most important. In these circumstances, a high wage-tax rate will have its greatest effect in decreasing disposable income, consumption and GNP. (iii) On the other hand, we find in the Klein–Goldberger system factors which are favourable for inflating the multiplier for GNP in that system in comparison with the multiplier in our UK model. First, Klein and Goldberger specify depreciations depending on the current level of private production, as well as capital stock in the middle of the year which is approximated by the average of the end-of-year and the beginning-of-year stock of private capital, whereas in our mixed Leontief–Keynes model for the UK, depreciations are regarded as constant. It is evident that the flexibility of depreciation contributes to increasing the value of the multiplier. Secondly, a more obvious difference is found between the UK and the US economies in their marginal propensities to import. If the latter had a propensity as high as the former, its multiplier would be calculated at a lower value. Thus there are found two classes of factors which tend to offset each other in their effects. Although we must restrain ourselves from making a heroic assertion, we may conclude from the considerable closeness of the multipliers of both economies that the favourable effects of a high propensity to consume and low tax rates on the multiplier for the UK economy are balanced by the favourable effects of flexible depreciations and a low propensity to import on the multiplier for the US economy.

A more recent study of the multiplier is the one by R. R. Rhomberg.[1] He calculates the effect of a unit change in government expenditure on GNP at current prices for Western Europe during the period 1948–60. In his system, the world is divided into three regions: North America (USA, Canada), other industrial countries (Western Europe, Japan) and the rest of the world (essentially the under-developed countries). The system consists of twenty-nine structural equations, and the method for calculating the multiplier is the same as that of Goldberger. Using a linearized version of the reduced form, Rhomberg has estimated the multiplier for Western Europe (including the UK) at 1.45 when the trade balance is fully flexible and at 1.38 when the imports of the rest of the world are stabilized, so that exports from Western Europe to the rest of the world are kept constant. While the estimate for Western Europe is not exactly applicable to the UK, it is remarkable that our estimate, 1.47, is not very far from his estimate, 1.38. (It is noted that in our input–output investigation the trade balance is only partly flexible, since exports are regarded as constant.)

[1] R. R. Rhomberg, 'A three-region world trade and income model, 1948–60', paper presented at the Summer Meeting of the Econometric Society, Ann Arbor, September 9–11, 1962.

3. EFFECTS OF COMPENSATING VARIATIONS IN GOVERNMENT EXPENDITURE

We have so far confined ourselves to discussing the case where a unit increase in government expenditure is either concentrated in a particular industry or distributed among all sectors in accordance with certain predetermined government expenditure ratios. Now let us focus our attention upon a more complicated and more general case, which is still a possibility open to the public authorities. As has already been mentioned, the Samuelson–LeChatelier principle is concerned with a unit increase in government expenditure that would leave outputs of a number of industries unchanged. Such a change in government expenditure is called a compensating variation of order one when output of only one industry is kept fixed, of order two when outputs of two industries are kept fixed, and so on until order $n-1$ when outputs are all fixed except that of a particular industry.

Let us begin by giving an example of a compensating variation of government expenditure of order one. We fix the output of the industry of 'public administration, etc.' at the level it has held before the variation in government expenditure. If the initial impulse is given to industry 1, the gross national income at factor cost, say, will increase by the amount,

$$\Delta Y_f = (f_1 L_{1,1}^{(1)} + f_2 L_{2,1}^{(1)} + \ldots + f_{11} L_{11,1}^{(1)}) \Delta G,$$

where $L_{ij}^{(1)}$ is the (i,j) element of the Leontief inverse of the transaction coefficient submatrix which is obtained by eliminating the last row and the last column from the original 12×12 matrix. At the same time, it induces an increase in the industrial and personal demand for public administration of the amount

$$\Delta Y_{12} = (A_{12,1} L_{1,1}^{(1)} + A_{12,2} L_{2,1}^{(1)} + \ldots + A_{12,11} L_{11,1}^{(1)}) \Delta G,$$

so that in order for Y_{12} to remain unchanged, the exogenous demand for Y_{12} must be diminished by exactly the same amount as ΔY_{12}. Consequently, the net increment of government expenditure would be

$$\Delta G^{\text{net}} = \Delta G - (A_{12,1} L_{1,1}^{(1)} + \ldots + A_{12,11} L_{11,1}^{(1)}) \Delta G.$$

Therefore, we find that a multiplier effect of a unit net increase in government expenditure on GNP is given as

$$\frac{\Delta Y_f}{\Delta G^{\text{net}}} = \frac{f_1 L_{1,1}^{(1)} + f_2 L_{2,1}^{(1)} + \ldots + f_{11} L_{11,1}^{(1)}}{1 - A_{12,1} L_{1,1}^{(1)} - \ldots - A_{12,11} L_{11,1}^{(1)}};$$

similarly for the cases where the original impulse is given to industries $2, 3, ..., 11$.

As the values of $L_{ij}^{(1)}$ are available in Table 9, it is easy to calculate the multiplier for each industry. When the output of industry 12 is fixed, the results are not very different from those originally obtained in the case of no sectoral output being fixed. This closeness is not surprising because each $L_{ij}^{(1)}$ is very close to the corresponding L_{ij} $(i, j = 1, ..., 11)$, while $A_{12, i}$ and $L_{12, i}$ are all of small magnitudes for $i = 1, ..., 11$. It must, however, be noticed that this is not a universal finding. Although it is true that the elements of the Leontief inverse are not much affected, whichever industry's output is chosen to be fixed, there are industries, $k_1, k_2, ...$, whose $A_{k_s i}$ and $L_{k_s i}$ are not small. A typical example is the industry 'services' labelled as 11, whose A_{k_i}s and L_{k_i}s are at least as high as 0.128 and 0.265, respectively. It is found that the partial multiplier of gross national income at factor cost is calculated at 1.70 when output of industry 11 is fixed and a unit increase of government expenditure is concentrated in industry 10. This value of the multiplier of order 1 is nearly 34 per cent higher than the value obtained when all outputs are flexible.

When the incremental government expenditure is distributed among industries $1, ..., 11$ in the ratios $g_1, g_2, ..., g_{11}$, so as to keep the output of industry 12 unchanged, then government expenditure of the net amount

$$\Delta G^{\mathrm{net}} = \sum_{i=1}^{11} (1 - A_{12, 1} L_{1, i}^{(1)} - ... - A_{12, 11} L_{11, i}^{(1)}) g_i \Delta G$$

will generate gross national income at factor cost in the amount

$$\Delta Y_f = \sum_{i=1}^{11} (f_1 L_{1, i}^{(1)} + ... + f_{11} L_{11, i}^{(1)}) g_i \Delta G.$$

Therefore, the formula for the general multiplier of order 1 can be written as

$$\frac{\Delta Y_f}{\Delta G^{\mathrm{net}}} = \frac{\sum_i (f_1 L_{1, i}^{(1)} + ... + f_{11} L_{11, i}^{(1)}) g_i}{\sum_i (1 - A_{12, 1} L_{1, i}^{(1)} - ... - A_{12, 11} L_{11, i}^{(1)}) g_i}.$$

By substituting actual values of g_is in 1954 into this formula, the general multiplier of order 1 is calculated at 1.20, which is compared with 1.33, the figure for the case where all outputs are flexible. Although we cannot say that the difference between the two multipliers is big in this case, we may obtain a bigger difference if the output of a different industry, say that of industry 11, is fixed. Thus we may conclude that the Samuelson–LeChatelier effects on the partial and general multipliers may be significantly large, whereas similar effects on elements of the Leontief inverse are generally negligible.

Next, let us consider a more general case in which the outputs of several industries, say $Y_{k+1}, Y_{k+2}, ..., Y_n$, are kept constant. When government expenditure is increased by one unit through the channel of industry i, GNP at factor cost will increase in the amount,

$$\Delta Y_f = (f_1 L_{1,i}^{(n-k)} + f_2 L_{2,i}^{(n-k)} + ... + f_k L_{k,i}^{(n-k)}) \Delta G,$$

where $L_{j,i}^{(n-k)}$ is the (j,i) element of the Leontief inverse of the $k \times k$ submatrix obtained by removing the last $n-k$ rows and columns from the original 12×12 transaction coefficient matrix. As the exogenous demands for the outputs of industries $k+1, ..., n$ must be adjusted so as to leave their outputs unchanged, the net increment in government expenditure will be

$$\Delta G^{\text{net}} = \left(1 - \sum_{j=k+1}^{n} A_{j,1} L_{1,i}^{(n-k)} - ... - \sum_{j=k+1}^{n} A_{j,k} L_{k,i}^{(n-k)} \right) \Delta G.$$

Dividing ΔY_f above by this ΔG^{net}, we get the formula for the partial multiplier of order k.

This general formula is now applied to the case of outputs other than those of industries 4, 5, 6 being kept constant; then the partial multipliers of order 9 of GNP at factor cost are calculated at 0.74, 0.93, and 1.35 when the incremental government expenditure is concentrated in each of these industries respectively. When the output of industry 5 is also fixed, it is found that one of the partial multipliers decreases from 0.74 to 0.73, while the other increases from 1.35 to 1.46. Comparing these values with the values of the partial multipliers with no fixed outputs in Table 10, we again observe fairly large (though not very large) differences between them.

Finally, in the extreme case we may have a compensating variation in government expenditure which increases output of industry i, all other outputs remaining unchanged. We then have

$$\Delta Y_f = f_i L_{i,i}^{(n-1)} \Delta G \quad \text{and} \quad \Delta G^{\text{net}} = (1 - \sum_{j \neq i} A_{j,i} L_{i,i}^{(n-1)}) \Delta G,$$

where $L_{i,i}^{(n-1)}$ stands for the ith Leontief inverse of order $n-1$ which is $1/(1-A_{ii})$. Consequently, it is found that the multiplier formula is reduced to the familiar traditional form,

$$\frac{\Delta Y_f}{\Delta G^{\text{net}}} = \frac{f_i}{1 - A_i} \quad (i = 1, ..., n),$$

where A_i represents the ith column sum of the transaction coefficient matrix. Similarly,

$$\frac{\Delta Y_m}{\Delta G^{\text{net}}} = \frac{m_i}{1 - A_i} \quad \text{and} \quad \frac{\Delta Y_d}{\Delta G^{\text{net}}} = \frac{d_i}{1 - A_i}$$

TABLE 11. *Impact multipliers of order 11 due to a unit change in government expenditure: the endogenous tax revenue case*

Industry where the additional government expenditure is made	Multiplier effects on		
	Y_f	Y_m	Y_d
1. Agriculture, forestry and fishing	0.89	1.22	0.69
2. Mining and quarrying	1.80	1.89	1.59
3. Food, drink and tobacco	0.36	0.87	0.23
4. Chemicals and allied industries	0.71	0.76	0.47
5. Metal manufacture	0.92	0.95	0.67
6. Engineering and allied industries	1.52	1.59	1.18
7. Textiles, leather and clothing	0.88	0.92	0.69
8. Other manufacturing	1.14	1.20	0.88
9. Construction	1.56	1.67	1.31
10. Gas, electricity and water	1.37	1.54	0.97
11. Services	1.34	1.52	0.98
12. Public administration, etc.	1.80	1.86	1.47

for gross national income at market prices and disposable personal income respectively. The values of these extreme multipliers are calculated and listed in Table 11. Comparing them with the simple Leontief–Keynes multipliers in Table 10, we observe a considerable variety of effects of the government's spending policy, so that the alternative budgets of the government may be assessed by their capability of generating gross national income or disposable personal income.

4. EFFICIENT GOVERNMENT EXPENDITURE

We now have to deal with the following two problems: (i) Of the various kinds of multipliers discussed in the previous sections, which should be consulted when the government budget is examined for efficiency in generating gross national income? (ii) Can the actual budget in 1954 be reckoned as an efficient one? Once the theoretical problem (i) is solved, it is no longer difficult to answer the econometric question (ii).

Let us consider the linear-programming problem of finding the budget $G_1, G_2, \ldots, G_n$ such that gross national income at factor cost,

$$Y_f = f_1 Y_1 + \ldots + f_n Y_n, \tag{3.22}$$

is as great as possible, subject to the input–output relations

$$\left. \begin{array}{l} A_{11}Y_1 + A_{12}Y_2 + \ldots + A_{1n}Y_n + G_1 + R_1 - Y_1 = 0, \\ A_{21}Y_1 + A_{22}Y_2 + \ldots + A_{2n}Y_n + G_2 + R_2 - Y_2 = 0, \\ \cdots\cdots\cdots\cdots\cdots\cdots\cdots\cdots\cdots\cdots\cdots\cdots \\ A_{n1}Y_1 + A_{n2}Y_2 + \ldots + A_{nn}Y_n + G_n + R_n - Y_n = 0, \end{array} \right\} \tag{3.23}$$

$$G_1 + G_2 + \ldots + G_n - \bar{G} \leqq 0, \tag{3.24}$$

$$Y_1 \geqq 0, \ldots, Y_n \geqq 0, G_1 \geqq 0, \ldots, G_n \geqq 0, \tag{3.25}$$

where R_i represents sectoral gross domestic capital formation plus stock appreciation plus exports plus the exogenous part of personal consumption and is regarded as constant, and $\bar{G}$ is the total amount of money allowed to the government for spending. To solve the problem we introduce Lagrangean multipliers, $\lambda_1, \ldots, \lambda_n$ and μ, to form the Lagrangean expression

$$f'Y + \lambda'[(A - I)Y + G + R] + \mu(\bar{G} - \Sigma G_i), \tag{3.26}$$

where f' and λ' are row vectors $(f_1, \ldots, f_n)$ and $(\lambda_1, \ldots, \lambda_n)$, respectively. Now maximize (3.26) with respect to Y and G. The Kuhn–Tucker conditions require that inequalities

$$f' + \lambda'(A - I) \leqq 0, \tag{3.27}$$

$$\lambda_i \leqq \mu \quad (i = 1, \ldots, n), \tag{3.28}$$

are satisfied at the efficient budget $(G_1^0, \ldots, G_n^0)$ and the corresponding production programme $(Y_1^0, \ldots, Y_n^0)$ which maximize the gross national income. It is noted that (i) $\lambda > 0$ because we have $\lambda' \geqq f'(I - A)^{-1} > 0$ from (3.27), (ii) if $\mu > 0$, (3.24) must hold with equality, (iii) if $Y_i^0 > 0$, the ith inequality of (3.27) must hold with equality, and (iv) if $G_i^0 > 0$, the ith inequality of (3.38) must hold with equality.

Suppose now $Y_i^0 > 0$ for all i. Then (3.27) becomes an equation, so that

$$f'(I - A)^{-1} = \lambda'.$$

Therefore, λ_i can be interpreted as the partial multiplier which will prevail when government expenditure is concentrated in industry i in a system with all outputs flexible. From (3.28) μ equals the largest among the n partial multipliers. As $G_i^0 = 0$ if $\lambda_i < \mu$, efficiency requires that government expenditure must be absorbed into those industries whose partial multipliers are greatest. Furthermore, as G_i^0s are non-negative and R_is are positive, all Y_i^0s are shown to be positive.

From the efficiency of the global budget of the government we now turn our attention to the efficiency of the marginal budget. The marginal budget is described as efficient if the given increment in government expenditure, ΔG, is allocated among n industries so that it maximizes the incremental gross national income, say, at factor cost,

$$\Delta Y_f = f'\Delta Y, \tag{3.29}$$

subject to

$$A_{11}\Delta Y_1 + \ldots + A_{1n}\Delta Y_n + \Delta G_1 - \Delta Y_1 = 0,$$
$$\ldots\ldots\ldots\ldots\ldots\ldots\ldots\ldots\ldots\ldots\ldots\ldots\ldots\ldots\ldots,$$
$$A_{n1}\Delta Y_1 + \ldots + A_{nn}\Delta Y_n + \Delta G_n - \Delta Y_n = 0,$$
(3.30)

$$\Delta G_1 + \Delta G_2 + \ldots + \Delta G_n \leqq \Delta G,$$
(3.31)

$$\Delta Y_1 \geqq 0, \Delta Y_2 \geqq 0, \ldots, \Delta Y_n \geqq 0,$$
(3.32)

$$G_1 + \Delta G_1 \geqq 0, G_2 + \Delta G_2 \geqq 0, \ldots, G_n + \Delta G_n \geqq 0,$$
(3.33)

where G_i is government expenditure on good i before the increase in government expenditure. The constraints (3.30) express incremental input–output relationships; (3.31) implies that the sum of the sectoral government expenditures cannot exceed the given amount, ΔG; (3.32) requires that no industry be adversely affected by the marginal spending of public authorities; finally (3.33) states the obvious fact that public authorities cannot be sellers of output i, so that government expenditure must be non-negative after, as well as before, the spending policy is introduced.

In order to solve this problem we start by ignoring (3.33) and maximize (3.29) subject to the other constraints. Then we obtain the Kuhn–Tucker conditions,

$$f' + \lambda'(A - I) \leqq 0,$$
(3.34)

$$\lambda_i = \mu \quad (i = 1, \ldots, n),$$
(3.35)

where λ_i and μ are the Lagrangean multipliers associated with (3.30) and (3.31) respectively. Note that λ_is are equated with each other by (3.35) because we have no restriction on ΔG_i other than (3.31). Also note that (i) all λ_is are at least as large as the partial multipliers by (3.34), (ii) if $\mu > 0$, (3.31) must hold with equality, and (iii) if the optimal increment of output i, ΔY_i^0, is positive, the ith inequality of (3.34) must be an equation. Substituting for λ_is from (3.35), we can write (3.34) in the form,

$$\frac{f_i}{1 - A_i} \leqq \mu,$$
(3.34′)

where A_i is the ith column sum of the transaction coefficient matrix.

As has been seen in the previous section, the term on the left-hand side of (3.34′) is the partial multiplier of order $n - 1$ of industry i. Rule (iii) above, therefore, states that when the partial multipliers of order $n - 1$ are compared with each other, ΔY_i^0 may be positive for the industry, i, which has the largest partial multiplier, while it must be zero for those industries whose partial multipliers do not reach the maximum. We find from (3.34′) that all

λ_i and μ are positive; consequently, by virtue of rule (ii), (3.31) must hold with equality.

Let us now rearrange the industries so that the partial multipliers of order $n-1$ of the first k industries are greatest. Then $\Delta Y_i^0 \geq 0$ for $i = 1, ..., k$, and $\Delta Y_i^0 = 0$ for $i = k+1, ..., n$. Therefore (3.30) are written as

$$A_{i1}\Delta Y_1^0 + ... + A_{ik}\Delta Y_k^0 + \Delta G_i^0 = \Delta Y_i^0 \quad (i = 1, ..., k),$$
$$A_{j1}\Delta Y_1^0 + ... + A_{jk}\Delta Y_k^0 + \Delta G_j^0 = 0 \quad (j = k+1, ..., n). \tag{3.36}$$

Hence,

$$(1 - A_1)\Delta Y_1^0 + ... + (1 - A_k)\Delta Y_k^0 = \Sigma \Delta G_i^0 = \Delta G. \tag{3.37}$$

Bearing in mind

$$\frac{f_1}{1 - A_1} = \frac{f_2}{1 - A_2} = ... = \frac{f_k}{1 - A_k},$$

we have from (3.37)

$$\Delta Y_f = f_1 \Delta Y_1^0 + ... + f_k \Delta Y_k^0 = \frac{f_1}{1 - A_1}\Delta G.$$

As $\Delta Y_i^0 \geq 0, i = 1, ..., k$, this means that ΔY_i^0s are bounded from above. Therefore, from (3.36), all ΔG_i^0s are bounded from below. When the given increment in government expenditure, ΔG, is small enough, ΔG_i^0s are small enough too, so that the constraints, (3.33), which we have so far ignored, will be fulfilled with strict inequality (we assume all $G_i > 0$). Hence ΔY_i^0s and ΔG_i^0s determined in this way are optimum solutions to our original linear-programming problem. Thus the criterion for the efficiency of the marginal budget is provided in terms of the partial multipliers of order $n-1$.

Let us finally apply the above theoretical conclusions to the 1954 UK economy. In examining a government budget for efficiency a crucial role is played by the relative magnitudes of partial multipliers; the criterion is given in terms of partial multipliers under perfect flexibility of outputs in the case of a global budget and partial multipliers of the highest order in the case of a marginal budget. From Tables 10 and 11, which list the values of these multipliers for the UK in 1954, we observe that industries may be classified, according to the order of magnitude of the multipliers, into two groups, one consisting of industries 2, 6, 9, 10, 11, and 12, and the other of all other industries, in the case of Table 10, and into four groups consisting of 2 and 12; 6 and 9; 10 and 11; and the remaining industries respectively, in the case of Table 11. The first classification is useful in the examination of the efficiency of the global budget of the government, while the second is useful in the examination of the marginal budget. It is noticed that there are rather substantial differences in the values of partial multipliers between groups, compared with those within any group. It is especially important for the following argument to point out that the multipliers of industries 2 and 12 greatly exceed those of 10 and 11 according to the second classification, whereas the difference between them is not so big in the first classification.

On the other hand, we find from the input–output table that more than 91 per cent of total government expenditure is concentrated in the top group of industries and only 8.5 per cent in the second group by the first classification. From this we may say that, globally speaking, the government budget of the UK in 1954 was efficient to a fairly satisfactory degree, so that the government's ability to generate national income was brought into nearly full play in that year. However, the same conclusion does not follow from Table 11. Although 48 per cent of total government expenditure is devoted to the industries in the top group by the second classification, which have the greatest partial multipliers of the highest order, half of the remaining 52 per cent is used to buy the outputs of the third and fourth groups. This suggests that it is still possible to increase national income by transfering government expenditure from industries belonging to the third and fourth groups to industries in the first (or second) group. We may therefore conclude that there remained margins for improving the UK government's budget in 1954, so that it might have generated more national income, although this budget might be conceded to be tolerably efficient from the global efficiency point of view. Finally, it is noted that more or less the same conclusion would be obtained even if we took gross national income at market prices or personal disposable income as the criterion of efficiency, instead of gross national income at factor cost, in terms of which our argument has been conducted.

Finally, it must be remembered that the above conclusions have been obtained under the restrictive assumptions that the scope of government activity is confined to the current period and that all tax rates are kept constant. In a wider perspective, it is obvious that the efficiency of government expenditure should be examined dynamically, by taking into consideration the fact that the government can change tax rates. Unfortunately we are unable to deal with the problem of the optimum budget on such a satisfactory level of generality, although dynamic multipliers and tax-rate reduction policies are topics of the next chapter.

4. *Generation of income through reduction of taxes*

1. TAXATION AS AN ALTERNATIVE FISCAL POLICY

We have so far been concerned with an examination of the effects of an increase in government expenditure on national income, as well as its effects on outputs of the component industries. We now turn to the other family of measures for encouraging the effective demand for outputs which may alternatively be taken by the government. These are effected by changing the bases and rates of various taxes.

Our model has taken account of four kinds of taxes: taxes on employment income, taxes on personal income from profits, excise taxes on industrial outlay, and taxes on final expenditure. They affect outputs in the following ways. A reduction of taxes on employment income, first of all, gives rise to an increase in the disposable income of employees, so that it raises the consumption coefficients,

$$c_{ij} = a_1(1-t_w)\beta_i l_j + a_1 b(1-t_\pi)$$

$$\times \beta_i \left[1 - (1+t_j) \left(\sum_{k=1}^{n} a_{kj} + a_{Mj} \right) - l_j \right], \quad (4.1)$$

defined as (2.22), since the effective tax rate t_w on employment income diminishes. When consumption coefficients become larger, it is obvious that intersectoral repercussions will be more vigorous than before, and outputs must be increased in order to meet increased demands.

Secondly, a reduction of taxes on personal income from profits influences outputs in two ways. Its immediate effect is, of course, an increase in the disposable income of persons receiving profits. However, profits consist of two parts: one is the part which is proportional to output, and the other is the part which is determined by subsidies to the industry and is therefore independent of the amount of output (see (2.16)). When taxes on personal income from profits are reduced, a greater fraction of each of the two parts of the profits is directed to consumption. Consequently, the consumption coefficients of profits earners, represented by the second term of (4.1), and also the consumption from subsidies, represented by the first term of the formula,

$$F_i = a_1 b(1-t_\pi)\beta_i \sum_{j=1}^{n} S_j + \beta_i S_c + G_i + I_i + E_i + D_i, \quad (4.2)$$

giving the autonomous part of the final demand for goods, are increased. The former accelerates interindustrial repercussions, whilst the latter causes an upward shift of equilibrium levels of outputs, since we continue to assume the multisectoral model,

$$Y_i = \sum_{j=1}^{n} A_{ij}Y_j + F_i + H_i \quad (i = 1, ..., n),$$ (4.3)

where $A_{ij} = a_{ij} + c_{ij}$.

Finally, the parameters of the model are influenced by excise taxes as follows. If excise taxes are levied on an industry j's outlay on goods at a lower rate than before, then the average excise tax rate for industry j, defined by (2.15), will be decreased and hence j's profits per output will be increased, *ceteris paribus*. Through this channel a reduction of excise taxes on industrial outlay has a favourable effect on consumption coefficients. On the other hand, although the outlay tax rates levied on personal expenditure have no explicit place in the formula, (4.1), of the consumption coefficient, they influence consumption coefficients by affecting the consumption quotas, β_is. In fact, we have in equation (2.11) the relation between the outlay tax rate on personal expenditure on good i, t_{ci}, the consumption quota, β_i, and the parameters of the utility function, γ_is. As the γ_is are assumed constant, the relation implies that a reduction of t_{ci} is an inducement to consumers to buy more of good i, so that it increases the consumption coefficients, $c_{i1}, ..., c_{in}$. Similarly, it stimulates consumption of good i by those persons and industrialists who are subsidized by the government; therefore the autonomous part F_i of the final demand for good i will be shifted upwards.

An experimental, macroeconomic analysis for reconnaissance purposes will facilitate the reader's comprehension, before we proceed to the multisectoral analysis of the effects of changes in tax rates. The macro-model consists of the *ex post* Keynesian identity,

$$Y_f = W + P = C + G + I + (E - M) + D - (T - S),$$ (4.4)

supplemented by the consumption function and other relationships.

We confine ourselves to the analysis of short-run effects, so that the consumption function can be given as

$$C = a_1[(1 - t_w)W + (1 - t_\pi)\Pi] + a_3,$$
$$a_3 = p_c N \left[a_2 \left(\frac{C}{p_c N} \right)_{-1} + a_0 \right],$$ (4.5)

where a_1 and a_3 are constant. C is the total personal consumption of goods and services (including imported ones), C^*, *plus* outlay taxes on personal expenditure, T_c, *minus* subsidies granted to persons, S_c. The constancy of

a_1 implies that a reduction of the outlay tax rate on personal expenditure induces an increase in the personal consumption of goods and services, C^*, such that there is no net effect on C, *ceteris paribus*. For the sake of simplicity, government expenditure, G, investment, I, exports, E, stock appreciation, D, and subsidies, S, are all assumed constant. For the total outlay taxes, T, however, the following formula is assumed:

$$T = t_c C^* + t_e \left(\sum_{i=1}^{n} \sum_{j=1}^{n} Y_{ij} + \sum_{i=1}^{n} M_i \right), \tag{4.6}$$

where t_c is the average tax rate on personal expenditure, and t_e is the average excise tax rate on industrial outlay; the part in parentheses represents total industrial input which is further assumed to be proportional to total output

$$\sum_{i=1}^{n} \sum_{j=1}^{n} Y_{ij} + \sum_{i=1}^{n} M_i = a \sum_{i=1}^{n} Y_i = a Y_o. \tag{4.7}$$

Taking the identities

$$C = C^* + t_c C^* - S_c$$

and

$$\sum_{i=1}^{n} Y_i = (1 + t_e) \left(\sum_{i=1}^{n} \sum_{j=1}^{n} Y_{ij} + \sum_{i=1}^{n} M_i \right) + \sum_{i=1}^{n} W_i + \sum_{i=1}^{n} P_i - \sum_{i=1}^{n} S_i$$

into account, we have respectively,

$$C^* = \frac{1}{1 + t_c} (C + S_c) \tag{4.8}$$

and

$$Y_o = \frac{1}{1 - a(1 + t_e)} \left(W + P - \sum_{i=1}^{n} S_i, \right), \tag{4.9}$$

where W is total wages and P total profits.

As for imports, M, they are the sum of $\sum_{i=1}^{n} M_i$ for industries, C_M for persons, G_M for public authorities, I_M for gross domestic capital formation, E_M for exports, and D_M for stock appreciation. Among them imports for industries may be assumed proportional to total output, because they are imported for current production; imports for personal consumption are equal to the consumption quota of imported goods and services multiplied by $C + S_c$; and all the other items of imports are regarded as constant throughout the subsequent analysis. Thus we may write

$$M = m Y_o + \beta_M (C + S_c) + \text{constant}. \tag{4.10}$$

Finally, we assume

$$W = l Y_o \quad \text{and} \quad \Pi = bP; \tag{4.11}$$

the former stating that wages are proportional to total output, while the latter states that a constant fraction of total profits is distributed to persons.

Equations (4.4)–(4.11) constitute our macroeconomic model. Eliminating C, W, Π, and so forth, we obtain

$$
\begin{aligned}
Y_f = {} & \frac{1}{1-(1+t_e)a}\left[a_1\left(\frac{1}{1+t_c}-\beta_M\right)\{(1-t_w)l\right. \\
& \left. +(1-t_\pi)b(1-l-(1+t_e)a)\}-(m+t_e a)\right]Y_f+\frac{1}{1-(1+t_e)a} \\
& \times\left[m+at_e-a_1 l\left(\frac{1}{1+t_c}-\beta_M\right)\{(1-t_w)-(1-t_\pi)b\}\right] \\
& \times\sum_{i=1}^{n}S_i-\frac{t_c}{1+t_c}(S_c+a_3)+\text{constant},
\end{aligned}
\tag{4.12}
$$

which is the equation from which the multiplier effects of changes in tax rates on the gross domestic income at factor cost Y_f are generated. On the right-hand side of (4.12) the coefficient of Y_f is denoted by k. By definition, $C^*/(C+S_c)$ equals $\sum_{i=1}^{n}\beta_i+\beta_M$, which is further equal to $1/(1+t_c)$ because of (4.8); therefore,

$$
0<\frac{1}{1+t_c}-\beta_M=\sum_{i=1}^{n}\beta_i<1.
\tag{4.13}
$$

Moreover, the excise tax rate on industrial outlay is sufficiently small for the sum of the labour-input coefficient and the material-input coefficient multiplied by $1+t_c$ not to reach one, i.e. $1>l+(1+t_e)a$; hence

$$
0<\frac{1}{1-(1+t_e)a}\{l(1-t_w)+(1-t_\pi)b(1-l-(1+t_e)a)\}<1 \tag{4.14}
$$

because both $1-t_w$ and $(1-t_\pi)b$ are positive fractions. Combining (4.13) and (4.14), and bearing in mind the fact that the marginal propensity to consume, a_1, is positive and less than unity, we finally find that k is less than one.

Defferentiating (4.12) with respect to t_w, we obtain

$$
\frac{dY_f}{dt_w}=\frac{1}{1-k}\frac{1}{1-(1+t_e)a}a_1 l(\sum_i S_i-Y_f)\left(\frac{1}{1+t_c}-\beta_M\right).
\tag{4.15}
$$

Similarly,

$$
\begin{aligned}
\frac{dY_f}{dt_\pi}= {} & \frac{1}{1-k}\frac{1}{1-(1+t_e)a}a_1 b\left(\beta_M-\frac{1}{1+t_c}\right) \\
& \times\{(1-l-(1+t_e)a)Y_f+l\sum_i S_{ij}\},
\end{aligned}
\tag{4.16}
$$

$$\frac{dY_f}{dt_c} = \frac{1}{1-k}\frac{1}{(1+t_c)^2}\left[\frac{-a_1}{1-(1+t_e)a}\right.$$

$$\times\left\{((1-t_w)l+(1-t_\pi)b(1-l-(1+t_e)a))\,Y_f\right.$$

$$\left.-l((1-t_w)-(1-t_\pi)b)\sum_i S_i\}-(S_c+a_3)\right], \tag{4.17}$$

$$\frac{dY_f}{dt_e} = \frac{-1}{1-k}\frac{1}{1-(1+t_e)a}\left[\left\{a_1\left(\frac{1}{1+t_c}-\beta_M\right)(1-t_\pi)\,ab-ak+a\right\}Y_f\right.$$

$$+\frac{a}{(1-(1+t_e)a)^2}\left\{a-1-m+a_1l\left(\frac{1}{1+t_c}-\beta_M\right)\right.$$

$$\left.\times((1-t_w)-(1-t_\pi)b)\right\}\sum_i S_i\right]. \tag{4.18}$$

Of these four effects, (4.16) is definitely negative, but the other three are indefinite in sign, because Y_f and $\sum_i S_i$ play counteracting roles in these formulas. However, in view of the fact that $\sum_{i=1}^{n} S_i$ is very small in size in comparison with Y_f, we can conclude that a reduction in the tax rate t_w or t_e also has a negative effect on gross domestic income at factor cost.

Let us neglect the effects of $\sum_{i=1}^{n} S_i$ and S_c. On the basis of the values of the parameters which are obtained from the data we have used in our multi-sectoral analysis, the elasticity of Y_f with respect to t_w is estimated at -0.03. That is to say, a 10 per cent decrease in the effective tax rate on employment income increases gross domestic income at factor cost by 0.3 per cent. In the same way, the other elasticities are estimated at:

$$\frac{t_\pi}{Y_f}\cdot\frac{dY_f}{dt_\pi} = -0.03;\quad \frac{t_c}{Y_f}\cdot\frac{dY_f}{dt_c} = -0.05;\quad \frac{t_e}{Y_f}\cdot\frac{dY_f}{dt_e} = -0.13.$$

It must, however, be admitted that the results derived from the macro-economic model (4.5)–(4.11) could be trusted only if the sum of the material-input coefficients, $a_j = \sum_{i=1}^{n} a_{ij}+a_{Mj}$, the labour-input coefficient, l_j, the import coefficient, a_{Mj}, and the excise tax rate on industrial outlay, t_j, all did not significantly differ from industry to industry. Unfortunately, Table 3 seems to offer evidence disproving any of these conditions for aggregation; the highest values of a_j, l_j, a_{Mj}, t_j are 0.64, 0.76, 0.25, 0.50, respectively, whilst the smallest are 0, 0.09, 0, 0, respectively. We are thus urged to undertake an alternative, multi-sectoral analysis.

Regarding all parameters, except the relevant tax rate, say t_w, as constant,

TABLE 12. *Elasticities of industrial outputs and gross domestic income at factor cost with respect to income and excise tax rates*[a]

	Y_1	Y_2	Y_3	Y_4	Y_5	Y_6	Y_7	Y_8	Y_9	Y_{10}	Y_{11}	Y_{12}	Y_f
t_w	−0.025	−0.026	−0.045	−0.021	−0.010	−0.010	−0.029	−0.024	−0.010	−0.029	−0.029	−0.015	−0.022
t_π	−0.028	−0.030	−0.052	−0.024	−0.011	−0.011	−0.032	−0.027	−0.011	−0.033	−0.033	−0.017	−0.025
t_c	−0.025	−0.026	−0.046	−0.021	−0.010	−0.010	−0.029	−0.024	−0.010	−0.030	−0.030	−0.015	−0.023
t_1	−0.003	−0.003	−0.005	−0.002	−0.001	−0.001	−0.003	−0.002	−0.001	−0.003	−0.003	−0.002	−0.002
t_2	*[b]	*	*	*	*	*	*	*	*	*	*	*	*
t_3	−0.014	−0.015	−0.027	−0.012	−0.006	−0.006	−0.017	−0.014	−0.006	−0.018	−0.017	−0.008	−0.013
t_4	*	*	−0.001	*	*	*	*	*	*	−0.001	−0.001	*	*
t_5	*	*		*	*	*	*	*	*	*	*	*	*
t_6	*	*	−0.001	*	*	*	*	*	*	*	−0.001	*	*
t_7	*	*	*	*	*	*	*	*	*	*	*	*	*
t_8		*	−0.001	*	*	*	*	*	*	*	*	*	*
t_9	−0.001	−0.001	−0.001			*	*	*	*	*	*	*	−0.001
t_{10}	−0.001	−0.001	−0.001	−0.001			−0.001	−0.001		−0.001	−0.001	*	−0.001
t_{11}	−0.009	−0.010	−0.016	−0.008	−0.004	−0.003	−0.011	−0.009	−0.003	−0.011	−0.011	−0.005	−0.008

[a] See footnote 2 on p. 82 for classification of industries.

[b] * stands for a number which is less than 0.0005.

we differentiate the multi-sectoral equations (4.1), (4.2) and (4.3) with respect to t_w and then solve them for $dY_j/dt_w, j = 1, \ldots, n$. As Y_f is the sum of $\sum_j W_j$ and $\sum_j P_j$ we obtain, from $W_j = l_j Y_j$ and (2.16),

$$Y_f = \sum_j [1 - (1 + t_j)(\sum_j a_{ij} + a_{Mj})] Y_j + \sum_j S_j. \qquad (4.19)$$

Since we have dY_j/dt_w, we can easily calculate dY_f/dt_w. In exactly the same way, dY_f/dt_π can be derived.

A reduction of the outlay tax rate, t_{ci}, levied on personal expenditure on good i implies an increase in the consumption quota β_i. In fact, differentiating (2.11), we have

$$\frac{d\beta_i}{dt_{ci}} = \frac{-\beta_i}{1 + t_{ci}}.$$

Therefore, differentiating (4.1)–(4.3) with respect to β_i and considering the above relation, we obtain $dY_j/dt_{ci}, j = 1, \ldots, n$, and hence dY_f/dt_{ci}. (Note that in (4.3) each H_i also depends on β_i.)

Finally, when we have a reduction of the excise tax rate, t_{ei}, on industrial outlay on good i, all $t_j, j = 1, \ldots, n$, will be changed according to the formula (2.15). In this case, it is noted that not only the coefficients of equations (4.1)–(4.3) but also those of (4.19) are affected by changes in the t_js. However $dY_j/dt_{ei}, j = 1, \ldots, n$, and dY_f/dt_{ei} are easily calculated.

Our results on the effects on Y_j and Y_f of changes in t_w, t_π, t_c and t_i are summarized in elasticity form in Table 12. It is interesting to compare them with our previous results from the macroeconomic model.

2. MULTIPLIER EFFECT OF A BALANCED BUDGET

An increase in government expenditure has a multiplier effect on national income, such that a part of the original increase in government expenditure will be compensated for by an increase in taxes collected, due to the increase in income and outlay. It is entirely compensated for in the extreme case of the marginal effective rate of tax being unity; in other cases deficits usually occur. If the effective tax rates are raised in order to maintain a balanced budget, the original multiplier effect of government expenditure on income will be reduced, because an increase in tax rates has negative effects on income, as has just been seen. Then what is the resultant of these opposed effects? The first answer was given by Haavelmo;[1] his theorem states that

[1] T. Haavelmo, *op. cit.*

a tax T that is fully spent will raise total gross national income by exactly the same amount, so that the multiplier of the balanced budget is unity.

Much attention has been paid to this problem by many economists; they have found that Haavelmo's theorem is true only under his restrictive assumptions and that if some of them are ruled out a balanced budget can easily affect national income with a multiplier which may be greater or smaller than one. This is numerically confirmed microeconomically as well as macroeconomically, even though our macro- and micro-models have, *inter alia*, the following assumptions in common with Haavelmo's model: (*a*) there are neither lags between tax collection and government expenditure of the same amount (which conforms to a final demand without leakage) nor effects on private investment; (*b*) there is unemployment of all kinds, so that prices and wage rates remain unchanged throughout the multiplier process; (*c*) there is also no complicated adjustment by transfers or by changes in the marginal propensity to consume. In addition to estimating the multiplier effects of a balanced budget numerically, we may ask what additional assumptions have to be made to obtain the Haavelmo result.

For convenience of explanation, let us recall our macroeconomic model (4.4)–(4.11). The reduced form, (4.12), can be written in a more abstract form:

$$Y_f = k(t_w, t_\pi, t_c, t_e) \, Y_f + G + h(t_w, t_\pi, t_c, t_e), \qquad (4.12')$$

where k and h are independent of Y_f but depend on tax rates t_i, $i = w, \pi, c, e$. Similarly, by eliminating W, Π, C^* and $\sum_{i=1}^{n} \sum_{j=1}^{n} Y_{ij} + \sum_{i=1}^{n} M_i$, the tax equation can be reduced to

$$T^* = t_w W + t_\pi \Pi + T = u(t_w, t_\pi, t_c, t_e) \, Y_f + v(t_w, t_\pi, t_c, t_e), \qquad (4.20)$$

where u and v are complexes of parameters and depend on t_i, $i = w, \pi, c, e$.

Let us now assume that when we have an increase in government expenditure a particular tax rate is adjusted, so that the expenditure and revenue of government continue to be balanced. Then, differentiating the budget equation of government, $G = t_w W + t_\pi \Pi + T$ and taking (4.20) into account, we find that a continually balanced budget requires the following condition to be fulfilled:

$$1 = u \frac{\partial Y_f}{\partial G} + \left(u \frac{\partial Y_f}{\partial t_i} + \frac{\partial u}{\partial t_i} \, Y_f + \frac{\partial v}{\partial t_i} \right) \frac{dt_i}{dG},$$

which can be solved for dt_i/dG. On the other hand, the simple multipliers of government expenditure and tax rate changes are obtained, from (4.12') as

$$\frac{\partial Y_f}{\partial G} = \frac{1}{1-k}, \quad \text{and} \quad \frac{\partial Y_f}{\partial t_i} = \frac{1}{1-k} \left(\frac{\partial k}{\partial t_i} \, Y_f + \frac{\partial h}{\partial t_i} \right),$$

respectively. Therefore, the multiplier of a balanced budget, denoted by dY_f/dB, is given as

$$\frac{dY_f}{dB} = \frac{\partial Y_f}{\partial G} + \frac{\partial Y_f}{\partial t_i}\frac{dt_i}{dG} = \frac{\Lambda_i + \Omega_i}{u\Lambda_i + (1-k)\Omega_i}, \tag{4.21}$$

where

$$\Lambda_i = \frac{\partial k}{\partial t_i}Y_f + \frac{\partial h}{\partial t_i} \quad \text{and} \quad \Omega_i = \frac{\partial u}{\partial t_i}Y_f + \frac{\partial v}{\partial t_i}. \tag{4.21'}$$

It is seen that dY_f/dB takes on the value of one if

$$\frac{\partial k}{\partial t_i}\Big/\frac{\partial u}{\partial t_i} = \frac{\partial h}{\partial t_i}\Big/\frac{\partial v}{\partial t_i} = k/(u-1); \tag{4.22}$$

otherwise it will be different from one.

The conditions (4.22) are very restrictive conditions. This is seen in the following way. Consider a case where only income taxes are in force, so that t_c and t_e are set at zero. Also, assume that income tax rates t_w and t_π change proportionately. Under these assumptions, both $(\partial k/\partial t_i)/(\partial u/\partial t_i)$ and $(\partial h/\partial t_i)/(\partial v/\partial t_i)$ are evaluated at $-a_1(1-\beta_M)$, but $k/(u-1)$ is evaluated at

$$-a_1(1-\beta_M)\frac{(1-t_w)l + (1-t_\pi)b(1-l-a) - m}{1 - a - t_w l - t_\pi b(1-l-a)}.$$

Hence (4.22) is fulfilled if the additional conditions $b = 1$ (all profits are distributed to persons) and $m = 0$ (there are no imports for current production) are satisfied; otherwise the multiplier dY_f/dB is not necessarily equal to unity. In fact on the basis of our macroeconomic parameters it is evaluated at 0.69 when t_c and t_e are fixed at their actual values in 1954 and t_w and t_π are adjusted proportionately.

We have seen in the previous chapter that the multiplier effects of an increase in government expenditure on national income are to a substantial extent dependent on the industries in which it is made. They depend also on whether a transfer of government expenditure from industry to industry is simultaneously made so as to keep outputs of certain industries constant. Likewise, it can be seen (and has been to some extent) that the effects of changes in tax rates on income are diversified in a similar way. Therefore the multiplier of a balanced budget can take on widely differing values, depending on the combination of expenditure and tax policies.

Table 13 summarizes the results of our investigation. The figures in column (*a*) show the multipliers which are obtained when an additional unit of government expenditure is spent in the corresponding industry and the effective tax rate on employment income is increased so that the incremental expenditure can be financed entirely by the increased tax revenue.

TABLE 13. *Multipliers of balanced budget on gross domestic national income at factor cost*

Industry where the additional government expenditure is made	Tax rates to be increased			
	(a) Tax rate on employment income	(b) Tax rate on personal income from profits	(c) Tax rates on employment income and personal income from profits	(d) Excise tax rates on personal and industrial outlays
1. Agriculture, forestry and fishing	0.93	0.94	0.94	0.94
2. Mining and quarrying	1.35	1.36	1.36	1.36
3. Food, drink and tobacco	0.64	0.66	0.65	0.66
4. Chemicals and allied industries	0.94	0.94	0.94	0.94
5. Metal manufacture	1.04	1.04	1.04	1.04
6. Engineering and allied industries	1.22	1.23	1.23	1.23
7. Textiles, leather and clothing	0.96	0.98	0.97	0.98
8. Other manufacturing	1.10	1.12	1.11	1.12
9. Construction	1.25	1.26	1.25	1.26
10. Gas, electricity and water	1.26	1.26	1.26	1.26
11. Services	0.98	1.09	1.06	1.10
12. Public administration, etc.	1.42	1.44	1.44	1.45
When the additional government expenditure is distributed among industries in the 1954 proportions	1.26	1.29	1.28	1.30

The figures in columns (*b*), (*c*), (*d*) show the similar effects of an increase in government expenditure which is accompanied by an increase in taxes on personal income from profits, a proportional increase in tax rates on employment income and personal income from profits, or a proportional increase in excise tax rates on industrial and personal outlays, in order to maintain the revenue and expenditure of government in equilibrium. The figures in the last row of the table show the global multipliers which are realized when additional government expenditure is distributed among industries in the actual 1954 proportions in the respective cases. It is seen from the table that the balanced-budget multiplier significantly depends on the industry where the additional government expenditure is made, but is not much influenced by the tax rate chosen to adjust itself in order to keep the government's budget in equilibrium.

3. CATALYTIC ACTION OF A TAX INCREASE

An increase in the effective rate at which personal income or an outlay (personal or industrial) is taxed has, by itself, a *negative* effect on national income; but it turns out to have a *positive* effect if it is combined appropriately with an increase in government expenditure. A tax increase can thus work as a catalyst bringing about a certain (sometimes considerable) increase in the value of the multiplier for government expenditure. This is not a paradoxical finding. The multiplier effect of a balanced budget is, as will be seen below, no more than an example of the catalysis of this kind which occurs in the extreme case of no deficits.

Let the net expenditure (or deficits) of government, Z, be defined as the excess of government expenditure over tax revenue. Consider alternative marginal fiscal policies which result in a given (prescribed) amount of marginal net expenditure. The government can choose among possible combinations of dG, dt_w, dt_π, dt_c, dt_e so that the resulting dZ is equated with the predetermined value, dZ^0. As

$$dZ^0 = dG - \left[u(t)\,dY_f + \left(\Sigma \frac{\partial u}{\partial t_i}\,dt_i \right) Y_f + \Sigma \frac{\partial v}{\partial t_i}\,dt_i \right]$$

from (4.20) and

$$dY_f = \frac{\partial Y_f}{\partial G}\,dG + \Sigma \frac{\partial Y_f}{\partial t_i}\,dt_i,$$

we obtain

$$\left[1 - u(t) \frac{\partial Y_f}{\partial G} \right] \frac{dG}{dZ^0} - \Sigma_i \left[u(t) \frac{\partial Y_f}{\partial t_i} + \Omega_i \right] \frac{dt_i}{dZ^0} = 1, \qquad (4.23)$$

where Ω_i is defined as in (4.21'), as before. On the other hand, regarding every variable as depending on Z^0 and differentiating (4.12') with respect to Z^0, we obtain

$$\frac{dY_f}{dZ^0} = \frac{1}{1-k}\left[\frac{dG}{dZ^0} + \sum_i \Lambda_i \frac{dt_i}{dZ^0}\right],$$
(4.24)

which, in turn, yields

$$\frac{dY_f}{dG} = \frac{1}{1-k}\left[1 + \sum_i \Lambda_i \frac{dt_i/dZ^0}{dG/dZ^0}\right].$$
(4.24')

In the particular case where only t_i responds to a change in G, other ts being kept constant, (4.24') is reduced to

$$\frac{dY_f}{dG} = \frac{1}{1-k}\left[1 + \Lambda_i \frac{(1-k-u)-(1-k)\zeta}{u\Lambda_i + (1-k)\Omega_i}\right],$$
(4.25)

where $\zeta = dZ^0/dG$, because we have

$$\partial Y_f/\partial G = 1/(1-k) \quad \text{and} \quad \partial Y_f/\partial t_i = \Lambda_i/(1-k).$$

(4.25) is the general formula of the expenditure multiplier which applies to the case where a change in the tax rate t_i accompanies an increase in government expenditure by one unit, so as to result in only ζ units of marginal net expenditure. (When $\zeta = 0$, it degenerates into the formula for the multiplier of the balanced budget (4.21), whilst when $\zeta = (1-k-u)/(1-k)$, it is reduced to the formula of the simple expenditure multiplier.) Consequently, when an extra deficit of £ζ is allowed to the public authorities, they can spend £1 more and £dY_f/dG of gross domestic income, given by (4.25), can be additionally produced by putting an appropriate tax policy into operation simultaneously. With no accompanying tax policies, however, an extra deficit of £ζ implies an amount of gross expenditure dG fulfilling

$$dG = u\,dY_f + \zeta,$$

so that $dG = \zeta(1-k)/(1-k-u)$ because $dY_f = dG/(1-k)$. Therefore, an increase in gross domestic income of the amount

$$\frac{dY_f}{dG}dG = \frac{1}{1-k}\frac{1-k}{1-k-u}\zeta = \frac{1}{1-k-u}\zeta$$
(4.26)

can be expected as the multiplier effect of the extra deficit of £ζ.

(4.25) and (4.26) are compared with each other. The difference between them gives the catalytic effect of a tax increase, which is

$$\frac{\Lambda_i + \Omega_i}{u\Lambda_i + (1-k)\Omega_i}\left[1 - \frac{1-k}{1-k-u}\zeta\right].$$

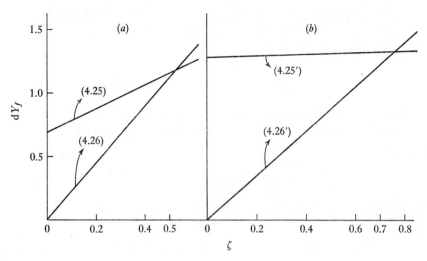

Figure 3

Catalytic effects of a proportional change in effective income-tax rates on gross domestic income at factor cost.

It is equated with the multiplier effect of a balanced budget at $\zeta = 0$ and vanishes at $\zeta = (1 - k - u)/(1 - k)$. Thus it is interesting to see that the entire effect of a balanced budget is no more than a catalytic effect of the associated tax policy, while it is evident that there is no catalytic effect when a simple expenditure policy is carried out without an accompanying revision of tax rates. Figure 3 a compares (4.25) and (4.26) in the case where excise tax rates, t_c and t_e, are fixed at their actual values in 1954 and personal income rates, t_w and t_π, are adjusted proportionately. In this case, (4.25) and (4.26) are evaluated at 0.88 and 0.47 respectively, when $\zeta = 0.2$; therefore the tax policy contributes to increasing the multiplier by 0.41.

The catalytic effects of tax policies can be analysed more precisely by using our mixed Leontief–Keynes model. Suppose one unit of additional expenditure is made by public authorities, exclusively in order to buy output of industry h. We have calculated $\partial Y_j/\partial G_h, j = 1, ..., n$, and $\partial Y_f/\partial G_h$. We have also calculated $\partial Y_j/\partial t_i$ and $\partial Y_f/\partial t_i, j = 1, ..., n; i = 1, ..., n, c, w, \pi$. The total tax revenue of public authorities is given as

$$T^* = t_w W + t_\pi \Pi + t_c C^* + \sum_j t_j \left(\sum_{i=1}^{n} a_{ij} + a_{Mj} \right) Y_j.$$

Therefore, we can calculate $\partial T^*/\partial G_h$ and $\partial T^*/\partial t_i$. Since the deficit Z is the excess of government expenditure G over revenue T^*, we have

$$dZ = dG_h - \frac{\partial T^*}{\partial G_h} dG_h - \sum_i \frac{\partial T^*}{\partial t_i} dt_i,$$

if the additional government expenditure dG_h is made in combination with a revision of tax rates, $dt_i, i = 1, ..., n, c, w, \pi$.

From this equation we can derive

$$\zeta_h = 1 - \frac{\partial T^*}{\partial G_h} - \sum_i \frac{\partial T^*}{\partial t_i} \frac{dt_i}{dG_h},$$

where $\zeta_h = dZ/dG_h$. Therefore, when only one t_i is revised in association with an increase in government expenditure, dG_h, we have

$$\frac{dt_i}{dG_h} = \frac{1 - \dfrac{\partial T^*}{\partial G_h}}{\dfrac{\partial T^*}{\partial t_i}} - \frac{1}{\dfrac{\partial T^*}{\partial t_i}} \zeta_h.$$

Hence we obtain

$$\frac{dY_f}{dG_h} = \frac{\partial Y_f}{\partial G_h} + \frac{\partial Y_f}{\partial t_i} \left[\frac{1 - \dfrac{\partial T^*}{\partial G_h}}{\dfrac{\partial T^*}{\partial t_i}} - \frac{1}{\dfrac{\partial T^*}{\partial t_i}} \zeta_h \right], \tag{4.25'}$$

which obviously corresponds to (4.25).

On the other hand, when there are no accompanying tax policies an extra definit of $\pounds\zeta_h$ implies an amount of gross expenditure

$$dG_h = \frac{\partial T^*}{\partial G_h} dG_h + \zeta_h.$$

Therefore

$$\frac{dY_f}{dG_h} dG_h = \frac{\partial Y_f}{\partial G_h} \frac{1}{1 - \dfrac{\partial T^*}{\partial G_h}} \zeta_h, \tag{4.26'}$$

which corresponds to the macroeconomic formula (4.26). On the basis of (4.25') and (4.26'), we can draw, for each industry h where the additional government expenditure is made and for each tax rate t_i that is changed, a figure which corresponds to Figure 3 *a*. Figure 3 *b* is drawn for the global case of the additional government expenditure being distributed among industries in the actual proportions of 1954 and the tax rates on employment income and personal income from profits being adjusted to retain the actual 1954 proportions. By superimposing Figure 3 *b* upon Figure 3 *a*, we can easily compare the results of the interindustrial, mixed Leontief–Keynes analysis with those of the macroeconomic analysis. We find that the catalytic effect derived from the aggregated model deviates from the one from the Keynes–Leontief model to a surprisingly large extent, especially when the deficit ζ takes on a small value. Also, it is seen that there is only an almost negligible difference between the balanced-budget and the pure expenditure multiplier calculated from the Keynes–Leontief model, whereas they differ from each other significantly in the aggregated model. These would illustrate the importance of the interindustrial analysis.

4. SHORT TERM BUILT-IN FLEXIBILITIES OF PERSONAL TAXES

In the preceding chapter we have examined the effects of an increase in government expenditure on the levels of industrial outputs and national income. When industrial outputs and national income expand, taxes will of course increase, as they are endogenous variables of the model. Next we have seen, in Section 1 of this chapter, that an increase in taxes has adverse effects on outputs and national income. It may therefore be deduced that the multipliers derived from a tax-endogenous model have to be considered as having already taken account of the negative effects of taxes. Isolated, pure effects of expenditure policies can be obtained only from a model which regards taxes as exogenous variables, and a comparison of such hypothetical multipliers with the real multipliers which work in the actual tax-endogenous economy would reveal the role of the tax system in stabilizing or dampening industrial outputs and national income.

Assuming the macroeconomic model (4.4)–(4.11), we may determine the values of the hypothetical multipliers in the following way. In the reduced form (4.12) of the model, we first set the effective tax rates on personal incomes, t_w and t_π, at zero, excise tax rates being held at their actual rates. Then the coefficient of Y_f on the right-hand side of (4.12) becomes 0.19; therefore we obtain a hypothetical multiplier of the magnitude 1.235. We may alternatively fix not only personal tax rates but also excise tax rates at zero; then the multiplier is estimated at 1.429.

These values are compared with the actual multiplier, which is 1.172. The ratio of the deviation of the actual multiplier from each of the hypothetical ones to the hypothetical multipliers gives the fraction of the change in income which is prevented by the existence of 'built-in flexibility'. This Musgrave–Miller measure of the effectiveness of built-in flexibility, which is denoted by α, is calculated, on the basis of the first and second hypothetical multipliers, at 0.05 and 0.18 respectively.[1] These figures, although they will have to be replaced later by more accurate estimates based on the mixed Leontief–Keynes model, may at this stage be compared with our predecessors' results.

Much of the literature on this subject is based on the economic system of

---

[1] R. A. Musgrave and M. H. Miller, 'Built-in flexibility', *American Economic Review* (March 1948).

the USA. First, Musgrave and Miller calculated the measure of built-in stability, using the average value of the marginal propensity to consume out of disposable income over the period 1929–47 and estimating the marginal income tax rate by the use of the average income elasticity of income tax revenue over 1929–47 and the average income tax rate in 1946–7. Their estimate of the measure α is 0.358, which means that about one-third of the change in income due to a change in autonomous investment will be offset by the built-in flexibility of income tax. Income tax in the USA, which was employed in their computation, includes personal income tax, corporation income tax and other federal income taxes. But Musgrave and Miller assumed that there was no induced investment and that the stabilizing effect of income tax appeared only through consumption. Thus their analysis and ours are effectively on the same basis, so that the estimates of α are comparable, apart from the fact that they are concerned with different economies and also that Musgrave and Miller differ from us in calculating α for net national income but not for gross domestic income at factor cost.

There is a large apparent difference between the two estimates of α: 0.358 versus 0.05. (The Musgrave–Miller estimate should be compared with our first estimate, because they take as the hypothetical tax-exogenous multiplier the multiplier which is obtained when only the effective income-tax rates are set at zero.) However it is found that a substantial portion of the difference may be ascribable to the difference between the assumed marginal propensities to consume. In fact, if we substitute our marginal propensity to consume out of disposable income, 0.255, for the Musgrave–Miller figure, 0.65 (no revision being made concerning the other data), then Musgrave and Miller's α is re-calculated at 0.09 by the same formula as they used. Since their figure for the marginal propensity to consume, simply derived from the time series data, may be considered, as usual, to be biased upwards, because the time trend and other appropriate explanatory variables are all ignored, we may safely conclude that their estimate of the measure of built-in stability is also biased upwards significantly.

The idea of tax flexibility originating with Musgrave and Miller has been improved in two types of analyses: the marginal approach by Lusher and Cohen, and the structural model approach by Goldberger and Smith.[1] Lusher introduced a new measure, and he himself translated his estimate of it for the US economy from the second quarter of 1953 to the first quarter

[1] D. W. Lusher, 'The stabilizing effectiveness of budget flexibility', *Conference on Policies to Combat Depressions* (National Bureau of Economic Research, 1956), pp. 77–89; L. Cohen, 'An empirical measurement of the built-in flexibility of the individual income tax', *American Economic Review* (May 1959); A. S. Goldberger, *op. cit.* pp. 39–48; P. E. Smith, 'A note on the built-in flexibility of the individual income tax', *Econometrica* (October 1963).

of 1955 into an estimate of Musgrave and Miller's α at 0.367, which is very close to their own estimate, 0.358. Lusher's approach is an improvement, in the sense that it was made on a step-by-step judgement basis embodying a detailed specification of the economic coefficients as well as estimates of taxes, transfers and public expenditures for major items. However, it must be borne in mind that he used time series data, so that the criticism levelled at Musgrave and Miller would also apply to him.

Another study was made by Cohen. He used another measure γ to express the magnitude of built-in flexibility of personal income tax:

$$\gamma = \frac{\Delta T}{\Delta AGI} = \frac{\Delta TI}{\Delta AGI} \frac{\Delta T}{\Delta TI},$$

where AGI represents adjusted gross income, TI taxable income, and T tax liability. This formula analyses the sensitivity of T to AGI into the flexibility of taxable income, $\Delta TI/\Delta AGI$, and the marginal rate of taxation, $\Delta T/\Delta TI$. He estimated each term and obtained $\gamma = 0.138$ for the US economy, 1949–53. No direct comparison is possible between Cohen and Musgrave–Miller. But if we are reminded of the identity

$$\frac{\Delta T}{\Delta Y} = \frac{\Delta T}{\Delta AGI} \frac{\Delta AGI}{\Delta Y_p} \frac{\Delta Y_p}{\Delta Y},$$

where Y_p denotes personal income, and assume $\Delta AGI/\Delta Y_p = 1$, then the marginal income tax rate $\Delta T/\Delta Y$ is estimated at 0.12, since $\Delta Y_p/\Delta Y$ is estimated at 0.85 from the time series data of 1949–53. Applying the Musgrave–Miller formula, Cohen's $\gamma = 0.138$ is translated as $\alpha = 0.04$ at the value of the marginal propensity to consume of 0.255 which our macro-economic model (4.4)–(4.11) assumes, and as $\alpha = 0.182$ at the Musgrave–Miller value.

The most elaborate study so far made is probably Goldberger's, which is based on the Klein–Goldberger model of the US economy, 1929–52. He computed the impact multiplier for GNP at market prices in the pre-determined tax yield case where not only income taxes (i.e. taxes on wage bill, corporate profits and distributed profits) but also outlay taxes on GNP at factor cost are taken as constant. By comparing this hypothetical multiplier with the 'actual' one in the endogenous tax yield case, he estimated the measure α at 0.113, which may be compared with Smith's estimate, $\alpha = 0.21$, obtained from a small structural model of the US economy, 1947–60. It must be noticed, however, that Goldberger's α is a figure relating to GNP *at market prices*. To compare it with our estimate, we must convert it into a figure relating to GNP at factor cost. Using the tables of impact multipliers computed by Goldberger, we obtain $\alpha = 0.20$ for GNP

TABLE 14. *Average effective individual income tax rates in postwar USA*

	Effective rate on personal income	Effective rate on adjusted personal income
1946–58	0.112	0.128
1945–59	0.113	0.129

Source: *Statistics of Income for 1952*, Part I (Washington: US Treasury Department, US Government Printing Office), 1956, p. 55; *Ibid. for 1960*, Part I, 1963, pp. 100–1; *Economic Report of the President, op. cit.* p. 226.

at factor cost, which is very close to our corresponding estimate for the UK economy, 0.18. It is also noted that our figure is not very different from the figure of 0.2 obtained by Hansen and the figures of 0.24–0.26 obtained by Balopoulos for the UK, from a simple model of the Keynesian type and a British econometric model respectively.[1]

It is noted that in the Klein–Goldberger model corporate income tax can influence investment only with a time lag of one period (i.e. a year); it has no impact effect on income through investment. Thus, so far as the short-run damping effect is concerned, the condition is the same as ours. Nevertheless his estimate is still greater than ours, although the discrepancy between them may be resolved if we take into account the differences between the effective income tax rates assumed by Goldberger and by us. In this respect, there is a point which should be taken into account: that is, the income tax rates employed by Goldberger may be the effective individual income tax rates on adjusted gross income, which are higher than the income tax rates on personal income before deducting some allowances, expenses, etc. He adopted heroic approximations to the income tax rates generally in effect in the United States in the postwar years. However, as the above time series data show, the average personal income tax rate did not exceed 0.113 on personal income and 0.129 on adjusted gross income. This may suggest that Goldberger's specification of the wage income tax rate, 0.15, and non-wage non-farm non-corporate income tax rate, 0.30, may be too high, even though they are marginal rates. Apart from this point, we would consider that Goldberger's method is most appropriate to this problem, and his estimate of the measure of built-in flexibility may have a high accuracy.

Let us now reconsider the problem in our interindustrial structural model. We calculate the value of the Musgrave–Miller measure of built-in

[1] See B. Hansen, *Fiscal Policy in Seven Countries, 1955–65* (OECD, 1969), and E. T. Balopoulos, *Fiscal Policy Models of the British Economy* (North-Holland Publishing Co. 1967).

TABLE 15. *Impact multipliers due to a unit change in government expenditure: the exogenous tax revenue case*

Industry where the additional government expenditure is made	Case I: Income taxes are exogenous Multiplier effects on			Case II: All taxes are exogenous Multiplier effects on		
	Y_f	Y_m	Y_d	Y_f	Y_m	Y_d
1. Agriculture, forestry and fishing	1.006	1.250	0.839	1.129	1.395	1.083
2. Mining and quarrying	1.456	1.574	1.289	1.528	1.660	1.362
3. Food, drink and tobacco	0.716	1.074	0.574	0.872	1.259	0.910
4. Chemicals and allied industries	1.002	1.102	0.815	1.067	1.179	0.928
5. Metal manufacture	1.100	1.191	0.912	1.167	1.271	1.021
6. Engineering and allied industries	1.309	1.411	1.101	1.388	1.504	1.227
7. Textiles, leather and clothing	1.049	1.136	0.884	1.114	1.213	0.989
8. Other manufacturing	1.190	1.292	1.001	1.264	1.379	1.122
9. Construction	1.322	1.440	1.140	1.408	1.541	1.282
10. Gas, electricity and water	1.339	1.480	1.113	1.428	1.584	1.268
11. Services	1.288	1.449	1.064	1.385	1.563	1.235
12. Public administration, etc.	1.539	1.635	1.336	1.626	1.737	1.466
When the additional government expenditure is distributed among industries in the actual 1954 proportions	1.396	1.508	1.192	1.482	1.609	1.329

flexibility not only for the entire economy but also for each extreme case where government expenditure is concentrated in one of the twelve industries. In principle there is no difficulty in doing so. In the previous chapter, we have calculated partial and global impact multiplier effects on gross domestic income at factor cost, Y_f, gross domestic income at market prices, Y_m, and disposable personal income, Y_d (see Table 10). In computing these multipliers, income and outlay tax rates have been fixed at their actual values. In exactly the same way, we can compute partial and global multiplier effects on Y_f, Y_m and Y_d in the two hypothetical cases: one where tax rates on employment income and personal income from profits are fixed at zero, and the other where not only effective income tax rates but also excise tax rates on personal and industrial expenditures are set at zero. For such simulations, adequate adjustments are required in consumption quotas β_i and consumption coefficients c_{ij}, but all other parameters remain unchanged. The results are presented in Table 15.

By the use of the Musgrave–Miller formula, we can now easily calculate the measure of built-in flexibility, α, for each industry as well as for the entire economy. The built-in flexibility may be analysed in terms of gross domestic income at factor cost, gross domestic income at market prices or disposable personal income. The results summarized in Table 16 show that the measure for industry 1 (agriculture, forestry and fishing) in the first

TABLE 16. *Short term built-in flexibility of taxes in the mixed Leontief–Keynes model of the UK, 1954* (%)

Industry where the additional government expenditure is made	Case I: Income taxes are exogenous The Musgrave–Miller measure α in terms of			Case II: All taxes are exogenous The Musgrave–Miller measure α in terms of		
	Y_f	Y_m	Y_d	Y_f	Y_m	Y_d
1. Agriculture, forestry and fishing	4.7	2.4	13.7	15.1	12.6	33.1
2. Mining and quarrying	5.8	3.4	12.9	10.0	8.5	17.6
3. Food, drink and tobacco	4.8	2.2	14.6	21.9	16.5	46.2
4. Chemicals and allied industries	4.9	3.1	14.7	10.8	9.5	25.0
5. Metal manufacture	4.7	2.9	14.0	10.2	9.0	23.2
6. Engineering and allied industries	4.6	2.7	13.5	10.0	8.7	22.4
7. Textiles, leather and clothing	4.7	2.7	13.5	10.2	8.9	22.7
8. Other manufacturing	4.7	2.8	13.6	10.3	8.9	22.9
9. Construction	4.5	2.4	12.7	10.3	8.9	22.4
10. Gas, electricity and water	5.0	3.1	14.2	10.9	9.5	24.7
11. Services	4.8	2.8	14.1	11.4	9.9	26.0
12. Public administration, etc.	4.4	2.4	12.6	9.5	8.1	20.3
When the additional government expenditure is distributed among industries in the actual 1954 proportions	4.5	2.6	13.1	10.1	8.7	22.0

column, 0.047, for example, indicates the ratio of the damping effect of personal taxes upon gross domestic income at factor cost to the impact multiplier which is realized, in the exogenous tax revenue case, when a unit injection of government expenditure is made into industry 1. We can also see from Table 15 that in the case where the additional government expenditure is distributed among industries in the actual 1954 proportions, the global impact effect of government expenditure upon gross domestic income at factor cost is raised from 1.33 to 1.40, if the actual endogenous personal tax revenue system is replaced by an exogenous one; and hence the global measure of built-in flexibility has been estimated at 0.045. This figure implies that a tax system such as the one prevailing in the postwar UK serves to reduce the impact effect of an autonomous change in expenditure upon gross domestic income at factor cost by about one-twentieth. Finally, it is seen that the damping effect is considerably higher if the injection is concentrated in the food, drink and tobacco industry, providing all taxes are made exogenous.

5. DYNAMIC PROPERTIES OF BUILT-IN FLEXIBILITY

The preceding section has dealt with built-in flexibility in the short term – the efficacy of the tax system as a stabilizer in a particular year. It is clear, though, that for most practical purposes knowledge of the 'instantaneous' effect is not sufficient. In this section we shall investigate the longer-run effects of taxes, by comparing the time path of income in the endogenous tax revenue case with that in the exogenous tax revenue case.

We must now be reminded that our system is provided with an aggregate consumption function which relates real consumption per capita in period t with disposable real personal income per capita in period t and real consumption per capita in $t-1$. This is the only intertemporal relationship in our system through which an injection of an autonomous expenditure propagates its effects in succeeding periods. In fact, if a unit increase in final demand, dF_{i0}, is made in period o, then the marginal Leontief–Keynes equations

$$dY_{i0} = \sum_{j=1}^{n} A_{ij} dY_{j0} + dF_{i0} \quad (i = 1, ..., n),$$

determine the increments of outputs $dY_{10}, ..., dY_{n0}$ in period o (the impact multiplier effects). Once incremental outputs are determined, they are distributed among persons as wages and profits, from which personal taxes are subtracted. We have an increase in the disposable personal income which raises the level of real consumption in period o. It, in turn, has lagged effects on the final demands for goods and services; that is, the constant terms of the final demand functions in period 1 are influenced by real consumption in period o as

$$dH_{it} = \beta_i a_2 dC_{t-1},$$

provided that the price level of consumption goods, p_c, and the population, N, do not change. Under the assumption that the autonomous increase in the final demands is sustained, we have $dF_{i1} = dF_{i0}, i = 1, ..., n$, which together with dH_{i1} determine $dY_{11}, ..., dY_{n1}$ such that

$$dY_{it} = \sum_{j=1}^{n} A_{ij} dY_{jt} + dF_{it} + dH_{it} \quad (i = 1, ..., n), \tag{4.27}$$

$$dY_{dt} = (1 - t_w) \sum_{j=1}^{n} l_j dY_{jt} + (1 - t_\pi) b$$
$$\times \sum_{j=1}^{n} \left\{ 1 - (1 + t_j) \left(\sum_{i=1}^{n} a_{ij} + a_{Mj} \right) - l_j \right\} dY_{jt}, \tag{4.28}$$

$$dC_t = a_1 dY_{dt} + a_2 dC_{t-1}, \tag{4.29}$$

$$dH_{it} = \beta_i a_2 dC_{t-1}, \tag{4.30}$$

which follow from (2.19), (2.16)–(2.18), (2.14) and (2.21) respectively. Repeating the same computations as those we did above, we obtain a dynamic path $dY_{it}, i = 1, ..., n; t = 0.1, 2, ...$

It is now easy to calculate the dynamic multipliers for gross domestic incomes at factor cost and at market prices. They are compared with hypothetical multipliers which are computed in the same way as above, on the presumption that tax revenues are predetermined. We have two kinds of hypothetical multiplier; one assumes that only income taxes are pre-determined, while the other takes the total tax yield (both income and outlay tax revenues) as predetermined. In order to obtain the former, we put $t_w = t_\pi = 0$ in (4.28), but t_j in (4.28) and β_i in (4.30) are kept at their actual values, whilst the multipliers of the second sort are obtained by fixing all t_w, t_π, and t_j at zero and β_i at $\gamma_i/(\Sigma\gamma_j + \gamma_M)$ (see (2.11)).

Following the same definition as the one given by Musgrave and Miller, the built-in flexibility of gross domestic income (say, at factor cost) in year t can be measured by the index,

$$\alpha_t^i = 1 - \frac{dY_{ft}}{dY_{ft}^i} \quad (i = \mathrm{I, II}),$$

where dY_{ft} denotes the multiplier effect on gross domestic income at factor cost in period t in the actual endogenous tax revenue economy and dY_{ft}^i the similar multiplier effect in the semi-totally or totally exogenous tax revenue economy. (i takes on I in the semi-total case, and II in the other case.) We can calculate thirteen αs; the first twelve α_{jt}^i ($j = 1, ..., 12$) give the measure of built-in flexibility which is obtained when a unit injection of government expenditure is concentrated in industry j, while the last gives the global measure which applies in the case where a unit injection is distributed among twelve industries in proportion to the actual distribution of govern-ment expenditure in 1954. Tables 17 and 18 present the dynamic multipliers for gross domestic income at factor cost in the endogenous and exogenous tax revenue cases respectively. Table 19 shows the movement of the Musgrave–Miller measure α of the effectiveness of built-in flexibility during the first six years. In view of the industrial distribution of government expenditure in the actual 1954 budget, we find from the tables that public authorities concentrated 90 per cent of their expenditure in 1954 in those industries which had rather high multipliers and were low in the effectiveness of built-in flexibility; so that we can conclude that they chose in that year a rather inflationary policy.

Next let us compare our estimates of the dynamic multipliers with Goldberger's results.[1] For this purpose, we first adjust his model so that

[1] A. S. Goldberger, *op. cit.* pp. 83–91.

TABLE 17. *Annual levels of GNP at factor cost in response to sustained unit increase in government expenditure: taxes endogenous*

Industry group[a]	Year					
	0	1	2	3	4	5
1	0.959	1.051	1.081	1.089	1.092	1.093
2	1.375	1.519	1.564	1.578	1.583	1.584
3	0.682	0.744	0.764	0.770	0.772	0.773
4	0.952	1.041	1.069	1.078	1.081	1.082
5	1.048	1.148	1.180	1.190	1.193	1.194
6	1.249	1.370	1.409	1.421	1.425	1.426
7	1.000	1.097	1.128	1.138	1.141	1.142
8	1.135	1.245	1.280	1.291	1.294	1.296
9	1.262	1.389	1.429	1.442	1.446	1.447
10	1.272	1.394	1.432	1.445	1.449	1.450
11	1.227	1.344	1.380	1.392	1.396	1.397
12	1.472	1.621	1.668	1.683	1.687	1.689
Global	1.333	1.465	1.507	1.520	1.524	1.526

[a] See Table 16 for the classification of industries.

TABLE 18. *Annual levels of GNP at factor cost in response to sustained unit increase in government expenditure: taxes exogenous*

Industry group[a]	Year					
	0	1	2	3	4	5
1	1.129	1.297	1.358	1.380	1.388	1.391
2	1.528	1.739	1.816	1.844	1.854	1.858
3	0.872	1.014	1.065	1.084	1.090	1.093
4	1.067	1.211	1.264	1.283	1.290	1.292
5	1.167	1.326	1.384	1.405	1.412	1.415
6	1.388	1.578	1.648	1.673	1.682	1.685
7	1.114	1.267	1.323	1.344	1.351	1.354
8	1.264	1.439	1.502	1.525	1.533	1.536
9	1.408	1.607	1.680	1.705	1.715	1.719
10	1.428	1.625	1.696	1.722	1.732	1.735
11	1.385	1.577	1.647	1.672	1.681	1.685
12	1.626	1.854	1.936	1.967	1.977	1.981
Global	1.482	1.688	1.763	1.791	1.800	1.804

[a] See Table 16 for the classification of industries.

it is subject to the same conditions as our model. Although both are structural models, there is no induced investment in our model (it is taken as constant), while there exists a co-variational relation between income and investment in the Klein–Goldberger model; investment increases income and vice versa. We have re-calculated the impact and dynamic multipliers of the

TABLE 19. *The Musgrave–Miller measure of the effectiveness of built-in flexibility of taxes in stabilizing GNP at factor cost* (%)

Industry group[a]	Year					
	0	1	2	3	4	5
1	15.1	18.9	20.4	21.1	21.3	21.4
2	10.0	12.7	13.9	14.4	14.7	14.7
3	21.9	26.6	28.3	28.9	29.2	29.3
4	10.8	14.1	15.4	16.0	16.2	16.3
5	10.2	13.4	14.7	15.3	15.5	15.6
6	10.0	13.2	14.5	15.1	15.3	15.4
7	10.2	13.4	14.7	15.3	15.5	15.6
8	10.3	13.5	14.8	15.4	15.6	15.7
9	10.3	13.5	14.9	15.5	15.7	15.8
10	10.9	14.2	15.6	16.1	16.4	16.5
11	11.4	14.8	16.2	16.7	17.0	17.1
12	9.5	12.6	13.9	14.4	14.7	14.8
Global	10.1	13.2	14.5	15.1	15.4	15.4

[a] See Table 16 for the classification of industries.

Klein–Goldberger system, abstracting all the effects of induced investment by fixing investment at zero. The resulting multipliers for GNP are displayed in Table 20, together with the corresponding figures for our model.

The table shows that our dynamic multipliers are generally higher than Goldberger's. In the adjusted Klein–Goldberger model, the GNP (at market prices) multiplier begins at 1.23 in year 0, reaches 1.38 in year 2 and then turns down to 1.25 in year 5. Our corresponding figures increase monotonically from 1.47 to 1.71 over the six years. The difference between the multipliers of the original and adjusted Klein–Goldberger models shows the effect of induced investment upon GNP. The table shows that it increases from 0.60 (31 per cent) of 1.95 in year 1 up to 0.98 (44 per cent) of 2.23 in year 5.

In order to obtain the value of the Musgrave–Miller measure α which is comparable with ours, we must eliminate the effects of induced investment not only from the multipliers in the actual endogenous tax revenue case but also from those in the hypothetical exogenous tax revenue case. However, we may assume, as a first approximation, that the effect of induced investment on income accounts for the same percentage of the t-year multiplier in the exogenous tax revenue case as it does in the endogenous tax revenue case; then induced investment has no effect upon the Musgrave–Miller measure. Thus Goldberger's estimate of the long-run built-in stabilizing effect of taxes, which amounts to 19.9 per cent of the multiplier effect in the case of no taxes, may be compared with our result for year 5, which is that

TABLE 20. *Comparison of dynamic multipliers for GNP*

Year	0	1	2	3	4	5
GNP at factor cost						
Adjusted K–G model	1.12	1.23	1.26	1.24	1.20	1.13
Our model	1.33	1.46	1.51	1.52	1.52	1.53
GNP at market prices						
Adjusted K–G model	1.23	1.35	1.38	1.36	1.31	1.25
Original K–G model	1.23	1.95	2.21	2.27	2.26	2.23
Our model	1.47	1.64	1.69	1.71	1.71	1.71

tax leakages reduce the six-year effect of autonomous expenditure injections on gross domestic income at market prices by some 14 per cent.

Some of these differences might be ascribed to differences in the values of the structural parameters between the USA, 1929–52 and the UK, 1954. We must, however, also recognize that the different assumptions underlying the two models may give rise to differences in the estimates. For example, in our model, the input coefficients are assumed to be constant throughout the dynamic process, although it would be plausible for them to become smaller in later periods than in earlier periods because of technical improvements. Evidently, the disregard of technical improvements will lead to over-estimation of the multipliers. On the other hand, in the Klein–Goldberger model, changes in prices will affect distribution of income, which will influence the estimates of the multipliers by affecting the aggregate propensity to consume, so that their marginal propensity to consume may become smaller in the course of time; this might offer another explanation of higher dynamic multipliers in our model than in theirs.

Finally, we have to note one defect which is common to both models. Since we have computed the multipliers on the assumption that all effective tax rates are constant, the effects of the progressiveness of income taxes have been neglected completely. If they were properly taken into account, the dynamic multipliers of the actual endogenous tax revenue economy would be estimated at smaller values, so that we would have a greater Musgrave–Miller measure. With the proviso that our conclusion is subject to secondary effects via the channels discussed above, we now conclude that in the 1954 UK economy tax leakages contributed to reducing the effect of autonomous expenditure upon GNP at factor cost by some 15 per cent and upon GNP at market prices by some 14 per cent in the fifth or sixth year after the injection was made.

SOURCES OF DATA

Annual Abstract of Statistics, Central Statistical Office (HMSO, 1962).

Census 1951, England and Wales, General Report, General Register Office (HMSO, 1958).

Census 1951, Scotland, Vol. III, General Volume, General Registry Office, Edinburgh (HMSO, 1954).

Census 1961, England and Wales, Preliminary Report, General Register Office (HMSO, 1961).

Civil Estimates 1954–55 (HMSO, 1954).

Customs and Excise Report, 51st Report of the Commissioners of Her Majesty's Customs and Excise for the year ended 31 March 1960 (HMSO, 1960).

Economic Report of the President (US Government Printing Office, 1964).

Family Expenditure Survey, Report for 1957–59, Ministry of Labour (HMSO, 1961).

Family Expenditure Survey, Report for 1960 and 1961, Ministry of Labour (HMSO, 1962).

Family Expenditure Survey, Report for 1962, Ministry of Labour (HMSO, 1963).

Inland Revenue Annual Report, Ninety-Ninth Report of the Commissioners of Her Majesty's Inland Revenue for the year ended 31 March 1956 (HMSO, 1957).

Inland Revenue Annual Report, One Hundredth Report of the Inland Revenue (HMSO, 1958).

Inland Revenue Annual Report, One Hundred and First Report of the Inland Revenue (HMSO, 1959).

Inland Revenue Annual Report, One Hundred and Second Report of the Inland Revenue (HMSO, 1960).

Inland Revenue Annual Report, One Hundred and Third Report of the Inland Revenue (HMSO, 1961).

Inland Revenue Annual Report, Hundred and Fourth Report of the Inland Revenue (HMSO, 1962).

Inland Revenue Annual Report, Hundred and Fifth Report of the Inland Revenue (HMSO, 1963).

Input–Output Tables for the United Kingdom, 1954, Board of Trade and Central Statistical Office (HMSO, 1961).

Input-Output Tables for the United Kingdom 1963, Central Statistical Office (HMSO, 1970).

National Income and Expenditure 1956, Central Statistical Office (HMSO, 1956).

National Income and Expenditure 1962, Central Statistical Office (HMSO, 1962).

National Income and Expenditure 1963, Central Statistical Office (HMSO, 1963).

Preliminary Report of the Sixteenth Census of Scotland 1961, General Registry Office, Edinburgh (HMSO, 1961).

Report of an Enquiry into Household Expenditure in 1953–54, The Interim Report of the Cost of Living Advisory Committee, Ministry of Labour and National Service (HMSO, 1951).

Statistics of Income for 1952, Part I, US Treasury Department (US Government Printing Office, 1956).

Statistics of Income for 1960, US Treasury Department (US Government Printing Office, 1963).

PART III

A general equilibrium analysis of prices
and outputs in Japan, 1953–1965

by M. Saito

1. *Introduction*

Most interindustry studies have hitherto been made on the assumption of stability of production coefficients of each commodity. Theoretical justification for this assumption may be found in the so called 'non-substitution' theorem, which was developed by Georgescu-Roegen, Samuelson and others.[1] Some empirical economists, however, have doubts about the conclusion that all relative prices as well as production coefficients should be kept constant irrespective of changes in final demand. On the other hand, Professor Klein's non-substitution theorem claims, on the assumption of the Cobb–Douglas production function and the marginal productivity relationships, that the ratios between the value of output and that of input, or the input coefficients in 'value' terms, should be kept constant while the input coefficients in 'quantity' terms and relative prices are flexible in response to changes in final demands.[2]

In this study I intend to make an empirical analysis of the inter-dependency of prices and outputs, on the basis of the latter theorem. Thus our empirical model is essentially a general equilibrium model of the Walras–Hicks type in which each industry has a production function of the Cobb–Douglas form. The general features of this model are explained in Chapter 2. Chapter 3 presents the results of estimating the model for the Japanese economy by using the 1960 input–output table (Table 1) and 1953–65 time series data for Japan. Chapter 4 is devoted to discussing the implications of the estimates of the excess supply functions. The estimated effects of a unit change in final demand on prices, outputs, employment and GNP originating in each industry are presented there. In connection with the theoretical problem, it is found that the Jacobian matrix of the estimated excess supply functions approximately satisfies the first and second Hicksian laws of comparative statics though it is not strictly gross-substitutive.[3] The third Hicksian law is also satisfied with the exceptions of the lumber and furniture and construction industries. Chapter 3 also deals with a testing of our

---

[1] N. Georgescu-Roegen, 'Some properties of a generalized Leontief model', *Activity Analysis of Production and Allocation*, ed. T. C. Koopmans (John Wiley and Sons, Inc., 1951), pp. 165–73, and P. A. Samuelson, 'Abstract of a theorem concerning substitutability in open Leontief models', pp. 142–6.

[2] L. R. Klein, 'On the interpretation of Professor Leontief's system', *Review of Economic Studies* (1952–3).

[3] Cf. M. Morishima, *Equilibrium, Stability and Growth*, Chapter I.

approach. The 1961 values of price, output, employment, and consumption for each industry, which are calculated from our estimated equations based on the 1960 input–output table (Table 1), are compared with their observed values. The results indicate that our estimated model reproduces, with a tolerable degree of accuracy, the actual fluctuations of the whole economy in 1960–1.

The factors causing shifts in demand and supply functions in this model can be grouped into demand (final demand), supply (capital accumulation and technological change), import (import prices), and tax categories. In the first half of Chapter 5, the causes of 1960–1 price changes are analysed into the first three categories, whilst in the second half the various multipliers are estimated for the predetermined tax yield case. The Musgrave–Miller measure of the effectiveness of built-in flexibility is calculated not only for GNP, but also for employment, relative prices, and the absolute levels of prices and wages, enabling us to obtain an idea of the overall effectiveness.

2. *Theoretical model*

The statistical study presented here may be best defined as an attempt to analyse the movement of prices and output empirically within the framework of the Walras–Hicks type general equilibrium of production.[1] The basic conceptual scheme of the model is so well known that it needs no special explanation apart from the following specifications.

Producers

We assume that each industry is confronted with a production function of the Cobb–Douglas type:

$$\ln X_i = \ln A_i + \gamma_i t + \sum_{j=1}^{n} \alpha_{ji} \ln X_{ji} + \xi_i \ln Z_i + \lambda_i \ln L_i$$
$$+ \kappa_i \ln K_i \quad (i = 1, ..., n); \quad (2.1)$$

where

X_i = output of the ith industry,

X_{ji} = output of the jth industry used in the ith industry,

Z_i = noncompetitive imports used in the ith industry,

L_i = labour input of the ith industry,

K_i = stock of capital of the ith industry,

t = time trend.

Since many empirical studies reveal approximately constant returns to scale,[2] we assume that output X_i is homogeneous of degree one in inputs, X_{ji}, Z_i, L_i and K_i, so that

$$\sum_{j=1}^{n} \alpha_{ji} + \xi_i + \lambda_i + \kappa_i = 1.$$

Neutral technological change is allowed for by a time trend. Imports are classified as competitive or noncompetitive. Noncompetitive imports, represented by Z_i, are treated as an independent variable, similarly to other material inputs. The treatment of competitive imports will be discussed later.

[1] L. Walras, *Elements of Pure Economics*, translated by W. Jaffé (Richard D. Irwin, 1954); J. R. Hicks, *Value and Capital*, second edition (Oxford University Press, 1946).

[2] A. A. Walters, 'Production and cost functions: an econometric survey', *Econometrica* (January–April 1963).

We are concerned with the behaviour of firms in the short-run (or Hicks' *temporary*) equilibrium under perfect competition. Evidently profits of the ith industry may be written as:

$$P_i = p_i(\mathrm{I} - t_i)X_i - \sum_{j=1}^{n} p_j X_{ji} - p_i^z Z_i - w_i L_i \quad (i = \mathrm{I}, ..., n), \quad (2.2)$$

where

P_i = profits of the ith industry,

p_i = price of the ith product,

p_i^z = price of noncompetitive imports used in the ith industry,

w_i = wage rate of labour employed in the ith industry,

t_i = the ratio of indirect taxation to output.

Given p_i, w_i, t_i, p_i^z, and K_i, each producer may maximize his profits subject to (2.1); we get the marginal productivity equations:

$$\left.\begin{aligned}
&\alpha_{ji} = p_j X_{ji}/p_i(\mathrm{I} - t_i)X_i \quad (i,j = \mathrm{I}, ..., n), \\
&\lambda_i = w_i L_i/p_i(\mathrm{I} - t_i)X_i \quad (i = \mathrm{I}, ..., n), \\
&\xi_i = p_i^z Z_i/p_i(\mathrm{I} - t_i)X_i \quad (i = \mathrm{I}, ..., n).
\end{aligned}\right\} \quad (2.3)$$

Solving (2.1), (2.2) and (2.3), the supply of output, the demand for inputs, the demand for labour and profits of each industry may be given as explicit functions of prices and wages:

$$\left.\begin{aligned}
\ln X_i &= -\ln(\mathrm{I} - t_i) + \ln H_i + \left(\frac{\mathrm{I}}{\kappa_i} - \mathrm{I}\right)\ln \pi_i - \sum_{r=1}^{n} \frac{\alpha_{ri}}{\kappa_i} \ln \pi_r \\
&\quad - \frac{\xi_i}{\kappa_i}\ln \pi_i^z - \frac{\lambda_i}{\kappa_i}\ln \omega_i + \ln K_i \quad (i = \mathrm{I}, ..., n), \\[6pt]
\ln X_{ji} &= \ln \alpha_{ji} + \ln H_i + \frac{\mathrm{I}}{\kappa_i}\ln \pi_i - \ln \pi_j - \sum_{r=1}^{n} \frac{\alpha_{ri}}{\kappa_i} \ln \pi_r \\
&\quad - \frac{\xi_i}{\kappa_i}\ln \pi_i^z - \frac{\lambda_i}{\kappa_i}\ln \omega_i + \ln K_i \quad (j,i = \mathrm{I}, ..., n), \\[6pt]
\ln Z_i &= \ln \xi_i + \ln H_i + \frac{\mathrm{I}}{\kappa_i}\ln \pi_i - \sum_{r=1}^{n} \frac{\alpha_{ri}}{\kappa_i} \ln \pi_r \\
&\quad - \left(\frac{\xi_i}{\kappa_i} + \mathrm{I}\right)\ln \pi_i^z - \frac{\lambda_i}{\kappa_i}\ln \omega_i + \ln K_i \quad (i = \mathrm{I}, ..., n), \\[6pt]
\ln L_i &= \ln \lambda_i + \ln H_i + \frac{\mathrm{I}}{\kappa_i}\ln \pi_i - \sum_{r=1}^{n} \frac{\alpha_{ri}}{\kappa_i} \ln \pi_r - \frac{\xi_i}{\kappa_i}\ln \pi_i^z \\
&\quad - \left(\frac{\lambda_i}{\kappa_i} + \mathrm{I}\right)\ln \omega_i + \ln K_i \quad (i = \mathrm{I}, ..., n), \\[6pt]
\ln P_i &= \ln w + \ln \kappa_i + \ln H_i + \frac{\mathrm{I}}{\kappa_i}\ln \pi_i - \sum_{r=1}^{n} \frac{\alpha_{ri}}{\kappa_i} \ln \pi_r \\
&\quad - \frac{\xi_i}{\kappa_i}\ln \pi_i^z - \frac{\lambda_i}{\kappa_i}\ln \omega_i + \ln K_i \quad (i = \mathrm{I}, ..., n);
\end{aligned}\right\} \quad (2.4)$$

where

$$\ln H_i = \frac{1}{\kappa_i}\left\{\ln A_i + \gamma_i t + \ln(1-t_i)\right.$$
$$\left. + \sum_{r=1}^{n}\alpha_{ri}\ln\alpha_{ri} + \xi_i\ln\xi_i + \lambda_i\ln\lambda_i\right\} \quad (i=1,\dots,n),$$

$$\left.\begin{aligned}
\pi_i &= \frac{p_i}{w} \quad (i=1,\dots,n),\\[4pt]
\pi_i^z &= \frac{p_i^z}{w} \quad (i=1,\dots,n),\\[4pt]
\omega_i &= \frac{w_i}{w} \quad (i=1,\dots,n),
\end{aligned}\right\} \qquad (2.5)$$

and w represents the average wage rate of the whole industry. Here, taking into account the homogeneity property of (2.3), we have represented all prices and wages in terms of their ratios to the average wage of the whole industry, w.

Consumers

The theory of consumer behaviour states that the combined effects of real income and relative prices determine the demand for any individual consumer good. It may be true that the consumer's decision on total consumption (or total savings) is not independent of his expenditure decision on individual consumption items, but the following formulation may be regarded as a realistic approximation. First let us assume that total consumption depends on income and lagged consumption. We also take the effect of population size into consideration by using per capita variables of income and consumption. The exponential consumption function may take the form of:

$$\ln\left(\frac{C}{L}\right) = \ln\bar{B} + \bar{\beta}\ln\left(\frac{Y/p^c}{L}\right) + \bar{\delta}\ln\left(\frac{C}{L}\right)_{-1}, \qquad (2.6)$$

where

C = total consumption expenditure in constant prices,

Y = disposable income in current prices,

p^c = index of general consumer prices,

$\bar{L}$ = population.

Taking total consumption as an income effect variable and the ratio of each individual commodity price to the general level of consumer prices as a price effect variable, we write the demand function for good k as

$$\ln\left(\frac{C_k'}{L}\right) = \ln B_k' + \beta_k'\ln\left(\frac{C}{L}\right) + \epsilon_k\ln\left(\frac{p_k^c}{p^c}\right) \quad (k=1,\dots,m), \quad (2.7)$$

where

C'_k = demand for the kth consumer good,

p^c_k = price of the kth consumer good.

Thus, from (2.6) and (2.7), the final form of the consumption functions is:[1]

$$\ln\left(\frac{C'_k}{L}\right) = \ln B_k + \beta_k \ln\left(\frac{Y/p^c}{L}\right) + \epsilon_k \ln\left(\frac{p^c_k}{p^c}\right)$$
$$+ \delta_k \ln\left(\frac{C}{L}\right)_{-1} \quad (k = 1, ..., m), \quad (2.8)$$

where
$$p^c = \sum_{k=1}^{m} v_k p^c_k, \quad (2.9)$$

$$\ln B_k = \ln B'_k + \beta'_k \ln \bar{B},$$
$$\ln \beta_k = \ln \bar{\beta} + \ln \beta'_k,$$
$$\ln \delta_k = \ln \bar{\delta} + \ln \beta'_k,$$
$$v_k = \text{constant weight.}$$

Equation (2.9) is a definitional identity for the general consumer price level.

The classification of goods in the consumer survey differs from that in the input–output table. In order to transform the former into the latter we may use a constant matrix representing the relationships between them in a base year. Then we have:

$$C_i = \sum_{k=1}^{m} s_{ik} C'_k \quad (i = 1, ..., n), \quad (2.10)$$

$$p^c_k = \sum_{i=1}^{n} s_{ik} p_i \quad (k = 1, ..., m), \quad (2.11)$$

$$C = \sum_{i=1}^{n} C_i; \quad (2.12)$$

where

C_i = consumption demand for the ith output, corresponding to final demand in the input–output table,

s_{ik} = the proportion of the value of the kth consumption good which corresponds to the ith input–output category.

By definition,

$$\sum_{i=1}^{n} s_{ik} = 1 \quad (k = 1, ..., m).$$

[1] The above two-stage budgeting procedure is permissible if the utility function is strongly or homogeneously separable. See W. M. Gorman, 'Separable utility and aggregation', *Econometrica* (July 1959).

Disposable income

Income consists of wage income and property income. Total wage income is $\sum_{i=1}^{n} w_i L_i$. Profits, as defined in equation (2.2) above, include not only rents, interests and dividends, but also corporate savings, corporate taxes and depreciation allowances. Thus property income may be expressed as a function of profits:

$$Pr/p = \eta_1 \left(\sum_{i=1}^{n} P_i/p \right) + \eta_0, \tag{2.13}$$

$$p = \sum_{i=1}^{n} u_i p_i, \tag{2.14}$$

where Pr = property income, i.e. rents and dividends,
          p = general price index,
          u_i = constant weight.

Then disposable income is defined as:

$$Y = (1 - T) \left\{ \sum_{i=1}^{n} w_i L_i + \eta_1 \left(\sum_{i=1}^{n} P_i \right) + \eta_0 p \right\}, \tag{2.15}$$

where T = the ratio of income tax to income.

Import functions

The demand for competitive imports will depend on total demand for that good and relative foreign and domestic prices. Our equation relates the ratio between imports and domestic output to relative prices. We also allow for the lag effects of this ratio, since substitution between foreign and domestic products will require some adjustment period.

Japanese imports have been greatly affected by the level of foreign exchange reserves. In 1953, 1957, 1961, and 1963, when this level dropped substantially, the Japanese authorities adopted a tight monetary policy, which resulted in a considerable decrease in imports. We therefore introduce the ratio of foreign exchange reserves to payments with a one-year lag into our equation.

$$\left(\frac{M_i}{X_i} \right) = \theta_1 \left(\frac{M_i}{X_i} \right)_{-1} + \theta_2 \left(\frac{p_i^m}{p_i} \right) + \theta_3 \left(\frac{R}{M} \right)_{-1} + \theta_0 \quad (i = 1, ..., n), \tag{2.16}$$

where M_i = competitive imports of the ith good at constant, prices,
          p_i^m = price of competitive imports of the ith good,
          R = end-of-period foreign exchange reserves in current prices,
          M = total payments of foreign exchange at current prices.

By putting

$$\pi_i^m = p_i^m/w \quad (i = 1, ..., n),$$

(2.16a)

the price variable, p_i^m/p_i, may be replaced by π_i^m/π_i.

Labour market

According to Blumenthal's extensive study, the main determinants of post-war Japanese wage differentials are socioeconomic factors, such as age, sex, education and type of labour.[1] He also found that the industry and scale wage differentials, which were not attributable to these socioeconomic factors, were not influenced much by short-run factors such as industrial differences in the vacancy rate, but were mainly explained by long-run factors such as productivity and differences in the rates of unionization among industries. Since the socioeconomic structure of labour in each industry does not change significantly in the short run, and the estimated elasticity of wages with respect to productivity, 0.13 per cent, is not very large, we may assume that wage differentials among industries, i.e. ω_i, are constant in the short run. In addition, the average wage rate, w, may be determined by the Phillips–Lipsey curve:

$$\frac{\Delta w}{w_{-1}} = \iota_1 \frac{\sum\limits_{i=1}^{n} L_i}{Lf} + \iota_2 \frac{\Delta p_{-1}^c}{p_{-2}^c} + \iota_0,$$

(2.17)

where Lf = total labour force.

Market equilibrium

Excess supply functions of each commodity are:

$$E_i = X_i + M_i - \sum\limits_{j=1}^{n} X_{ij} - C_i - F_i \quad (i = 1, ..., n),$$

(2.18)

where

E_i = excess supply of the ith good,

F_i = final demand for the ith good, excluding consumption; i.e. fixed investment *plus* government expenditure *plus* inventory investment *plus* exports.

We assume that final demands, excluding consumption, are exogenously determined. This modifies to some extent the conclusions drawn below, since effects such as those on induced investment are neglected.

[1] T. Blumenthal, 'The determination of wage differentials in the Japanese economy', *Discussion Paper No. 41*. The Institute of Social and Economic Research, Osaka University (1965).

Finally we have market equilibrium conditions:

$$E_i = 0 \quad (i = 1, ..., n). \tag{2.19}$$

Now the economic model, which consists of equations (2.4), (2.5), and (2.8) to (2.19), determines a set of equilibrium prices. By counting the numbers of equations and unknowns, it is found that the system is consistent and able to determine the equilibrium values of the unknowns uniquely. Before proceeding to a detailed examination, we sum up the essential character of price formation in our model as follows.

(i) Homogeneous case. Suppose that the non-competitive and competitive import prices relative to the average wage, i.e. $\pi_i^z (= p_i^z/w)$ and $\pi_i^m (= p_i^m/w)$, are exogeneously given. Outputs, X_is, and inputs, X_{ji}s, as shown in equation (2.4), are functions of the π_is only, since the ω_is are assumed to be constant. As regards consumption functions, substitute equations (2.9), (2.10) and (2.11) into (2.8). Then, taking into account the fact that these equations are homogeneous of degree zero in p_i, p_i^c, p^c, and Y, we may express all C_is as functions of $\pi_i (= p_i/w)$ and Y/w, the last being seen in turn to be a function of the π_is only because of (2.14), (2.15) and (2.4). Further, equation (2.16) shows that, apart from the lagged variables, competitive imports are functions of X_i, π_i, and π_i^m, and thus only of the π_is. Therefore, given the final demands F_i, equation (2.19) will determine a set of equilibrium relative prices. Let this set of relative prices be π_i^*. Substitution of the π_i^*s into equations (2.4) and (2.8)–(2.15) will yield a set of equilibrium outputs, inputs, employment and consumption. Finally, by putting total equilibrium employment into the wage-determination equation (2.17), which implies that there is a money illusion in the labour market, we obtain the average money wage, and thereby all absolute prices from equation (2.5). Our system, thus interpreted, may be called 'homogeneous' in the sense that all equations, except the wage equation, are homogeneous functions in the monetary variables, and all relative prices, outputs, and employment are determined independently of absolute prices and wages.

(ii) Nonhomogeneous case. An alternative and more realistic assumption is to take p_i^z and p_i^m, instead of π_i^z and π_i^m, as constant.[1] In what follows, however, we shall refer exclusively to the homogeneous system, partly because the feed-back effect of wage changes through demand for imports turned out to be small and partly because the computational treatment of the homogeneous system was much easier than that of the nonhomogeneous one.

[1] Other important factors which make the system nonhomogeneous are liquid assets, held by households and firms, and foreign prices in the export functions. An empirical analysis allowing for all these factors is left for later study.

3. *The estimation of the model*

The estimation of the model was made for the Japanese economy on the basis of yearly data over the period 1953–65, the consumer surveys in 1953–65, and the 1960 input–output table. Sources and units of all statistical data are listed in Appendix A, pp. 228–36.

(1) PRODUCTION FUNCTIONS

(i) *Exponents of labour, capital, and materials*

Our estimation of these parameters of the production functions (2.1) is basically due to Klein's interpretation of Leontief's system.[1] On the assumption of Cobb–Douglas production functions, marginal productivity equations (2.3) are obtained which imply that the value of output of industry i is proportional to each value of input of i. We may take, as estimates of the α_{ji}s, ξ_is, and λ_is, the ratios of values of input and output (excluding indirect taxes) derived from the 1960 input–output table. The assumption of constant returns to scale enables us to estimate the κ_is at one *minus* the sum of the estimated α_{ji}s, ξ_i and λ_i.

Table 1 presents the 1960 input–output table. Here the original 56 sectors are aggregated into 27, because the consistent time series of output, labour, and capital necessary for our later analysis are only available at this level of aggregation. Details of aggregation and other modifications to the table are described in Appendix B (p. 237–40). Now, let us take 1960 as a base year of the price index; then each figure expressed in billions of 1960 yen represents both quantity and value. Thus, for example, α_{16} is simply computed as:

$$\alpha_{1,6} = \frac{p_1 X_{1,6}}{p_6 (1 - t_6) X_6}$$

$$= \frac{58.353}{2310.268 - 12.308}$$

$$= 0.0254.$$

Here 58.353 billion yen is the value of input of sector 6 (textiles) from sector 1 (agriculture and fishery); 2310.268 and 12.308 billion yen are the

[1] L. R. Klein, 'On the interpretation of Professor Leontief's System'.

[156]

TABLE I. The 1960 input-output table (unit: billion yen)

Industry	1 Agriculture	2 Forestry	3 Petroleum & coal	4 Metal, nonmetal mining	5 Food	6 Textiles	7 Lumber & furniture	8 Pulp & paper	9 Printing & publishing	10 Leather
1. Agriculture & fishery	205.061	-1.814	0.0	0.001	1535.847	58.353	0.107	7.537	0.002	0.036
2. Forestry	8.310	278.148	10.427	1.596	4.887	2.653	331.950	38.279	0.001	0.913
3. Petroleum & coal mining	0.218	0.012	3.417	1.761	4.484	6.099	0.742	11.371	0.0	0.235
4. Metal & nonmetal mining	0.850	0.002	0.0	1.132	8.210	0.0	0.003	2.966	0.006	0.0
5. Food	124.683	0.001	0.0	0.0	527.104	6.079	0.0	0.676	0.006	18.032
6. Textiles	33.357	1.518	1.882	0.322	2.338	892.148	5.035	3.952	1.589	4.418
7. Lumber & furniture	5.975	0.499	1.578	0.353	14.579	5.218	90.138	16.328	0.942	0.095
8. Pulp & paper	3.763	0.090	1.081	0.532	28.209	7.924	3.151	279.629	119.626	0.209
9. Printing & publishing	0.355	0.122	2.232	0.716	3.907	7.418	0.0	20.290	6.337	0.019
10. Leather	0.0	0.009	0.0	0.0	0.521	17.568	0.048	0.009	0.159	8.238
11. Rubber	1.679	0.073	0.0	0.004	0.252	7.234	0.739	0.039	0.048	0.262
12. Chemicals	146.953	1.692	4.159	3.303	84.757	247.482	20.589	19.257	15.310	2.107
13. Petroleum, coal products	34.720	6.213	1.224	2.532	19.111	10.444	3.192	6.890	0.014	0.361
14. Stone, clay & glass	3.637	0.092	0.229	0.009	37.605	0.044	1.404	0.625	0.016	0.081
15. Primary metals	0.094	0.145	4.235	1.392	2.179	3.747	16.744	0.143	1.868	0.0
16. Fabricated metals	5.690	1.680	1.185	0.569	23.052	6.834	15.419	1.542	0.104	2.066
17. Machinery	12.346	1.697	4.259	1.829	1.674	10.741	1.250	2.875	3.771	0.011
18. Electrical machinery	5.111	1.517	1.563	1.298	1.169	2.839	1.387	0.0	1.105	0.059
19. Transportation equipment	10.382	3.425	1.101	0.159	1.239	0.040	1.391	0.0	0.0	0.0
20. Miscellaneous manufacturing	7.031	0.219	0.418	0.119	8.395	4.281	3.415	0.167	1.032	2.051
21. Construction	15.028	0.569	2.273	4.902	11.535	4.500	2.759	1.355	0.941	0.457
22. Utilities	5.895	0.186	16.542	5.967	17.375	24.336	5.515	32.551	2.161	0.323
23. Trade	31.625	2.371	4.395	3.112	145.149	87.949	30.007	20.218	10.720	2.867
24. Transportation & communication	23.568	2.296	5.137	4.937	64.018	31.196	19.307	20.730	19.472	0.668
25. Services	23.264	4.783	6.435	3.437	47.783	31.947	11.014	9.535	11.764	0.513
26. Unallocated	17.378	3.155	6.150	12.203	114.201	40.604	10.495	9.953	18.638	0.509
27. Government	-1.267	0.0	0.0	0.0	0.0	0.0	0.0	0.0	0.0	0.0
28. Noncompetitive imports	0.0	0.0	0.0	0.0	0.0	277.593	0.0	0.0	0.0	0.0
29. Subtotal	726.965	308.699	79.921	52.179	2709.571	1795.268	576.902	506.912	215.624	44.527
30. Business consumption	4.396	2.630	6.608	5.500	33.016	20.009	12.803	5.126	15.362	0.085
31. Wages	1088.122	126.144	107.883	63.160	211.295	323.640	139.009	75.066	99.669	10.509
32. Surplus	375.324	249.318	9.130	25.095	146.219	111.863	17.310	50.823	47.675	0.168
33. Depreciation	186.207	23.666	20.634	13.069	47.355	47.090	11.334	24.323	7.992	0.762
34. Indirect taxes	42.732	5.354	5.752	4.216	510.588	12.308	7.032	3.742	2.400	0.226
35. (Less) subsidies	-1.207	-0.030	-0.029	-0.099	-29.299	0.0	0.0	0.0	0.0	0.0
36. Value added	1695.511	407.682	149.977	110.940	919.172	515.000	187.487	159.080	173.098	11.750
37. Output	2422.477	715.780	229.897	163.118	3628.745	2310.268	764.389	665.992	388.721	56.277

TABLE I (cont.)

Industry	11 Rubber	12 Chemicals	13 Petroleum products	14 Stone, clay & glass	15 Primary metals	16 Fabricated metals	17 Machinery	18 Electrical machinery	19 Transportation equipment
1. Agriculture & fishery	0.0	54.007	0.0	0.186	0.009	0.002	5.167	0.984	-0.700
2. Forestry	0.0	4.242	4.589	1.540	0.725	0.742	0.0	0.0	0.0
3. Petroleum & coal mining	1.450	24.666	254.557	21.571	4.120	0.653	0.463	0.632	0.663
4. Metal & nonmetal mining	0.137	33.388	0.079	46.037	176.065	0.0	0.0	0.0	0.0
5. Food	0.0	19.993	0.0	0.247	0.0	0.0	0.009	0.0	0.0
6. Textiles	37.941	6.697	0.790	2.034	2.732	1.876	10.794	9.676	5.528
7. Lumber & furniture	0.088	20.904	1.852	1.725	3.084	2.816	12.458	11.611	15.022
8. Pulp & paper	0.316	70.087	2.052	16.245	3.712	1.170	6.887	9.610	2.797
9. Printing & publishing	0.338	5.243	1.189	1.963	8.098	1.971	10.254	3.438	1.423
10. Leather	0.0	0.208	0.0	0.0	0.0	0.040	5.398	0.424	0.597
11. Rubber	4.780	0.951	0.0	0.037	1.657	1.935	12.057	14.667	94.740
12. Chemicals	25.670	468.338	6.994	10.754	120.973	5.471	14.701	25.252	16.005
13. Petroleum, coal products	4.633	54.668	19.131	24.386	120.468	4.087	10.924	10.942	5.201
14. Stone, clay & glass	2.126	7.920	2.412	44.308	24.967	2.203	9.697	21.836	9.649
15. Primary metals	0.627	12.277	2.084	14.759	1931.122	230.889	411.277	253.463	148.996
16. Fabricated metals	0.212	9.381	1.446	0.606	4.472	19.680	27.699	10.898	19.288
17. Machinery	1.646	7.378	1.785	1.520	20.585	3.719	427.678	42.968	202.842
18. Electrical machinery	0.349	6.408		1.979	13.566	2.664	40.667	370.423	56.507
19. Transportation equipment	0.0	0.021	0.008	1.083	2.355	0.064	6.944	4.969	203.014
20. Miscellaneous manufacturing	3.111	0.650	1.286	0.297	0.520	0.212	11.078	29.009	8.044
21. Construction	0.511	7.939	2.410	4.551	5.939	3.526	4.805	3.923	4.604
22. Utilities	3.199	53.181	3.183	22.698	61.461	4.200	12.841	13.153	12.860
23. Trade	11.325	57.436	7.648	26.660	56.536	14.442	35.528	38.278	35.810
24. Transportation & communication	4.107	47.504	14.707	33.565	55.174	11.587	42.242	28.868	24.242
25. Services	3.350	52.248	5.564	12.216	56.124	4.971	39.193	29.913	25.839
26. Unallocated	6.091	54.309	33.549	13.380	64.087	25.551	68.927	59.081	47.266
27. Government	0.0	0.0	0.0	0.0	0.0	0.0	0.0	0.0	0.0
28. Noncompetitive imports	49.552	0.0	0.0	0.0	0.0	0.0	0.0	0.0	0.0
29. Subtotal	161.558	1080.037	367.603	304.347	2608.549	344.468	1227.684	994.016	940.234
30. Business consumption	2.833	22.291	6.151	6.851	17.762	11.656	37.892	19.306	15.165
31. Wages	37.394	150.585	16.666	104.622	203.507	140.173	279.306	177.568	224.157
32. Surplus	33.421	167.292	78.012	78.012	289.363	69.298	240.171	172.383	108.105
33. Depreciation	5.203	90.902	20.822	22.071	91.301	8.894	45.635	28.672	42.176
34. Indirect taxes	1.372	19.568	123.405	7.419	5.001	8.112	25.943	35.157	32.198
35. (Less) subsidies	0.0	-0.095	0.0	0.0	0.0	0.0	0.0	0.0	0.0
36. Value added	80.223	450.543	265.924	218.975	606.934	238.133	628.949	433.087	421.801
37. Output	241.781	1530.581	633.527	523.322	3215.482	582.601	1856.632	1427.103	1362.036

TABLE I (*cont.*)

Industry	20 Miscellaneous manufacturing	21 Construction	22 Utilities	23 Trade	24 Transportation & communication	25 Services	26 Unallocated	27 Government	28 Subtotal
1. Agriculture & fishery	9.264	2.031	0.0	-1.175	0.0	0.601	23.899	0.0	1899.402
2. Forestry	3.210	23.876	0.0	0.031	0.003	6.377	0.0	0.0	722.498
3. Petroleum & coal mining	0.018	0.120	88.259	0.0	15.037	6.964	2.040	0.0	449.546
4. Metal & nonmetal mining	1.578	50.990	-0.451	0.0	0.0	0.0	3.144	0.0	324.128
5. Food	1.465	0.0	0.0	2.082	0.0	0.200	23.904	0.0	724.478
6. Textiles	2.695	32.669	1.158	21.198	11.687	16.748	100.924	0.0	1211.695
7. Lumber & furniture	15.254	380.082	0.589	21.454	1.832	17.905	3.005	0.0	645.441
8. Pulp & paper	15.002	12.426	0.430	30.576	2.557	14.525	17.757	0.0	650.368
9. Printing & publishing	1.001	5.897	1.261	31.248	11.014	127.659	0.403	0.0	254.896
10. Leather	2.676	0.010	0.0	0.0	0.0	0.143	1.226	0.0	37.270
11. Rubber	0.031	3.509	0.0	0.227	1.380	5.689	10.796	0.0	162.784
12. Chemicals	91.789	24.939	0.148	0.979	1.050	93.412	41.008	0.0	1393.991
13. Petroleum, coal products	4.279	53.072	12.856	49.923	122.412	20.775	26.364	0.0	628.755
14. Stone, clay & glass	0.635	293.373	1.156	-1.219	0.237	5.114	11.157	0.0	477.190
15. Primary metals	18.441	258.546	3.245	0.817	-0.938	1.066	40.814	0.0	3358.354
16. Fabricated metals	1.640	265.009	0.530	11.747	2.652	7.256	16.344	0.0	457.641
17. Machinery	0.975	84.842	4.141	4.227	2.467	39.141	18.080	0.0	904.101
18. Electrical machinery	0.234	166.588	28.864	0.0	4.966	8.023	31.404	0.0	750.471
19. Transportation equipment	0.0	44.910	0.060	32.952	123.156	3.025	25.181	0.0	465.478
20. Miscellaneous manufacturing	5.241	29.611	0.130	2.670	0.040	19.920	25.338	0.0	164.882
21. Construction	0.924	3.161	24.490	30.462	16.228	134.545	0.372	0.0	292.705
22. Utilities	3.166	5.619	5.270	22.811	23.981	57.647	6.155	0.0	422.267
23. Trade	15.531	154.893	8.663	39.280	28.906	78.242	23.153	0.0	970.743
24. Transportation & communication	7.950	131.979	23.083	103.599	76.426	114.605	99.056	0.0	1010.020
25. Services	12.636	49.483	4.629	172.994	33.702	298.942	107.329	0.0	1029.594
26. Unallocated	14.743	98.987	11.570	0.0	99.881	87.538	0.002	0.0	918.176
27. Government	0.0	0.0	0.0	0.0	0.0	0.0	0.0	0.0	0.0
28. Noncompetitive imports	0.0	0.0	0.0	0.0	0.0	0.0	0.0	0.0	327.145
29. Subtotal	230.375	2176.619	220.075	576.884	580.107	1166.049	658.850	0.0	20654.020
30. Business consumption	6.305	39.553	11.865	199.626	44.518	148.906	145.684	43.115	885.101
31. Wages	59.701	561.757	91.225	1147.503	640.451	1497.416	14.116	530.067	8126.680
32. Surplus	38.742	340.654	62.515	334.025	223.040	835.308	56.674	159.319	4340.117
33. Depreciation	4.907	55.748	124.832	149.140	283.249	344.437	0.0	92.769	1793.195
34. Indirect taxes	8.729	7.161	79.692	82.057	26.339	155.406	86.990	0.0	1298.898
35. (Less) subsidies	0.0	0.0	0.0	0.0	-0.030	0.0	-3.056	0.0	-33.905
36. Value added	118.383	1004.873	370.129	1912.356	1223.566	2981.473	300.407	825.271	16410.121
37. Output	348.758	3181.492	590.203	2489.240	1803.673	4147.520	959.257	825.271	37064.145

TABLE I (cont.)

Industry	29 Business consumption	30 Personal consumption	31 Government consumption	32 Gross fixed investment	33 Net inventory change	34 Exports	35 Final demand, total	36 Imports	37 Gross output, total
1. Agriculture & fishery	28.963	495.702	0.269	17.775	102.414	57.791	702.913	−179.838	2422.477
2. Forestry	0.428	60.232	0.706	−4.130	−2.212	3.192	58.216	−64.934	715.780
3. Petroleum & coal mining	0.0	9.496	1.677	0.0	−5.777	0.180	5.575	−225.224	229.897
4. Metal & nonmetal mining	0.0	2.966	0.0	0.0	4.689	0.687	8.342	−169.351	163.118
5. Food	372.223	2556.027	0.0	0.0	86.023	60.893	3075.175	−170.908	3628.745
6. Textiles	23.734	646.807	5.429	2.595	66.769	364.002	1109.427	−10.855	2310.208
7. Lumber & furniture	6.060	50.274	1.491	20.133	7.025	36.626	122.509	−3.562	764.389
8. Pulp & paper	1.524	−8.180	3.297	0.0	14.186	17.390	28.216	−12.592	665.992
9. Printing & publishing	2.399	112.543	15.125	0.0	5.400	2.769	138.235	−4.410	388.721
10. Leather	0.0	14.539	0.335	0.0	1.483	4.256	20.612	−1.605	56.277
11. Rubber	0.820	34.944	0.455	0.0	12.572	31.380	80.170	−1.174	241.781
12. Chemicals	41.287	122.152	6.519	0.0	37.097	61.397	268.452	−131.864	1530.581
13. Petroleum, coal products	0.025	33.009	17.588	0.0	21.468	12.532	84.621	−79.849	633.527
14. Stone, clay & glass	1.544	−10.115	−0.144	0.0	14.416	45.801	51.791	−5.659	523.322
15. Primary metals	0.0	−4.639	−0.395	−112.025	31.089	140.828	54.858	−197.732	3215.482
16. Fabricated metals	3.769	19.561	1.957	34.466	20.278	48.286	128.316	−3.356	582.601
17. Machinery	1.576	95.852	5.990	791.522	82.054	92.498	1069.494	−116.963	1856.612
18. Electrical machinery	8.421	128.708	6.132	379.445	78.585	92.779	694.070	−17.438	1427.103
19. Transportation equipment	0.0	70.986	42.815	597.096	35.743	177.767	924.407	−27.850	1362.036
20. Miscellaneous manufacturing	3.122	86.530	1.320	4.646	11.702	80.466	187.786	−3.910	348.758
21. Construction	0.0	0.0	6.433	2876.641	0.0	5.885	2888.958	−0.171	3181.492
22. Utilities	0.0	157.043	7.401	0.0	0.001	4.140	168.585	−0.649	590.203
23. Trade	102.414	1099.056	13.230	158.331	22.901	136.062	1531.994	−13.497	2489.240
24. Transportation & communication	9.900	486.077	50.952	13.395	7.000	145.435	712.757	80.896	1803.673
25. Services	276.896	2195.735	645.221	0.0	0.0	5.417	3123.266	−5.338	4147.520
26. Unallocated	0.0	0.942	−10.663	0.0	21.900	90.008	102.888	−61.107	959.257
27. Government	0.0	0.0	825.271	0.0	0.0	0.0	825.271	0.0	825.271
28. Noncompetitive imports	0.0	0.0	0.0	0.0	0.0	0.0	0.0	−327.145	
29. Subtotal	885.101	8456.335	1648.697	4779.890	677.716	1718.465	18166.205	−1756.081	37064.145

values of total output and indirect taxes of sector 6 respectively. Similarly, from 343.739 billion yen of wages in the same sector, we may compute:

$$\lambda_6 = \frac{w_6 L_6}{p_6(1 - t_6) X_6}$$
$$= 0.1496.$$

Table 2 shows the exponents of the Cobb–Douglas functions thus computed.

Profits of the original table include not only corporate profits, but also income of self-employed and family workers. Although there is a distinct downward tendency in the proportion of self-employed and family workers in the total of persons engaged, they make up a significant percentage of persons engaged in some industries.[1] For example, their share in total persons engaged in 1960 amounts to 26.0 per cent in textiles, and to 43.9 per cent in leather (the highest for any manufacturing industry); it is 15.9 per cent in total manufacturing, and 23.2 per cent in all industries, excluding agriculture, fishery and forestry.[2] Self-employed persons have characteristics of both capitalists and workers. Therefore we have made an adjustment by allocating part of the original profits to labour income. The imputed labour income of self-employed and family workers may be computed as:

(the number of the self-employed and family workers)

× (the average wage rate in that industry).

This amount is subtracted from profits, and added to wages.

In Japanese agriculture nearly all farmers (96.7 per cent in 1960) are self-employed and family workers. The number of wage workers is too small to estimate imputed labour income of self-employed and family workers from the average wage rate. Instead we obtain an estimate of 0.4588 for the labour exponent of the Cobb–Douglas function from Torii's study based on cross-section data for 1959.[3] It might be argued that the marginal productivity theory of the firm is irrelevant to the Japanese agricultural

[1] By persons engaged I mean the total of employees, self-employed and family workers.
[2] Computed from the figures in Ministry of Labour, *An Interindustry Analysis of Labour Employment* (Showa 35 nen Sangyorenkanhyo niyoru Rodokeizai no Bunseki), (Ministry of Labour, 1964), pp. 138–41.
[3] See Y. Torii, 'Economic development and labour supply' (Keizai-hatten to Rohdo-kyokyu-shutai no Kinkoh-zushiki) *Keizaigaku Nempoh* (Keio Gijuku Keizaigakkai, 1966). He has related gross output to hours worked by males, hours worked by females, construction, land, domestic animals, power input, fertilizers, feeds, agricultural chemicals and a regional dummy. The sum of the coefficients of the first two inputs refers to labour, and that of the next two inputs to capital. We get the value of 0.4588 by allocating the value added ratio of the input–output table, 0.6997, between labour and capital in the proportions of the corresponding estimates by Torii.

6

TABLE 2. *The estimated exponents of the Cobb–Douglas functions*[a]

Industry	1 Agriculture	2 Forestry	3 Petroleum & coal	4 Metal, non-metal mining	5 Food	6 Textiles	7 Lumber & furniture	8 Pulp & paper	9 Printing & publishing
1	0.0861	−0.0026	0.0	0.0000	0.4880	0.0254	0.0001	0.0114	0.0000
2	0.0035	0.3915	0.0465	0.0100	0.0016	0.0012	0.4383	0.0578	0.0000
3	0.0001	0.0000	0.0152	0.0111	0.0014	0.0027	0.0010	0.0172	0.0
4	0.0004	0.0000	0.0	0.0071	0.0026	0.0	0.0	0.0045	0.0
5	0.0524	0.0000	0.0084	0.0	0.1675	0.0026	0.0000	0.0010	0.0000
6	0.0140	0.0021	0.0070	0.0020	0.0007	0.3882	0.0066	0.0060	0.0041
7	0.0025	0.0007	0.0048	0.0022	0.0046	0.0023	0.1190	0.0247	0.0024
8	0.0016	0.0001	0.0100	0.0033	0.0090	0.0034	0.0042	0.4222	0.3097
9	0.0001	0.0002	0.0100	0.0045	0.0012	0.0032	0.0015	0.0306	0.0164
10	0.0	0.0000	0.0	0.0	0.0002	0.0076	0.0001	0.0000	0.0004
11	0.0007	0.0001	0.0186	0.0000	0.0001	0.0031	0.0010	0.0001	0.0001
12	0.0617	0.0024	0.0055	0.0208	0.0269	0.1077	0.0272	0.0291	0.0396
13	0.0146	0.0087	0.0010	0.0159	0.0061	0.0045	0.0042	0.0104	0.0000
14	0.0015	0.0001	0.0189	0.0001	0.0119	0.0000	0.0019	0.0009	0.0000
15	0.0000	0.0002	0.0053	0.0088	0.0007	0.0016	0.0221	0.0002	0.0048
16	0.0024	0.0024	0.0190	0.0036	0.0073	0.0030	0.0204	0.0023	0.0003
17	0.0052	0.0024	0.0070	0.0115	0.0005	0.0047	0.0017	0.0043	0.0098
18	0.0021	0.0021	0.0049	0.0082	0.0004	0.0012	0.0018	0.0	0.0029
19	0.0044	0.0048	0.0019	0.0010	0.0004	0.0000	0.0018	0.0	0.0
20	0.0030	0.0003		0.0007	0.0027	0.0019	0.0045	0.0003	0.0027
21	0.0063	0.0008	0.0101	0.0308	0.0037	0.0020	0.0036	0.0020	0.0024
22	0.0025	0.0003	0.0738	0.0375	0.0055	0.0106	0.0073	0.0492	0.0056
23	0.0133	0.0033	0.0196	0.0196	0.0461	0.0383	0.0396	0.0305	0.0277
24	0.0099	0.0032	0.0229	0.0311	0.0203	0.0136	0.0255	0.0313	0.0504
25	0.0098	0.0067	0.0287	0.0216	0.0152	0.0139	0.0145	0.0144	0.0305
26	0.0073	0.0044	0.0274	0.0767	0.0363	0.0177	0.0139	0.0150	0.0482
27	0.0	0.0	0.0	0.0	0.0	0.0	0.0	0.0	0.0
28	0.0	0.0	0.0	0.0	0.0	0.1208	0.0	0.0	0.0
Labour	0.4588	0.1813	0.5107	0.4318	0.0776	0.1496	0.2004	0.1211	0.2978
Capital	0.2358	0.3842	0.1328	0.2400	0.0615	0.0692	0.0378	0.1135	0.1441

[a] See Table 1 for the classification of industries.

TABLE 2 (*cont.*)

Industry	10 Leather	11 Rubber	12 Chemicals	13 Petroleum products	14 Stone, clay & glass	15 Primary metals	16 Fabricated metals	17 Machinery	18 Electrical machinery
1	0.0006	0.0	0.0357	0.0	0.0004	0.0000	0.0000	0.0028	0.0007
2	0.0163	0.0	0.0028	0.0090	0.0030	0.0002	0.0013	0.0	0.0
3	0.0042	0.0060	0.0163	0.4990	0.0418	0.0013	0.0011	0.0003	0.0005
4	0.0	0.0006	0.0221	0.0002	0.0892	0.0548	0.0	0.0000	0.0
5	0.3217	0.0	0.0132	0.0	0.0005	0.0	0.0	0.0000	0.0
6	0.0788	0.1578	0.0044	0.0015	0.0039	0.0009	0.0033	0.0059	0.0070
7	0.0017	0.0004	0.0139	0.0036	0.0033	0.0010	0.0049	0.0068	0.0083
8	0.0037	0.0013	0.0464	0.0040	0.0315	0.0012	0.0020	0.0038	0.0069
9	0.0003	0.0014	0.0035	0.0023	0.0038	0.0025	0.0034	0.0056	0.0025
10	0.1470	0.0	0.0001	0.0	0.0	0.0	0.0001	0.0029	0.0003
11	0.0047	0.0199	0.0006	0.0	0.0001	0.0005	0.0034	0.0066	0.0105
12	0.0376	0.1068	0.3099	0.0137	0.0208	0.0065	0.0095	0.0080	0.0181
13	0.0064	0.0193	0.0361	0.0375	0.0473	0.0375	0.0071	0.0060	0.0079
14	0.0014	0.0088	0.0052	0.0006	0.0859	0.0078	0.0038	0.0053	0.0157
15	0.0	0.0026	0.0081	0.0047	0.0286	0.6015	0.4019	0.2247	0.1821
16	0.0369	0.0009	0.0062	0.0041	0.0012	0.0014	0.0343	0.0151	0.0078
17	0.0002	0.0068	0.0049	0.0028	0.0029	0.0064	0.0065	0.2336	0.0309
18	0.0011	0.0015	0.0042	0.0035	0.0038	0.0042	0.0046	0.0222	0.2661
19	0.0	0.0	0.0000	0.0000	0.0021	0.0007	0.0001	0.0038	0.0036
20	0.0366	0.0129	0.0004	0.0025	0.0006	0.0002	0.0004	0.0061	0.0208
21	0.0082	0.0021	0.0053	0.0047	0.0088	0.0018	0.0061	0.0026	0.0028
22	0.0058	0.0133	0.0352	0.0062	0.0440	0.0191	0.0073	0.0070	0.0094
23	0.0511	0.0471	0.0380	0.0150	0.0517	0.0176	0.0251	0.0194	0.0275
24	0.0119	0.0171	0.0314	0.0288	0.0651	0.0172	0.0202	0.0231	0.0207
25	0.0092	0.0139	0.0346	0.0109	0.0237	0.0081	0.0087	0.0214	0.0215
26	0.0091	0.0253	0.0359	0.0658	0.0259	0.0200	0.0445	0.0377	0.0424
27	0.0	0.0	0.0	0.0	0.0	0.0	0.0	0.0	0.0
28	0.0	0.2061	0.0	0.0	0.0	0.0	0.0	0.0	0.0
Labour	0.1890	0.1673	0.1144	0.0447	0.2161	0.0689	0.2643	0.1733	0.1414
Capital	0.0166	0.1607	0.1709	0.2347	0.1940	0.1186	0.1361	0.1561	0.1444

TABLE 2 (cont.)

Industry	19 Transportation equipment	20 Miscellaneous manufacturing	21 Construction	22 Utilities	23 Trade	24 Transportation & communication	25 Services	26 Unallocated	27 Government
1	-0.0005	0.0272	0.0006	0.0	-0.0005	0.0	0.0002	0.0273	0.0
2	0.0	0.0094	0.0075	0.0	0.0000	0.0000	0.0016	0.0	0.0
3	0.0005	0.0001	0.0000	0.1729	0.0	0.0085	0.0017	0.0023	0.0
4	0.0	0.0046	0.0161	-0.0009	0.0009	0.0	0.0	0.0036	0.0
5	0.0	0.0043	0.0	0.0	0.0009	0.0	0.0001	0.0273	0.0
6	0.0042	0.0079	0.0103	0.0023	0.0088	0.0066	0.0042	0.1153	0.0
7	0.0113	0.0449	0.1197	0.0012	0.0089	0.0010	0.0045	0.0034	0.0
8	0.0021	0.0441	0.0039	0.0008	0.0127	0.0014	0.0036	0.0203	0.0
9	0.0011	0.0029	0.0019	0.0025	0.0130	0.0062	0.0320	0.0005	0.0
10	0.0004	0.0079	0.0000	0.0	0.0	0.0	0.0000	0.0014	0.0
11	0.0712	0.0001	0.0011	0.0	0.0001	0.0008	0.0014	0.0123	0.0
12	0.0120	0.2699	0.0079	0.0003	0.0004	0.0011	0.0234	0.0468	0.0
13	0.0039	0.0126	0.0167	0.0252	0.0207	0.0689	0.0052	0.0301	0.0
14	0.0073	0.0019	0.0924	0.0023	-0.0005	0.0001	0.0013	0.0127	0.0
15	0.1120	0.0542	0.0814	0.0064	0.0003	-0.0005	0.0003	0.0466	0.0
16	0.0145	0.0048	0.0835	0.0010	0.0049	0.0015	0.0018	0.0187	0.0
17	0.1525	0.0029	0.0267	0.0081	0.0018	0.0014	0.0098	0.0207	0.0
18	0.0425	0.0007	0.0525	0.0565	0.0	0.0028	0.0020	0.0359	0.0
19	0.1527	0.0	0.0141	0.0001	0.0137	0.0693	0.0008	0.0288	0.0
20	0.0060	0.0154	0.0093	0.0003	0.0011	0.0004	0.0050	0.0289	0.0
21	0.0035	0.0027	0.0010	0.0480	0.0127	0.0091	0.0337	0.0004	0.0
22	0.0097	0.0093	0.0018	0.0103	0.0095	0.0135	0.0144	0.0070	0.0
23	0.0269	0.0457	0.0488	0.0170	0.0163	0.0163	0.0196	0.0265	0.0
24	0.0182	0.0234	0.0416	0.0452	0.0430	0.0430	0.0287	0.1132	0.0
25	0.0194	0.0372	0.0156	0.0091	0.0719	0.0190	0.0749	0.1226	0.0
26	0.0355	0.0434	0.0312	0.0227	0.0	0.0562	0.0219	0.0000	0.0
27	0.0	0.0	0.0	0.0	0.0	0.0	0.0	0.0	0.0
28	0.0	0.0	0.0	0.0	0.0	0.0	0.0	0.0	0.0
Labour	0.1800	0.1941	0.1894	0.2019	0.5596	0.3888	0.4124	0.1826	0.6945
Capital	0.1130	0.1284	0.1249	0.3670	0.2007	0.2849	0.2955	0.0647	0.3055

sector, which consists mostly of small-scale proprietors.[1] But we can derive the same relationships as equation (2.3) if we maximize the self-employed person's utility, which depends on income and leisure, subject to the production function, budget restraint and the restriction of hours available. This is the justification for applying equations (2.3) to the agriculture sector.

The original input–output table of 56 sectors makes no distinction between competitive and non-competitive imports. All imports are treated as competitive; for example, wool imports used by the textile industry are treated as if they are bought from the agricultural sector. In view of the importance of noncompetitive imports in Japan, we have made some modifications: in the textile industry, we regard wool and cotton as noncompetitive imports by separating them from other material inputs. A similar treatment has been applied to crude rubber in the rubber industry. At the aggregative level being adopted, these are the most important noncompetitive commodities.[2]

(ii) The rate of technological change

From equations (2.1) and (2.3) we obtain:

$$\ln \overline{X}_i = \ln A_i + \gamma_i t \quad (i = 1, \ldots, n), \tag{3.1}$$

where

$$\ln \overline{X}_i = \ln X_i - \sum_{j=1}^{n} \alpha_{ji} \ln \left\{ \alpha_{ji} \frac{p_i(1 - t_i) X_i}{p_j} \right\} - \xi_i \ln \left\{ \xi_i \frac{p_i(1 - t_i) X_i}{p_i^z} \right\}$$
$$- \lambda_i \ln L_i - \kappa_i \ln K_i.$$

Let us suppose that the indirect tax ratio, t_i, is constant, and adopt the value of this ratio in the 1960 input–output table as our estimate. Then, if the time series of X_i, L_i, K_i, p_i and p_i^z are available, one can compute a time series of $\overline{X}_i$, defined above, by using the estimates of α_{ji}, ξ_i, λ_i, and κ_i already

---

[1] Let us suppose that the utility function and budget restraint of a farm household are respectively:

$$U = f(y, \overline{L}_1 - L_1 - L_1^n),$$

$$py = wL_1^n + p_1 X_1 - \sum_{i=1}^{n} p_i X_{i1},$$

where y represents its real income, and L_1, L_1^n and $\overline{L}_1$ are the hours worked in agriculture, the hours worked in the nonagricultural sector and total hours available, respectively; w is the average wage of the nonagricultural sector. The inclusion of L_1^n is necessary because it is common practice for the older members of many Japanese families to engage in agriculture, while the younger members hold jobs in industry. Given, $p, p_i, w, \overline{L}_1$ and K_1, maximize U, subject to the budget restraint and the production function. Then one may get equations (2.2) and (2.3), for industry 1, in which w_1 is put as w (or $\omega_1 = 1.0$).

[2] Bauxite, nickel ores and phosphate ores are other important noncompetitive imports. See Appendix B.

obtained. Hence the logarithmic regression of the computed series on time trend yields estimates of γ_i and A_i. The point of this estimation is that

$$\alpha_{ji}\{p_i(1-t_i)X_i/p_j\}$$

is used as a proxy for material input X_{ji}, whose time series is not available.

Due to the limited availability of consistent data, equation (3.1) is estimated using the yearly time series for 1955–63 rather than for 1953–65; the degree of freedom is reduced to seven. The capital stock series are those of tangible fixed assets in constant dollars, while the labour inputs are given in terms of total hours worked. The capital variable in forestry and 'unallocated' is suppressed, since reliable series are not available; this implies that the coefficients of time trend in these industries might reflect the effects of both technological change and capital accumulation.

Results of the estimation of equations (3.1) are tabulated in Table 3. Columns (1) and (3) are estimates of γ_i and $\ln A_i$ respectively. Columns (2) and (4) are the values of the t-statistics which are used for testing the null hypothesis that the corresponding coefficients are not significantly different from zero; its critical value at the 5 per cent level of significance is 2.365. The measure of goodness of fit $\bar{R}^2$ in column (5) is adjusted for degrees of freedom; d in column (6) is the Durbin–Watson statistic.

It is seen from the table that there is a significant upward trend in $\bar{X}_i$ in most industries (22 out of 26), whereas both the t-value and $\bar{R}^2$ are very low in lumber and leather. In construction and fabricated metals the estimated coefficients of γ_i are less than zero, and are not presented here.

During these years the heavy and chemical industries played a central role in the remarkable economic growth of Japan, with rapid introduction of new techniques and a high rate of investment. In fact it is seen that the five industries which enjoyed the highest rate of technical progress in manufacturing were transportation equipment, printing and publishing, chemicals, electrical machinery and rubber. These, except printing and publishing, belong to the heavy and chemical industries. By contrast the five industries with the lowest rate of technical change were fabricated metals, lumber, food, leather and textiles, four of which belong to the light industries.[1] As

[1] The Japanese fabricated metal industry included many small-scale firms with less modern equipment. The share of total sales of this industry accounted for by firms employing at least 500 persons was 13.3 per cent in 1963, while it was 76.3 per cent in transportation equipment, 18.8 per cent in food and 43.9 per cent in all manufacturing. See *Japan Statistical Year Book* (Nippon Tohkei Nenkan), (Office of the Prime Minister, 1966), pp. 184–5. The petroleum products industry was admittedly one of the most modernized industries. But its capacity utilization decreased drastically in the last three years of our period. Therefore our estimation, which is based on the existing stock of capital, but not on the utilized capital, might underestimate the rate of technical change.

TABLE 3. *Estimates of the rate of technical change*

Industry	1 γ_i	2 t-value of γ_i	3 $\ln A_i$	4 t-value of $\ln A_i$	5 R^2	6 d	7 γ_i/σ_i	8 Massel's estimate
1. Agriculture	0.0205	6.83	−0.12	7.05	0.85	1.73	0.0295	—
2. Forestry	0.0095	3.35	2.96	185.6	0.56	2.12	0.0168	—
3. Coal & petroleum	0.0495	6.17	0.38	8.49	0.82	0.71	0.0769	—
4. Metal & nonmental mining	0.0357	4.00	0.41	8.23	0.65	1.27	0.0531	0.0137[a]
5. Food	0.0060	5.93	1.69	297.0	0.81	1.32	0.0431	
6. Textiles	0.0113	5.33	1.43	119.4	0.77	2.12	0.0516	0.0121[b]
7. Lumber & furniture	0.0020	1.27	1.27	143.1	0.07	1.16	0.0084	0.0279[c]
8. Pulp & paper	0.0175	6.58	1.59	106.6	0.84	1.97	0.0746	0.0234
9. Printing & publishing	0.0343	25.6	0.95	125.7	0.99	1.85	0.0776	0.0244
10. Leather	0.0060	1.16	1.63	56.1	0.04	1.27	0.0292	0.0106
11. Rubber	0.0235	5.02	1.61	61.3	0.75	1.84	0.0716	0.0098
12. Chemicals	0.0285	17.4	1.81	195.8	0.97	2.38	0.0999	0.0346
13. Petroleum products	0.0205	6.30	1.58	86.2	0.83	1.79	0.0734	0.0189
14. Stone, clay & glass	0.0145	3.16	1.71	66.1	0.53	1.96	0.0354	0.0248
15. Primary metals	0.0192	9.38	1.17	101.9	0.92	1.33	0.1024	0.0043
16. Fabricated metals	—	—	—	—	—	—	—	0.0025
17. Machinery	0.0175	4.38	1.65	73.5	0.70	1.79	0.0531	0.0179[d]
18. Electrical machinery	0.0272	6.69	1.71	74.8	0.85	1.92	0.0952	0.0369
19. Transportation equipment	0.0372	6.20	1.69	50.2	0.82	1.81	0.1270	0.0239
20. Other manufacturing	0.0230	6.42	1.65	81.7	0.83	1.62	0.0713	—
21. Construction	—	—	—	—	—	—	—	—
22. Utilities	0.0137	3.61	0.71	33.2	0.60	1.14	0.0241	—
23. Trade	0.0512	9.86	−0.30	10.2	0.92	1.11	0.0673	—
24. Transport. & communication	0.0383	10.6	0.26	13.0	0.93	1.72	0.0569	—
25. Services	0.0392	12.8	0.35	20.1	0.95	1.13	0.0554	—
26. Unallocated	0.0340	11.3	2.41	141.9	0.94	1.00	0.1375	

[a] A weighted average of food and tobacco.
[b] A weighted average of textiles and clothing.
[c] A weighted average of lumber and furniture.
[d] A weighted average of machinery and instruments.

TABLE 4. *Weighted average of the rate of technical change*

Industry	(1) Average of γ_i (weighted by 1960 gross output)	(2) Average of γ_i/σ_i (weighted by 1960 value added)	(3) Average of Massel's estimate (weighted by 1954 value added)
(1) Mining	0.0438	0.0668	–
(2) Manufacturing	0.0172	0.0682	0.0193
(3) Light industries[a]	0.0095	0.0467	0.0171
(4) Heavy and chemical industries[b]	0.0220	0.0800	0.0204
(5) Services and construction	0.0301	0.0497	–
(6) Services[c]	0.0407	0.0574	–

[a] Light industries include (5), (6), (7), (9), (10) and (20) in Table 1.
[b] Heavy and chemical industries include (8), (11), (12), (13), (14), (15), (16), (17), (18) and (19) in Table 1.
[c] Services include (22), (23), (24) and (25).

shown in Table 4, the average rate of technical progress is 2.20 per cent in the heavy and chemical industries, while it is 0.95 per cent in the light industries. In computing the average of the table, the gross outputs of each industry in 1960 are used as weights.

Technical change in agriculture, fishery, and forestry is estimated at low rates. (Note that the coefficient of time trend in forestry includes the effects of capital accumulation as well.) On the other hand, the estimated rates for mining are very high: 4.95 per cent in coal and petroleum and 3.57 per cent in metal and nonmetal mining. Japanese mineral resources were very limited and the mining industries hardly competed with imported minerals. The Japanese coal mining industry attempted, with the cooperation of the government under the Five Year Coal Industry Rationalization Program, to increase efficiency and to reduce prices. The higher rate of technical change may partly reflect the outcome of this rationalization. It is also noted, however, that the computed sampling errors of the coefficient are high.

The average rate in all service industries, which include utilities, trade, transportation and communication as well as services, is estimated at 4.07 per cent. One might have some doubts about the reliability of this estimate because the value is much higher than that of all manufacturing, 1.72 per cent. As will be shown later, however, this result is not as unreasonable as it appears at first glance.

(iii) *Value added version of the production functions*

It may be of some interest to compare these results with other estimates of the production functions in which value added is related to capital and labour. Value added in constant prices may be defined as:

$$V_i = X_i - \sum_{j=1}^{n} X_{ji} - Z_i \quad (i = 1, ..., n), \tag{3.2}$$

where V_i represents the value added in constant prices of the ith industry. Substituting equation (2.3) for X_{ji} and Z_i gives:

$$V_i = \frac{p_i(1 - t_i) X_i}{p_i^v} \left(\frac{1}{1 - t_i} - \sum_{j=1}^{n} \alpha_{ji} - \xi_i \right) \quad (i = 1, ..., n), \tag{3.3}$$

where

$$p_i^v = \frac{1/(1 - t_i) - \sum_{j=1}^{n} \alpha_{ji} - \xi_i}{1/p_i(1 - t_i) - \sum_{j=1}^{n} \alpha_{ji}/p_j - \xi_i/p_i^z},$$

p_i^v = the value added price in industry i.[1]

Equations (2.1) and (2.3) may yield:

$$\ln X_i = \left(\frac{1}{\sigma_i} - 1 \right) \ln(1 - t_i) + \ln \bar{H}_i + \left(\frac{\gamma_i}{\sigma_i} \right) t + \sum_{j=1}^{n} \frac{\alpha_{ji}}{\sigma_i} \ln \left(\frac{p_i}{p_j} \right)$$

$$+ \frac{\xi_i}{\sigma_i} \ln \frac{p_i}{p_i^z} + \frac{\lambda_i}{\sigma_i} \ln L_i + \frac{\kappa_i}{\sigma_i} \ln K_i, \tag{3.4}$$

where

$$\sigma_i = 1 - \sum_{j=1}^{n} \alpha_{ji} - \xi_i$$

$$= \lambda_i + \kappa_i,$$

$$\ln \bar{H}_i = \frac{1}{\sigma_i} \left(\ln A_i + \sum_{j=1}^{n} \alpha_{ji} \ln \alpha_{ji} + \xi_i \ln \xi_i \right).$$

From equations (3.3) and (3.4) we obtain:

$$\ln V_i = \frac{1}{\sigma_i} \ln(1 - t_i) + \ln \left(\frac{1}{1 - t_i} - \sum_{j=1}^{n} \alpha_{ji} - \xi_i \right) + \ln \bar{H}_i$$

$$+ \frac{\gamma_i}{\sigma_i} t + \frac{1}{\sigma_i} \ln Q_i + \frac{\lambda_i}{\sigma_i} \ln L_i + \frac{\kappa_i}{\sigma_i} \ln K_i \quad (i = 1, ..., n), \tag{3.5}$$

where

$$\ln Q_i = \sigma_i \ln \frac{p_i}{p_i^v} + \sum_{j=1}^{n} \alpha_{ji} \ln \frac{p_i}{p_j} + \xi_i \ln \frac{p_i}{p_i^z}.$$

---

[1] Here the value added price is defined as the ratio between value added in current prices and that in constant prices, V_i.

This value added production function has a relative price term, Q_i, as well as the capital, labour and technology terms; material inputs are eliminated by (2.3) which implies optimum utilization of materials. When output X_i is increased, material inputs X_{ji} and Z_i increase proportionately, provided prices and tax rates remain constant. This is always implied by production functions (3.3) and (3.5). Therefore a proportional change in labour and capital gives rise to a proportional change in X_i, because of the assumed constant returns to scale of the original production function (2.1). This is, in fact, assured by the fact that the sum of the exponents of the labour and capital variables of the production functions (3.3) and (3.5), λ_i/σ_i and κ_i/σ_i, is obviously unity. It is also seen that the exponent of the technological improvement variable of (3.3) or (3.5) is γ_i/σ_i.

The estimated values of the rate of technical change in the value added version and their weighted average are shown in column (7) of Table 3 and in column (2) of Table 4. It is seen that for the typical heavy and chemical industries, such as transportation equipment, chemicals, electrical machinery and primary metals, there has been a fairly high rate of technical change (over 9.0 per cent). The average rate of the heavy and chemical industries, 8.00 per cent, is much higher than that of the light industries, 4.67 per cent. Further, in contrast to the results of the gross output version, the average rate for all services, 5.74 per cent, is exceeded by that of the heavy and chemical industries, and even by that of all manufacturing, 6.82 per cent.

The estimates of 5.16 per cent for textiles and 8.00 per cent for the heavy and chemical industries are close to Ueno's estimates of 5.5 per cent and 8.6 per cent respectively.[1] He also estimated a rate of 3.0 per cent for agriculture, which is very close to our estimate of 2.95 per cent. The finding that the rate for all manufacturing is somewhat higher than that for all services is comparable with Dhrymes' results for the United States.[2] Massell's estimates for two-digit manufacturing industries of the United States in 1946–57 and their averages are shown in column (8) of Table 3 and column (3) of Table 4 respectively.[3] It should be pointed out that, except

---

[1] H. Ueno and S. Kinoshita, 'A simulation experiment for growth with a long-term model of Japan', *International Economic Review* (February 1968).

[2] P. J. Dhrymes, 'A comparison of productivity behavior in manufacturing and service industries', *Review of Economics and Statistics* (February 1963), p. 68. His estimates are 1.73 per cent in all manufacturing and 1.61 per cent in all services for the sample period, 1945–58.

[3] See B. F. Massell, 'A disaggregated view of technical change', *Journal of Political Economy* (December 1961). The average is computed by taking values added in 1954 from the United States Department of Commerce, *The National Income and Product Accounts of the United States, 1929–1965* (A supplement to the Survey of Current Business), (Washington: Department of Commerce, 1966), p. 20. Comparisons among the estimated rates of technical change in the United States are found in E. Mansfield, 'Comment on

for lumber and fabricated metals, our estimates are higher than Massell's for every manufacturing industry. 'Imitating technology', it appears, is mainly responsible for the large difference between the rates of technical progress in Japan and the United States. It is very likely that countries introducing high technology from more advanced countries can enjoy a faster rate of technical progress than the countries which originally develop these techniques.[1] Japan, which had no access to the technical progress of the Western countries during World War II, rapidly introduced many newly developed and perfected techniques as she recovered from the ravages of war.

Finally, it should be added that, in spite of the large difference in the levels of the estimated rates between the US and Japan, the rank orderings of industries by these rates in the two countries are roughly similar. Major differences in this ordering are found only in lumber, primary metals and stone. Apart from these three industries the coefficient of rank correlation between the estimates of the two countries is as high as 0.87.

(2) CONSUMPTION FUNCTION

The estimation of the consumption functions is made mainly on the basis of consumer surveys and the time series data of the commodity classification of the consumer surveys. The sixteen consumption items used here are shown in Table 5 and in more detail in Appendix B.

The estimation of the parameters is made in several steps. For the overall marginal propensity to consume and the lagged consumption effect (or the parameters $\bar{\beta}$ and $\bar{\delta}$ in equation (2.6)), we use the annual consumer surveys, which present household consumption by income classes for each year in 1953–65. In the preliminary calculation the following regression has been tried for each year:

$$\ln \left(\frac{C_{j,t}^*}{\bar{L}_{j,t}^*}\right) = \bar{\beta} \ln \left(\frac{Y_{j,t}^*/p_t^c}{\bar{L}_{j,t}^*}\right) + \ln \bar{B}, \qquad (3.6)$$

where the subscripts t and j refer to year and income class respectively, and the asterisk stands for the household figure; $C_{j,t}^*$, $Y_{j,t}^*$, and $\bar{L}_{j,t}^*$ are consumption, disposable money income and the number of persons in the household respectively. The calculated results enable us to observe a gradual shift in the estimated intercept, $\ln \bar{B}$, during the sample period 1953–65, while the yearly estimate for $\bar{\beta}$ was fairly stable throughout this period. Therefore all

Marc Nerlove's " Recent empirical studies of the CES and related production functions "', *The Theory and Empirical Analysis of Production*, ed. M. Brown (New York: National Bureau of Economic Research, 1967).

[1] See P. A. Samuelson, *Economics: An Introductory Analysis*, 6th ed. (McGraw–Hill, 1964), pp. 770–1.

TABLE 5. *Estimates of consumption functions*

	(1) β'_k	(2) t-value of β'_k	(3) ln B'_k	(4) t-value of ln B'_k	(5) $\bar{R}^2$	(6) ϵ_k	(7) t-value of ϵ_k	(8) ln B'_k	(9) t-value of ln B'_k	(10) $\bar{R}^2$	(11) ρ	(12) d	(13) Prais and Houthakker's estimate for β'_k	(14) Stone's estimate for β'_k	(15) Stone's estimate for ϵ_k
(1) Cereals	0.04	2.33	6.32	40.3	0.26	−0.35	1.32	2.39	88.0	0.44	0.69	1.24	0.12	−0.01	−0.19
(2) Vegetables	0.53	54.0	0.88	10.1	0.995	−0.77	15.3	−1.16	134.2	0.96	0.12	1.87	0.41	0.66	−0.52
(3) Meat, fish & dairy	0.73	28.8	0.05	0.24	0.98	−0.77	2.64	−0.76	5.08	0.88	0.94	2.63	0.45	0.56	−0.48
(4) Processed food & condiments	0.25	15.5	3.76	25.7	0.94	−0.70	3.30	0.11	1.50	0.95	0.88	2.44	0.38	0.40	−0.44
(5) Cakes, fruit & beverages	0.76	17.5	−0.68	1.75	0.96	−1.80	16.0	−1.07	512.8	0.93	−0.27	1.06	0.63	0.77	−0.61
(6) Meals away from home	1.06	15.0	−4.21	6.64	0.94	−0.97	1.13	−6.20	28.6	0.94	0.94	2.31	0.97	2.66	–
(7) Clothing[a]	0.87	10.3	–	–	–	−1.11	3.03	−1.39	3.60	0.99	0.22	1.12	0.99	–	–
(8) Fuel and light	0.75	34.7	−0.76	3.98	0.99	−0.96	6.64	−2.08	189.4	0.84	0.26	2.19	0.79	0.39	−0.23
(9) Water	0.53	10.2	−1.22	2.64	0.88	−1.17	2.47	−3.09	18.6	0.84	0.92	1.85	–	–	–
(10) Rent[b]	0.81	14.8	–	–	–	–	–	−1.62	6.59	0.98	0.37	1.37	0.92	–	–
(11) Furniture & repairs[b]	1.45	3.21	–	–	–	–	–	−4.24	1.74	0.99	0.93	1.45	1.52	–	–
(12) Medical and toilet care	0.66	19.4	0.06	0.21	0.96	−2.53	6.43	−1.09	17.5	0.97	0.74	1.86	1.55	–	–
(13) Transportation & communication	1.24	24.8	−5.93	13.3	0.98	−1.40	1.87	−4.95	58.0	0.58	0.77	1.39	1.57	–	–
(14) Amusement & literary activity[b]	1.41	23.7	–	–	–	–	–	−4.47	16.7	0.99	0.18	2.01	1.24	–	–
(15) Tobacco[a]	0.70	6.21	–	–	–	−0.47	2.09	−2.45	4.94	0.99	0.60	1.52	0.90	–	–
(16) Education & others	1.82	24.1	−9.34	13.9	0.98	−3.82	4.59	−6.41	120.6	0.82	0.70	2.28	1.26	–	–

[a] Estimates for equation (3.10).

[b] Estimates for equation (3.10), in which ϵ_k is assumed to be zero.

the survey data are pooled and the average consumption of the previous year is introduced to explain the shift in the intercept. This regression yields the following estimation of equation (2.6):

$$\ln\left(\frac{C_{j,t}^*}{\bar{L}_{j,t}^*}\right) = \underset{(141.6)}{0.695} \ln\left(\frac{Y_{j,t}^*/p_t^c}{\bar{L}_{j,t}^*}\right) + \underset{(16.45)}{0.186} \ln\left(\frac{C_{t-1}^*}{\bar{L}_{t-1}^*}\right) + \underset{(10.14)}{0.998}$$

$$\bar{R}^2 = 0.992, \text{ d.f.} = 192, \quad (3.7)$$

where C_{t-1}^* and $\bar{L}_{t-1}^*$ are household averages of $C_{j,t-1}^*$ and $\bar{L}_{j,t-1}^*$ respectively.

As regards the income and price elasticities of each consumption item (or the parameters of equation (2.7)), the following regressions are first calculated on the basis of the consumer survey in 1960:

$$\ln\left(\frac{C_{k,j}^{\prime*}}{\bar{L}_j^*}\right) = \beta_k' \ln\left(\frac{C_j^{\prime*}}{\bar{L}_j^*}\right) + \ln B_k'' \quad (k = 1, ..., 16); \quad (3.8)$$

where the subscripts k and j refer to the individual item of consumption and the income class, and the prime stands for the figure in the consumption survey category rather than in the input–output category. Then, by using this estimate for β_k' (denote it by $\hat{\beta}_k'$) and the time series of the national aggregate of each consumption item and population, we calculate the regression equation:

$$\ln\left(\frac{C_{k,t}'}{\bar{L}_t}\right) - \hat{\beta}_k' \ln\left(\frac{C_t}{\bar{L}_t}\right) = \epsilon_k \ln\left(\frac{p_{k,t}^c}{p_t^c}\right) + \ln B_k' \quad (k = 1, ..., 16).$$
$$(3.9)$$

Our method of pooling the cross-section and time series data was used by Stone *et al.* in estimating the demand for a wide variety of food products in the United Kingdom.[1] He adopted the first-difference form of equation (3.9) in the estimation of the price elasticities, rather than its form in terms of the absolute values of the variables, in order to eliminate the possible presence of serial correlation in the errors. Here, intending to make a more general treatment of the problem, we apply the Cochrane–Orcutt iterative method for first-order autocorrelated disturbances to the estimation of equation (3.9).[2] There is another difference from Stone's method; he measured the consumption variable in terms of adult-equivalents while this study works in per capita terms.

The results thus estimated are presented in Table 5. Columns (1) to (5) refer to the estimates for equation (3.8), and columns (6) to (12) to those for equation (3.9). ρ in column (11) stands for the autocorrelation coefficient of the disturbances, and other notations are the same as in Table 3. This table,

[1] See R. Stone *et al. The Measurement of Consumers' Expenditure and Behaviour in the United Kingdom, 1920–38*, vol. I (Cambridge University Press, 1954).

[2] D. Cochrane and G. H. Orcutt, 'Application of least squares regressions to relationships containing auto-correlated error terms', *Journal of the American Statistical Association* (March 1949).

as explained later, also includes better estimates for the five items of clothing, rent, furniture, amusement and tobacco, obtained from equations other than (3.8) and (3.9). In the ordinary least squares estimates for equation (3.9), the calculated Durbin–Watson statistics show that positive serial correlation is significant at the 5 per cent level in ten out of fourteen equations, while it is not significant in three equations and inconclusive in one equation.[1] In the estimates by the Cochrane–Orcutt method, however, thirteen out of sixteen d values, as shown in column (12) of the table, are higher than the approximate critical value at the 5 per cent level, 1.34, and therefore indicate insignificant positive serial correlation, while the remaining three values are inconclusive at the same level.

Let us focus attention on food consumption. The point estimates for the elasticity of food consumption with respect to total consumption expenditure are less than unity for all food items, excluding meals-away-from-home, illustrating the well-accepted Engel's law. Among them, the expenditure elasticity of cereals, 0.04, is the lowest, and that of processed food, 0.25, is relatively low. Processed food here includes canned meat, canned fish and margarine as well as sugar, salt, etc.; its details are shown in Appendix B. Meals-away-from-home, whose elasticity is estimated at 1.06, may be regarded as a luxury food item. Columns (13) to (15) present two comparable estimates by Prais and Houthakker, and Stone *et al.*;[2] the former is based on cross-section data for 1937–8 in the United Kingdom, and the latter on the same cross-section data and a time series for 1920–38 in the United Kingdom. Figures in the table are weighted averages of their estimates, according to our classification of commodities.[3] Comparison between the estimates of total expenditure elasticities reveals (i) that the elasticities, except those for meals-away-from-home, are less than unity; (ii) that the ordering of the magnitude of the estimates from highest to lowest is meals-away-from-home, cakes and fruits, meat and fish, vegetables, processed food and cereals, except for a reversed ordering between meat and vegetables in Stone's estimates, (iii) that for each item other than meals-away-from-home and meat, fish and dairy products the discrepancies among the three estimates of the expenditure elasticity (by us, by Stone *et al.* and by Prais–Houthakker) do not exceed 0.25, and (iv) that the Japanese expenditure elasticity for meat, fish and dairy products, 0.73, is larger than Stone's British estimate of 0.56 and Prais–Houthakker's of 0.45. The last finding

[1] Rent and tobacco are excluded from this test, for a reason which will be explained later.

[2] See S. J. Prais and H. S. Houthakker, *The Analysis of Family Budgets* (Cambridge University Press, 1955) and R. Stone *et al.*, *op. cit.*

[3] While Stone uses per equivalent adult consumption, Prais–Houthakker proceeded with per capita consumption. The classification of items was somewhat different between them. For details of the way in which the average was computed see Appendix B.

might be ascribed to the difference in consumption patterns between the two countries – meat, fish and dairy products being regarded as luxury food items in Japan.

Comparison of the price elasticities shows that the Japanese values are higher in the five food items than Stone's British estimates. The orderings of the elasticities in the two countries are substantially the same, with cereals being lowest and cakes, fruits and beverages highest in both cases.

A simple application of the above method of pooling the cross-section and time series data has resulted in a small positive price elasticity for clothing; therefore, for clothing, we directly estimate the following equation:

$$\ln\left(\frac{C'_{k,t}}{\bar{L}_t}\right) = \beta'_k \ln\left(\frac{C_t}{\bar{L}_t}\right) + \epsilon_k \ln\left(\frac{p^c_{k,t}}{p^c_t}\right) + \ln B'_k \qquad (3.10)$$

by the Cochrane–Orcutt method, without estimating β'_k by the use of cross-section data. By this treatment we obtain a negative price elasticity of -1.11, which is presented in Table 5. The corresponding expenditure elasticity, 0.87, adopted by us is somewhat less than Prais–Houthakker's estimate, 0.99.

The estimates for fuel and light and water are obtained by the pooling method. The expenditure elasticity of fuel and light, 0.75, is close to Prais–Houthakker's, 0.79, but much higher than Stone's 0.39. The price elasticity, 0.96, is also higher than Stone's 0.23.

Rent in the cross-section data excludes imputed rents for house owners, while that of the time series used here includes them. In view of the consistency of the national income accounts and the input–output table, it might be preferable to estimate the elasticities for the rent item solely from the time series. Thus the estimate of the total expenditure elasticity in Table 5 is obtained by regressing the time series of rent on that of total expenditure by the Cochrane–Orcutt method. Here the price variable is suppressed because its estimated coefficient is positive in the regression which includes it.

In furniture and amusement, the estimates of the price elasticity are small positive or very small negative values in equation (3.10) as well as (3.9). Thus the expenditure elasticities of these items, as for clothing and rent, are calculated from the time series of the national aggregates. Total expenditure elasticity of furniture, 1.45, is close to Prais–Houthakker's, 1.52, while that of amusement, 1.41, is somewhat higher than his estimate, 1.24.

Medical care, transportation, amusement, education and others constitute the principal consumption output of the tertiary industry. Their expenditure elasticities are estimated to be more than unity, except that of medical care. Corresponding estimates by Prais–Houthakker all exceed unity; their estimates are somewhat higher than the Japanese estimates in transportation but lower in education and others.

TABLE 6. *The proportion of the value of consumption good k which corresponds to input–output category i.*[a] s_{ik}

Industry	1 Cereals	2 Vegetables	3 Meat, fish & dairy	4 Processed food	5 Cakes & beverages	6 Meals-away-from-home	7 Clothing	8 Fuel & light
1	0.0444	0.8212	0.5549	0	0.0712	0.1410	−0.0181	0
2	0	0	0.0013	0	0.0058	0	0	0.1679
3	0	0	0	0	0	0	0	0.0298
4	0.7763	0	0.2644	0.8208	0.0028	0	0	0
5	0	0	0	0	0.7395	0	0	0
6	0	0	0	0	0	0.3614	0.5950	0
7	0	0	0	0	0	0	0	0
8	0	0	0	0	0	0	0	0
9	0	0	0	0	0	0	0	0
10	0	0	0	0	0	0	0.0140	0
11	0	0	0	0	0	0	0.0337	0
12	0	0	0	0	0.0004	0	0.0004	0.0094
13	0	0	0	0	0	0	0	0.1036
14	0	0	0	0	0	0	0	0
15	0	0	0	0	0	0	0	0
16	0	0	0	0	0	0	0	0
17	0	0	0	0	0	0	0	0
18	0	0	0	0	0	0	0	0
19	0	0	0	0	0	0	0.0162	0
20	0	0	0	0	0	0	0	0
21	0	0	0	0	0	0	0	0
22	0	0	0	0	0	0	0	0
23	0.1597	0.1594	0.1598	0.1598	0.1607	0.0414	0.3080	0.4930
24	0.0196	0.0193	0.0196	0.0194	0.0196	0.0051	0.0063	0.1660
25	0	0	0	0	0	0.4511	0.0445	0.0304
26	0	0	0	0	0	0	0	0
27	0	0	0	0	0	0	0	0
Total	1.0000	1.0000	1.0000	1.0000	1.0000	1.0000	1.0000	1.0000

[a] See Table 1 for the classification of industries.

TABLE 6 (cont.)

Industry	9 Water	10 Rent	11 Furniture & repairs	12 Medical care	13 Transportation & communication	14 Amusement	15 Tobacco	16 Education & others
1	0	0	0	0	0	0	0	0
2	0	0	0	0	0	0	0	0
3	0	0	0	0	0	0	0	0
4	0	0	0	0	0	0	0	0
5	0	0	0.0643	0	0	0	0.8351	0
6	0	0	0.1038	0	0	0	0	0
7	0	0	0	0	0	0	0	0
8	0	0	0	0.0078	0	−0.0465	0	0.0070
9	0	0	0	0	0	0.02924	0	0
10	0	0	0	0	0	0	0	0
11	0	0	0	0.1681	0	0	0	0
12	0	0.0050	0.0027	0	0	0	0	0
13	0	0	0	0	0	0	0	0
14	0	0	−0.0209	0	0	0	0	0
15	0	0	−0.0095	0	0	0	0	0
16	0	0	0.0405	0	0	0	0	0
17	0	0	0.1433	0.0105	0	0.0504	0	0
18	0	0	0.2661	0	0	0	0	0
19	0	0	0.1468	0	0	0	0	0
20	0	0	0.0724	0	0	0.0577	0	0.0198
21	0	0	0	0	0	0	0	0
22	0	0	0	0	1.0000	0	0	0
23	0.1826	0	0.1821	0.0382	0	0.0696	0.1649	0.0052
24	0	0	0.0085	0	0	0	0	0.0006
25	0.8174	0.9950	0	0.7754	0	0.5764	0	0.9660
26	0	0	0	0	0	0	0	0.0014
27	0	0	0	0	0	0	0	0
Total	1.0000	1.0000	1.0000	1.0000	1.0000	1.0000	1.0000	1.0000

It is said that Japanese household surveys tend to underestimate tobacco consumption substantially, since few husbands report their tobacco expenses accurately to their wives. Thus the consumption function of tobacco, like that of clothing, is estimated by fitting the time series data to (3.10). The expenditure elasticity obtained, 0.70, is somewhat lower than the British estimate, 0.90.

To sum up: the total expenditure elasticities estimated from the Japanese survey are less than unity for each food item (except meals-away-from-home), fuel and water, and more than unity in almost all the items of service consumption. They are comparable with Prais–Houthakker's and Stone's estimates, though the elasticity of meat, fish and dairy products is relatively higher and that of medical care is much lower in Japan.

Apart from cereals, rent, furniture, amusement and tobacco, the price elasticities are found to be fairly high, ranging between -0.77 and -3.82. They are much higher than those of Stone.

The consumer demand model presented here is essentially static, apart from the inclusion of the lagged consumption variable in the total consumption function. The demand for consumer durables, and probably that for clothing, might be more appropriately treated by taking into account the dynamic aspect of demand, e.g. the effect of stocks of these commodities or accumulated liquid assets on demand.[1] It is noted, however, that expenditure on cars constituted a very small part of total expenditure in Japan during the sample period, and the approach adopted here would not seriously distort the conclusions in the later parts of our study, although it is true that an allowance for the dynamic forces in the demand for consumer durables is required for more elaborate analysis.

Finally, Table 6 shows the proportion, s_{ik}, of consumption expenditure spent on the kth consumption good which is classified as the final demand for the ith industry, according to the input–output table. For example, $s_{11} = 0.0444$ means that 4.44 per cent of expenditure on cereals is directed to the agricultural industry. These ratios enable us to transform the above estimates for the consumption functions according to the input–output classification, and to give them the resulting estimates as functions of disposable income and relative prices.

[1] Empirical investigations in this direction have been made, e.g. by Chow, Stone–Rowe, Houthakker–Taylor, and Harberger. See G. C. Chow, *Demand for Automobiles in the United States: A Study in Consumer Durables* (North-Holland Publishing Co., 1957), R. Stone and D. A. Rowe, 'The market demand for durable goods', *Econometrica* (July 1957), H. S. Houthakker and L. D. Taylor, *Consumer Demand in the United States, 1929–1970* (Harvard University Press, 1966), and A. C. Harberger, ed. *The Demand for Durable Goods* (University of Chicago Press, 1960).

(3) IMPORT FUNCTIONS

In 1960, the share of imports in total supply was 49.5 per cent for coal and crude petroleum, and 50.9 per cent in ferrous, nonferrous and other mining. Apart from these two industries, the share was highest in petroleum and coal products (11.2 per cent), whilst in all other industries it did not exceed 10 per cent at the level of industrial disaggregation adopted here. Therefore import functions (2.16) are estimated solely for the two mining sectors on the basis of the annual time series data for the period 1953–65. In all other industries the share of imports in total supply is assumed to be constant in the short run. Since these imports are of small magnitude, this approximation will not cause large errors in the estimation of excess supply of each product. The observations of 1956 and 1957 are ignored, because the Suez crisis in 1956 caused a violent increase in the foreign prices of mining products. The results are:

coal and crude petroleum:

$$\frac{M_3}{X_3} = \underset{(39.87)}{1.246} \left(\frac{M_3}{X_3}\right)_{-1} - \underset{(1.215)}{0.299} \frac{p_3^m}{p_3} + \underset{(2.283)}{0.601} \left(\frac{R}{M}\right)_{-1} + \underset{(0.285)}{0.091},$$

$$\bar{R}^2 = 0.99, \ d = 1.53, \quad (3.11)$$

ferrous, nonferrous and other mining:

$$\frac{M_4}{X_4} = \underset{(2.335)}{0.822} \left(\frac{M_4}{X_4}\right)_{-1} - \underset{(0.993)}{0.564} \frac{p_4^m}{p_4} + \underset{(1.788)}{0.870} \left(\frac{R}{M}\right)_{-1} + \underset{(0.562)}{0.487},$$

$$\bar{R}^2 = 0.77, \ d = 1.50. \quad (3.12)$$

The elasticity of imports with respect to import prices is computed for 1960 as −0.31 in coal and crude petroleum, and as −0.54 in ferrous, nonferrous and other mining.[1]

(4) WAGE EQUATION

The estimated wage equation is:

$$\frac{\Delta w}{w_{-1}} = \underset{(4.629)}{0.677} \frac{L}{Lf} + \underset{(1.997)}{0.488} \frac{\Delta p_{-1}^c}{p_{-2}^c} + \underset{(3.961)}{1.449} \frac{\Delta L_{-1}'}{L_{-2}'} - \underset{(3.946)}{0.386},$$

$$\bar{R}^2 = 0.70, \ d = 2.46. \quad (3.13)$$

Here L is the total of the L_is and w is the average wage per hour in the industrial sector. Agriculture, fishery and forestry are excluded from L and

---

[1] The elasticity is computed by inserting the observed values of 1960 into the following formula:

$$\frac{p^m}{M} \frac{\partial M}{\partial p^m} = \frac{X}{M} \frac{p^m}{p} \frac{\partial (M/X)}{\partial (p^m/p)}.$$

w, since the great majority of Japanese agricultural workers were self-employed and family workers, and the labour market of the agricultural sector differed substantially from that of the industrial sector. *Lf* is the total available labour hours, computed as the product of the size of the labour force and the maximum average annual labour hours during the sample period.

Throughout these years supply of labour to the industrial sector increased, not only through the natural growth of the labour force but also through inflow from the agricultural or rural sector. In 1953–65 the number of persons engaged in the industrial sector increased on average at an annual rate of 3.7 per cent, while the persons engaged in agriculture decreased at a rate of 2.7 per cent per year and the labour force grew at a rate of 1.5 per cent. Thus L/Lf rose over time, revealing a tendency towards increasing labour scarcity in spite of the persistent drainage of labour from the agricultural sector. As an increase in L/Lf implies that wage increase is accelerated, there is a tendency to long-run cost-push inflation. The rate of increase of wages, on the other hand, is also related to the phases of the business cycle. If the economy is in the early stages of recovery, the potential labour supply in the industrial or urban sector is relatively abundant and the wage rise will not be much, whilst if labour demand has been increasing for some time, further recruiting of labour will be much harder, and the wage rise will be larger. Because of this consideration, the rate of change in employment in the previous year is introduced as a variable to explain the cyclical behaviour of the industrial wage rate.[1]

(5) PROPERTY INCOME EQUATION

Based on the national income statistics, the following regression equation explaining property income *Pr* by profits *P* is obtained:

$$Pr/p = \underset{(16.23)}{0.614}(P/p) - \underset{(1.462)}{189.9}, \quad \bar{R}^2 = 0.96, d = 1.40. \qquad (3.14)$$

Here it is noted that profits include the excess of the proprietors' income over their imputed labour income.

---

[1] More specifically, L' represents the number of persons engaged in the industrial sector at the end of the year.

4. *Comparative statics of general equilibrium*

We are indebted to Sir John Hicks for deriving the laws of change of the price system in general equilibrium, i.e. for working out how a shift in the demand or supply function of a particular product affects the prices of all products.[1] Following his line of thought I make an empirical analysis of the price formation in this chapter.

As has been explained, the empirical excess supply of each good, E_i, defined as (2.18), is a function of relative prices π_is and the predetermined variables:[2]

$$E_i = f_i(\pi_1, ..., \pi_{26}; G_1, ..., G_{138}) \quad (i = 1, ..., 26). \tag{4.1}$$

Here, G_k stands for the kth predetermined variable. All the G_ks are defined as follows:

$$F_i \qquad\qquad (i = 1, ..., 27, \text{ are referred to as } G_i);$$

$$K_i \qquad\qquad (i = 1, ..., 26, \text{ as } G_{27+i});$$

$$\bar{A}_i = A_i e^{\gamma_i t} \quad (i = 1, ..., 26, \text{ as } G_{53+i});$$

$$\omega_i \qquad\qquad (i = 1, ..., 26, \text{ as } G_{79+i});$$

$$m_i = M_i/X_i \quad (i = 1, 2, \text{ and } 5, ..., 26, \text{ as } G_{106}, ..., G_{129});$$

$$\pi_i^m \qquad\qquad (i = 3, 4, \text{ as } G_{130}, \text{ and } G_{131});$$

$$\left(\frac{M_i}{X_i}\right)_{-1} \qquad (i = 3, 4, \text{ as } G_{132} \text{ and } G_{133});$$

$$\pi_i^z, \qquad\qquad (i = 6, 11, \text{ as } G_{134} \text{ and } G_{135});$$

$$\left(\frac{R}{M}\right)_{-1}, \ \left(\frac{C}{L}\right)_{-1}, \text{ and } \bar{L} \text{ (as } G_{136}, G_{137} \text{ and } G_{138}).$$

---

[1] Hicks, *op. cit.* Chapters V and VIII.

[2] In the public administration sector (sector 27 of our input–output table), output equals the sum of wage payments to public officers and a small amount of property income. Therefore we treat this sector as exogenous and do not define the excess supply function for it. Our assumption is that an increase in the final demand for this sector raises wage payments by the same amount, and raises employment at the same rate as the wage payments increase. Since the increase in wage payments affects the demand for products of other sectors through the consumption functions, the partial derivative of the excess supply of the ith sector with respect to the final demand for sector 27 is computed as

$$\partial E_i/\partial F_{27} = -\partial C_i/\partial(Y/p^c).$$

In this chapter the 'homogeneous system' will be considered, treating π_i^m and π_i^z as predetermined.

Given all the predetermined variables, the equilibrium conditions,

$$E_i = f_i(\pi_1, ..., \pi_{26}; G_1, ..., G_{138}) = 0 \quad (i = 1, ..., 26), \qquad (4.2)$$

will determine a set of equilibrium relative prices. Hence, differentiating each equation with respect to all the predetermined variables, we get

$$\Phi_P \Gamma_P + \Phi_G = 0, \qquad (4.3)$$
where

$$\Phi_P = \left[\frac{\partial E_i^0}{\partial \pi_j}\right], \quad \text{(a } 26 \times 26 \text{ matrix)},$$

$$\Gamma_P = \left[\frac{\partial \pi_j}{\partial G_k}\right], \quad \text{(a } 26 \times 138 \text{ matrix)},$$

$$\Phi_G = \left[\frac{\partial E_i^0}{\partial G_k}\right], \quad \text{(a } 26 \times 138 \text{ matrix)};$$

and the partial derivatives with superscript 0 are evaluated at the equilibrium point. Solving (4.3), we obtain:

$$\Gamma_P = -\Phi_P^{-1}\Phi_G, \qquad (4.4)$$

which gives the effects of changes in predetermined variables on the equilibrium relative prices of goods.

Table 7 presents the calculated Φ_P, which was obtained by substituting the estimated values of the parameters of the equations and the actual 1960 values of the variables into the algebraic formulas of the partial derivatives.[1] Table 8 gives the inverse of Φ_P. It is noted that, since all the relative prices, π_i, are unity in 1960, Γ_P gives the rates as well as the absolute magnitudes of price changes.

It is clear from equation (2.18) that

$$\frac{\partial E_i}{\partial F_j} = \begin{cases} 0, \text{ if } i \neq j \\ -1, \text{ if } i = j \end{cases} \quad (i,j = 1, ..., 26); \qquad (4.5)$$

so that the (i,j) element of Φ_P^{-1} represents the change in the ith relative price induced by a unit increase in the jth final demand. For example, if the final demand for the machinery sector (sector 17) increases by 100 units or 100 billion yen (which amounts to 3.8 per cent of total government expenditure or 2.1 per cent of total capital formation in 1960), the relative price of

[1] Since our model is based on input coefficients calculated from the 1960 input–output table, the 1960 values of the variables satisfy the equilibrium conditions (4.2) with small errors, though not exactly.

TABLE 7. *The Jacobian matrix of the excess supply functions,^{a} Φ_P (unit: billion yen)*

Industry	1 Agriculture	2 Forestry	3 Petroleum & coal	4 Metal, non-metal mining	5 Food	6 Textiles	7 Lumber & furniture	8 Pulp & paper	9 Printing & publishing
1	20918	45	35	73	−21260	−677	47	204	20
2	6	4623	−129	−7	−55	32	−7706	−153	23
3	42	−131	6961	1	−56	−73	−32	−57	−25
4	71	−7	0	2752	−104	10	52	3	1
5	−26508	97	−103	−119	42514	−213	−501	−404	−157
6	−744	92	−88	14	−157	12060	−214	−39	−93
7	99	−7814	−33	53	−195	−130	16035	−125	−17
8	196	−163	−59	2	−374	−47	−127	2301	−917
9	19	40	−28	2	−59	−88	−39	−926	2524
10	6	−47	−12	0	−973	−382	−6	−8	−1
11	−6	12	−8	1	−4	−256	−7	6	−1
12	−45	261	−142	−153	−1227	−2110	−515	−302	−105
13	39	19	−1469	62	−237	−32	−21	−6	9
14	294	27	−104	−170	−502	42	249	−59	−2
15	52	212	−61	−653	−10	96	−87	53	−11
16	173	194	−14	35	−265	−9	−121	10	−6
17	−66	33	−60	9	−22	−118	−7	−24	−71
18	−16	43	−11	21	−10	−23	47	−27	−21
19	−26	23	−19	8	−8	−2	−118	−8	−5
20	−42	29	−4	−7	−96	−4	−185	−103	−13
21	21	−157	−14	−444	−143	−292	−3105	−94	−35
22	109	124	−494	0	−263	−219	121	−131	1
23	986	467	−39	55	−1864	−734	−759	−143	−239
24	355	293	−74	35	−949	−211	−376	16	−152
25	−275	354	−159	28	−1710	−658	−675	95	−610
26	440	139	−31	−98	−1957	−2140	−166	−276	−105
27 Complementary (total: 180)	16	19	2	17	0	4	4	7	5
28 Substitutive (total: 470)	9	6	23	8	25	21	21	18	20
30 Correlation	0.9997	0.9993	0.9935	0.9969	0.9985	0.9861	0.9980	0.9969	0.9875

^{a} See Table 1 for the classification of industries.

TABLE 7 (cont.)

Industry	10 Leather	11 Rubber	12 Chemicals	13 Petroleum products	14 Stone, clay & glass	15 Primary metals	16 Fabricated metals	17 Machinery	18 Electrical Machinery
1	0	0	-25	48	293	84	165	-80	-18
2	-47	9	252	25	28	216	190	17	22
3	-12	-7	-126	-1036	-101	-60	-14	-58	-7
4	0	1	-135	61	-164	-559	35	7	20
5	-968	9	-1309	-201	-603	187	-360	-141	-61
6	-390	-250	-2087	0	43	145	-21	-145	-31
7	-6	-2	-481	-11	248	-85	-123	13	76
8	-8	5	-272	-5	-57	54	9	-21	-26
9	-5	0	-83	20	-4	12	-109	-76	-24
10	2534	-12	-78	-16	-0	139	5	-26	-4
11	-12	1438	-126	-15	-30	85	-7	64	-33
12	-77	-127	5359	-185	-56	-306	15	-37	-111
13	-17	-16	-172	2887		103	191	-22	-16
14	-3	0	-30	-59	2464			32	16
15	12	136	60	-368	92	6886	-1387	-1761	-1084
16	-105	6	1	21	190	-1416	4094	-72	58
17	-31	61	-21	-16	27	-1946	-86	6823	-319
18	-8	-35	-96	-5	11	-1128	53	-317	4877
19	-7	-742	-93	17	-42	-1113	-114	-1622	-440
20	-129	-5	-678	-11	27	-38	21	-689	-123
21	-23	-26	-196	-415	-2369	-2062	-2142		-1347
22	-17	-7	-117	27	-92	-126	-13	-48	-145
23	-153	-20	162	-122	53	227	-9	-146	-125
24	-43	11	63	-300	-14	199	50	-143	-56
25	-94	-2	66	163	28	443	-20	-439	-217
26	-41	-189	-748	-508	-148	-568	-365	-548	-785
27 Complementary	3	11	6	8	11	13	10	5	5
28 Substitutive	22	14	19	17	14	12	15	20	20
30 Correlation	0.9976	0.9989	0.9930	0.9739	0.9991	0.9941	0.9991	0.9926	0.9967

TABLE 7 (cont.)

Industry	19 Transportation equipment	20 Miscellaneous manufacturing	21 Construction	22 Utilities	23 Trade	24 Transportation & communication	25 Services	26 Unallocated
1	−54	−30	−100	140	992	457	230	442
2	8	18	−172	115	368	243	94	140
3	−17	−1	−17	−459	−21	−63	−91	−28
4	7	−7	−445	−2	47	30	8	−93
5	−134	−126	−642	−283	−2903	−1016	−1321	−3122
6	−51	2	−493	−193	−820	−152	−325	−1913
7	−105	−164	−3124	−102	−645	−301	−245	−173
8	−7	−100	−90	−140	−164	5	33	−237
9	−20	−12	−89	11	−229	−143	−485	−104
10	−5	−129	−28	−14	−140	−30	−25	−38
11	−707	−6	−37	−7	−32	10	−6	−162
12	−103	−661	−237	−156	−16	5	−167	−771
13	12	−19	−427	23	−179	−364	14	496
14	−37	27	−2359	−95	43	−19	5	−126
15	−1061	−42	−2058	−166	109	127	159	−498
16	−107	24	−2148	−9	−2	61	31	−335
17	−1552	−36	−735	−39	−124	−127	−250	−532
18	−433	−127	−1410	−122	−140	−41	−116	−730
19	8014	−48	−423	−85	−424	−540	−155	−715
20	−56	2501	−279	−12	−114	−1	−84	−477
21	−387	−239	22563	−92	−1355	−1073	−792	−763
22	−96	−17	−142	1551	−67	−75	−178	−46
23	−480	−91	−1641	−18	10702	−412	−1189	−314
24	−572	−4	−1255	−49	−547	5685	−372	−1679
25	−407	−115	−1712	−141	−2133	−378	11450	−2358
26	−767	−536	−763	−63	−167	−1949	−2084	15901
27 Complementary	3	4	0	4	5	8	8	2
28 Substitutive	22	21	25	21	20	17	17	23
30 Correlation	0.9889	0.9933	0.9724	0.9818	0.9443	0.9863	0.9363	0.9551

TABLE 8. *The relative price change induced by a unit change in final demand,*[a] $\Phi_P^{-1} \times 10^6$

Industry	1	2	3	4	5	6	7	8	9	10	11	12	13
1	158	53	16	16	89	36	42	44	39	52	31	57	33
2	53	1494	60	39	50	51	767	229	113	80	49	82	70
3	15	60	170	12	14	17	39	36	26	17	18	29	77
4	14	38	12	391	15	16	29	28	23	17	18	33	21
5	112	64	20	20	91	37	50	56	47	55	34	61	39
6	38	54	19	18	30	116	43	51	44	43	48	75	34
7	38	773	39	30	36	39	467	139	76	53	38	64	52
8	48	243	40	31	47	52	150	605	255	54	48	99	57
9	39	118	28	25	37	43	83	254	522	42	41	71	43
10	60	85	20	19	50	44	59	54	43	436	36	59	37
11	31	50	20	19	26	47	41	46	40	35	765	66	40
12	68	102	37	41	57	82	83	113	85	64	74	278	70
13	41	94	107	27	37	40	70	68	55	43	47	51	430
14	30	78	34	62	32	30	59	70	51	34	37	56	61
15	32	72	36	82	31	35	64	59	52	39	42	46	81
16	28	68	26	46	28	30	60	50	44	42	36	48	55
17	30	67	26	42	27	32	55	55	50	34	45	48	54
18	33	76	28	42	30	35	61	62	53	36	51	57	57
19	28	67	23	34	26	31	53	51	44	32	104	48	47
20	49	128	29	33	42	49	92	100	71	66	52	116	55
21	28	164	26	41	26	29	108	63	47	33	35	46	52
22	49	58	80	41	46	58	61	117	81	53	60	88	72
23	24	48	16	14	24	27	42	47	45	30	28	32	32
24	39	63	30	25	38	39	57	62	63	41	46	53	68
25	46	72	22	22	39	38	59	60	70	40	39	50	37
26	41	67	26	30	37	46	55	67	57	40	52	65	57
A[b]	4	1	3	0	15	11	1	2	1	0	0	2	0
B[c]	21	24	22	25	10	14	24	23	24	25	25	23	25
C[d]	0.257	0.074	0.193	0.083	0.401	0.339	0.196	0.131	0.121	0.099	0.058	0.219	0.121

[a] See Table 1 for the classification of industries.
[b] The number of elements whose values are over $\frac{1}{3}$ of the diagonal element

[c] The number of elements whose values are under $\frac{1}{3}$ of the diagonal element.
[d] The average of the ratios of the values of the off-diagonal elements to the value of the diagonal.

TABLE 8 (cont.)

Industry	14	15	16	17	18	19	20	21	22	23	24	25	26
1	34	33	33	34	36	32	46	34	39	31	35	27	40
2	82	70	74	68	77	69	119	170	42	56	58	50	61
3	32	30	24	24	25	22	25	26	71	17	26	15	21
4	61	72	43	37	38	30	29	40	35	15	23	14	25
5	45	39	41	38	41	37	51	41	49	39	45	32	46
6	34	36	35	35	38	35	48	36	53	33	39	27	44
7	59	60	62	52	59	53	83	112	45	45	50	38	47
8	77	60	58	59	67	56	97	73	113	57	63	47	65
9	56	53	51	53	56	49	67	56	71	52	62	52	54
10	39	40	49	37	40	35	66	40	48	36	40	27	40
11	40	42	40	45	52	102	49	39	53	32	44	27	47
12	66	65	61	59	69	60	122	63	97	49	63	45	71
13	73	85	66	61	66	55	62	65	82	45	79	35	62
14	501	69	55	51	63	49	47	95	86	36	55	31	47
15	75	277	146	123	120	96	63	88	93	40	60	34	62
16	56	143	341	79	77	66	49	84	66	35	49	29	51
17	56	129	85	223	84	89	53	63	68	36	54	33	52
18	67	121	82	82	282	74	66	73	83	40	56	35	59
19	52	97	70	90	75	188	50	55	64	37	58	30	50
20	55	67	58	57	71	56	476	63	72	45	56	40	65
21	94	82	82	58	68	51	52	108	56	37	51	30	44
22	98	96	78	76	94	73	75	71	743	53	73	50	64
23	35	34	35	33	36	35	36	38	37	119	39	30	32
24	61	60	56	57	60	62	54	60	65	48	234	41	65
25	49	48	49	50	53	48	53	52	58	51	54	120	54
26	55	66	60	57	65	56	66	53	62	39	70	42	112
A^b	0	5	1	5	1	7	0	22	0	12	1	7	22
B^c	25	20	24	20	24	18	25	3	25	13	24	18	3
C^d	0.116	0.245	0.175	0.253	0.217	0.295	0.128	0.591	0.087	0.337	0.223	0.288	0.454

machinery will be raised by 0.0223 (or 2.23 per cent), that of primary metals (sector 15) by 0.0123, that of trade (sector 23) by 0.0033 and so on.

Let us now derive some salient implications of the calculated Φ_P^{-1}. First, the matrix Φ_P^{-1} shows that in most industries the diagonal elements are significantly larger than the off-diagonal elements of the corresponding columns; in other words, a change in the final demand for a good influences its own price, much more than the other prices. A general idea of this fact may be given by the figures in rows A, B and C of Table 8; row A shows the number of off-diagonal elements which are greater in magnitude than one third of the corresponding diagonal elements, while row B shows the number of other off-diagonal elements; row C presents an average of the ratios of off-diagonals to diagonals for each column. In the case of machinery, as shown in column (17), the induced price change is more than one third of the price change of machinery in the following five industries: primary metals, fabricated metals, electrical machinery, transportation equipment and utilities. These industries are closely related to machinery; an increase in the demand for machinery gives rise to an increase in the demand for its materials and fuels, such as primary metals, fabricated metals, gas and electricity, and thereby induces a rise in their prices. This, in turn, will lead to price rises in transportation equipment and electrical machinery, which consume much of the primary and fabricated metals. On the other hand, the prices of the products of other industries do not increase as much as the prices of these products, and the average of the ratios of the cross effects to the diagonal effect is 0.253. Only two industries, lumber and construction, have off-diagonal elements which exceed the corresponding diagonal elements. These industries require as inputs much of the output of forestry, whose elasticity of supply is relatively small. Therefore it is not surprising to find that the price of the product of forestry increases at a higher rate than the prices of the products of the lumber and construction industries.

It is seen from Table 8 that food, textiles, construction, trade and 'unallocated' are the industries which have large repercussion effects on other prices, in comparison with the direct effects on their own prices. They have the figures in the range (0.337–0.591) in row C. It is noted that final demand has a large share in total demand in these industries, except 'unallocated'. In agriculture, chemicals, primary metals, machinery, electrical machinery, transportation equipment, transportation and services the corresponding figures are between 0.217 and 0.295. In all other industries, most of which are extractive industries or material-producing industries, they are lower than 0.196, with the industries in which the cross effects are greater than one third of the corresponding diagonal effects being no more than three in number.

Second, it is pointed out that the matrix Φ_P^{-1} is a positive matrix although Φ_P is not a strict gross-substitute matrix; in other words, an increase in the final demand for any good will lead, more or less, to some increase in the prices of all goods in terms of labour.

Hicks showed that if all goods in the system are gross substitutes for each other, or if all the principal minors of the Jacobian matrix Φ_P are positive and all its off-diagonal elements are negative, then an increase in demand for any good induces changes in prices in such a way that the prices of all the other goods would rise proportionately less than its own price.[1] Rows 27 and 28 of Table 7 present the numbers of negative and positive off-diagonal elements in each column of Φ_P, respectively. Clearly the off-diagonal elements of Φ_P are very largely negative; 470 out of the 650 off-diagonal elements (72.3 per cent) are negative. Therefore, the properties of Φ_P^{-1} mentioned above may be attributed to the fact that gross sub-stitutability is nearly realized in the estimated Jacobian, Φ_P.

Third, the estimated Jacobian and its inverse are found to be approximately symmetric matrices. Although this fact is easily discovered by a glance at Φ_P, it may also be revealed by the high correlations between corresponding columns and rows shown in row 30 of Table 7. The approximate symmetry of Φ_P may be due to the fact that the Jacobian matrix of the excess supply functions is highly symmetrical when consumption demand for each good is taken as constant. This conditional Jacobian is given in Table 9, which may be compared with Table 7.[2]

Now let us turn to the effects on employment. Employment, as shown in equation (2.4), is a function of relative prices. Therefore the change in employment in the ith sector induced by a change in a certain predetermined variable may be calculated according to the following formula:

$$\Gamma_L = \Lambda_P \Gamma_P + \Lambda_G, \tag{4.6}$$

or by the use of equation (4.4),

$$\Gamma_L = -\Lambda_P \Phi_P^{-1} \Phi_G + \Lambda_G, \tag{4.7}$$

---

[1] The Jacobian matrix Φ_P must have positive elements on the diagonal, except for the Giffen case. If an off-diagonal element of the matrix is negative, the two goods concerned are 'gross substitutes', and if it is positive they are 'gross complements'. See M. Morishima, *Equilibrium, Stability and Growth* (1964), pp. 3–11.

[2] It is also found that the computed Φ_P is positive quasi-definite, indicating that both the Hicksian and Samuelsonian stability conditions are satisfied by our general equilibrium system. See P. A. Samuelson, *Foundations of Economic Analysis* (1948), pp. 140–141. The conditional Jacobian (or the Jacobian of the production sector) is a matrix with

$$\partial\left(X_i - \sum_{k=1}^{26} X_{ik}\right) \Big/ \partial\pi_j \quad (i, j = 1, \ldots, 26),$$

as the (i, j) element. It can be seen from equations (2.4) that this matrix is exactly symmetrical if the indirect tax rate t_i is the same for all sectors.

TABLE 9. *The conditional Jacobian matrix of the excess supply functions[a] (unit: billion yen)*

Industry	1 Agriculture	2 Forestry	3 Petroleum & coal	4 Metal, non-metal mining	5 Food	6 Textiles	7 Lumber & furniture	8 Pulp & paper	9 Printing & publishing
1	20818	14	44	71	-21305	-594	102	198	36
2	18	4611	-129	-7	-46	42	-7699	-154	25
3	44	-133	6961	1	-53	-72	-31	-57	-25
4	71	-7	-68	2752	-107	11	53	3	1
5	-26431	-62	-72	-135	41614	43	-240	-462	-64
6	-590	42	-31	11	50	11776	-121	-47	-70
7	105	-7822	-60	53	-190	-122	16047	-126	-17
8	198	-162	-24	2	-367	-47	-129	2301	-917
9	36	25	-12	0	-51	-69	-16	-927	2525
10	10	-48			-968	-389	-4	-8	-1
11	3	9	-7	1	7	-272	-2	5	0
12	-17	248	-139	-154	-1136	-2084	492	-310	-94
13	45	11	-1469	62	-228	-26	-17	-7	10
14	292	28	-104	-170	-503	40	248	-59	-2
15	51	212	-61	-653	-10	95	-88	53	-11
16	175	191	-14	35	-263	-6	-116	9	-6
17	-49	21	-56	8	-11	-100	12	-25	-70
18	1	25	-6	20	0	-1	76	-29	-19
19	-14	14	-17	-8	-4	10	-104	-9	-5
20	-21	18	-1	7	-73	5	-167	-104	-10
21	21	-157	-14	-444	-143	-292	-3105	-94	-35
22	142	90	-495	-0	-219	-192	-103	-132	5
23	1096	377	-18	48	-1894	-786	-619	-163	-201
24	485	247	-59	32	-801	-98	-292	10	-132
25	359	114	-86	11	-581	-116	-231	10	-473
26	441	139	-31	-99	-1956	-2139	-166	-276	-105

[a] See Table 1 for the classification of industries.

TABLE 9 (cont.)

Industry	10 Leather	11 Rubber	12 Chemicals	13 Petroleum products	14 Stone, clay & glass	15 Primary metals	16 Fabricated metals	17 Machinery	18 Electrical machinery
1	10	2	-43	32	290	51	172	-51	-1
2	-46	9	250	17	28	213	191	20	24
3	-11	-7	-126	-1038	-101	-61	-14	-58	-6
4	0	1	-135	61	-164	-559	35	7	20
5	-935	6	-1410	-292	-629	-18	-340	-17	-4
6	-382	-271	-2116	-27	40	96	-7	-96	1
7	-4	-3	-487	-15	247	-92	-121	18	78
8	-8	5	-273	-5	-57	55	9	-22	-26
9	-1	0	-93	12	-2	-7	-5	-65	-18
10	2534	-12	-79	-17	-4	11	-109	-25	-3
11	-12	1437	-128	-16	0	137	6	67	-31
12	-75	-127	5302	-193	-33	65	-6	-29	-106
13	-16	-16	-173	2883	-56	-308	16	-20	-15
14	-3	-0	-30	-59	2464	104	190	32	16
15	11	136	61	-368	92	6886	-1387	-1762	-1085
16	-105	6	-1	19	190	-1419	4094	-70	59
17	-27	61	-32	-23	27	-1956	-83	6831	-314
18	-3	-35	-109	-15	10	-1144	56	-304	4883
19	-4	-742	-99	12	-42	-1120	-112	-1616	-436
20	-125	-5	-684	-17	27	-47	24	-29	-117
21	-23	-26	-196	-415	-2369	-2062	-2142	-689	-1347
22	-13	-6	-123	7	-92	-134	-10	-39	-138
23	-135	-30	100	-172	45	137	7	-78	-86
24	-27	13	37	-324	-16	156	63	-98	-26
25	-19	5	-301	32	3	172	36	-223	-76
26	-41	-189	-748	-508	-148	-568	-365	-547	-784

TABLE 9 (cont.)

Industry	19 Transportation equipment	20 Miscellaneous manufacturing	21 Construction	22 Utilities	23 Trade	24 Transportation & communication	25 Services	26 Unallocated
1	−18	−22	15	140	1084	476	350	495
2	13	19	−156	90	376	246	114	138
3	−17	−1	−15	−463	−20	−62	−88	−28
4	7	−7	−444	−2	48	31	10	−93
5	−8	−101	−182	−278	−2383	−1016	−742	−2280
6	13	5	−292	−195	−795	−104	−119	−1887
7	−98	−163	−3098	−105	−626	−299	−233	−162
8	−8	−100	−94	−139	−161	5	10	−233
9	−4	−10	−35	6	−196	−135	−457	−107
10	−4	−129	−24	−14	−140	−28	−20	−39
11	−704	−6	−26	−7	−31	13	5	−162
12	−93	−658	−200	−155	66	9	−319	−675
13	15	−18	−418	7	−175	−362	25	−498
14	−38	27	−2364	−95	41	−20	2	−121
15	−1062	−42	−2060	−166	107	127	158	−497
16	−104	25	−2138	−10	7	61	36	−327
17	−1538	−34	−690	−43	−95	−120	−237	−536
18	−415	−125	−1345	−129	−96	−34	−83	−719
19	8024	−47	−388	−88	−404	−534	−137	−721
20	−44	2502	−238	−14	−84	7	−96	−476
21	−387	−239	22563	−92	−1355	−1073	−792	−763
22	−83	−13	−103	1477	−46	−67	−127	−52
23	−396	−80	−1358	−47	10887	−374	−945	−107
24	−511	10	−1069	−55	−350	5175	−152	−1684
25	−127	−96	−810	−133	−922	−171	9277	−1824
26	−766	−536	−762	−63	−166	−1949	2087	15900

where

$$\Lambda_P = \left[\frac{\partial L_i^0}{\partial \pi_j}\right], \quad \text{(a 26} \times \text{26 matrix)},$$

$$\Gamma_L = \left[\frac{\delta L_i}{\delta G_k}\right], \quad \text{(a 26} \times \text{138 matrix)},$$

$$\Lambda_G = \left[\frac{\partial L_i^0}{\partial G_k}\right], \quad \text{(a 26} \times \text{138 matrix)}.$$

The superscript o attached to a partial derivative indicates that it is evaluated at the equilibrium point. Table 10 shows the calculated matrix, $\Lambda_P \Phi_P^{-1}$, with elements of Λ_P and Φ_P which are evaluated at actual 1960 values. Since that part of $-\Phi_G$ or Λ_G whose elements are partial derivatives of $-E_i$ or L_i with respect to the final demand for commodities is either an identity matrix (in the case of $-\Phi_G$) or a null matrix (in the case of Λ_G), the (i,j) element of $\Lambda_P \Phi_P^{-1}$ represents the effect of a unit increase in final demand for sector j on employment in sector i. Row 'Total' of Table 10 gives the column sums, so that the jth figure of it gives the total effect on employment of a unit increase in the final demand for sector j. For example, if the final demand for the machinery sector (sector 17) increases by 100 units or 100 billion yen, total industrial employment will increase by 0.908 billion hours per year, which implies an increase of 0.0083 in the employment ratio L/Lf.

Further, substituting this increase into equation (3.13), we find that the money wage is increased at a rate of 0.56 per cent per year. Therefore, returning to column (17) of Table 8, we can see that the increase in final demand for the machinery sector will raise the money price of machinery at the rate of 2.80 per cent per year, and so on.[1]

Now the value added of industry i is defined as:

$$w_i L_i + P_i + T_i,$$

where T_i is indirect taxes less subsidies of industry i. It is then evident that the value added of industry i deflated by its price, V_i, is reduced to a function of relative prices.[2] Therefore the effects of a change in the predetermined variables on the values added of the individual sectors in the economy are given by

$$\Gamma_V = \Upsilon_P \Gamma_P + \Upsilon_G, \tag{4.8}$$

or, in view of equation (4.4),

$$\Gamma_V = -\Upsilon_P \Phi_P^{-1} \Phi_G + \Upsilon_G, \tag{4.9}$$

---

[1] $2.80 = 100 \times (1.0223 \times 1.0056 - 1.0)$.

[2] It is noted that this definition of value added at constant prices is different from that in Chapter 3. The deflator here is the price of each industry, while there it is an implicit deflator.

TABLE 10. *The change in hours worked induced by a unit change in final demand,[a]* $\Lambda_P \Phi_P^{-1}$ *(unit: million hours per year/billion yen)*

Industry	1 Agriculture	2 Forestry	3 Petroleum & coal	4 Metal, non-metal mining	5 Food	6 Textiles	7 Lumber & furniture	8 Pulp & paper	9 Printing & publishing
1	15.677	2.850	0.916	0.933	8.366	2.554	2.481	2.664	2.638
2	0.109	3.169	0.121	0.079	0.103	0.103	1.622	0.478	0.231
3	0.089	0.123	1.891	0.065	0.085	0.099	0.115	0.190	0.127
4	0.038	0.079	0.025	1.794	0.041	0.042	0.070	0.067	0.054
5	0.403	0.316	0.101	0.101	1.261	0.216	0.272	0.269	0.286
6	0.516	0.602	0.201	0.205	0.405	4.271	0.531	0.515	0.507
7	0.129	0.571	0.089	0.101	0.128	0.133	3.509	0.339	0.216
8	0.078	0.108	0.040	0.040	0.086	0.093	0.103	2.073	0.733
9	0.089	0.141	0.054	0.049	0.081	0.093	0.125	0.288	2.646
10	0.014	0.018	0.005	0.006	0.012	0.044	0.015	0.013	0.014
11	0.027	0.042	0.014	0.017	0.023	0.031	0.037	0.032	0.032
12	0.163	0.134	0.051	0.057	0.138	0.249	0.142	0.159	0.159
13	0.010	0.014	0.006	0.006	0.010	0.010	0.013	0.013	0.011
14	0.061	0.159	0.039	0.056	0.082	0.053	0.122	0.092	0.076
15	0.068	0.159	0.058	0.073	0.066	0.073	0.157	0.109	0.102
16	0.090	0.223	0.061	0.083	0.100	0.096	0.234	0.139	0.116
17	0.122	0.233	0.097	0.127	0.107	0.126	0.195	0.189	0.185
18	0.090	0.190	0.068	0.093	0.081	0.092	0.158	0.144	0.131
19	0.086	0.168	0.057	0.073	0.078	0.082	0.141	0.126	0.118
20	0.084	0.142	0.040	0.046	0.076	0.074	0.125	0.106	0.099
21	0.256	1.124	0.207	0.324	0.240	0.253	0.773	0.486	0.384
22	0.045	0.029	0.049	0.036	0.042	0.055	0.044	0.113	0.073
23	0.943	1.422	0.486	0.522	1.047	1.118	1.495	1.451	1.460
24	0.452	0.618	0.226	0.260	0.437	0.432	0.612	0.648	0.690
25	1.720	2.073	0.665	0.675	1.442	1.307	1.835	1.626	1.852
26	0.0	0.0	0.0	0.0	0.0	0.0	0.0	0.0	0.0
27	0.0	0.0	0.0	0.0	0.0	0.0	0.0	0.0	0.0
Total	21.357 / 5.571[b]	14.704 / 8.685[b]	5.568 / 4.531[b]	5.819 / 4.808[b]	14.534 / 6.065[b]	11.701 / 9.044[b]	14.926 / 10.823[b]	12.329 / 9.188[b]	12.941 / 10.072[b]

[a] See Table 1 for the classification of industries.   [b] Total excluding agriculture and forestry.

TABLE 10 (cont.)

Industry	10 Leather	11 Rubber	12 Chemicals	13 Petroleum products	14 Stone, clay & glass	15 Primary metals	16 Fabricated metals	17 Machinery	18 Electrical machinery
1	4.373	1.957	3.077	1.553	2.111	1.992	2.161	2.220	2.334
2	0.165	0.096	0.164	0.130	0.165	0.137	0.145	0.134	0.153
3	0.102	0.114	0.177	0.762	0.233	0.174	0.134	0.126	0.138
4	0.046	0.049	0.101	0.043	0.235	0.279	0.149	0.123	0.124
5	0.594	0.197	0.280	0.170	0.233	0.216	0.237	0.237	0.250
6	0.738	0.958	0.537	0.322	0.436	0.432	0.460	0.478	0.520
7	0.154	0.132	0.215	0.143	0.225	0.204	0.218	0.201	0.234
8	0.093	0.082	0.196	0.063	0.147	0.086	0.087	0.096	0.114
9	0.090	0.086	0.111	0.072	0.116	0.112	0.115	0.125	0.122
10	2.837	0.014	0.013	0.009	0.012	0.013	0.013	0.024	0.016
11	0.034	1.887	0.033	0.025	0.033	0.043	0.043	0.057	0.068
12	0.168	0.212	1.035	0.086	0.118	0.111	0.113	0.116	0.144
13	0.011	0.012	0.017	0.159	0.019	0.023	0.017	0.015	0.017
14	0.074	0.082	0.090	0.071	2.572	0.146	0.127	0.116	0.162
15	0.092	0.093	0.106	0.095	0.149	1.078	0.520	0.419	0.393
16	0.221	0.095	0.131	0.110	0.152	0.186	3.096	0.197	0.183
17	0.125	0.170	0.165	0.161	0.192	0.350	0.261	2.154	0.324
18	0.097	0.118	0.134	0.118	0.165	0.235	0.187	0.222	2.009
19	0.088	0.184	0.114	0.102	0.135	0.193	0.154	0.188	0.171
20	0.192	0.107	0.109	0.072	0.089	0.098	0.095	0.115	0.183
21	0.300	0.284	0.378	0.387	0.696	0.607	0.613	0.450	0.522
22	0.049	0.054	0.083	0.042	0.088	0.083	0.066	0.065	0.073
23	1.335	1.146	1.190	0.810	1.392	1.285	1.340	1.306	1.459
24	0.464	0.440	0.556	0.398	0.679	0.588	0.585	0.596	0.631
25	1.429	1.286	1.431	1.034	1.566	1.495	1.590	1.652	1.762
26	0.0	0.0	0.0	0.0	0.0	0.0	0.0	0.0	0.0
27	0.0	0.0	0.0	0.0	0.0	0.0	0.0	0.0	0.0
Total	13.871 9.333[b]	9.857 7.805[b]	10.443 7.203[b]	6.935 5.252[b]	11.957 9.681[b]	10.165 8.037[b]	12.527 10.221[b]	11.433 9.079[b]	12.106 9.620[b]

TABLE 10 (*cont.*)

Industry	19 Transportation equipment	20 Miscellaneous manufacturing	21 Construction	22 Utilities	23 Trade	24 Transportation & communication	25 Services	26 Unallocated	27 Government
1	2.124	2.988	2.242	2.277	2.087	2.227	1.912	2.918	1.242
2	0.137	0.243	0.353	0.078	0.113	0.113	0.100	0.121	0.044
3	0.119	0.135	0.137	0.401	0.090	0.156	0.076	0.124	0.032
4	0.098	0.085	0.137	0.058	0.036	0.049	0.034	0.068	0.014
5	0.229	0.277	0.243	0.256	0.239	0.248	0.362	0.304	0.139
6	0.508	0.500	0.505	0.466	0.372	0.476	0.135	0.796	0.216
7	0.213	0.341	0.628	0.170	0.165	0.161	0.080	0.167	0.057
8	0.090	0.206	0.103	0.078	0.099	0.080	0.160	0.120	0.031
9	0.110	0.121	0.119	0.099	0.133	0.117	0.160	0.106	0.053
10	0.016	0.037	0.014	0.012	0.009	0.012	0.010	0.018	0.006
11	0.203	0.033	0.041	0.035	0.026	0.045	0.025	0.055	0.012
12	0.128	0.372	0.122	0.104	0.086	0.100	0.084	0.163	0.043
13	0.014	0.015	0.017	0.012	0.011	0.020	0.008	0.015	0.003
14	0.116	0.090	0.353	0.101	0.059	0.079	0.060	0.103	0.021
15	0.312	0.159	0.264	0.131	0.078	0.111	0.070	0.151	0.029
16	0.188	0.142	0.421	0.132	0.106	0.121	0.088	0.159	0.036
17	0.566	0.180	0.261	0.213	0.135	0.197	0.128	0.205	0.055
18	0.252	0.146	0.259	0.240	0.102	0.141	0.092	0.180	0.046
19	1.830	0.122	0.162	0.136	0.118	0.243	0.082	0.160	0.039
20	0.118	2.907	0.128	0.090	0.074	0.088	0.068	0.152	0.038
21	0.408	0.418	2.970	0.522	0.333	0.416	0.322	0.355	0.101
22	0.064	0.068	0.058	0.852	0.045	0.055	0.046	0.054	0.019
23	1.362	1.422	1.568	1.040	7.127	1.193	0.994	1.237	0.544
24	0.574	0.584	0.678	0.555	0.537	3.376	0.447	0.725	0.208
25	1.632	1.664	1.702	1.518	1.868	1.661	5.228	1.909	0.887
26	0.0	0.0	0.0	0.0	0.0	0.0	0.0	0.0	0.0
27	0.0	0.0	0.0	0.0	0.0	0.0	0.0	0.0	3.427
Total	11.412 9.150[b]	13.253 10.021[b]	13.484 10.890[b]	9.574 7.220[b]	14.051 11.852[b]	11.483 9.143[b]	10.824 8.812[b]	10.365 7.327[b]	7.342 6.056[b]

TABLE 11. *Changes in GNP, NNP and NI induced by a unit change in the final demand for the individual sector*

Industry	(1) GNP	(2) NNP	(3) NI
1. Agriculture	1.246	1.097	1.033
2. Forestry	0.904	0.812	0.758
3. Coal & petroleum mining	0.519	0.449	0.424
4. Metal & nonmetal mining	0.522	0.456	0.419
5. Food	1.157	1.034	0.836
6. Textiles	0.984	0.866	0.802
7. Lumber & furniture	1.098	0.985	0.915
8. Pulp & paper	1.039	0.892	0.822
9. Printing & publishing	1.207	1.076	1.000
10. Leather	1.161	1.039	0.923
11. Rubber	0.950	0.846	0.785
12. Chemicals	0.952	0.803	0.729
13. Petroleum products	0.701	0.628	0.458
14. Stone, clay & glass	1.144	1.003	0.921
15. Primary metals	0.986	0.850	0.777
16. Fabricated metals	1.203	1.078	0.996
17. Machinery	1.205	1.069	0.982
18. Electrical machinery	1.272	1.132	1.025
19. Transportation equipment	1.245	1.101	1.001
20. Other manufacturing	1.178	1.047	0.951
21. Construction	1.293	1.158	1.078
22. Utilities	0.949	0.741	0.602
23. Trade	1.293	1.155	1.067
24. Transportation & communication	1.176	0.973	0.895
25. Services	1.077	0.944	0.866
26. Unallocated	1.040	0.927	0.773
27. Public administration	1.297	1.143	1.110

where

$$\Upsilon_P = \left[\frac{\partial V_i^0}{\partial \pi_j}\right], \quad \text{(a 26} \times \text{26 matrix),}$$

$$\Gamma_V = \left[\frac{\delta V_i}{\delta G_k}\right], \quad \text{(a 26} \times \text{138 matrix),}$$

$$\Upsilon_G = \left[\frac{\partial V_i^0}{\partial G_k}\right], \quad \text{(a 26} \times \text{138 matrix).}$$

The superscript o, as before, denotes evaluation at the equilibrium point. The jth column sum of $\Upsilon_P \Phi_P^{-1}$ represents the change in GNP induced by a unit change in the final demand for industry j. Column (1) of Table 11 shows

TABLE 12. *Changes in GNP, NNP and NI induced by a unit change in government expenditure, fixed investment and exports*

	(1) GNP	(2) NNP	(3) NI
(1) Government expenditure	1.194	1.048	0.991
(2) Fixed investment	1.276	1.139	1.053
(3) Export	1.118	0.981	0.892

the column sums of the calculated $\Upsilon_P \Phi_P^{-1}$, that is the multiplier effects on GNP. For example, 1.205 for industry 17 implies that an increase of 1 billion yen in the final demand for machinery will bring about an increase of 1.205 billion yen in GNP. Further, columns (2) and (3) of the same table give similar effects on NNP and NI (national income), respectively. These values have been calculated by assuming that depreciation allowances and indirect taxes of each industry are a certain percentage of its value added, i.e.

$$\text{NNP originating in industry } i = (1 - d_i)V_i,$$
$$\text{NI originating in industry } i \quad = (1 - d_i - t_i)V_i,$$

where d_i and t_i represent the observed rates of depreciation allowances and indirect taxes calculated from the 1960 input–output table respectively.

The multipliers for macroeconomic variables are presented in Table 12. Here the GNP multiplier is given as the induced total change in GNP obtained when an additional final demand of one unit or one billion yen, in the form of government consumption (or fixed investment, or exports), is distributed among industries, in proportion to the actual 1960 distribution of government consumption (or fixed investment, or exports). The NNP and NI multipliers are similar effects with relation to NNP and NI. We can see from the table that the GNP multipliers of government consumption, fixed investment and exports were estimated at 1.194, 1.276 and 1.118 respectively. In the 1960 input–output table, fixed investment in the final demand section includes private and government gross fixed investment; separate figures for government fixed investment are not available. However, 1.276 may be considered as a good approximation for the GNP multiplier of *government* fixed investment.[1] An average of 1.194 and 1.276, weighted

[1] As is shown in Table 11, the GNP multipliers of the final demands for the machinery (including electrical machinery and transportation equipment) and construction industries are relatively close to each other: they range from 1.205 to 1.293. In view of the great importance of these items in private and government fixed investment, we may suppose that the GNP multipliers of private and government fixed investment do not much differ from each other, even if there is some difference between the composition of private and government expenditure.

with the 1960 shares of consumption and investment in total government expenditure (i.e. 0.523 and 0.477 respectively), is computed at 1.233. This value is close to the 1.40 of the Klein–Goldberger model and the 1.304 of the Research Seminar in Quantitative Economics model, but lower than the 2.12 of the Wharton forecasting model and the 2.1 of the Brookings quarterly econometric model for the US economy, though comparable with the figures obtained for the USA, Japan and the UK in other parts of this book.[1] Finally, it must be remembered that in our computations final demands, apart from consumption, are kept constant. If the effects of changes in prices and output on capital formation or inventory investment are allowed for, the multiplier will be higher than the values we have obtained.

Let us next test our econometric model for its ability to forecast. Since the model is estimated by the use of the 1960 input–output table, the observed 1960 values satisfy the whole system of equations approximately. Assuming that there was another equilibrium in 1961 corresponding to the shift in the predetermined variables between the two years, we compare the changes in the endogenous variables observed in 1960–1 with the corresponding computed changes obtained by substituting the observed changes in the predetermined variables into the estimated equations.

Let a column vector ΔG represent the observed changes in the

---

[1] Our Klein–Goldberger figure is obtained by substituting the values of impact multipliers in the endogenous tax yield case into the formula:

$$\frac{\partial Q}{\partial G} (1.00) + \frac{\partial Q}{\partial W_2} (0.50) + \frac{\partial Q}{\partial N_G} (0.50) (0.64),$$

where $\partial Q / \partial G$, $\partial Q / \partial W_2$, and $\partial Q / \partial N_G$ represent the effects on Q (GNP) of a unit increase in total government expenditure (G), in the government wage bill (W_2), and in the number of government employees (N_G), respectively. Goldberger derives this formula by specifying a reasonable package for a unit increase in the government budget as:

$$\Delta G = 1.00, \quad \Delta W_2 = 0.50 \Delta G \quad \text{and} \quad \Delta N_G = 0.64 \Delta W_2.$$

He applies the formula to the case of exogenous tax yields and obtains a multiplier of 1.575. See A. S. Goldberger, *op. cit.* p. 35. The Wharton figure is the average of the dynamic multipliers of the first four quarters. See M. K. Evans and L. R. Klein, *The Wharton Econometric Forecasting Model*, 2nd ed. (University of Pennsylvania, 1968). Suits' multiplier of 1.304 was obtained for the case in which additional expenditure is spent for purchases of goods and services from private firms. He also presented a value of 1.690 for the case in which half of additional expenditure is spent for producers' durable equipment and a value of 1.692 for the case in which additional expenditure of one billion dollars is spent for government wages to hire 0.2 million new workers. See D. Suits, 'Forecasting with an econometric model', *American Economic Review* (March 1962). For the Brookings estimates see G. Fromm and P. Taubman, *Policy Simulations with an Econometric Model* (North-Holland Publishing Co. 1968), pp. 95–98. The increase in real GNP at the end of four quarters induced by a sustained increase of one unit of government durables expenditures was estimated at 2.1. Government expenditures on nondurables and construction were estimated to have a multiplier of 2.4.

predetermined variables, i.e. the difference between the 1960 G and the 1961 G. By virtue of equation (4.4), we may get

$$\Delta\pi = \Gamma_P \Delta G, \tag{4.10}$$

or

$$\Delta\pi = -\Phi_P^{-1}\Phi_G \Delta G, \tag{4.11}$$

where the ith element of the column vector $\Delta\pi$ represents the estimated change in the ith relative price between 1960 and 1961.

We take the figures for final demands in 1961 from the 1961 table compiled by Miyazawa and Sakiyama.[1] Substituting the observed changes in all the predetermined variables, except the ω_is and m_is, into (4.11) we obtain the values of $\Delta\pi_i$s.[2] In calculation, the entire observed changes in inventory investment, together with those in government expenditure, fixed investment and exports, are taken as changes in final demands, in spite of the fact that observed inventory investment is made up of both intended and unintended inventory investment. For the purpose of calculating equilibrium prices, the final demand should include intended but not unintended inventory investment one. We have ignored unintended inventory investment by assuming that the greater part of the actual change in inventory investment in 1960–1 either accompanied increases in sales or was for speculative purposes.[3]

The observed and computed changes in relative prices are shown in columns (1) and (2) of Table 13 respectively. All the observed changes are between – 17.4 per cent and 7.1 per cent, while the estimates are confined to a narrower range (– 15.7 per cent to 3.9 per cent). However, the average of the estimated values, –9.7 per cent, is very close to that of the observed values, –9.6 per cent.[4] Eighteen of the price changes for the twenty-five

[1] Their 1961 table was compiled by extrapolating the 1960 table. We have made some further adjustments, considered appropriate for removing discords due to the differences in industrial classification between the two tables.

[2] All the ω_is and the m_is other than m_3 and m_4 are assumed to be constant in the short run, whilst m_3 and m_4 (the import ratios of the mining sectors) are subject to change through the import functions.

[3] In 1961 inventory investment in agriculture and fishery was lower than in 1960 by 75.243 billion yen; nevertheless output increased by 8.4 per cent in the same period. This suggests that a large proportion of inventories may be withdrawn to meet excess demand for output. Therefore this figure is replaced by a more appropriate estimate of the change in intended inventory investment, amounting to 22.8 billion yen, which is estimated by taking the product of the 1960 inventory-sales ratio and output change in 1960–61 as the 1961 intended inventory investment. Further, inventory investment in primary metals increased by 117.102 billion yen in the period 1960–61; this figure is thought to be too large by comparison with other sources. Therefore we use 32.6 billion yen, an estimate calculated in the same way.

[4] The observed relative price of a commodity is computed as the ratio between its absolute price and the average wage. For example, the 1961 price index of agriculture and fishery

industries are estimated with errors of less than 3.0 per cent. The absolute errors of the remaining seven industries are between 3.1 per cent and 5.5 per cent. These results are graphically represented by the use of Theil's pre-diction–realization diagram (Figure 1 a).[1] The horizontal axis refers to actual changes and the vertical axis to calculated changes; hence the 45-degree line is the line of prefect forecasts. The points in the diagram are fairly well clustered round the 45-degree line, indicating that our estimates traced out the general feature of price changes between 1960 and 1961.

Perhaps a better way of looking at this performance is to express the change in the price structure between 1960 and 1961 in terms of the change in the divergence of each price from the average price level, or the change in the *normalized price*. More specifically, let us define the normalized price of commodity i, π_i^n, as:

$$\pi_i^n = \pi_i - \bar{\pi},$$

where $\bar{\pi}$ is the weighted average of the π_is. By definition each π_i^n in 1960 is zero (π_is are equal to each other for all i in 1960); hence the changes in normalized prices between 1960 and 1961 are represented simply by 1961 normalized prices, whose observed and estimated values are shown in columns (4) and (5) of Table 13 respectively. It is remarkable that the sign of the estimated normalized price change coincides with that of the observed change in twenty-one of the twenty-five industries. This implies that the direction of change in the price structure in 1960–1 is almost perfectly predicted by our approach.

A picture of these results in terms of normalized prices is given by the prediction–realization diagram of Figure 1 b, in which actual changes in normalized prices are measured horizontally and estimated changes verti-cally. Here twenty-one points are in the first and third quadrants, indicating that the directions of change in the normalized prices have been correctly predicted, and even the few points in the second and fourth quadrants are near to the origin, showing that the errors are fairly small. However, most of the points in the first quadrant (six out of eight) are below the line of perfect forecasts, and eight out of thirteen in the third quadrant are above it. This

is 1.041 and the 1961 average wage index is 1.150; hence the 1961 relative price is com-puted at 0.905 ($= 1.041/1.150$). In computing the average price, the sum of gross output and imports of each commodity is used as a weight. The observed and estimated price changes of 'unallocated' (industry 26) are not shown in the table and not used in computing the average price, because the general wholesale price index is arbitrarily adopted as its actual price.

[1] See H. Theil, *Applied Economic Forecasting* (North-Holland Publishing Co. 1966), pp. 19–21, and *Economic Forecasts and Policy*, 2nd ed. (North-Holland Publishing Co. 1965), p. 30.

TABLE 13. *Price changes in 1960–1: observed v. estimated*

Industry	(1) Observed change in π_i	(2) Estimated change in π_i	(3) Error (1)–(2)	(4) Observed change in π_i^n (1)+0.096	(5) Estimated change in π_i^n (2)+0.097	(6) Error (4)–(5)	(7) Observed change in p_i	(8) Estimated change in p_i	(9) Error (7)–(8)
1. Agriculture	-0.095	-0.074	-0.021	0.002	0.023	-0.022	0.041	0.068	-0.027
2. Forestry	0.071	0.039	0.032	0.168	0.137	0.031	0.232	0.199	0.034
3. Coal & petroleum mining	-0.160	-0.130	-0.030	-0.064	-0.033	-0.030	-0.034	0.003	-0.037
4. Metal & nonmetal mining	-0.064	-0.112	0.047	0.032	-0.015	0.047	0.076	0.024	0.052
5. Food	-0.106	-0.086	-0.020	-0.010	0.011	-0.021	0.028	0.054	-0.026
6. Textiles	-0.127	-0.099	-0.028	-0.031	-0.002	-0.029	0.004	0.039	-0.035
7. Lumber & furniture	0.035	-0.005	0.040	0.131	0.092	0.039	0.190	0.148	0.043
8. Pulp & paper	-0.114	-0.135	0.021	-0.018	-0.038	0.020	0.019	-0.003	0.022
9. Printing & publishing	-0.110	-0.131	0.021	-0.013	-0.034	0.021	0.024	0.002	0.022
10. Leather	-0.092	-0.078	-0.014	0.004	0.019	-0.015	0.044	0.063	-0.019
11. Rubber	-0.148	-0.155	0.008	-0.051	-0.058	0.007	-0.020	-0.026	0.006
12. Chemicals	-0.153	-0.143	-0.010	-0.057	-0.046	-0.011	-0.026	-0.012	-0.014
13. Petroleum products	-0.173	-0.118	-0.055	-0.076	-0.021	-0.056	-0.049	0.017	-0.066
14. Stone, clay & glass	-0.116	-0.093	-0.023	-0.019	0.004	-0.024	0.017	0.046	-0.029
15. Primary metals	-0.156	-0.134	-0.021	-0.059	-0.037	-0.022	-0.029	-0.002	-0.027
16. Fabricated metals	-0.111	-0.107	-0.005	-0.015	-0.009	-0.006	0.022	0.030	-0.008
17. Machinery	-0.121	-0.111	-0.010	-0.025	-0.013	-0.011	0.011	0.026	-0.015
18. Electrical machinery	-0.174	-0.157	-0.017	-0.078	-0.060	-0.017	-0.050	-0.029	-0.022
19. Transportation equipment	-0.137	-0.140	0.002	-0.041	-0.042	0.002	-0.008	-0.008	0.000
20. Other manufacturing	-0.108	-0.143	0.036	-0.011	-0.046	0.035	0.026	-0.012	0.038
21. Construction	-0.036	-0.079	0.044	0.061	0.018	0.043	0.109	0.062	0.047
22. Utilities	-0.075	-0.106	0.031	0.021	-0.009	0.030	0.064	0.031	0.033
23. Trade	-0.054	-0.080	0.026	0.043	0.017	0.026	0.088	0.060	0.028
24. Transportation & communication	-0.050	-0.078	0.028	0.047	0.019	0.027	0.093	0.063	0.030
25. Services	-0.068	-0.079	0.010	0.028	0.019	0.009	0.071	0.062	0.009
Average	-0.096	-0.097	0.001	0.0	0.0	0.0	0.039	0.041	-0.002

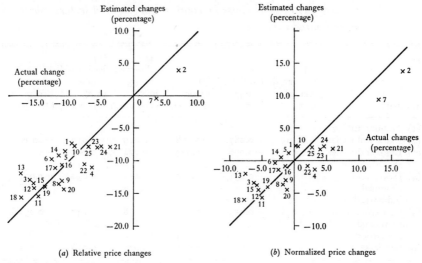

(*a*) Relative price changes   (*b*) Normalized price changes

Figure 1

Prediction–realization diagram: prices.

implies that there is some tendency towards underestimation of the magnitudes of changes.

A closer examination of the observed and estimated changes in the normalized prices reveals the following points:

(1) The actual increase in the normalized price was very large in construction (6.1 per cent) and the industries producing construction materials, such as forestry (16.8 per cent), lumber (13.1 per cent), and metal and nonmetal mining (3.2 per cent).[1] This was brought about by the construction boom of 1960 and 1961. The rate of growth of the output of construction was as high as 17.6 per cent in 1959–60 and 27.7 per cent in 1960–1. Further, the price rise was unusually accelerated by speculative demand for construction materials, such as lumber, gravel, stones and so on. Our estimates reflect this general tendency of the price movements in construction and its related industries very well, but on the other hand they have resulted in considerable underestimation. In fact, as is shown in column (5) of Table 14, the weighted average of the estimated changes in the normalized prices is 4.5 per cent, which is 3.3 per cent lower than that of the observed change, 7.8 per cent.

(2) The actual normalized prices in the heavy and chemical industries fell in 1960–1. The weighted average of the changes in their normalized prices was −5.5 per cent. The directions of the changes were correctly forecast in all the heavy and chemical industries except stone, clay and glass.

[1] The normalized price is found to have risen 5.4 per cent in nonmetal mining, in which gravel, sand, building stones, etc. are included.

TABLE 14. *Price changes in 1960–1: (aggregated sectors) observed v. estimated*

Industry	(1) Observed change in π_i	(2) Estimated change in π_i	(3) Error (1)−(2)	(4) Observed change in π_i^n (1)+0.096	(5) Estimated change in π_i^n (2)+0.097	(6) Error (4)−(5)
(1) Manufacturing						
(2) Light industries[a]	−0.105	−0.087	−0.018	−0.009	0.010	−0.019
(3) Light industries, excluding lumber	−0.120	−0.096	−0.024	−0.024	0.001	−0.025
(4) Heavy and chemical industries[b]	−0.151	−0.131	−0.020	−0.055	−0.034	−0.021
(5) Construction & its related industries[c]	−0.018	−0.052	0.034	0.078	0.045	0.033
(6) Services[d]	−0.069	−0.081	0.012	0.027	0.016	0.011

[a] Light industries include (5), (6), (7), (9), (10) and (20) in Table 1.

[b] Heavy and chemical industries include (8), (11), (12), (13), (14), (15), (16), (17), (18) and (19) in Table 1.

[c] Construction and its related industries include (2), (4), (7) and (21) in Table 1.

[d] Services include (22), (23), (24) and (25) in Table 1.

The magnitude of errors, except for petroleum products, are between −2.4 and 2.0 per cent. The average of the estimated values (−3.4 per cent) is higher than that of the observed values by 2.1 per cent. Towards the end of 1961 there occurred a sudden slump in the petroleum products industry, which gave rise to a decline of 7.6 per cent in its normalized price. The estimated decrease of 2.1 per cent is much smaller than this.

(3) The actual changes in the prices of the light industries (other than those of lumber and furniture) converged upon the average for the whole group of industries. The largest decline in normalized price was −3.1 per cent in textiles, while the largest rise was 0.4 per cent in leather; the average change was a decline of 2.4 per cent. The estimated changes range from 1.9 per cent to −4.6 per cent, and their average, 0.1 per cent, is 2.5 per cent higher than the observed average. The forecast errors of the individual normalized prices are all less than 3.5 per cent in absolute value.

(4) Tables 13 and 14 show that the actual changes in the normalized prices of the outputs of the service industries were all between 2.1 per cent and 4.7 per cent, and their average was 2.7 per cent. Our estimation has resulted in a slight underestimation of them (i.e. an underestimation of 1.1 per cent on the average), but the directions of the changes are correctly forecast, except for utilities.

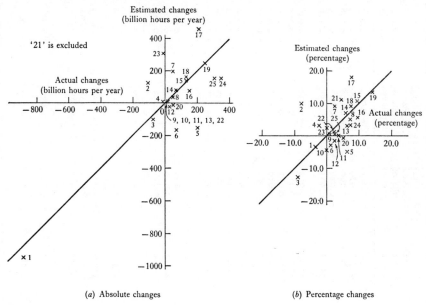

(a) Absolute changes (b) Percentage changes

Figure 2
Prediction–realization diagram: employment.

As will be shown later, the rate of change in the average wage, w, is estimated at 15.2 per cent. As the absolute price of a commodity may be given as the product of its relative price and the average wage, we can easily calculate the rate of change in the absolute price. The result for each industry is shown in columns (7) to (9) of Table 13. The average of the estimated changes in absolute prices, 4.1 per cent, is very close to that of the observed average, 3.9 per cent. In view of the small errors, we may conclude that the absolute prices are almost perfectly forecast.

Let us turn to the results concerning the real variables. As equation (2.4) shows, employment in industry i depends on the relative prices of commodities, the price of noncompetitive imports, the capital stock the industry holds, and the rate of technical change in the industry. From (4.6) we have

$$\Delta L = \Gamma_L \Delta G, \tag{4.12}$$

or

$$\Delta L = (\Lambda_P \Gamma_P + \Lambda_G) \Delta G, \tag{4.13}$$

where the ith element of ΔL gives the (estimated) change in employment in industry i during 1960–1. It is calculated by substituting the above estimates of the changes in relative prices in 1960–1 and the observed changes in the predetermined variables in the same period into equation (4.13).

The changes in employment thus calculated, together with the observed

TABLE 15. *Changes in hours worked 1960–1: observed v. estimated*

Industry	(1) Observed change[a]	(2) Estimated change[a]	(3) Error[a] (1) − (2)	(4) Observed rate of growth	(5) Estimated rate of growth	(6) Error (4) − (5)
1. Agriculture	−873.3	−958.8	85.6	−0.031	−0.034	0.003
2. Forestry	−105.7	133.8	−239.5	−0.079	0.100	−0.179
3. Coal & petroleum mining	−71.0	−101.2	30.1	−0.090	−0.128	0.038
4. Metal & nonmetal mining	−14.0	15.2	−29.2	−0.026	0.028	−0.054
5. Food	201.6	−157.8	359.4	0.065	−0.051	0.116
6. Textiles	74.2	−166.7	240.9	0.014	−0.032	0.046
7. Lumber & furniture	57.9	194.2	−136.4	0.027	0.092	−0.065
8. Pulp & paper	55.6	37.0	18.5	0.073	0.048	0.025
9. Printing & publishing	9.0	5.3	3.8	0.010	0.006	0.004
10. Leather	0.0	6.5	−6.5	0.000	0.047	−0.047
11. Rubber	16.3	0.5	15.8	0.039	0.001	0.038
12. Chemicals	27.2	−17.1	44.4	0.026	−0.016	0.042
13. Petroleum products	6.7	2.9	3.8	0.066	0.028	0.038
14. Stone & glass	68.6	82.6	−13.9	0.059	0.071	−0.012
15. Primary metals	130.7	142.0	−11.4	0.097	0.106	−0.009
16. Fabricated metals	154.4	73.1	81.4	0.096	0.045	0.051
17. Machinery	201.8	459.5	−257.7	0.079	0.179	−0.100
18. Electrical machinery	131.3	158.8	−27.4	0.076	0.092	−0.016
19. Transportation equipment	251.1	243.1	8.0	0.140	0.135	0.005
20. Other manufacturing	46.0	−7.8	53.8	0.051	−0.009	0.060
21. Construction	317.6	801.5	−483.8	0.045	0.114	−0.069
22. Utilities	9.5	5.5	4.0	0.022	0.012	0.010
23. Trade	−8.5	304.1	−312.6	−0.001	0.023	−0.024
24. Transportation & communication	345.8	154.7	191.2	0.074	0.033	0.041
25. Services	311.5	157.9	153.6	0.021	0.010	0.011
26. Unallocated	–	–	–	–	–	–
27. Public administration	111.4	111.4	0.0	0.039	0.039	0.0
Total	1455.7 / 2434.7[b]	1680.2 / 2505.2[b]	−224.5 / −70.5[b]	0.015 / 0.035[b]	0.017 / 0.036[b]	−0.002 / −0.001[b]

[a] Unit: millions of manhours per year.

[b] Total excluding agriculture and forestry.

TABLE 16. *Output changes in 1960–1: observed v. estimated*

Industry	(1) Observed change[a]	(2) Estimated change[a]	(3) Error[a] (1)−(2)	(4) Observed rate of growth	(5) Estimated rate of growth	(6) Error (4)−(5)
1. Agriculture	204.0	97.2	106.8	0.084	0.040	0.044
2. Forestry	6.4	43.0	−36.6	0.009	0.060	−0.051
3. Coal & petroleum mining	17.1	−6.1	23.2	0.074	−0.027	0.101
4. Metal & nonmetal mining	20.4	21.2	−0.8	0.125	0.130	−0.005
5. Food	373.8	127.0	246.8	0.103	0.035	0.068
6. Textiles	184.8	156.3	28.5	0.080	0.068	0.012
7. Lumber & furniture	45.1	73.9	−28.8	0.059	0.100	−0.041
8. Pulp & paper	115.9	122.2	−6.3	0.174	0.184	−0.010
9. Printing & publishing	54.4	53.2	1.2	0.140	0.137	0.003
10. Leather	16.9	7.1	9.8	0.300	0.125	0.175
11. Rubber	33.4	37.9	−4.5	0.138	0.157	−0.019
12. Chemicals	208.2	194.7	13.5	0.136	0.127	0.009
13. Petroleum products	128.0	93.1	34.9	0.202	0.147	0.055
14. Stone & glass	75.4	85.6	−10.2	0.144	0.164	−0.020
15. Primary metals	989.8	771.1	218.7	0.308	0.240	0.068
16. Fabricated metals	154.0	88.5	65.5	0.264	0.152	0.112
17. Machinery	525.0	538.3	−13.3	0.283	0.290	−0.007
18. Electrical machinery	408.1	355.8	52.3	0.286	0.249	0.037
19. Transportation equipment	375.9	374.6	1.3	0.276	0.275	0.001
20. Other manufacturing	86.2	47.0	39.2	0.247	0.135	0.112
21. Construction	881.3	615.7	265.6	0.277	0.194	0.083
22. Utilities	97.6	70.0	27.6	0.165	0.119	0.046
23. Trade	326.1	256.3	69.8	0.131	0.103	0.028
24. Transportation & communication	404.0	200.1	203.9	0.224	0.111	0.113
25. Services	390.4	369.6	20.8	0.094	0.089	0.005
26. Unallocated	183.1	65.5	117.6	0.194	0.086	0.108
27. Public administration	36.2	36.2	0.0	0.044	0.044	0.0
Total	6338.8	4695.0	1443.8	0.171	0.132	0.039

[a] Unit: billions of 1960 yen.

employment changes, are shown in terms of both absolute changes and rates of change in Table 15 and Figure 2. In Figure 2*b* of the prediction–realization diagram it is seen that the results in terms of the rates of change are more or less clustered around the 45-degree line with the few significant exceptions of forestry (2), machinery (17), and food (5). Columns (4) to (6) of Table 15 shows that the errors in the growth rate are less than 5.0 per cent in absolute value in seventeen of the twenty-five industries, while those of the remaining industries are less than 11.6 per cent, apart from the error of 17.9 per cent in forestry. Further, Figure 2*a* and columns (1) to (3) of Table 15 confirm similar results in terms of the absolute changes with large errors in machinery (17), food (5), textiles (6) and construction (21). We may conclude from these observations that the general features of the changes in employment are reproduced by our approach.

The last two rows of the table give changes in total employment (including agriculture, fishery and forestry) and total industrial employment respectively. It is seen that the change in total industrial employment is estimated with an error of -70.5 million man-hours per year, or with an error of 0.1 per cent in the growth rate. Substituting this estimate of the change in industrial employment, 2,505.2 million manhours, into the wage equation (3.13), we obtain an estimate of the increase in the average wage rate of 15.2 per cent. This is further used to obtain estimates of money prices (presented in Table 13).

Equation (2.4) shows that the output of each industry is a function of the relative prices of commodities, the price of noncompetitive imports, its own capital stock and the rate of technical change of that industry. Thus changes in outputs between 1960 and 1961 are estimated, in the same way as we estimated changes in employment. The results are presented in Table 16. The observed rates of change (column (4)) were between 0.9 per cent and 30.8 per cent and the observed rate of growth of total output was 17.1 per cent, reflecting the remarkable boom in 1961 throughout the whole economy. These are compared with the estimated rates of changes (column (5)) which are between -2.7 per cent and 29.0 per cent, and with the estimated rate of growth of total output, 13.2 per cent, which is, though fairly high, still less than the actual rate by 3.9 per cent. Fifteen of the twenty-five industries are estimated with errors of less than 5.0 per cent in absolute value.[1] The errors for the remaining ten industries are less than 11.3 per cent, except for leather, where the change in output is underestimated by 17.5 per cent. The absolute error, 3.9 per cent, in the estimation of the growth rate of total output is not very high, compared with the high average rate of growth of 17.1 per cent.

Figure 3 shows the prediction–realization diagram of output. It is seen

[1] Twenty-five industries excluding 'unallocated' and public administration.

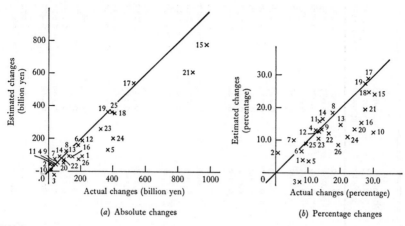

Figure 3
Prediction–realization diagram: output.

from Figure 3*b* that there is a general tendency to underestimation, particularly for the outputs of industries such as coal and petroleum (3), food (5), leather (10), primary metals (15), fabricated metals (16), miscellaneous manufacturing (20), construction (21) and transportation and communication (24).

Columns (1) to (3) of Table 16 and Figure 3*a* refer to absolute changes in output, in billions of 1960 yen. The results for absolute changes enable us to find those industries which have made the biggest contribution to the increase in total output. It is seen from Figure 3*a* that a major part of the underestimation in total output is due to the underestimation of the industrial outputs of primary metal (15), construction (21), transportation and communications (24) and food (5).

Finally, Table 17 and Figure 4 compare the estimated with the actual changes in consumption expenditure. It is seen from column (6) of the table that the errors in estimating the growth rate are substantial for the products of several industries, such as coal and petroleum (− 20.0 per cent), petroleum products (28.8 per cent), stone, clay and glass (− 64.2 per cent), other manufacturing (39.9 per cent), and 'unallocated' (407.2 per cent). The large errors in these industries are, however, mainly due to the fact that consumption expenditures on these products were so small that their rates of change were very unstable. The absolute error in the growth rate is under 5.0 per cent for thirteen out of the twenty-five outputs, and between 5.2 and 13.8 per cent for another seven outputs.[1] The last row of Table 17 shows that total consumption change is underestimated with an absolute error of

[1] Construction is excluded because there is no consumption demand for it.

TABLE 17. *Consumption changes in 1960–1: observed v. estimated*

Industry	(1) Observed change[a]	(2) Estimated change[a]	(3) Error[a] (1)−(2)	(4) Observed rate of growth	(5) Estimated rate of growth	(6) Error (4)−(5)
1. Agriculture	84.4	32.9	51.5	0.170	0.066	0.104
2. Forestry	4.9	4.6	0.3	0.082	0.077	0.005
3. Coal & petroleum mining	−1.2	0.7	−1.9	−0.124	0.076	−0.200
4. Metal & nonmetal mining	0.2	0.2	−0.1	0.055	0.080	−0.025
5. Food	173.1	126.4	46.8	0.068	0.050	0.018
6. Textiles	98.8	69.2	29.6	0.153	0.107	0.046
7. Lumber & furniture	10.1	7.7	2.4	0.201	0.153	0.048
8. Pulp & paper	−1.6	−1.5	−0.1	0.192	0.183	0.009
9. Printing & publishing	8.1	16.8	−8.7	0.072	0.149	−0.077
10. Leather	1.5	1.5	0.0	0.102	0.104	−0.002
11. Rubber	5.5	3.7	1.8	0.157	0.105	0.052
12. Chemicals	7.5	10.3	−2.8	0.061	0.084	−0.023
13. Petroleum products	12.0	2.5	9.5	0.364	0.076	0.288
14. Stone & glass	4.9	−1.5	6.5	−0.489	0.153	−0.642
15. Primary metals	−0.1	−0.7	0.6	0.014	0.152	−0.138
16. Fabricated metals	3.9	3.0	0.9	0.202	0.154	0.048
17. Machinery	25.3	14.1	11.2	0.264	0.147	0.117
18. Electrical machinery	23.3	19.7	3.6	0.181	0.153	0.028
19. Transportation equipment	4.3	10.9	−6.6	0.061	0.154	−0.093
20. Other manufacturing	47.0	12.5	34.6	0.544	0.145	0.399
21. Construction	0.0	0.0	0.0	0.0	0.0	0.0
22. Utilities	24.7	11.9	12.8	0.157	0.075	0.082
23. Trade	36.2	87.0	−50.8	0.033	0.079	−0.046
24. Transportation & communication	63.8	53.1	10.7	0.131	0.109	0.022
25. Services	292.1	255.9	36.2	0.133	0.116	0.017
26. Unallocated	4.0	0.1	3.8	4.226	0.154	4.072
27. Public administration	0.0	0.0	0.0	0.0	0.0	0.0
Total	932.9	740.9	192.0	0.110	0.088	0.022

[a] Unit: billions of 1960 yen.

TABLE 18. *The various statistics of the prediction errors*

	(1) Relative price	(2) Normalized price	(3) Employment, million man-hours	(4) Employment, growth rate	(5) Employment, million man-hours, excluding (2), (5), (17)	(6) Employment, growth rate, excluding (2), (5), (17)	(7) Gross output, 1960 million yen	(8) Gross output, growth rate	(9) Consumption, 1960 million yen, excluding (13), (14), (20), (21)	(10) Consumption, growth rate, excluding (13), (14), (20), (21)
(1) Average error (unweighted)	−0.004	−0.003	9.0	0.002	3.9	−0.005	−55.6	−0.040	−6.5	0.000
(2) Average error (weighted)	−0.001	0.000	6.6	0.002	8.6	0.001	−99.9	−0.039	−23.4	−0.017
(3) Average absolute error (unweighted)	0.024	0.024	112.5	0.044	88.9	0.032	63.4	0.051	13.3	0.057
(4) Average absolute error (weighted)	0.023	0.023	178.6	0.029	169.2	0.022	104.5	0.045	37.2	0.033
(5) RMS: root-mean-square error	0.027	0.027	172.5	0.059	145.8	0.038	101.2	0.068	22.0	0.075
(6) $\bar{R}$: correlation coefficient	0.89	0.89	0.79	0.48	0.85	0.74	0.95	0.75	0.96	0.36
(7) Slope of regression line	0.67	0.67	1.03	0.63	1.07	0.89	0.76	0.75	0.81	0.19
(8) U: inequality coefficient	0.24	0.47	0.75	0.95	0.63	0.63	0.29	0.35	0.27	0.54

Note 1. Columns (1) to (4) cover industries (1) to (25).
2. Columns (5) and (6) cover industries (1) to (25), excluding (2), (5) and (17).
3. Columns (7) and (8) cover industries (1) to (26).
4. Columns (9) and (10) cover industries (1) to (25), excluding (13), (14), (20) and (21).

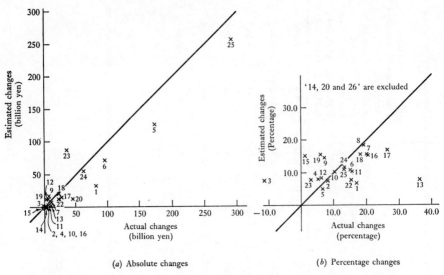

(a) Absolute changes

(b) Percentage changes

Figure 4

Prediction–realization diagram: consumption.

192.0 billion yen, or with an error of 2.2 per cent in the growth rate. It is also seen from Figure 4a that the estimates for services (25), foods (5), agriculture (1) and other manufacturing (20) are largely responsible for the under-estimation of total consumption. Relatively poor results for consumption may have been caused by the fact that we have converted consumption of commodities according to the classification of the consumer survey into the input–output categories by use of a base-year matrix.

Table 18 summarizes the above results of the *ex post* forecasting in terms of various statistics. Denote the actual and predicted changes in some variable of industry i by A_i and P_i, respectively, and let the number of industries be n. Then the following statistics measure the magnitude of prediction error:

(1) average error (unweighted) $= \sum_{i=1}^{n} (P_i - A_i)/n,$

(2) average error (weighted) $= \sum_{i=1}^{n} r_i(P_i - A_i)/n,$

(3) average absolute error (unweighted) $= \sum_{i=1}^{n} |P_i - A_i|/n,$

(4) average absolute error (weighted) $= \sum_{i=1}^{n} r_i |P_i - A_i|/n,$

(5) root-mean-square (or RMS) error $= \sqrt{\left(\sum_{i=1}^{n} (P_i - A_i)^2/n \right)}$,

where the weights, r_i, are taken to be proportional to the distribution of gross output *plus* imports among industries for columns (1) and (2), to the distribution of employment among industries for columns (3), (4), (5) and (6), to the distribution of gross output among industries for columns (7) and (8), and to the distribution of consumption among industries for columns (9) and (10); all distributions are those in 1960. Evidently, average errors (unweighted and weighted) measure bias in predicting the average change, while other statistics measure dispersion of errors.

A regression of predicted changes on actual changes gives two statistics:

(6) $\bar{R} =$ the correlation coefficient, adjusted for degrees of freedom,

(7) $\beta =$ the slope of the regression line, which may be considered to measure the degree of systematic underestimation or overestimation.

The last statistic is Theil's inequality coefficient:[1]

(8) $U = \sqrt{\left(\sum_{i=1}^{n} (P_i - A_i)^2 \Big/ \sum_{i=1}^{n} A_i^2 \right)}$.

$U = 0$ means perfect prediction. If one predicts no change for every industry when there are actual changes at least in one industry, all P_is are zero and $U = 1$. Thus the value of U expresses the degree of prediction error relative to the simple prediction of no changes.

(1) Price. The unweighted average errors of -0.4 per cent (relative price) and -0.3 per cent (normalized price) imply that there is practically no systematic bias in predicting the average change, as overestimations (or underestimations) of the increases are almost offset by overestimations (or underestimations) of the decreases. However, the slope of the regression line of predicted on actual changes, 0.67, means that the regression line is rotated clockwise around the line of accurate estimation, i.e. the 45° line, approximately by 11°. RMS of 2.7 per cent, $\bar{R}$ of 0.89, and U of 0.24 indicate our model's good capacity for predicting changes in relative prices.

(2) Employment. The low values of the unweighted average error of 9.0 million manhours (in terms of the absolute change) and 0.2 per cent (in terms of the growth rate) show that bias in predicting the average change is negligible. The slope of the regression line of 1.03 implies that the regression line for employment changes is practically parallel to the accurate

---

[1] See H. Theil, *Applied Economic Forecasting*, pp. 26–9.

estimation line. Although in seventeen out of twenty-five industries the absolute error in predicting the growth rate is less than 5.0 per cent, the errors of a few industries are fairly large. Thus the variances of errors are large in prediction of the absolute changes as well as in prediction of the growth rates, as is seen in Table 18. The values of U, 0.75 (for prediction of the absolute changes) and 0.95 (for prediction of the growth rates), are rather close to the value of U for simple prediction. It is seen from columns (5) and (6) of the table, however, that these statistics are improved by excluding three exceptional industries: forestry, foods and machinery.

(3) Output. By and large, the striking industrial rates of growth throughout the whole economy are reproduced by the simulation of our model. The growth rates of outputs of eighteen industries are estimated with an absolute error of less than 5.0 per cent. However, as is shown in columns (7) and (8), the unweighted average errors of -55.6 billion yen and of -4.0 per cent indicate negative biases in predicting the average change in output and the average rate of growth of output respectively. The actual growth rate of total output, 17.1 per cent, is underestimated with an error of -3.9 per cent. The slope of the regression line is 0.76 between the predicted and the actual changes and 0.75 between the predicted and the actual rates of growth. These figures imply that the regression lines for absolute changes and growth rates are rotated clockwise around the 45° line approximately by 8°. The predictions of both the absolute changes and the growth rates have resulted in fairly good values of $\bar{R}$ and U.

(4) Consumption. The observed growth rate of total consumption, 11.0 per cent, is underestimated by 2.2 per cent. For the reasons stated above, petroleum products, stone, clay and glass, other manufacturing and 'unallocated' are excluded in calculating the eight statistics. Even these statistics show that the growth rates have been poorly predicted: the correlation coefficient is 0.36 and the regression slope is 0.19. On the other hand, the prediction of absolute changes in consumption is much better, as the correlation coefficient of 0.96 and the regression slope of 0.81 show.

We may now conclude that the empirical model of general equilibrium with Cobb–Douglas production functions is able to reproduce, with a tolerable degree of accuracy, overall short-run fluctuations in prices, outputs, consumption and employment. For later study along these lines, however, possible sources of remaining errors may be point out:

(1) 1961 is one of the most prosperous years during the postwar period, characterized by a phenomenal growth rate in Japan. Underestimation in real variables, such as output and consumption, can probably be ascribed to the unusually high rates of growth.

(2) Our model is based on industrial production functions of the

Cobb–Douglas type and the marginal productivity principle. These assumptions may or may not be satisfied.

(3) This model is essentially non-linear. Comparative static results, however, have been derived from the formulas given in terms of partial derivatives which are only locally true. It is likely that an improved solution of the nonlinear system would reduce the errors in forecasting.

(4) Fixed investment, inventory investment, exports, and government expenditure are all treated as exogenous. Introduction of additional possible feed-back effects may significantly affect the results from our model.

5. A factor analysis of price and output changes

The predetermined variables of our model will be grouped into four major categories, associated respectively with (1) demand, (2) supply, (3) imports and (4) tax rates. The variables associated with demand include lagged consumption, population and final demands (excluding consumption). The effect of this last on relative prices and outputs has already been discussed in Chapter 4. The supply category includes capital accumulation and technological change. An increase in the capital stock of an industry will induce the firms of that industry to expand output, and thereby result in a fall in the price of the output. The expansion of output will have repercussions upon other prices through the channel of technical substitution and complementarity as well as the channel of income and substitution effects on consumers' demands. According to our calculations on $-\Phi_P^{-1}\Phi_G$ of equation (4.4), the total effect of an increase in the capital stock of an industry is to lower the relative prices of all other industries as well as of that industry. The effect of technological progress on relative prices is fairly similar to that of capital accumulation. The import category includes competitive and noncompetitive import prices and other variables in the import function. From $-\Phi_P^{-1}\Phi_G$ we can show that a rise in these prices leads to a price rise in the corresponding domestic industry, with minor effects in other industries. Assuming that tax rates remain constant, in the first half of this chapter we analyse the changes in prices between 1960 and 1961 into the effects of the other factors, demand, supply and imports.

For this purpose let us rewrite equation (4.11) of the previous chapter as:

$$\Delta\pi = -\Phi_P^{-1}\Phi_G(\Delta G_D + \Delta G_S + \Delta G_M), \tag{5.1}$$

where $\Delta G_D(\Delta G_S$ or $\Delta G_M)$ is a vector which has the observed 1960–1 changes in the demand (supply, or imports) variables in the appropriate places and zero in the other places. Then the three terms of the right-hand side represent the demand, supply and imports effects, whose calculated results are presented in columns (1), (2), and (3) of Table 19 respectively. Column (4) presents their total, and hence the figures are the same as those of column (2) of Table 13 above. In columns (5) to (8) the change in each relative price is expressed in terms of its divergence from the average of each effect for the whole industry, or in terms of the normalized price. Thus column (8), presenting the total of all three effects, is equal to column (5) of Table 13.

[216]

TABLE 19. *The effects of the demand, supply, and imports on the price changes: 1960–1*

Industry	Changes in the relative prices				Changes in the normalized prices			
	(1) Demand effect	(2) Supply effect	(3) Imports effect	(4) Total (1)+(2)+(3)	(5) Demand effect (1)−0.107	(6) Supply effect (2)+0.187	(7) Imports effect (3)+0.017	(8) Total (5)+(6)+(7)
1. Agriculture	0.066	−0.133	−0.007	−0.074	−0.041	0.054	0.010	0.023
2. Forestry	0.199	−0.149	−0.011	0.039	0.092	0.038	0.011	0.137
3. Coal & petroleum	0.040	−0.078	−0.093	−0.130	−0.066	0.109	−0.076	−0.033
4. Metal & nonmetal mining	0.058	−0.098	−0.071	−0.112	−0.049	0.089	−0.055	−0.015
5. Food	0.074	−0.152	−0.009	−0.090	−0.032	0.035	0.008	0.011
6. Textiles	0.061	−0.128	−0.032	−0.099	−0.046	0.059	−0.015	−0.002
7. Lumber & furniture	0.135	−0.131	−0.010	−0.005	0.029	0.056	0.009	0.092
8. Pulp & paper	0.122	−0.243	−0.014	−0.135	0.016	−0.056	0.003	−0.038
9. Printing & publishing	0.096	−0.218	−0.009	−0.131	−0.011	−0.031	0.008	−0.034
10. Leather	0.069	−0.136	−0.011	−0.078	−0.038	0.051	0.006	0.019
11. Rubber	0.081	−0.159	−0.077	−0.155	−0.026	0.028	−0.060	−0.058
12. Chemicals	0.110	−0.235	−0.018	−0.143	0.003	−0.048	0.000	−0.046
13. Petroleum products	0.102	−0.164	−0.055	−0.118	−0.005	0.023	−0.038	−0.021
14. Stone, clay & glass	0.111	−0.182	−0.023	−0.093	0.005	0.005	−0.006	0.004
15. Primary metals	0.154	−0.263	−0.025	−0.134	0.047	−0.076	−0.008	−0.037
16. Fabricated metals	0.118	−0.209	−0.015	−0.107	0.011	−0.022	0.002	−0.009
17. Machinery	0.164	−0.260	−0.015	−0.111	0.057	−0.073	0.002	−0.013
18. Electrical machinery	0.150	−0.292	−0.016	−0.157	0.043	−0.105	0.001	−0.060
19. Transportation equipment	0.138	−0.259	−0.018	−0.140	0.031	−0.072	−0.002	−0.042
20. Other manufacturing	0.104	−0.235	−0.013	−0.143	−0.003	−0.048	0.004	−0.046
21. Construction	0.122	−0.187	−0.014	−0.079	0.015	0.000	0.003	0.018
22. Utilities	0.125	−0.203	−0.027	−0.106	0.018	−0.016	−0.010	−0.009
23. Trade	0.068	−0.143	−0.005	−0.080	−0.038	0.044	0.012	0.017
24. Transportation & communication	0.102	−0.168	−0.012	−0.078	−0.005	0.019	0.005	0.019
25. Services	0.093	−0.165	−0.007	−0.079	−0.013	0.022	0.010	0.019

Now the general feature of price changes in 1960–1 described in Chapter 4 is analysed in terms of the demand, supply and imports components:

(1) Construction and its related industries. Because of the striking demand pressure for these industries, demand effects on their prices are seen to be greater than the whole industry average of demand effects, which is 10.7 per cent. As shown in column (5) of Table 19, the demand effect in terms of normalized prices is 9.2 per cent in forestry, 2.9 per cent in lumber and 1.5 per cent in construction. On the other hand, the decreasing effects of capacity expansion on the relative prices of these industries are smaller than or equal to the whole industry average of this effect, − 18.7 per cent. The normalized supply effects are computed as 3.8 per cent, 5.6 per cent and 0.0 per cent in forestry, lumber and construction respectively. (See column (6) of Table 19.) Thus these effects, together with the small positive imports effects, lead to large increases in normalized prices, such as 13.7 per cent in forestry, 9.3 per cent in lumber and 1.8 per cent in construction. Since 'metal and nonmetal mining' includes not only construction materials (stone, gravel, etc.) but also metal and nonmetal ores, the price changes in its products did not follow the typical pattern of price changes in construction materials. Instead the import price effect, − 5.5 per cent, is fairly large, reflecting the fact that the industry is substantially influenced by import competition.

(2) The heavy and chemical industries. The demand effects on the prices of outputs of these industries are larger than the average over all industries, excluding petroleum products and rubber. The average of the demand effects of the heavy and chemical industries is 13.8 per cent in relative prices and 3.1 per cent in normalized prices. (See Table 20.) In contrast to construction, however, the effects of capacity expansion in reducing relative prices are even stronger than the demand effects.[1] The supply effects on the prices of the outputs of these industries are computed, on average, at − 24.7 per cent in relative and at − 6.0 per cent in normalized prices. The import effects are relatively small in industries other than rubber and petroleum products. Hence, in total, the normalized prices of the heavy and chemical industries decline, on average, by 3.4 per cent. Rubber and petroleum products are among the industries susceptible to changes in import prices.

(3) Light industries (excluding lumber). The average demand effect on the prices of outputs of light industries is lower than the average for all

[1] In 1960–1, there was a considerable amount of investment and rapid technological change in the heavy and chemicals industries. Apart from rubber, petroleum products and stone, clay and glass, the supply effects on all the heavy and chemical industries are computed to be larger than the whole industry average.

TABLE 20. *The effects of the demand, supply, and imports on the price changes: 1960–1*

	Changes in the relative prices				Changes in the normalized prices			
	(1) Demand effect	(2) Supply effect	(3) Imports effect	(4) Total (1)+(2)+(3)	(5) Demand effect	(6) Supply effect	(7) Imports effect	(8) Total (5)+(6)+(7)
(1) Agriculture	0.066	−0.133	−0.007	−0.074	−0.041	0.054	0.010	0.023
(2) Coal and petroleum	0.040	−0.078	−0.093	−0.130	−0.066	0.109	−0.076	−0.033
(3) Light industries, excluding lumber[a]	0.073	−0.151	−0.017	−0.096	−0.034	0.036	0.000	0.001
(4) Heavy and chemical industries[b]	0.138	−0.247	−0.022	−0.131	0.031	−0.060	−0.006	−0.034
(5) Construction and its related industries[c]	0.132	−0.167	−0.017	−0.052	0.025	0.020	0.000	0.045
(6) Services[d]	0.090	−0.162	−0.009	−0.081	−0.017	0.025	0.008	0.016
Average	0.107	−0.187	−0.017	−0.097	0.0	0.0	0.0	0.0
General consumer price	0.084	−0.159	−0.011	−0.087	−0.023	0.028	0.005	0.010

[a] Includes (5), (6), (9), (10) and (20) in Table 1.
[b] Includes (8) and (11) to (19) in Table 1.
[c] Includes (2), (4), (7) and (21) in Table 1.
[d] Includes (22) to (25) in Table 1.

industries. The effects of capacity expansion in reducing the relative prices of food, textiles and leather are less than the average for all industries, while the supply effects on printing and publishing and other manufacturing are greater; on average the normalized supply effect for the light industries has a *positive* value of 3.6 per cent, which neutralizes the negative average demand effect, −3.4 per cent. Further the import effect is close to the whole industry average. Hence, in total, the change in the normalized price of the light industries is practically zero.

(4) Services and agriculture. The demand, supply and imports effects on the prices of the outputs of these industries are opposite in direction to those of the heavy and chemical industries. In all the service industries, excluding utilities, the positive supply effects on normalized prices are greater than the moduli of the negative demand effects, so that their normalized prices become larger, on average. Agriculture is very similar to the service industries in price behaviour. On the other hand, 'utilities' is similar to the heavy and chemical industries.

(5) General consumer price index. The last row of Table 20 shows the results for the general consumer price. The general consumer price level relative to the average wage, i.e. p^c/w, is estimated to fall by 8.7 per cent.[1] This value may be regarded as a result of a demand effect of 8.4 per cent, a supply effect of −15.9 per cent and an imports effect of −1.1 per cent. After normalization, the demand, supply and imports effects on the general consumer price level are −2.3, 2.8 and 0.5 per cent respectively, and hence, in total, the general consumer price level relative to wages is 1.0 per cent higher than the average over all industries. Since the products of agriculture, the light industries and services account for a large proportion of consumer goods, the fluctuations in the general consumer price level are very similar to the movements in the prices of these products.

Let us next examine our model for the effects of changes in tax rates. We have assumed in equations (2.2) and (2.15) the following tax functions:

$$T_i = t_i(p_i X_i) \quad (i = 1, ..., n), \tag{5.2}$$

$$T_p = T\left(\sum_{i=1}^{n} w_i L_j + Pr\right), \tag{5.3}$$

where T_i represents indirect business taxes in industry i, T_p personal income taxes, t_i the indirect tax rate for industry i and T the personal tax rate. In the previous chapters the personal tax rate is set at the observed 1960 ratio of

[1] From the estimates for the general relative consumer price level and the money wage (0.913 and 1.153 respectively), the general absolute consumer price level is calculated at 1.053, which is close to the observed value of 1.051.

TABLE 21. *Changes in GNP, NNP and NI induced by a unit change in the final demand for the individual sector (tax yield predetermined)*

Industry	Multiplier			Musgrave–Miller's α			Indirect business tax rates
	(1) GNP	(2) NNP	(3) NI	(4) GNP	(5) NNP	(6) NI	
1. Agriculture	1.303	1.146	1.146	0.043	0.043	0.098	0.017
2. Forestry	1.020	0.912	0.912	0.114	0.109	0.168	0.007
3. Coal and petroleum mining	0.593	0.514	0.514	0.124	0.128	0.175	0.025
4. Metal and nonmetal mining	0.604	0.529	0.529	0.136	0.138	0.209	0.025
5. Food	1.408	1.302	1.302	0.178	0.206	0.358	0.133
6. Textiles	1.103	0.972	0.972	0.108	0.109	0.175	0.005
7. Lumber and furniture	1.235	1.105	1.105	0.111	0.109	0.173	0.009
8. Pulp and paper	1.177	1.018	1.018	0.118	0.124	0.193	0.006
9. Printing and publishing	1.345	1.200	1.200	0.102	0.103	0.166	0.006
10. Leather	1.357	1.213	1.213	0.145	0.144	0.240	0.004
11. Rubber	1.066	0.949	0.949	0.109	0.108	0.173	0.006
12. Chemicals	1.105	0.944	0.944	0.139	0.149	0.228	0.013
13. Petroleum products	1.015	0.904	0.904	0.309	0.305	0.493	0.195
14. Stone, clay and glass	1.290	1.133	1.133	0.113	0.115	0.187	0.014
15. Primary metals	1.118	0.967	0.967	0.118	0.122	0.196	0.002
16. Fabricated metals	1.347	1.205	1.205	0.107	0.105	0.173	0.014
17. Machinery	1.359	1.205	1.205	0.113	0.113	0.185	0.014
18. Electrical machinery	1.456	1.295	1.295	0.126	0.126	0.208	0.025
19. Transportation equipment	1.420	1.256	1.256	0.123	0.123	0.203	0.024
20. Miscellaneous manufacture	1.344	1.195	1.195	0.124	0.124	0.204	0.025
21. Construction	1.441	1.290	1.290	0.103	0.102	0.164	0.002
22. Utilities	1.224	0.988	0.988	0.224	0.250	0.390	0.135
23. Trade	1.433	1.277	1.277	0.098	0.096	0.165	0.033
24. Transportation and communication	1.302	1.094	1.094	0.097	0.110	0.182	0.015
25. Services	1.214	1.066	1.066	0.113	0.114	0.188	0.037
26. Unallocated	1.319	1.173	1.173	0.211	0.210	0.342	0.087
27. Public administration	1.350	1.190	1.190	0.039	0.040	0.067	0.000

personal taxes to personal income, 0.081. The indirect industrial tax rates are set at the observed 1960 ratios of indirect business taxes to the outputs of the respective industries, which are shown in the last column of Table 21.

On the other hand, corporate income taxes have no explicit place in our model. The excess of profits P over property income Pr gives the sum of corporate savings, depreciation and corporate income taxes which is determined by (2.13). In our model it is impossible to separate corporate income taxes from the rest.

Now for the purpose of analysing the effect of built-in flexibility in the Japanese economy, let us consider a hypothetical system in which the yields of indirect business taxes and personal income taxes are treated as exogenous.

TABLE 22. *Changes in GNP, NNP and NI induced by a unit change in final demands of the 1960 composition (tax yield predetermined)*

	Multiplier			Musgrave–Miller's α		
	(1) GNP	(2) NNP	(3) NI	(4) GNP	(5) NNP	(6) NI
(1) Government consumption	1.291	1.135	1.135	0.075	0.077	0.127
(2) Fixed investment	1.431	1.277	1.277	0.108	0.108	0.175
(3) Exports	1.271	1.118	1.118	0.120	0.123	0.202

More specifically, in this system (2.2) and (2.15) are replaced by

$$P_i = p_i X_i - T_i - \sum_{j=1}^{n} p_j X_{ji} - p_i^z Z_i - w_i L_i \quad (i = 1, \ldots, n), \qquad (5.4)$$

$$Y = \sum_{i=1}^{n} w_i L_i + Pr - T_p, \qquad (5.5)$$

respectively, and T_i and T_p are regarded as given. All the t_is in equations (2.4) are set at zero, and all other equations are kept unchanged. This is a system in which tax yields rather than tax rates are considered as direct instruments of government policy, subject to legislative decision; following Goldberger's terminology[1] it is called the 'predetermined tax yield model', while the original model is called the 'endogenous tax yield model'.[2]

By a procedure similar to that adopted in Chapter 4, the GNP, NNP and NI multipliers are computed for the predetermined tax yield case.[3] Columns (1),(2) and (3) of Table 21, which correspond to columns (1) to (3) of Table 11 in the endogenous tax yield case, present respectively the changes in GNP, NNP, and NI induced by a unit change in the final demand for an individual sector. Columns (1), (2) and (3) of Table 22, which correspond to columns (1) to (3) of Table 12 in the endogenous tax yield case, give respectively the GNP, NNP and NI multipliers, i.e. the effects on GNP, NNP and NI of a unit increase in government consumption (or gross fixed investment, or exports) with the 1960 industrial distribution. It is seen that the GNP multipliers of government consumption, fixed investment and exports are computed at 1.291, 1.431 and 1.271 respectively, exceeding the corresponding multipliers in the endogenous tax yield case by 0.097, 0.155 and 0.153 respectively.

---

[1] A. S. Goldberger, *op. cit.* p. 37.

[2] It is noted that, since we make no change in the property income equation (2.13) or (3.14), corporate tax yields are still endogenous in our predetermined tax yield model.

[3] For the sake of computational simplicity Φ_P and Φ_G are evaluated at the point of the observed 1960 values, although the relative prices (all unity in 1960) do not necessarily satisfy the set of equations in the predetermined tax yield system.

The effectiveness of built-in flexibility may be measured by Musgrave and Miller's α:[1]

$$\alpha = 1 - \frac{\Delta Y}{\Delta Y_a},$$

where ΔY_a is the income change that would occur in response to an injection of autonomous expenditure if tax yields remained constant, while ΔY is the income change that would occur under a given tax rate system in response to the same injection. Columns (4) to (6) of Table 22 show the Musgrave–Miller coefficients for GNP, NNP and NI respectively. The Musgrave–Miller α with respect to government consumption, 0.075, implies that the response of tax yields to income changes reduces the income changes by 7.5 per cent when the income changes are induced by a change in government consumption. As has been stated in Chapter 4, the α of 0.108 with respect to gross fixed investment may be considered as an approximation to the coefficient for *government* investment expenditures. An average of 0.075 and 0.108, weighted with the 1960 share of consumption and investment in total government expenditures, is computed at 0.092. This value is comparable with Goldberger's finding, 0.113,[2] but is somewhat less than one third of the figure obtained by Musgrave and Miller, 0.358.[3] Goldberger considered that the difference between Musgrave and Miller's estimate and his own might be largely ascribed to the facts that the Musgrave–Miller estimate was obtained by predetermining personal income taxes only and that Goldberger's estimate referred to impact (or one-year) effects rather than to longer-run effects.

These figures may also be compared with the following recent estimates. Using a simple model of the Keynesian type, Hansen estimated the Musgrave–Miller α at 0.1 for Belgium, 0.3 for France, 0.4 for Germany, 0.2 for Italy, 0.2 for Sweden, 0.2 for the UK and 0.4 for the USA.[4] Balopoulos' estimate of α, based on a British econometric model with a set of detailed tax functions, is 0.246 when exports are increased by one unit at 1958 factor cost, 0.265 when public corporations increase productive investment by one unit at current prices, and 0.246 and 0.244 when public authorities increase purchases of goods and services, and investment on housing, respectively, by one unit at current prices.[5]

It may be of some interest to calculate the reduction in GNP in 1960–1 due to built-in flexibility of taxes. Columns (1) and (2) in Table 23 present the GNP multipliers in the endogenous and predetermined tax yield cases.

[1] R. A. Musgrave and M. H. Miller, *op. cit.* p. 123.   [2] Goldberger, *op. cit.* p. 46.
[3] Musgrave and Miller, *op. cit.* p. 127.   [4] B. Hansen, *op. cit.* p. 65.
[5] E. T. Balopoulos, *op. cit.*

TABLE 23. *The reduction in income due to built-in flexibility, 1960–1*

	GNP multipliers		1960–1 observed changes in final demands (1960 billion yen) (3)	1960–1 GNP changes due to final demand changes (1960 billion yen)	
	Tax yield endogenous (1)	Tax yield predetermined (2)		Tax yield endogenous (1) × (3) (4)	Tax yield predetermined (2) × (3) (5)
(1) Government consumption	1.194	1.291	105.6	126.0	136.3
(2) Gross fixed investment	1.276	1.431	1,312.2	1,674.3	1,877.7
(3) Net inventory change	1.140	1.305	150.9	172.0	196.9
(4) Exports	1.118	1.271	30.8	34.4	39.2
(5) Total	–	–	1,599.5	2,006.7	2,250.1

	Income reduction (1960 billion yen) (5) − (4) (6)	1960–1 GNP growth due to final demand changes (%)		Growth rate reduction (%) (8) − (7) (9)
		Tax yield endogenous $(4)/A^a$ (7)	Tax yield predetermined $(5)/A^a$ (8)	
(1) Government consumption	10.3	0.81	0.88	0.07
(2) Gross fixed investment	203.4	10.78	12.09	1.31
(3) Net inventory change	24.9	1.11	1.27	0.16
(4) Exports	4.8	0.22	0.25	0.03
(5) Total	243.4	12.93	14.49	1.56

[a] A is the observed 1960 GNP in the input–output table, i.e. 15,525.0 billion yen.

The products of the 1960–1 observed changes in final demands and the respective multipliers give the changes in GNP due to these changes in final demands, which are shown in colums (4) and (5) for the endogenous and predetermined tax yield cases respectively. The differences between the corresponding figures in columns (4) and (5) are given in column (6), whose total is 243.4 billion yen, which is the estimated GNP reduction due to built-in flexibility. The GNP reductions in terms of the growth rate of GNP are derived from columns (7) and (8) and given in column (9). The total GNP reduction of 243.4 billion yen amounts to a reduction of 1.56 per cent in terms of the growth rate.

TABLE 24. *The changes in relative prices induced by a unit change in the 1960 composition of final demands*

	Tax yield predetermined			Tax yield endogenous			Musgrave–Miller's coefficient		
	(1) Government consumption	(2) Fixed investment	(3) Exports	(4) Government consumption	(5) Fixed investment	(6) Exports	(7) $1-\frac{(4)}{(1)}$	(8) $1-\frac{(5)}{(2)}$	(9) $1-\frac{(6)}{(3)}$
1. Agriculture	24	39	44	22	34	42	0.083	0.128	0.046
2. Forestry	41	120	82	40	132	85	0.024	-0.100	-0.037
3. Coal and petroleum mining	13	25	24	12	24	23	0.077	0.040	-0.042
4. Metal and nonmetal mining	12	34	28	11	36	29	0.083	-0.059	-0.036
5. Food	24	40	43	25	40	46	-0.042	0.000	-0.070
6. Textiles	22	36	54	21	36	56	0.046	0.000	-0.037
7. Lumber and furniture	30	81	59	29	89	62	0.033	-0.099	-0.051
8. Pulp and paper	36	63	65	37	68	69	-0.028	-0.079	-0.062
9. Printing and publishing	41	55	55	40	54	55	0.024	0.018	0.000
10. Leather	21	38	42	21	39	45	0.000	-0.026	-0.071
11. Rubber	23	48	61	23	49	63	0.000	-0.021	-0.033
12. Chemicals	35	59	72	35	62	78	0.000	-0.051	-0.083
13. Petroleum products	26	49	48	32	62	61	-0.231	-0.265	-0.271
14. Stone, clay and glass	24	69	54	24	77	58	0.000	-0.116	-0.074
15. Primary metals	28	86	78	28	91	82	0.000	-0.058	-0.051
16. Fabricated metals	24	72	60	23	78	64	0.042	-0.083	-0.067
17. Machinery	27	87	64	26	92	67	0.037	-0.058	-0.047
18. Electrical machinery	28	82	67	28	89	71	0.000	-0.085	-0.060
19. Transportation equipment	26	71	63	27	77	67	-0.039	-0.085	-0.064
20. Miscellaneous manufacture	31	58	72	31	61	78	0.000	-0.052	-0.083
21. Construction	23	82	48	23	87	50	0.000	-0.061	-0.042
22. Utilities	38	66	65	41	73	72	-0.079	-0.106	-0.108
23. Trade	23	39	40	22	39	39	0.044	0.000	0.025
24. Transportation and communication	36	58	65	36	60	67	0.000	-0.035	-0.031
25. Services	62	55	52	64	51	48	-0.032	0.073	0.077
26. Unallocated	28	47	50	30	54	58	-0.071	-0.149	-0.160
Average	31	61	56	31	63	58	0.000	-0.033	-0.036

The unit of the figures in columns (1) to (6): 10^{-6} (index point)/billion yen.

The effects of built-in flexibility on relative prices are similarly estimated. Columns (1) to (3) of Table 24 present the effects on relative prices of a unit increase in government consumption (or fixed investment, or exports) with the 1960 composition. The bottom row of the table shows the change in the average relative price;[1] for example, an increase of 100 units (or 100 billion yen) in fixed investment will raise the average relative price by 0.61 per cent in the predetermined tax yield case and by 0.63 per cent in the endogenous tax yield case. It is noted that in either case the effect of a unit increase in government consumption on the average relative price is drastically smaller than that of a unit increase in fixed investment. This is largely due to the fact that expenditure for public administration (sector 27) accounts for a large proportion of government consumption whereas its effect on relative prices is relatively small, because a change in the output of that sector affects the relative prices only through the change in income of government employees.

Musgrave and Miller's formula may be used to measure the effects of built-in flexibility on relative prices; that is to say, a coefficient α_{π_i} is defined as:

$$\alpha_{\pi_i} = 1 - \frac{\Delta\pi_i}{\Delta\pi_{ia}},$$

where $\Delta\pi_{ia}$ is the change in the relative price of output i that would occur in response to an injection of autonomous expenditure if tax yields remained constant, while $\Delta\pi_i$ is the similar effect in the endogenous tax yield case. The values of α_{π_i} are calculated for the cases of government consumption, fixed investment or exports being increased, as shown in columns (7), (8) and (9) of Table 24.

Finally, similar calculations are made with respect to aggregate industrial employment (i.e. total hours worked in all sectors except agriculture and forestry), the average wage and the average money price. The results are presented, together with those on GNP and the average relative price, in Table 25. Our analysis may be concluded by saying that the existence of built-in flexibility will result in (1) a reduction of about 10 per cent (7.5 to 12.0 per cent) in GNP at constant prices, (2) a reduction of about 20 per cent (17.0 to 21.8 per cent) in aggregate industrial employment, (3) a reduction of about 20 per cent (17.1 to 21.9 per cent) in the average wage, (4) practically no change (0.0 to 3.6 per cent increase) in the average relative price, and (5) a reduction of about 10 per cent (9.3 to 11.5 per cent) in the average money price.

[1] The average price here is an average of the relative prices of all industries weighted by their gross outputs.

TABLE 25. *The effects of an increase of 100 billion yen in final demand on employment, the average wage and the average money price*

	Tax yield predetermined			Tax yield endogenous			Musgrave–Miller's coefficient		
	(1) Government consumption	(2) Fixed investment	(3) Exports	(4) Government consumption	(5) Fixed investment	(6) Exports	(7) $1 - \frac{(4)}{(1)}$	(8) $1 - \frac{(5)}{(2)}$	(9) $1 - \frac{(6)}{(3)}$
(1) Change in GNP in 1960 prices (billion yen)	129.1	143.1	127.1	119.4	127.6	111.8	0.075	0.108	0.120
(2) Change in industry employment (billion hours per year)	0.898	1.269	1.144	0.746	1.034	0.894	0.170	0.185	0.218
(3) Rate of change in the average wage (%)	0.56	0.79	0.71	0.46	0.64	0.56	0.171	0.190	0.219
(4) Rate of change in the average relative price (%)	0.31	0.61	0.56	0.31	0.63	0.58	0.000	−0.033	−0.036
(5) Rate of change in the average money price (%)	0.87	1.40	1.28	0.77	1.27	1.14	0.115	0.093	0.109

Appendix A: *Sources and units of statistical data*

Sources and units of statistical data are listed below. For details of X_i, N_i, h_i, K'_i, and p_i, see Table A1.

X_i: Gross output of industry i, billions of 1960 yen.
X_i = Table A1, (col. 1)+(col. 2)+(col. 3).

N_i: Number of persons engaged in industry i, thousands of persons.
N_i = Table A1, (col. 4)+(col. 5)+(col. 6).

h_i: Number of hours worked per month per person in industry i, hours.
h_i = Table A1, (col. 7)+(col. 8).

L_i: Total hours worked of industry i, millions of hours per year.
$L_i = (N_i) \times (h_i) \times 12.0/1000.0$.

K'_i: End-of-year stock of capital in industry i, billions of 1960 yen.
K'_i = Table A1, [(col. 9)+(col. 10)] or (col. 11).

K_i: Yearly average of capital stock in industry i, billions of 1960 yen.
$K_i = \frac{1}{2}(K'_{i-1}+K'_i)$.

p_i: Price index of output in industry i, 1960 = 1.0.
p_i = Table A1, (col. 12), (col. 13) or (col. 14).

$C'_{k,t}$:   Consumption of consumer survey category k (time series of national aggregate), billions of 1960 yen.
$C'_{k,t} = (S_{27})$.

$p^c_{k,t}$:   Consumer price index of consumer survey category k, 1960 = 1.0.
$p^c_{k,t} = (S_{28})$.

p^c_t: Average of $p^c_{k,t}$, 1960 = 1.0.
$p^c_t = (S_{28})$.

$\bar{L}_t$:   Population, thousands of persons.
$\bar{L}_t = (S_{29})$.

$C'^*_{k,j}$:   Consumption of consumer survey category k of income class j (1960 survey data), thousand yen per household.
$C'^*_{k,j} = (S_{30})$.

$\bar{L}^*_j$:   Number of persons per household, units.
$\bar{L}^*_j = (S_{30})$.

TABLE A1

Industry	X_i (1) Source (S_1)	(2) Source (S_2)	(3) Other sources	N_i (4) Source (S_5)	(5) Source (S_6)	(6) Other sources	h_i (7) Source (S_{10})	(8) Other sources
(1)		(1)+(2)+(3)+(4)+(6)		(1)		$-N_2$ (S_7)		$4.345 \times (S_{11})$
(2)		(5)						$4.345 \times (S_{11})$
(3)				(2)			Mining	
(4)				(3)			Mining	
(5)				(4)			Food and related products	
(6)				(5)			Textile mill products	
(7)				(6)			Lumber and wood products	
(8)				(7)			Pulp, paper, etc.	
(9)				(8)			Publishing, printing, etc.	
(10)				(9)			Leather and leather products	
(11)				(10)			Rubber products	
(12)				(11)			Chemical and allied products	
(13)				(12)			Petroleum and coal products	
(14)				(13)			Ceramic, stone and clay products	
(15)		(33)+(34)+(35)			(7)		Iron and steel	
(16)		(36)					Fabricated metal products	
(17)		(37)+(41)			(8)		Machinery and precision instruments	
(18)		(38)			(9)		Electrical machinery	
(19)		(39)+(40)		(16)	(10)		Transportation equipment	
(20)	(17)			(17)		(S_8)	Miscellaneous manufacturing	
(21)	(18)			(18)			Construction	
(22)	(19)			(19)			Electricity, gas and water	
(23)	(20)			(20)			Wholesale and retail trade	
(24)	(22)		$-X_{27}$	(22)	(16)		Transportation and communications	
(25)	(23)	(16)		(23)		$-N_{27}$	Real estate plus wholesale and retail trade	
(26)			(S_3)	-	-	-	Communications	
(27)			(S_4)	-	-	(S_9)	All industries	

TABLE A1 (cont.)

Industry	K_i'			p_i		
	(9) Source (S_{12})	(10) Source (S_{13})	(11) Source (S_{15})	(12) Source (S_{16})	(13) Source (S_{17})	(14) Other sources
(1)	$0.8405 \times (1)$		(1)			(S_{18})
(2)	—	—	—			(S_{19})
(3)	(2)		(2)			(S_{20})
(4)	(3)		(2)			(S_{20})
(5)	(4)		(3)			(S_{21})
(6)	(5)		(4)	Textiles		
(7)	(6)		(12)	Timber and products		
(8)	(7)		(5)	Pulp, paper and products		
(9)	(8)		(12)	$0.3077 \times p_8 + 0.6923 \times p_{20}$		
(10)	(9)		(12)		Leather plus leather goods	
(11)	(10)		(12)	Chemical goods		
(12)	(11)		(6)	Oil, coal and products		
(13)	(12)		(12)	Ceramics		
(14)	(13)		(12)	Iron and steel plus nonferrous metals		
(15)		(7)			Rubber products	
(16)		(8)		Metal products		
(17)		(9)+(S_{14})			General industrial machinery	
(18)		(10)			Electrical machinery	
(19)		(11)			Transportation machinery	
(20)	(17)		(12)			(S_{22})
(21)	(18)		(13)			(S_{23})
(22)	(19)		(14)		Electric power plus gas	
(23)	(20)		(15)			(S_{24})
(24)	(22)		(17)			(S_{25})
(25)	(23)	(16)	(19)			(S_{26})
(26)	—	—	—	—	—	—
(27)	—	—	—	—	—	—

$p_t^c C_{j,t}^*$:   Total consumption of income class j (yearly survey data), thousand yen per household.
$$p_t^c C_{j,t}^* = (S_{31}).$$

$p_t^c Y_{j,t}^*$:   Disposable income of income class j (yearly survey data), thousand yen per household.
$$p_t^c Y_{j,t}^* = (S_{31}).$$

$\bar{L}_{j,t}^*$:   Number of persons in the household, units.
$$\bar{L}_{j,t}^* = (S_{31}).$$

$p_t^c C_t^*$:   Average of $p_t^c C_{j,t}^*$, thousand yen per household.
$$p_t^c C_t^* = (S_{31}).$$

p_i^z: Price index of noncompetitive imports used in industry i, 1960 = 1.0.
$$p_i^z = (S_{32}).$$

p_i^m: Price index of competitive imports of good i, 1960 = 1.0.
$$p_i^m = (S_{33}).$$

M_i: Competitive imports of good i, billions of 1960 yen.
$$M_i = (S_{34}).$$

R: End-of-year gold and foreign exchange reserves, millions of US dollars.
$$R = (S_{35}).$$

M: Net payments of foreign exchange, millions of US dollars.
$$M = (S_{36}).$$

w: Index of average wage earnings, excluding agriculture, forestry and fishery.
$$w = [(S_{37}) + (S_{38})]/L.$$

L: Total hours worked, excluding agriculture, forestry and fishery, millions of hours per year.
$$L = (S_{43}).$$

Lf: Total available labour hours, millions of hours per year.
$$Lf = (S_{46}).$$

L':   End-of-year number of persons engaged, excluding agriculture, forestry and fishery, thousands of persons.
$$L' = (S_{48}).$$

P: Profits, billions of current yen.
$$P = (S_{49}) - (S_{37}) - (S_{50}) + (S_{51}).$$

Pr: Property income, billions of current yen.
$$Pr = (S_{52}) - (S_{37}) - (S_{50}) + (S_{53}).$$

p: Implicit price deflator of GNP, 1960 = 1.0.
           $p = (S_{57})$.

(S_1):   Ministry of Labour [14],[1] Table 8–4, p. 164. The number in parentheses in Table A 1 indicates row number.

(S_2):   EPA [6], Table 4–2, pp. 29–30. The number in parentheses in Table A 1 indicates row number.

(S_3):   [6], Table 4–1, p. 28, row 20.

(S_4):   EPA [6], Table 4–2, p. 30, for 1960–3; and Ministry of Labour [14], Table 6–7, p. 156, for 1955. The figures for 1956–9 are interpolated by the series for NNP produced by the government (EPA [5], p. 68).

(S_5):   Ministry of Labour [14], Table 8–2, p. 162. The number in parentheses in Table A 1 indicates row number.

(S_6):   EPA [6], Table 6–1, p. 38. The number in parentheses in Table A 1 indicates row number.

(S_7):   For 1960 and 1963, Ministry of Labour [14], Table 5–2, pp. 138–9. The figures for 1955–9 are extrapolated back by the series for employed persons in agriculture and forestry in the 'labour force survey', Ministry of Labour [13]. The figures for 1961 and 1962 are interpolated by the series for employed persons in agriculture and forestry as above.

(S_8):   Employed persons in precision instrument manufacturing. Ministry of Labour [14], Table 5–2, pp. 138–9, for 1955, 1960 and 1963. The figures for other years are interpolated by the employment index for precision instruments (Ministry of Labour [13]).

(S_9):   For 1960, Ministry of Labour [14], Table 5–2, p. 138. The figures for other years are extrapolated by employed persons in government in the 'labour force survey,' Ministry of Labour [13].

(S_{10}): Average monthly hours worked per regular employee, Ministry of Labour [13].

(S_{11}): Average weekly hours worked in agriculture and forestry in the 'labour force survey,' Ministry of Labour [13], 4.345 = (365/12)/7.

(S_{12}): Ministry of Labour [14], Table 8–5, p. 165. The number in parentheses in Table A 1 indicates row number. 0.8405 is the ratio

---

[1] Numbers in square brackets refer to the references on p. 236.

of capital stock in agriculture and forestry to that in agriculture, forestry and fishery in the Wealth Survey.

The series in source (S_{12}) are known for 1955–63; hence they are extrapolated back to 1954 by the series of capital stock in source (S_{15}).

(S_{13}): EPA [6], Table 5–1, p. 31. The number in parentheses in Table A 1 indicates row number.

(S_{14}): End-of-year capital stock for precision instruments, EPA [7], Table 1, p. 7.

(S_{15}): EPA [8], Table 1, pp. 60–1. The number in parentheses in Table A 1 indicates row number. See (S_{12}).

(S_{16}): Index numbers for industrial products by groups, Bank of Japan [1]. *Plus* indicates weighted average of prices of both industries. The weights are gross output of both industries. The weight of 0.3077 (printing and publishing) is the share of the cost of paper and pulp in total cost.

(S_{17}): Index numbers for commodity classes in basic indices, Bank of Japan [1], for 1960–3. For 1955–9, the price index with 1952 base (Bank of Japan, [2], pp. 299–433) is converted to a 1960 base.

(S_{18}): Weighted average of prices of agricultural and aquatic products ('nonindustrial products by groups', Bank of Japan [1]), and of perishable food stuffs (Bank of Japan [1] for 1960–3 and extrapolated by the retail price index of perishable food stuffs, Bank of Japan [3], for 1955–9). The weights, 0.7914 and 0.2086 respectively are those of the wholesale price index, Bank of Japan [1].

(S_{19}): The price index for timber and products, 'nonindustrial products by groups,' Bank of Japan [1].

(S_{20}): The price of output (i.e. X_3 or X_4) is the domestic price. The price of input (i.e. X_{3i} or X_{4i}) is a weighted average of the domestic and import prices; the weights are, respectively, domestic output and imports of the 1960 input–output table. The domestic price is the ratio between the value and quantity of output, Ministry of International Trade and Industry [12]. The import price is the ratio of the value and quantity of imports, Ministry of Finance, [11].

(S_{21}): EPA [9], Table 18, row 3, p. 18.

(S_{22}): The price index of miscellaneous manufacturing, excluding leather, leather goods and rubber products, Bank of Japan [1].

(S_{23}): Annual average of quarterly construction cost index, Ministry of

Construction [10], which is a weighted average of cost indices of construction (Table 3, pp. 6–8) and building (Table 6, pp. 15–17).

(S_{24}): The sales index divided by $(X_{21}/2489.2)$. The sales index comes from 'Indexes of Wholesale and Retail, Total', Ministry of International Trade and Industry. 2489.2 is gross output of trade in 1960.

(S_{25}): Weighted average of charges of freight, mail, telephone and telegram, Bank of Japan [4], pp. 309–10.

(S_{26}): Weighted average of price indices of rent (Office of the Prime Minister [15]), of water (Bank of Japan [4], p. 309–10), of banking and insurance (*EPA* [9], Table 18, row 18, p. 18), and of services (weighted average of consumer price indices of medical and toilet care, education and recreation, Office of the Prime Minister [15]). The weights, respectively, are gross output of real estate, water services, banking and insurance and public *plus* miscellaneous services in the 56-sector input–output table of 1960.

(S_{27}): EPA [6], Table 1–2, p. 2.

(S_{28}): EPA [6], Table 1–3, p. 3.

(S_{29}): Ministry of Labour [13], 'labour force survey'.

(S_{30}): Office of the Prime Minister [15], 1960 issue, Table 2, pp. 14–19.

(S_{31}): Office of the Prime Minister [15], 'yearly average of monthly receipts and disbursements per household by money income groups – December excluded, worker households, all Japan'.

(S_{32}): For p_{11}^z, 'rubber' from the same source as (S_{17}). For p_6^z, Bank of Japan [4], Table 162– (2), p. 308, 'textile fibres'.

(S_{33}): See the import price of (S_{20}).

(S_{34}): The quantity series of imports are available in Ministry of Finance [11]. They are adjusted so as to equal the corresponding imports of the 1960 input–output table in the base year.

(S_{35}): Bank of Japan [3], for 1954–64. The figures for 1952 and 1953 are extended by 'gold and foreign exchange holdings by the Bank of Japan and Government' Bank of Japan [3].

(S_{36}): Bank of Japan [4], Table 152, pp. 279–80, 'payment of foreign exchange, total of visible and invisible trade'.

(S_{37}): EPA [5], Table 2, row 1, pp. 70–1, 'employment compensation'.

(S_{38}): Imputed wages of self-employed and family workers, $((S_{39}) - (S_{40})) \times (S_{41})$.

(S_{39}): Number of persons engaged, excluding agriculture, forestry and fishery, Ministry of Labour [14], p. 162, for 1955–63. The figures for 1952–4 and 1964–5 are extended by the series for the corresponding category in 'labour force survey', Ministry of Labour [13].

(S_{40}): Number of employees, excluding agriculture, forestry and fishery, Ministry of Labour [14], p. 163, for 1955–63. The figures for 1952–4 and 1964–5 are extended by the series for the corresponding category in 'labour force survey', Ministry of Labour [13].

(S_{41}): The imputed wage earnings of self-employed and family workers, $((S_{37})/(S_{42})) \times (0.1677/0.2681)$.
$0.2681 =$ the 1960 value of $(S_{37})/(S_{42})$.
$0.1677 =$ the 1960 value of the imputed wage earnings of self-employed and family workers, excluding agriculture, forestry and fishery. See Appendix B.

(S_{42}): Number of employees, all industries. The same source as (S_{40}).

(S_{43}): $\sum_{i=3}^{27} L_i$ for 1955–63, $0.943 \times (S_{44})$ for 1952–4, and $0.982 \times (S_{44})$ for 1964–5.

(S_{44}): $((S_{42})+(S_{39})-(S_{40})) \times (S_{45}) \times 12.0/1000.0$.

(S_{45}): 'Average monthly hours worked per regular worker: total', Ministry of Labour [13].

(S_{46}): $(S_{47}) \times 202.7 \times 12.0/1000.0$.
$202.7 =$ maximum of (S_{45}) during the sample period.

(S_{47}): Total labour force, Ministry of Labour [13], 'labour force survey'.

(S_{48}): Ministry of Labour [13], 'labour force survey'.

(S_{49}): National income, EPA [5], Table 2, row 10, pp. 70–1.

(S_{50}): Unincorporated income, EPA [5], Table 2, row 2, pp. 70–1.

(S_{51}): Imputed profits of self-employed and family workers. $(S_{54})-(S_{38})$.

(S_{52}): Personal income, EPA [5], Account 3, pp. 60–1.

(S_{53}): Imputed dividend. $(S_{51}) \times (S_{55})/((S_{55})+(S_{56}))$.

(S_{54}): Unincorporated income, excluding agriculture, forestry and fishery, EPA [5] Table 2, row $2.b$, pp. 70–1.

(S_{55}): Dividends, EPA [5], Table 2, row $3.c$, pp. 70–1.

(S_{56}): Corporate profits, EPA [5], Table 2, the last row, pp. 70–1.

(S_{57}): EPA [5], Table 5, row 5, pp. 82–3.

REFERENCES

[1]   Bank of Japan, *Wholesale Price Index Annual* (Oroshiuri Bukka Shisū Nempō), 1955 to 1963 (The Bank of Japan).

[2]   —, *Wholesale Price Undex, 1887–1962* (Oroshiuri Bukka Shisū, 1887–1962), (The Bank of Japan, 1964).

[3]   —, *Economic Statistics of Japan* (Hompō Keizai Tōkei), (The Bank of Japan).

[4]   —, *Economic Statistics of Japan, 1965* (Hompō Keizai Tōkei), (The Bank of Japan, 1966).

[5]   EPA (Economic Planning Agency), *Annual Report on National Income Statistics 1966* (Kokuminshotoku Tōkei Nempō), (Economic Planning Agency, 1967).

[6]   —, *Basic Data I on the Input–output Model* (Sangyōrenkan-model Kankei Kiso-shiryō I), mimeograph (Economic Planning Agency, 1967).

[7]   —, *Estimates of Gross Capital Stock by Industries* (Minkankigyō no Sangyō-betsu Sō-shihon-stock no Suikei), mimeograph (Economic Planning Agency, 1967).

[8]   —, '*Estimates of Gross Capital Stock*' (Sō-shihon-stock no Suikei), *Economic Analysis* (Keizai Bunseki), (March, 1966), pp. 59–95.

[9]   —, *Basic Data on a Study of Prices* (Kakaku Bunseki-yō Kisoshiryō), mimeograph (Economic Planning Agency, 1967).

[10]   Ministry of Construction, *Quarterly Index of Construction Cost, 1951–65*, (Shihanki-betsu Kensetsu-hi Shisū, 1951–65), mimeograph (Ministry of Construction, 1966).

[11]   Ministry of Finance, *Monthly Report on International Trade* (Nippon Gaikokubōeki Geppyō), 1953 to 1965 (Ministry of Finance).

[12]   Ministry of International Trade and Industry, *The Statistical Yearbook of Japanese Mining* (Hompō Kōgyō no Sūsei), 1953 to 1965 (Ministry of International Trade and Industry).

[13]   Ministry of Labour, *The Statistical Yearbook of Labour* (RōdōTōkei Nempō), 1953 to 1965 (Ministry of Labour).

[14]   —, *An Interindustry Analysis of Labour Employment* (Shōwa-35-nen Sangyōren-kanhyō niyoru Rōdōkeizai no Bunseki), (Ministry of Labour, 1964).

[15]   Office of the Prime Minister, *Annual Report on the Family Income and Expenditure Survey* (Kakei-chōsa Nempō), 1953 to 1965 (Office of the Prime Minister).

Appendix B: *Computational notes on the aggregated input–output table*

(1) Table B1 gives the correspondence between the industries of the aggregated 27-sector table (shown in Table 1) and the original 56-sector table.

TABLE B1. *Industrial classification scheme*

27 Sectors (Aggregated)	56 Sectors (Original)
(1) Agriculture and fisheries	(1) Fruits and crops (except crops for industrial use) (2) Crops for industrial use (3) Livestock, and poultry for clothing (4) Other livestock and poultry (including agricultural services) (6) Fisheries
(2) Forestry	(5) Forestry and logging (including hunting)
(3) Coal and crude petroleum	(7) Coal and lignite (10) Crude petroleum and natural gas
(4) Metal and nonmetal mining	(8) Iron ores (9) Nonferrous metallic ores (11) Other mining
(5) Food	(12) Slaughtered livestocks (13) Manufactured sea foods (14) Grain mills (15) Miscellaneous processed foods (16) Beverages (17) Tobacco
(6) Textiles	(18) Spinning fibres, vegetable and animal (19) Spinning fibres, chemical and synthetic (20) Fabrics, miscellaneous textile products (21) Clothing
(7) Lumber and furniture	(22) Sawed products, veneer, plywood and wooden products (23) Furniture
(8) Pulp and paper	(24) Pulp, paper
(9) Printing and publishing	(25) Printing and publishing
(10) Leather	(26) Leather and leather products

TABLE B1 (*cont.*)

27 Sectors (Aggregated)	56 Sectors (Original)
(11) Rubber	(27) Rubber products
(12) Chemicals	(28) Basic chemicals
	(29) Raw materials of chemical and synthetic fibres
	(30) Miscellaneous chemicals
(13) Petroleum and coal products	(31) Petroleum products
	(32) Coal products
(14) Stone, clay and glass	(33) Nonmetallic mineral products, except petroleum and coal products
(15) Primary metals	(34) Pig iron, ferroalloys and steel ingots
	(35) Basic iron and steel products
	(36) Basic nonferrous metal products
(16) Fabricated metals	(37) Metal products
(17) Machinery	(38) Machinery, except electrical machinery
	(41) Precision instruments (including optical instruments, watches and clocks)
(18) Electrical machinery	(39) Electrical machinery, apparatus, appliances and supplies
(19) Transportation equipment	(40) Transportation equipment
(20) Miscellaneous manufacturing	(42) Miscellaneous manufacturing
(21) Construction	(43) Building (including repairing)
	(44) Construction except building
(22) Utilities	(45) Electricity
	(46) Gas
(23) Trade	(48) Wholesale and retail trade
(24) Transportation and communication	(51) Transportation (including storage and warehousing)
	(52) Communications
(25) Services	(47) Water services (including sewage disposal)
	(49) Banking, insurance
	(50) Real estate
	(54) Public services
	(55) Miscellaneous services
(26) Unallocated	(56) Unallocated
(27) Public administration	(53) Public administration and defence

TABLE B2. *Consumption classification scheme*

Items of this paper	Prais and Houthakker's items	Stone's items
(1) Cereals	C_i $(i = 1$, and 3 to 6)	1, 2 and 4
(2) Vegetables	G_i $(i = 1$ to 5)	21 and 22
(3) Meat, fish and dairy	D_i $(i = 1$ to 6, 9 to 10) H_i $(i = 1$ to 3) and I_i $(i = 7, 9$ and 10)	5, 6, 8 to 11 and 13 to 17
(4) Processed food and condiments	C_2, D_i $(i = 7, 8$ and 11) E_i $(i = 4$ to 7), F_i $(i = 5, 6)$ G_6, I_8, and J_i $(i = 1$ to 3)	7, 12, 18 to 20, 23, 25 to 27 and 31 to 33
(5) Cakes, fruit and beverages	C_i $(i = 7$ and 8) E_i $(i = 1$ to 3), F_i $(i = 1$ to 4), and K_1	3, 24 and 28 to 30
(6) Meals away from home	J_i $(i = 4$ to 7)	34
(7) Clothing	N_i $(i = 1$ to 6) and T_1	
(8) Fuel and light	M_i $(i = 1$ to 11)	
(9) Water	L_i $(i = 1$ and 2)	
(10) Rent	L_i $(i = 1$ and 2)	
(11) Furniture and repairs	O_i $(i = 1$ to 9)	
(12) Medical and toilet care	S_i $(i = 1$ to 4)	
(13) Transportation and communications	P_4 and R_i $(i = 1$ to 6)	
(14) Amusement and literary activity	P_i $(i = 2$ and 3), and Q_i $(i = 1$ to 3)	
(15) Tobacco	K_i $(i = 2$ and 3)	
(16) Education and others	P_1 and T_i $(i = 2$ to 10)	

(2) The imputed labour income:

The imputed labour income of self-employed and family workers of industry i is computed as:

[(the number of persons engaged in industry i) − (the number of employees in industry i)] × (the average wage of industry i).

The figures come from the Ministry of Labour [14,] Table Fu-6, pp. 194–8. This imputed labour income of each industry is added to the wages, and subtracted from the surpluses, of the original table to get wages (row 31) and surplus (row 32) of Table 1 respectively.

(3) Noncompetitive imports:

The noncompetitive imports of textiles, 277.593, are the sum of the $X_{02,j}$s and $X_{03,j}$s ($j = 18, ..., 21$), where the suffix (i,j) refers to the industrial classification of the original 56-sector table (see Table B1). The noncompetitive imports of rubber products, 49.552 billion yen, are $X_{02,27}$ of the original table. These X_{ij}s are put as 0.0 and the corresponding amount is subtracted from imports of the second and third industries of the original table to get imports of the first industry of the aggregated table.

(4) In the estimation of the Cobb–Douglas exponents labour income is defined as the sum of wages and business consumption (rows 31 and 30 of Table 1 respectively), profits as the sum of surpluses and depreciation (rows 32 and 33 respectively), and indirect taxes as the difference between indirect taxes and subsidies (rows 34 and 35 respectively). Business consumption is included in labour income because its greater part is regarded as a subsidiary wage payment in Japan.

(5) The consumption classification scheme of this paper is compared with those of Prais–Houthakker and Stone in Table B 2. See Prais, S. J. and H. S. Houthakker, *op. cit.* pp. 179–83; and R. Stone *et al.*, *op. cit.* pp. 315–27.

PART IV

An input–output analysis of disguised
unemployment in Japan, 1951–1965

by M. Morishima and Y. Murata

1. *Introduction*

I. DEFINITION OF DISGUISED UNEMPLOYMENT

In the *General Theory*, Keynes confined himself to investigating causes of involuntary unemployment, as distinct from voluntary unemployment, and proposing remedies for it. In Keynes' world complete unemployment is forced upon a worker if he is not employed. In reality, especially in those economies in which a well-organized labour market has not yet been established, there is a mixture of employment and unemployment, i.e. disguised or latent unemployment which might superficially be considered as employment but in substance has to be regarded as a kind of unemployment. Then what are the causes of disguised unemployment? What are the remedies for it? In the present studies we try to extend the Keynes–Leontief theory so as to be able to deal with these problems.

Our concept of disguised unemployment corresponds to Marx's relative surplus-population in its latent and stagnant forms. With respect to the surplus-population in its latent form, Marx wrote:

> As soon as capitalist production takes possession of agriculture, and in proportion to the extent to which it does so, the demand for an agricultural labouring population falls absolutely...Part of the agricultural population is therefore constantly on the point of passing over into an urban or manufacturing proletariat...This source of relative surplus-population is thus constantly flowing. But the constant flow towards the towns presupposes, in the country itself, a constant latent surplus-population, the extent of which becomes evident only when its channels of outlet open to exceptional width. The agricultural labourer is therefore reduced to the minimum wages...[1]

He also wrote:

> The third category of the relative surplus-population, the stagnant, forms a part of the active labour army, but with extremely irregular employment. Hence it furnishes to capital an inexhaustible reservoir of disposable labour-power. Its conditions of life sink below the average normal level of the working class; this makes it at once the broad basis of special branches of capitalist exploitation. It is characterized by maximum of working-time, and minimum of wages. We have learnt to know its chief form under the rubric of 'domestic industry'. It recruits itself constantly from the supernumerary forces of modern industry and agriculture, and specially from those decaying branches of industry...[2]

[1] K. Marx, *Capital, A Critical Analysis of Capitalist Production*, vol. 1, translated by S. Moore and Edward Aveling (Moscow: 1965), p. 642.

[2] K. Marx, *op. cit.* p. 643.

[243]

Naturally, Marxian economists have emphasized the importance of disguised unemployment during the fifties in the Japanese economy, which still had much agriculture and many domestic industries, as well as modern industries. It is said that in Japan there were 6.7 million persons who might be considered to be in disguised unemployment in March 1952, when 35.56 million persons were employed and 0.53 million unemployed. From these figures, we have to say that the problem of pseudo-employment is at least as important as the problem of genuine unemployment in 'dual' economies, such as Japan's, where non-capitalistic elements are still active and powerful.

Although a more rigorous definition is given later, we now define disguised unemployment roughly as follows.[1] A man is said to be in a state of disguised unemployment if he is employed at a wage rate which is lower than the normal or equilibrium rate. If the labour market is perfectly organized and workers can move freely between industries ('industry' is used here in an extended sense including agriculture), then the wage rate is 'equalized' throughout all industries, after allowing for differences in skill, risks, etc. which are normally required or expected for work in the respective industries. Let $\bar{w}_1, ..., \bar{w}_n$ be the wage rates which would prevail in sectors $1, ..., n$, when there exists a perfect labour market. Let $w_1, ..., w_n$ be the actual wage rates in these sectors. If the actual wage rate, w_i, is lower than the equilibrium rate, $\bar{w}_i$, then workers in sector i are in a state of disguised unemployment.

Since we assume that a uniform wage rate prevails within each sector, all employment in a sector becomes disguised if the wage rate there is lower than its equilibrium rate. But we do not measure the magnitude of disguised unemployment in that sector by the total number of labourers working there. In fact, if some (but not all) workers are removed, the output of that industry is decreased so that its price will be increased. The industry then becomes able to pay its workers wages at a higher rate; when wages are raised to the normal level, disguised unemployment vanishes in that sector. Thus, the removal of part of the total employment in the sector is sufficient to normalize the rest. By the size of the part which needs to be removed in order to bring about normalization we measure the magnitude of disguised unemployment in the sector. This gives the excess of the actual number of workers employed in the sector over the equilibrium number at which disguised unemployment is zero.

It may appear to be so far so good. However, it is obvious that the above argument must be re-developed so as to take into account factors which determine employment, other than the wage rate in the sector, since the

[1] A similar (but *prima facie* different) definition of disguised unemployment is given by Joan Robinson. See her *Essays in the Theory of Employment* (Macmillan, 1937), p. 84.

wage rate is not the sole determinant. The above argument does hold true if the only wage rate which deviates from its equilibrium value is that in sector i. If there are several sectors where the prevailing wage rate differ from the respective equilibrium rate, some modification is necessary.

Let z_i be the actual employment of labour in sector i and γ_i the share of wages in the total value of output of sector i. γ_i is assumed to be constant. By definition, we have

$$\gamma_i = \frac{w_i z_i}{p_i x_i} \quad \text{or} \quad z_i = \frac{\gamma_i}{w_i} p_i x_i, \tag{1.1}$$

where x_i is the output of industry i, p_i its price and w_i the wage rate in industry i. Next, let $\overline{w}_i$ be the equilibrium wage rate; the values which p_i, x_i, and z_i take on when the equilibrium wage rate in each industry prevails are denoted by the corresponding symbols with a bar. According to the previous definition of disguised unemployment, it is measured by $z_i - \overline{z}_i$, provided that the actual wage rate is lower than the equilibrium rate in industry i, i.e. $w_i < \overline{w}_i$. If the differences between p_i and $\overline{p}_i$ and between x_i and $\overline{x}_i$ are ignored, disguised unemployment, $z_i - \overline{z}_i$, is positive if, and only if, $w_i < \overline{w}_i$. But, if they are allowed for, it may be negative even if $w_i < \overline{w}_i$, and positive even if $w_i \geqslant \overline{w}_i$. As will in fact be verified in the next chapter, this is not possible, though repercussions upon prices and outputs are not negligible, if the wage rates other than that in industry i are given at their equilibrium levels. But such possibilities always exist if wage rates deviate from the equilibrium values in two or more industries.

On the basis of a general equilibrium system, we approach the problem of disguised unemployment in the following way. Suppose the equilibrium wage rates, $\overline{w}_1, ..., \overline{w}_n$, which would prevail in the economy if it were provided with a perfectly organized labour market, are known to us. The absolute level of the wage rates does not matter; equilibrium prices and wage rates in terms of the equilibrium wage rate in industry 1 are denoted by

$$\overline{p}'_i = \overline{p}_i/\overline{w}_1 \quad (i = 1, ..., n) \quad \text{and} \quad \overline{w}'_i = \overline{w}_i/\overline{w}_1 \quad (i = 2, ..., n).$$

Because of the imperfection of the labour market, the actual wage structure $w'_i = w_i/w_1, i = 2, ..., n$, may differ from the equilibrium structure, $\overline{w}'_i$, $i = 2, ..., n$. Such a distortion in the wage structure will cause a distortion in the price structure, from $\overline{p}'_i, i = 1, ..., n$, to $p'_i = p_i/w_1, i = 1, ..., n$, which in turn induces changes in outputs. Allowing for such changes in prices and outputs, actual employment z_i is calculated according to formula (1.1) and is compared with the equilibrium employment $\overline{z}_i$ calculated in a similar way. We say, irrespective of the relationship of w_i to $\overline{w}_i$, that there is disguised unemployment in industry i if z_i is greater than $\overline{z}_i$.

According to this definition positive disguised unemployment may occur in an industry whose wage rate is higher than the equilibrium one, so that it may be thought at first sight that this definition is not appropriate. However, the level of the actual wage rate should be examined not only in comparison with the equilibrium wage rate but also with the actual value of output. Our definition amounts to saying that w_i is lower than $\overline{w}_i$ if $w_i/(p_i x_i)$ is lower than $\overline{w}_i/(\overline{p}_i \overline{x}_i)$; therefore, w_i is 'lower' than $\overline{w}_i$ even though $w_i > \overline{w}_i$, if $\overline{p}_i \overline{x}_i$ is sufficiently greater than $p_i x_i$. It seems that this arithmetic paradox is legitimate enough from the point of view of economics.

Disguised unemployment, thus viewed as the result of a direct effect of a distortion of the wage structure upon employment and its indirect effects through changes in prices and outputs, may conveniently be analysed into two components. For this purpose, the value of output, $p_i x_i$, in (1.1) is substituted by a linear combination of the final demands for goods, the constants of the combination being supplied by the input–output table. Then (1.1) can be written as

$$z_i = \frac{\gamma_i}{w_i'} \sum_j b_{ij} \, p_j' D_j, \tag{1.2}$$

where b_{ij}s are the elements of the Leontief inverse of the (augmented) input coefficients and D_j represents the final demand for good j. One of the components is a partial effect of w_i' on z_i, which is obtained when the repercussions upon prices $p_1', \ldots, p_n'$ are neglected. The other is an additional change in z_i arising from the adjustments of prices to the change in the wage rate w_i'. When the distortion of the wage structure from the equilibrium structure is infinitesimally small, the total effect is given by the sum of these two components. In the case of a finite distortion, the sum does not give the true total effect but only approximates it.

Similarly, the effect of an increase in final demand D_k upon disguised unemployment, $z_i - \overline{z}_i$, may be analysed into two components: the direct partial effect and the roundabout effect via changes in prices. In this case it is noted that not only the actual prices corresponding to actual wage rates, but also the equilibrium prices corresponding to equilibrium wage rates, are disturbed by a change in D_k.

For a long time, Japan suffered from the existence of severe, inveterate disguised unemployment which arose from persistent wage differentials among industries (especially the low wage rate in agriculture). However, the period 1951–65, which we have examined in this study, was a period during which Japan managed drastically to reduce disguised unemployment. During the period she was also very successful in expanding her GNP. We present a method of estimating disguised unemployment in Chapter 2 and actually estimate it in Chapter 3 for the four years 1951, 1955, 1960 and 1965, for which an input–output table is available.[1] According to our estimates, the percentages of disguised unemployment to total actual employment were 18.4 per cent and 15.0 per cent in 1951 and 1955, respectively; then they were reduced to 10.7 per cent in 1960 and 9.6 per cent in 1965. These are results of changes in the wage structure and expansion of final demand. In Chapter 4, we shall see how these observed decreases in disguised unemployment are analysed into partial effects of changes in the wage structure and partial effects of the expansion of final demand. It will be interesting to see which of them was efficacious in curing Japan's chronic disease.

2. WAGE DIFFERENTIALS IN JAPAN

Since the Restoration of 1868 it has been the ultimate purpose of the Japanese to build *Seiyo* (the West) in Japan. It was of course impossible for a poor country to westernize itself completely in a reasonable period of time. So the Japanese had to be content with building up within the country a thoroughly Occidentalized core, *Kindai Nippon* (modern Japan), which would do credit to them. Only selected people could be full citizens of the privileged sub-country; a few more could spend only their daytime lives there, working in its offices; but all Japanese are very proud of the products of *Kindai Nippon*, such as Zero fighters, the *Hikari* express, mammoth tankers, and even the Tokyo Tower, more so than historic inheritances such as *Horyuji* temple, *Himeji* castle and the *kabuki*.

Before the War, although the majority of the people had little chance of benefiting from the 'priority' policy, they supported it, because of their patriotic feelings; and after the War, they were still not very antagonistic towards it, because of the high probability for those parents who have clever sons, that they would gain entry into the upper strata of society. If a boy could graduate from one of the good universities (say, the best 50 out of 800 universities) it was almost certain that he would be given some comfortable, if not exciting, position in *Kindai Nippon*. It seems that a high propensity to go to university in Japan is closely related to the dual structure of the society.

Discrimination between the modern sector and the traditional sector has created very big wage differentials between agriculture and industry, between big and small business, between skilled and unskilled labour, and so on.[2]

---

[1] The first two tables were compiled by the Ministry of International Trade and Industry, and the last two by the Administrative Management Agency, Japan.

[2] The duality in the Japanese economy is neatly reviewed by S. Broadbridge. See his *Industrial Dualism in Japan* (London: Frank Cass and Co. 1966).

Such differentials evidently conflict with competition and have to be eliminated eventually; but, although there are indications that some of them have recently begun to vanish, their existence has continued for a long time, for social reasons specific to Japan. This is not a surprising, exceptional resistance against rationality. In the West too, it is taking a long time to remove wage differentials between the sexes.

The labour market in Japan is also divided into two distinct sections: one for *Kindai* and the other for *Zen-kindai Nippon* (pre-modern Japan). Companies belonging to the former pick the best newcomers to the labour market, and the failures knock on the door of the second section. The most important factors governing selection are the 'intellectual ability' which is attributed to the candidates according to the conventionalized classification of the universities and schools, and the 'agreeability' or obedience of the candidates. There is some family favouritism, but nepotism is far less influential in *Kindai Nippon*, compared with school fraternity. In fact, this part of society is dominated by the graduates of a few top universities.[1]

The jobs in *Kindai Nippon* are 'permanent', but the retiring ages are comparatively low. Winners in the struggle for careers remain in that sector, as directors, after the initial retiring age, and the rest are rusticated to sub-contracting firms in *Zen-kindai Nippon*, as directors or employees. These firms are controlled directly or indirectly by parent companies and are destined to be the first victims in serious business depressions, in their role as buffers or guards for the parent companies.

The essence of the *Yamato-damashii* (Japanese spirit) lies in allowing concord between persons to take precedence over any other virtue. The first Japanese constitution promulgated in the twelfth year to the Empress Suiko (AD 604) stated, in its first article, that concord between persons was the most precious principle of the community. But it is clear that the concord emphasized there was not one between equal persons, because it was also stated in the same article that the people should make it their principle *not* to contradict their sovereign, their parents, and the majority of the community. It is not surprising that in such a society, where consideration is given to the 'whole' before individuals, sacrifices of individuals for the 'whole' have always been encouraged. The *Kamikaze* suicide-bombing corps were not wartime exceptions; even after the War, there were numerous hopeless individuals who were forced to be loyal to a small group of selected persons in the name of the 'majority' of the society.

There is little of the spirit of Western individualism; there is little ethic

---

[1] It is remarkable that feudal Japan was reformed into a paradise for intellectuals and professionals by the Meiji restoration in 1868 – a revolution whose leaders were poor, highly educated, subordinate samurai.

of competition and fair play. It is true that in Japan extremely severe competition is imposed upon boys and girls up to the stage of high school, but as soon as they are graded in the academic hierarchy by the university entrance examinations their future careers are almost completely determined. Further competition is not welcomed; they must stand on the stairs of the escalator in the order of the quality of their universities. 'A taller stake will be hammered.' 'Select a big tree for your shelter.' 'A loyal retainer would not serve a second master.' Various vulgar arts of succeeding in life are recommended to youths in support of the prevailing social order. The notorious system of grading wages by seniority is preserved by the same reasoning; it assures the 'majority' of tranquillity.

If the labour market was competitive, there would be no large wage differentials between the *Kindai* and *Zen-kindai* sectors, because workers in the latter would offer to work for entrepreneurs in the *Kindai* sector at a wage rate lower than the ruling wage rate in the *Kindai* sector, but still higher than their current wage rate. However, because *Yamato-damashii* values concord between persons above everything else, entrepreneurs in *Kindai Nippon* prefer new graduates from the universities and schools to disloyal *samurai* who leave their masters and colleagues in the lurch and look for second lords, even though fresh men are much more expensive than the 'betrayers'. It is usually extremely difficult for a man in the *Zen-kindai* sector to move to a company in the *Kindai* sector, unless he is strongly recommended by a powerful man in the company.

Clearly, it is ridiculous to pay unnecessarily high wages because of psychological and ethical inclinations. There must also be some economic reason for the fact that the labour aristocrats in *Kindai Nippon* receive higher wages. In this respect, as has been pointed out, Japan's powerful subcontracting system must play a crucial role. Suppose that wage differentials vanish between the two sectors. Then, in the short run, *Kindai* firms will certainly benefit, because they will be able to employ workers at a cheaper wage rate, whereas *Zen-kindai* firms will find themselves in a difficult position, since they have to compete with *Kindai* firms. Many of them will be defeated, and only a few strong firms will be able to survive, so that the subcontracting system will lose its foundation. This implies that *Kindai* firms will be placed in a risky position such that they will be confronted with the impact of business depression without buffers. High wages at ordinary times might thus be considered as including insurance premiums against damages due to depression.

Now it is seen from Table 1 that Japan is one of those countries which have large wage differentials between agriculture and industry. The ratio of the agricultural to the industrial wage is calculated for 1955 for all the

TABLE I. *International comparison of wage differentials between agriculture and industry*

Country (1)	The ratio of the agricultural to the industrial wage (2)	Composition of labour in agriculture		(Number of employees in manufacturing industries) ÷ (number of persons engaged in manufacturing industries) (5)	Remarks
		(Number of employees) ÷ (number of persons engaged) (3)	(Number of unpaid family workers) ÷ (number of persons engaged) (4)		
New Zealand	0.89	0.42	0.08	0.91	1956, $m+f+l$
Portugal	0.83	0.61	0.11	0.82	1950, *
UK	0.70	0.66	0.02	0.96	1951
Sweden	0.67	0.50	–	0.95	1960
Colombia	0.67	0.42	0.14	0.56	1951, *
W. Germany	0.59	0.15	0.53	0.91	1960, m
Austria	0.57	0.21	0.50	0.79	1951, $m+f+l$, *
Finland	0.55	0.22	0.46	0.87	1950
Canada	0.50	0.26	0.16	0.95	1962, *
USA	0.47	0.28	0.13	0.95	1960, $m+l$
Japan	0.47	0.05	0.58	0.86	1960, m, *
Peru	0.46	0.33	0.19	0.32	1940
Philippines	0.46	0.18	0.35	0.43	1960, $m+f$
Norway	0.43	0.25	0.43	0.88	1950, $m+f+l$
France	0.41	0.23	0.40	0.86	1954, m, *
India	0.34	–	–	0.38	m
Mexico	0.24	0.30	0.18	0.68	1950, m, *
Cyprus	1.09	0.29	–	0.66	1946, m, *
S. Korea	1.01	0.03	0.58	0.47	1955, $m+f$, *
Belgium	0.80	0.14	0.31	0.85	1947
Bulgaria	0.83	0.71	–	0.91	1956, m
Hungary	0.81	0.19	0.28	0.88	1960, m
Czecho-Slovakia	0.76	0.14	0.51	0.92	1950, *
Yugoslavia	0.75	0.05	0.51	0.84	1953
Poland	0.70	0.08	0.54	0.95	1950

Source: International Labour Office, *Yearbook of Labour Statistics 1962*, Geneva.

TABLE 2. *The ratio of employees to the total number of persons engaged in some major countries*

Year	Japan	USA	UK	W. Germany	France	Italy	Canada
1950	35.4%	79.5%	92.0%	–	–	–	–
1951	37.8	80.8	92.1	–	–	–	–
1952	38.1	81.4	91.7	–	–	–	–
1953	39.9	81.7	92.3	–	–	–	–
1954	40.6	81.3	92.4	72.7%	64.3%	54.7%	75.5%
1955	41.0	81.8	92.4	73.8	65.3	54.6	77.1
1956	43.4	82.4	92.5	74.7	66.3	58.1	78.6
1957	45.5	82.7	92.6	75.1	67.6	59.2	79.2
1958	47.4	82.9	92.4	75.3	68.4	59.1	79.9
1959	49.4	83.2	92.3	75.9	68.9	59.4	80.7
1960	51.0	83.7	92.5	77.2	69.7	61.0	81.2
1961	52.7	83.9	92.7	77.7	70.5	62.6	81.1
1962	54.6	84.6	92.8	78.3	71.3	64.2	81.8
1963	55.9	85.4	93.1	78.9	72.6	64.4	82.2
1964	57.1	85.7	93.2	79.5	73.5	64.1	82.7
1965	58.6	86.4	–	–	–	–	–

Source: OECD, *Manpower Statistics*.

countries in the table apart from South Korea and Yugoslavia. For these two countries the figures for 1955 are unavailable, so that the figures listed for South Korea and Yugoslavia are for 1956 and 1959, respectively. The figures in the remarks column represent the years for which the figures in column 3 (the ratio of agricultural employees to the total population engaged in agriculture), column 4 (the ratio of unpaid agricultural family workers to the total population engaged in agriculture), and column 5 (the ratio of industrial employees to the total population engaged in industry) are calculated for the corresponding countries. The symbol m indicates that only money wages are taken into account for agricultural wages where there is also a payment in kind; l (or f) indicates that lodgings (or food) provided for agricultural workers are included in their wages. Finally, * indicates that the average agricultural wage of male workers is compared with the average industrial wage of both male and female workers. The figures with * will naturally overestimate the true values, while those with m, $m+f$ or $m+l$ may underestimate them.

Table 2 shows how the ratio of employees to the total number of persons engaged has changed in recent years in some major industrial countries. This ratio may be considered as an index of the degree to which the capitalistic sector is dominant in each country. From the table it is seen that although the Japanese figures have improved very much during the 1950s and 1960s, the only figure with which her 1965 figure is comparable, is Italy's 1956

TABLE 3. *Wage differentials in some major countries*

(Average wage in plants of 1000 or more workers = 100)

Scale of plant (number of workers)	Wage differentials				
	Japan (1960)	USA (1958)	France (1958)	W. Germany (1958)	Britain (1949)
1000 or more	100	100	100	100	100
500–999	79	85	91	85	89
300–499	70	79^a	86^e		86^h
200–299	64			83^g	
100–199	59	77^b	79		85
50–99	54	74	79	81	84
30–49	50	74^c	78^f	–	
20–29	47			–	83^i
10–19	42	71	78	–	84^j
4–9	33	67^d	–	–	–

^{a} 250–499; ^{b} 100–249; ^{c} 20–49; ^{d} 5–9; ^{e} 200–499; ^{f} 20–49;

^{g} 100–499; ^{h} 200–499; ^{i} 25–49; ^{j} 11–24.

Source: S. Broadbridge, *Industrial Dualism in Japan* (London: Frank Cass and Co. 1966), p. 51.

figure. Therefore, we may say that in this respect Japan was still eight or ten years behind Italy in 1965.

Table 3 compares wage differentials in Japan with those in the major countries. Other data show that about two-thirds of Japan's industrial and commercial labour force work in minor enterprises. In sectors such as construction, distribution, services, and manufacturing industries producing wood and wood products, pulp, paper and printing, and stone, pottery and glass, particularly high proportions of smaller businesses are found, while in sectors producing chemical products, iron, steel and non-ferrous metals and electricity the proportions are rather low. These facts suggest that the proportions of *Kindai* and *Zen-kindai Nippon* differ among sectors, so that there are wage differentials between sectors. For example, the average wage in the wood-and-wood-products sector, which is about 50 per cent of the wage level prevailing in the big firms of 1000 or more workers in that sector, is less than half of the average wage in the electricity sector.

Table 4 compares agricultural and industrial wages in Japan in four different years with those in the United Kingdom in 1960. The Japanese figures are derived, by making some adjustments, from the input–output tables for the years 1951, 1955, 1960 and 1965, respectively, while the British figures are obtained by dividing the industrial wages and salaries given in *National Income and Expenditure* (Central Statistical Office, 1963) by the numbers of workers employed in the respective industries, given in

TABLE 4. *Industrial relative wages: Japan and the United Kingdom*

| Industry | Japan | | | | UK |
	1951	1955	1960	1965	1960
(1) Agriculture, fishing and forestry	0.56	0.57	0.61	0.60	1.00
(2) Mining	1.57	1.61	1.43	1.22	1.35
(3) Food, beverages and tobacco	0.69	1.07	0.76	1.03	1.01
(4) Textiles and clothes	0.82	0.81	0.75	0.81	0.85
(5) Wood and wood products	0.68	0.95	0.80	0.99	1.10
(6) Pulp, paper and printing	1.91^a	1.61	1.31	1.16	1.32
(7) Leather and rubber products	1.11^b	0.85	1.03	0.97	0.96
(8) Chemical products	1.37	1.37	1.55	1.92	1.27
(9) Stone, pottery and glass	1.08	1.01	1.09	0.84	1.18
(10) Iron, steel and nonferrous metals	1.63	1.28	1.49	1.40	1.31
(11) General machinery and equipment	0.96	1.16	1.39	1.30	1.21^c
(12) Electrical machinery	1.24	0.94	1.21	1.13	1.21^c
(13) Ship-building and vehicles	1.22	1.09	1.51	1.44	1.34
(14) Precision machinery	1.17	1.14	1.18	1.10	1.21^c
(15) Other manufacturing	1.11^b	0.70	0.79	0.97	1.06
(16) Construction	0.52	1.44	0.98	1.18	1.34
(17) Electricity	2.27	2.47	2.16	1.92	1.41
(18) Distributive trades	1.26	0.86	1.14	1.08	1.13
(19) Transport and storage	1.61	1.46	1.56	1.58	1.44
(20) Communication, gas, water and business services	1.18	1.59	1.28	1.44	1.28

[a] Excluding 'printing'.

[b] Including 'printing', 'leather and rubber products' and 'other manufacturing'.

[c] Including 'general machinery and equipment', 'electrical machinery' and 'precision machinery'.

Annual Abstract of Statistics (Central Statistical Office, No. 101, 1964). It is noted that each wage vector is normalized so that the sums of the elements (i.e. the sum of the figures in each column) are all equal. Sectoral wage differentials depend upon the divisions between permanent and daily employees and skilled and unskilled labour, the sex and age compositions of the workers, and so on, as well as wage differentials between big and small businesses within the sectors. We assume throughout this study that wage differentials within sector i in year t are similar to those in year t', except for the wage differentials due to the scale of firms. We also assume that the sex and age compositions of the workers, etc. in each sector do not change significantly. Then a change in the wages of sector i from year t to t' will only reflect a change in the wage differentials between big and small business from year t to t'. As well as assuming that the wage differentials within the Japanese sector i remain the same in $t = 1951, 1955, 1960$ and

1965, we also assume that they are similar to those within the UK sector i in 1960. We might then expect that the UK relative wages will prevail in Japan when the wage differentials between big and small businesses are improved to such an extent as to approach the situation in the UK economy in 1960.

These assumptions are satisfied to some extent. For example, it is seen that the sex composition of the workers is more or less stable in Japan in the period 1951–60 and the wage differentials due to sex are similar in Japan and the United Kingdom. In this study we take the UK 1960 relative wages as the equilibrium relative wages which would prevail in Japan if wage differentials due to the scale of the firms could be removed. As has been pointed out, there are a number of grounds for justifying this heroic assumption. First, capitalism is most advanced in the United Kingdom in the sense that the ratio of employees to the total number of persons engaged in every major industry is the highest among developed economies. Secondly, the ratio of agricultural to industrial wages in the UK is very high compared with capitalist economies and is comparable with those in socialist economies, where the same wages are paid, in principle, to all kinds of labour of the same efficiency. Thirdly, wage differentials due to the scale of the firms are negligible in every industry in the UK economy. Fourthly, wage differentials between industries in the UK are the smallest among advanced capitalist economies.[1]

Now we can state what we want to deal with in this study. As is often maintained, some disguised unemployment is caused by the intraindustrial dual structure of production, i.e. the coexistence of big and small business within the same industry. However, the input–output tables of the Japanese economy unfortunately have not been so constructed that such a kind of disguised unemployment can be analysed. In this study we give up the idea of dealing with the intraindustrial disguised unemployment and reluctantly confine ourselves to discussing disguised unemployment caused by interindustrial wage differentials. We assume, together with the assumptions stated above, that firms which belong to the same industry are all homogeneous, and by doing so, we preclude intraindustrial unemployment from existing. Even under this assumption, firms of an industry may be distinguishable from those of other industries in the scale, due to which

---

[1] It is interesting to see that what Marx said about England is still true in the second half of this century. He said: 'In this work I have to examine the capitalist mode of production, and the conditions of production and exchange corresponding to that mode. Up to the present time, their classic ground is England. That is the reason why England is used as the chief illustration in the development of my theoretical ideas'. (Marx, *op. cit.* vol. 1, p. 8.) This is also the reason why the British relative wages are taken as the equilibrium wages in our study.

TABLE 5. *The time series of the Liapounoff indices*

Indices	1951	1955	1960	1965
D	5.24	4.40	3.64	3.44
D^+	2.64	2.20	1.80	1.67
V	1.60	1.41	1.13	1.07
V^+	1.12	0.77	0.73	0.62

wages may be different from industry to industry. The Japanese relative wages will approach those of the UK (1960) when the labour market in Japan is improved so that there are no significant wage differentials between big and small businesses. It is evident that our results could be revised so as to allow for intraindustrial disguised unemployment when we were provided with input–output tables which were so constructed as to dis-aggregate each industry into big-firm and small-firm sectors.

Finally, let w_i^t be the relative wages per person in the Japanese industry i in year t, and w_i^B the relative wages per person in the same British industry in 1960. They are normalized so that

$$\sum_i w_i^t = \sum_i w_i^B \quad (t = 1951, 1955, 1960, 1965).$$

The distance between the vectors w^t and w^B may be defined in various ways. We define them as,

$$D_t = \sum_i |w_i^B - w_i^t|, \qquad D_t^+ = \sum_i \max (w_i^B - w_i^t, 0),$$
$$V_t = \sqrt{(\sum_i (w_i^B - w_i^t)^2)}, \qquad V_t^+ = \sqrt{(\sum_i (\max (w_i^B - w_i^t, 0))^2)}.$$

The values of these Liapounoff indices calculated from Table 4 are summarized in Table 5, which shows that each of these indices was decreasing in the period 1951–65, so that we may conclude that the wage vector w^t in Japan was approaching the British wage vector w^B in this period. Our analysis below finds that there are disguised unemployment in those industries whose wage rates are relatively lower than the corresponding wage rates in the UK economy. The amount of disguised unemployment is seen to have decreased considerably in the period, but it is found that there still remained, in 1965, a substantial amount of disguised unemployment in industries such as agriculture, fishing and forestry; pulp, paper and printing; stone, pottery and glass; construction; and a few others.

2. Disguised unemployment in a re-interpreted input–output model

In this chapter we develop a method of estimating disguised or latent unemployment of labour – a new method based on Leontief's input–output analysis. The great advantage of this method lies in the fact that it enables us to discover those sectors which act as reservoirs for disguised unemployment. However, most available input–output tables, or at least those for the Japanese economy, have not been so constructed as to make them ideally suited for this purpose. They entirely neglect the dual structure within each sector by paying no attention to the simultaneous existence of big and small factories, developed and underdeveloped technologies, modern and traditional social and economic elements, and so on, within each sector. We must therefore recognize a limitation of the application of our method to the existing actual input–output tables; nevertheless, the reader will be convinced of the effectiveness of our method by the very plausible results derived in the next chapter.

Four input–output tables for Japan have so far been published; they are for the years 1951, 1955, 1960 and 1965. In the first two tables, inputs of imported goods are distinguished from those of domestic goods, whilst in the last two a sectoral input given in a cell of the input–output tables includes not only domestic input but also imported input. Although our method is applicable to both kinds of input–output table with no significant differences in principle, we first confine ourselves to its application to the first two tables, and then explain the necessary adjustments which have to be made for the treatment of imports when we apply the method to the other two tables.

1. MODEL I FOR THE 1951 AND 1955 TABLES

An actual input–output table describes the interindustrial relations in an actual economy where (i) there are differences in scale among firms belonging to the same sector, (ii) big firms play the role of price maker, while small firms cannot influence market prices, and (iii) each firm may produce by-products as well as its main product. We, however, construct, as a first approximation to reality, a model economy where entrepreneurs can only adjust their operations to market prices, which are viewed as parameters by them. It is also assumed that each firm produces a single output which is a

[256]

composition of elementary commodities, by using such 'outputs' of other sectors as inputs. Furthermore, it is assumed that firms belonging to the same sector are all homogeneous.

Let x_i^k be the output of firm k in sector i, $x_{ij,k}$ the output of sector i used as input by firm k in sector j, $y_{j,k}$ the imported input of firm k in sector j, and $z_{j,k}$ the labour input of firm k in sector j, where $i, j = 1, ..., n$. We assume a short-run production function of the extended Cobb–Douglas form:

$$x_j^k = G_j x_{1j,k}^{\alpha_{1j}} \cdots x_{nj,k}^{\alpha_{nj}} y_{j,k}^{\beta_j} z_{j,k}^{\gamma_j}, \tag{2.1}$$

where G_j, α_{ij}, β_j, γ_j depend *inter alia* upon fixed capital goods endowed in firm k and are regarded as constant throughout the following short-run analysis. It follows from the assumed homogeneity of the firms that G_j, α_{ij}, β_j, γ_j are common to all firms in the same sector.

Next, let p_i be the price of the output of sector i, q the price of imported goods, and w_j the wage rate in sector j. The short-run economic problem for firm k in sector j is to maximize the profit

$$p_j x_j^k - (\sum_i p_i x_{ij,k} + q y_{j,k} + w_j z_{j,k})$$

subject to the production function (2.1). For a given set of prices

$$(p_1, ..., p_n, q, w_j)$$

this implies the marginal conditions:

$$\alpha_{ij} = \frac{p_i x_{ij,k}}{p_j x_j^k}, \quad \beta_j = \frac{q y_{j,k}}{p_j x_j^k}, \quad \gamma_j = \frac{w_j z_{j,k}}{p_j x_j^k} \quad (i = 1, ..., n). \tag{2.2}$$

These hold for all firms in sector j; we have, therefore,

$$\alpha_{ij} = \frac{p_i x_{ij}}{p_j x_j}, \quad \beta_j = \frac{q y_j}{p_j x_j}, \quad \gamma_j = \frac{w_j z_j}{p_j x_j} \quad (i, j = 1, ..., n), \tag{2.3}$$

where x_j is the total output of sector j, x_{ij} the total input in sector j of goods produced by sector i, y_j the total imported input in sector j, and z_j the total employment of labour in sector j. Obviously $x_j = \sum_k x_j^k$, $x_{ij} = \sum_k x_{ij,k}$, etc.

The basic equations of the input–output analysis can be written as

$$x_i = \sum_j x_{ij} + C_i + F_i \quad (i = 1, ..., n), \tag{2.4}$$

where C_i represents the consumption of output of sector i by workers and F_i the remaining final demand for output of sector i, which consists of consumption of the non-working class, investment, exports and government expenditure. Multiplying (2.4) by p_i and considering (2.3), we obtain

$$X_i = \sum_j \alpha_{ij} X_j + p_i C_i + p_i F_i \quad (i = 1, ..., n), \tag{2.5}$$

where X_i denotes the money value of the output of section i, $p_i x_i$. If the workers' consumption of output i, $p_i C_i$, is a function of the form

$$p_i C_i = \Sigma c_{ij} W_j + p_i d_i \quad (i = 1, ..., n), \tag{2.6}$$

where W_j denotes wage income from sector j, c_{ij} the marginal propensity to consume domestic good i and $p_i d_i$ the basic consumption of good i, then equation (2.5) can further be rewritten, because of (2.3), in the form,

$$X_i = \sum_j (\alpha_{ij} + c_{ij} \gamma_j) X_j + p_i D_i \quad (i = 1, ..., n), \tag{2.7}$$

where $D_i = d_i + F_i$.

Let us now define $\alpha_{ij} + c_{ij} \gamma_j$ as a_{ij}, the $n \times n$ matrix (a_{ij}) as A, and its Leontief inverse, i.e. $(I - A)^{-1}$, as (b_{ij}). Solving (2.7) with respect to X_i and bearing $X_i = p_i x_i$ in mind, we get

$$x_i = \frac{1}{p_i} \Sigma b_{ij} (p_j D_j). \tag{2.8}$$

Therefore, from (2.3),

$$z_i = \frac{\gamma_i}{w_i} \Sigma b_{ij} (p_j D_j) = \frac{\gamma_i}{w_i'} \Sigma b_{ij} \left(\frac{p_j}{w_1} D_j \right), \tag{2.9}$$

where w_i' denotes the relative wage rate, w_i / w_1. As we are provided with the values of $\alpha_{ij}, c_{ij}, \gamma_j, w_i', D_j, i, j = 1, ..., n$, by input–output tables and other statistics, the sectoral employment of labour, $z_i, i = 1, ..., n$, can easily be calculated as soon as the values of prices in terms of w_1 are known.

The relative prices, $p_1 / w_1, ..., p_n / w_1$, are obtained in the following way. Writing $p_j' = p_j / w_1$ and $q' = q / w_1$, we have from (2.2)

$$x_{ij,k} = \alpha_{ij} \frac{p_j'}{p_i'} x_j^k, \quad y_{j,k} = \beta_j \frac{p_j'}{q'} x_j^k, \quad z_{j,k} = \gamma_j \frac{p_j'}{w_j'} x_j^k.$$

Substituting these into (2.1), we obtain

$$(x_j^k)^{\alpha_j} = G_j \alpha_{1j}^{\alpha_{1j}} ... \alpha_{nj}^{\alpha_{nj}} \beta_j^{\beta_j} \gamma_j^{\gamma_j} \left(\frac{p_j'}{p_1'} \right)^{\alpha_{1j}} ... \left(\frac{p_j'}{p_n'} \right)^{\alpha_{nj}} \left(\frac{p_j'}{q'} \right)^{\beta_j} \left(\frac{p_j'}{w_j'} \right)^{\gamma_j}, \tag{2.10}$$

where

$$\alpha_j = 1 - \sum_i \alpha_{ij} - \beta_j - \gamma_j. \tag{2.11}$$

As $x_j = \theta_j x_j^k$, where θ_j is the number of firms in sector j, we have from (2.10)

$$x_j^{\alpha_j} = H_j \left(\frac{p_j'}{p_1'} \right)^{\alpha_{1j}} ... \left(\frac{p_j'}{p_n'} \right)^{\alpha_{nj}} \left(\frac{p_j'}{q'} \right)^{\beta_j} \left(\frac{p_j'}{w_j'} \right)^{\gamma_j},$$

where

$$H_j = G_j \alpha_{1j}^{\alpha_{1j}} \ldots \alpha_{nj}^{\alpha_{nj}} \beta_j^{\beta_j} \gamma_j^{\gamma_j} \theta_j^{\alpha_j}. \qquad (2.12)$$

This, together with (2.8), yields

$$(\Sigma p_k' m_{jk})^{\alpha_j} = H_j \left(\frac{p_j'}{p_1'}\right)^{\alpha_{1j}} \ldots \left(\frac{p_j'}{p_n'}\right)^{\alpha_{nj}} \left(\frac{p_j'}{q'}\right)^{\beta_j} (p_j')^{\gamma_j + \alpha_j} \left(\frac{1}{w_j'}\right)^{\gamma_j},$$

$$(2.13)$$

where $m_{jk} = b_{jk} D_k$.

It is now seen that the price of imported goods q' is a weighted average of the prices of the n outputs, $p_1', \ldots, p_n'$. Imports are classified into two categories: competitive imports are imports of those goods which can be and are produced within the country, while non-competitive imports are imports of those goods which either cannot be produced in the country or can be produced only in a very limited amount. Let u_{kj} be the part of competitive imports of good k used as current input by sector j, and let qu be the total value of competitive imports for the purpose of current production. Obviously,

$$qu = \sum_j (\sum_k p_k u_{kj}), \quad \text{or} \quad q' = \Sigma p_k' n_k,$$

where $n_k = \sum_j u_{kj}/u$. Substituting for q' from this, (2.13) becomes

$$(\Sigma p_k' m_{jk})^{\alpha_j} (\Sigma p_k' n_k)^{\beta_j} = H_j (p_1')^{\delta_{1j} - \alpha_{1j}} \ldots (p_n')^{\delta_{nj} - \alpha_{nj}} (w_j')^{-\gamma_j}, \qquad (2.14)$$

where δ_{ij} is the Kronecker delta, so that it takes on values of zero for $i \neq j$ and one for $i = j$. When the logarithms of both sides are taken, the equations (2.14) may be written, in matrix form, as

$$\begin{bmatrix} 1-\alpha_{11} & -\alpha_{21} & \ldots & -\alpha_{n1} \\ -\alpha_{12} & 1-\alpha_{22} & \ldots & -\alpha_{n2} \\ \vdots & \vdots & & \vdots \\ -\alpha_{1n} & -\alpha_{2n} & \ldots & 1-\alpha_{nn} \end{bmatrix} \begin{bmatrix} \log p_1' \\ \log p_2' \\ \vdots \\ \log p_n' \end{bmatrix}$$

$$= \begin{bmatrix} k_1 + \alpha_1 \log(\Sigma p_k' m_{1k}) + \beta_1 \log(\Sigma p_k' n_k) \\ k_2 + \alpha_2 \log(\Sigma p_k' m_{2k}) + \beta_2 \log(\Sigma p_k' n_k) \\ \vdots \\ k_n + \alpha_n \log(\Sigma p_k' m_{nk}) + \beta_n \log(\Sigma p_k' n_k) \end{bmatrix}, \qquad (2.15)$$

where

$$k_j = -\log H_j + \gamma_j \log w_j'. \qquad (2.16)$$

Evidently, the equations (2.15) are non-linear but determine $\log p_1'$, $\log p_2', \ldots, \log p_n'$ uniquely. To show this, we calculate the Jacobian. As

$$\frac{\partial \log(\Sigma p_k' m_{jk})}{\partial \log p_i} = \frac{p_i' m_{ji}}{\Sigma p_k' m_{jk}} \equiv \xi_{ji}, \quad \text{and} \quad \frac{\partial \log(\Sigma p_k' n_k)}{\partial \log p_i} = \frac{p_i' n_i}{\Sigma p_k' n_k} \equiv \eta_i, \qquad (2.17)$$

the Jacobian is given as

$$
J = \begin{bmatrix}
1-(\alpha_{11}+\alpha_1\xi_{11}+\beta_1\eta_1) & -(\alpha_{21}+\alpha_1\xi_{12}+\beta_1\eta_2) \\
-(\alpha_{12}+\alpha_2\xi_{21}+\beta_2\eta_1) & 1-(\alpha_{22}+\alpha_2\xi_{22}+\beta_2\eta_2) \\
\vdots & \vdots \\
-(\alpha_{1n}+\alpha_n\xi_{n1}+\beta_n\eta_1) & -(\alpha_{2n}+\alpha_n\xi_{n2}+\beta_n\eta_2)
\end{bmatrix}
$$

$$
\begin{matrix}
\cdots & -(\alpha_{n1}+\alpha_1\xi_{1n}+\beta_1\eta_n) \\
\cdots & -(\alpha_{n2}+\alpha_2\xi_{2n}+\beta_2\eta_n) \\
& \vdots \\
\cdots & 1-(\alpha_{nn}+\alpha_n\xi_{nn}+\beta_n\eta_n)
\end{matrix} \; .
$$

Now from the definitions of α_{ij}, β_j, and γ_j as input coefficients, and c_{ij} as the marginal propensity to consume, they are all non-negative. We assume (i) that the sum of the input coefficients of each sector j, i.e. $\Sigma\alpha_{ij}+\beta_j+\gamma_j$, is less than one, and (ii) that the aggregate marginal propensity to consume of the workers of sector j, $\sum_i c_{ij}$, is positive and less than one for each j. By definition, all α_j are positive when (i) holds. (i) and (ii) imply that the column sums of the non-negative matrix

$$
A = \begin{bmatrix}
\alpha_{11}+c_{11}\gamma_1 & \alpha_{12}+c_{12}\gamma_2 & \cdots & \alpha_{1n}+c_{1n}\gamma_n \\
\alpha_{21}+c_{21}\gamma_1 & \alpha_{22}+c_{22}\gamma_2 & \cdots & \alpha_{2n}+c_{2n}\gamma_n \\
\vdots & \vdots & & \vdots \\
\alpha_{n1}+c_{n1}\gamma_1 & \alpha_{n2}+c_{n2}\gamma_2 & \cdots & \alpha_{nn}+c_{nn}\gamma_n
\end{bmatrix}
$$

are all non-negative and less than one, so that the augmented input coefficient matrix A satisfies the so-called Hawkins–Simon conditions (or A is 'productive'). Therefore, its Leontief inverse is non-negative, to the effect that $m_{ij} \geqslant 0$ as $D_j \geqslant 0$. It is now seen from (2.17) that all $\xi_{ji} \geqslant 0$ with $\sum_i \xi_{ji} = 1$.

On the other hand, by definition, all n_i are non-negative; hence, all $\eta_i \geqslant 0$, with $\sum_i \eta_i = 1$.[1]

We can now at once see that all the off-diagonal elements of the Jacobian J are non-positive, and each row sum is non-negative and less than one; this is shown because, considering the definition of α_j in addition to $\sum_i \xi_{ji} = 1$

$\Sigma\eta_i = 1$, we find that the jth row sum equals γ_j. Thus J satisfies all the requirements for the Hawkins–Simon result. Therefore it is a matrix the principal minors of which are all positive. That is to say, the Jacobian of

[1] Note that ξ_{ji} and η_i depend upon $p_1', \ldots, p_n'$, having these properties everywhere.

equations (2.15) is a P-matrix everywhere, so that the uniqueness of solutions to (2.15) is assured by a theorem due to Gale and Nikaido.[1]

Once the uniqueness is established, it is not difficult to find the solutions. Assuming some arbitrary values of $p'_1, ..., p'_n$ on the right-hand side of (2.15), we solve (2.15) with respect to $\log p'_1, ..., \log p'_n$ on the left-hand side. The $p'_1, ..., p'_n$ thus obtained are substituted into the right-hand side and then equations (2.15) are solved with respect to $\log p'_1, ..., \log p'_n$ again. The new values of $p'_1, ..., p'_n$ are substituted into the right-hand side again, and so forth. By this iterative method we can finally find the true solutions, because the sequences of the pseudo-solutions are convergent. Being provided with the relative prices, $p'_1, ..., p'_n$, we can calculate the sectoral employment of labour $z_i, i = 1, ..., n$ by formula (2.9).

2. MODEL II FOR THE 1960 AND 1965 TABLES

In the 1960 and 1965 tables, imported inputs are resolved into their component commodities. Coefficients of imported inputs $\beta_j, j = 1, ..., n$, are now zero, and each interindustrial input x_{ij} includes domestic and imported inputs. The production functions have no term of imported input and are rewritten as

$$x_j^k = G_i x_{1j,k}^{\alpha_{1j}} ... x_{nj,k}^{\alpha_{nj}} z_{j,k}^{\gamma_j}, \tag{2.1'}$$

where, for each j, the sectoral sum of the indices α_{ij}, i.e. $\sum_i \alpha_{ij}$, has to equal the corresponding sum of those indices (α_{ij}s and β_j) of the old production function (2.1) which would be obtained if the 1960 and 1965 tables were constructed as the 1951 and 1955 tables.

This alteration in the treatment of imported inputs gives rise to a revision in the balance equation (2.4) between input and output. Now, as interindustrial inputs x_{ij} include imported inputs, imports must be substracted in order for the total demand for domestic output i to be equated with its supply, x_i. Let v_i be the total imports of good i, and redefine the final demands C_i and F_i so that they include the corresponding demands for imported good i. Then we have, instead of (2.4),

$$x_i = \sum_j x_{ij} + C_i + F_i - v_i \quad (i = 1, ..., n). \tag{2.4'}$$

Let us now assume that imports of good i are proportional to output of good i.

We denote the proportionality coefficient by μ_i. This assumption, together with the marginal conditions,

$$\alpha_{ij} = \frac{p_i x_{ij}}{p_j x_j}, \quad \gamma_j = \frac{w_j z_j}{p_j x_j} \quad (i,j = 1, ..., n), \tag{2.3'}$$

which are obtained in exactly the same way as before, enables us to rewrite (2.4′) in the form

$$(1 + \mu_i) X_i = \sum_j \alpha_{ij} X_j + p_i C_i + p_i F_i \quad (i = 1, ..., n). \tag{2.5'}$$

These balance equations in terms of money are further specified as

$$(1 + \mu_i) X_i = \Sigma(\alpha_{ij} + c_{ij} \gamma_j) X_j + p_i D_i \quad (i = 1, ..., n), \tag{2.7'}$$

since we assume the same consumption functions (2.6) as before.[1] In (2.7′) D_i stands for $d_i + F_i$ as before.

Let us now define

$$A^* = \begin{bmatrix} \alpha_{11} + c_{11}\gamma_1 - \mu_1 & \alpha_{12} + c_{12}\gamma_2 & \cdots & \alpha_{1n} + c_{1n}\gamma_n \\ \alpha_{21} + c_{21}\gamma_1 & \alpha_{22} + c_{22}\gamma_2 - \mu_2 & \cdots & \alpha_{2n} + c_{2n}\gamma_n \\ \vdots & \vdots & & \vdots \\ \alpha_{n1} + c_{n1}\gamma_1 & \alpha_{n2} + c_{n2}\gamma_2 & \cdots & \alpha_{nn} + c_{nn}\gamma_n - \mu_n \end{bmatrix},$$

$$B^* = (b_{ij}^*) = (I - A^*)^{-1},$$

$$m_{ij}^* = b_{ij}^* D_j.$$

Since A^* fulfils the Hawkins–Simon conditions, its Leontief inverse $B^* = (b_{ij}^*)$ is non-negative. We get the formulas for determining the sectoral outputs and employment of labour, in the same way as before:

$$x_i = \frac{1}{p_i} \sum_j b_{ij}^* (p_j' D_j), \tag{2.8'}$$

$$z_i = \frac{\gamma_i}{w_i'} \sum_j b_{ij}^* (p_j' D_j). \tag{2.9'}$$

The equations for determining the relative prices, $p_1', ..., p_n'$, are also derived in the same way as before. But some minor alterations are necessary since $\beta_j = 0$ for all j in this case. We define:

$$\alpha_j = 1 - \sum_i \alpha_{ij} - \gamma_j, \tag{2.11'}$$

$$H_j = G_j \alpha_{1j}^{\alpha_{1j}} ... \alpha_{nj}^{\alpha_{nj}} \gamma_j^{\gamma_j} \theta_j^{\alpha_j}, \tag{2.12'}$$

$$k_j = -\log H_j + \gamma_j \log w_j'; \tag{2.16'}$$

---

[1] Notice, however, that the consumption of good i now includes the consumption of imported good i too.

then the final equations are given as

$$
\begin{bmatrix}
1-\alpha_{11} & -\alpha_{21} & \cdots & -\alpha_{n1} \\
-\alpha_{12} & 1-\alpha_{22} & \cdots & -\alpha_{n2} \\
\vdots & \vdots & & \vdots \\
-\alpha_{1n} & -\alpha_{2n} & \cdots & 1-\alpha_{nn}
\end{bmatrix}
\begin{bmatrix}
\log p_1' \\
\log p_2' \\
\vdots \\
\log p_n'
\end{bmatrix}
$$

$$
= \begin{bmatrix}
k_1 + \alpha_1 \log \left(\Sigma p_k' m_{1k}^* \right) \\
k_2 + \alpha_2 \log \left(\Sigma p_k' m_{2k}^* \right) \\
\vdots \\
k_n + \alpha_n \log \left(\Sigma p_k' m_{nk}^* \right)
\end{bmatrix}, \qquad (2.15')
$$

where $m_{ij}^* \equiv b_{ij}^* D_j \geqslant 0$ because $D_j \geqslant 0$. We can show that $(2.15')$ has unique solutions, $p_1', \ldots, p_n'$, which can be calculated, say, by an iterative method. Substituting these solutions into $(2.8')$ and $(2.9')$, we get the sectoral outputs and employment of labour, corresponding to the given final demands, $D_1, \ldots, D_n$. Finally, it is noted that the Jacobian J^* of $(2.15')$ is given as

$$
J^* = \begin{bmatrix}
1-(\alpha_{11}+\alpha_1\xi_{11}^*) & -(\alpha_{21}+\alpha_1\xi_{12}^*) & \cdots & -(\alpha_{n1}+\alpha_1\xi_{1n}^*) \\
-(\alpha_{12}+\alpha_2\xi_{21}^*) & 1-(\alpha_{22}+\alpha_2\xi_{22}^*) & \cdots & -(\alpha_{n2}+\alpha_2\xi_{2n}^*) \\
\vdots & \vdots & & \vdots \\
-(\alpha_{1n}+\alpha_n\xi_{n1}^*) & -(\alpha_{2n}+\alpha_n\xi_{n2}^*) & \cdots & 1-(\alpha_{nn}+\alpha_n\xi_{nn}^*)
\end{bmatrix},
$$

where $\xi_{ji}^* = p_i' m_{ji}^* / \sum_k p_k' m_{jk}^*$, which is the partial derivative of $\log \left(\Sigma p_k' m_{jk}^* \right)$ with respect to $\log p_i'$.

3. CALCULATION OF DISGUISED UNEMPLOYMENT

As has been pointed out, the actual sectoral relative wage rates, $w_2', \ldots, w_n'$, may differ from the equilibrium relative wage rates (denoted by $\bar{w}_2', \ldots, \bar{w}_n'$) for various reasons. If the given relative wage rate of sector i, w_i', is lower than its equilibrium value, $\bar{w}_i'$, then entrepreneurs in sector i are encouraged to employ more labour than the equilibrium amount. This is the direct effect, to which must be added the following indirect effects. A distortion of the inter-sectoral wage structure induces deviations of the actual relative prices from their equilibrium values. If the actual relative prices of outputs, $1, \ldots, n$, in terms of the wage rate in sector 1, i.e. $p_1', \ldots, p_n'$, are so determined that they are all greater than the respective equilibrium values, then the final demand for every good, $p_j' D_j$, is increased, so that entrepreneurs in every sector are encouraged to expand their output and therefore increase their demand for labour.

To obtain such effects of an inter-sectoral distortion of the wage structure upon the employment of labour, we compare the demands for labour effective at the actual relative wage rates with those at the equilibrium rates.

In order to calculate the latter, we fix the relative wage rates in (2.16) or (2.16′) at their equilibrium values (which are exogenously given) and substitute the parameters k_j thus determined into (2.15) or (2.15′). Solving (2.15) or (2.15′), we get the equilibrium relative prices corresponding to the prescribed equilibrium relative wage rates, which enables us to find the equilibrium employment, denoted by $\bar{z}_i$, according to the formula (2.9) or (2.9′). If the equilibrium employment is less (or greater) than the actual employment in some sector, then there is over-employment (or under-employment) in that sector; and the excess of the actual employment of labour in sector i over its equilibrium employment, if it is positive, gives the 'disguised unemployment' in sector i, which is over-employment due to the distortion of the inter-sectoral relative wage structure.

4. ANALYSIS OF THE DISGUISED UNEMPLOYMENT

As we have seen above, a change in the relative wage rate in sector i has, in addition to the direct effect, indirect effects on the employment of labour in sector i via induced changes in prices. If prices $p'_1, \ldots, p'_n$ change in the same direction as the wage rate w'_i, the direct and indirect effects work in opposite directions, so that in this case the relative importance of these effects must be examined. In this section we are concerned with assessing the repercussions following a change in a wage rate. We shall show that when the wage rate w'_i in sector i increases, all other wages remaining unchanged, then (i) all prices will rise, (ii) the price of the output of sector i will rise proportionately more than the prices of all the other outputs, and (iii) the prices of outputs will increase with elasticity less than one.

First, we differentiate (2.15) with respect to $\log w'_i$; then we obtain

$$\begin{pmatrix} j_{11} & j_{21} & \cdots & j_{n1} \\ j_{12} & j_{22} & \cdots & j_{n2} \\ \vdots & \vdots & & \vdots \\ j_{1n} & j_{2n} & \cdots & j_{nn} \end{pmatrix} \begin{pmatrix} e_{1i} \\ e_{2i} \\ \vdots \\ e_{ni} \end{pmatrix} = \begin{pmatrix} 0 \\ \vdots \\ \gamma_i \\ \vdots \\ 0 \end{pmatrix}, \qquad (2.18)$$

where e_{ki} represents the partial elasticity of p'_k with respect to w'_i, i.e. $\partial(\log p'_k)/\partial(\log w'_i)$; j_{ki} is the (k,i)-element of the Jacobian matrix J, i.e. $j_{ii} = 1 - (\alpha_{ii} + \alpha_i \xi_{ii} + \beta_i \eta_i)$ and $j_{ki} = -(\alpha_{ki} + \alpha_i \xi_{ik} + \beta_i \eta_k)$. J is a matrix of the 'gross-substitute' type; that is to say, the diagonal elements are all positive, the off-diagonal elements are all non-positive, and all row sums are positive. Throughout the following, we assume, for the sake of simplicity, the 'indecomposability' of J, which is harmless because the J's derived from actual input–output tables are really indecomposable, as will be seen in the next chapter. Then it is well known that all elements of the inverse of J are positive.[1] Therefore, the elasticities (e_{ki}s) obtained by solving (2.18) are all positive; this establishes the proposition (i) asserted above.

Next, for any k, the kth row sum of J equals γ_k, which is positive and less than one. This condition, together with the positiveness of the diagonal elements and the non-positiveness of the off-diagonal elements of J, implies that the inverse of J has diagonal elements which are all greater than the off-diagonal elements of the corresponding columns.[2] That is to say, let

$$J^{-1} = \begin{pmatrix} J_{11} & J_{21} & \cdots & J_{n1} \\ J_{12} & J_{22} & \cdots & J_{n2} \\ \vdots & \vdots & & \vdots \\ J_{1n} & J_{2n} & \cdots & J_{nn} \end{pmatrix},$$

then $J_{ii} > J_{ik}, k = 1, \ldots, i-1, i+1, \ldots, n$, for all i. It then follows from

$$\begin{pmatrix} e_{1i} \\ e_{2i} \\ \vdots \\ e_{ni} \end{pmatrix} = J^{-1} \begin{pmatrix} 0 \\ \vdots \\ \gamma_i \\ \vdots \\ 0 \end{pmatrix} = \begin{pmatrix} J_{i1}\gamma_i \\ J_{i2}\gamma_i \\ \vdots \\ J_{in}\gamma_i \end{pmatrix} \tag{2.19}$$

that $e_{ii} > e_{ki}, k = 1, \ldots, i-1, i+1, \ldots, n$, for all i. Thus the direct elasticities are greater than the corresponding cross-elasticities; in other words, the price of the output of sector i, where the wage rate is increased, will rise at the largest rate, as was asserted in proposition (ii) above.

Finally, let us show $e_{ki} < 1$ for all i and k. As we have already seen $e_{ii} > e_{ki} > 0$ for all $k \neq i$, we only prove $e_{ii} < 1$. The ith expression of (2.18) is written as

$$\sum_k j_{ki} e_{ki} = \gamma_i. \tag{2.20}$$

Since $j_{ki}, k = 1, \ldots, i-1, i+1, \ldots, n$, are non-positive and at least one of them is negative (because of the assumed indecomposability of J), we find, in view of the inequality concerning e_{ii} and e_{ki} mentioned above, that the left-hand side of (2.20) is greater than $\sum_k j_{ki} e_{ii}$. On the other hand, we have $\sum_k j_{ki} = \gamma_i$; therefore, $\gamma_i e_{ii} < \sum_k j_{ki} e_{ki} = \gamma_i$; hence $e_{ii} < 1$. Thus we obtain proposition (iii), to the effect that the elasticities of prices, $p'_1, \ldots, p'_n$, with respect to the wage rate w'_i in any sector i are less than one.

These economic propositions (i)–(iii) were originally empirically found by Leontief and then mathematically proved for an input–output model, in which each sector has a production function with an elasticity of substitution

[1] See, for example, M. Morishima *Equilibrium, Stability and Growth*, Chapter I.
[2] This is no more than a direct application of a theorem due to Metzler. See Morishima, *op. cit.* p. 18.

of zero.[1] The above argument confirms the same results for the opposite case where the elasticities of substitution are infinite, provided that the assumed exogenous change of the relative wage rate w'_i is infinitesimally small. These local results may, however, be extended to global theorems by repeated use of the corresponding local results.

In combination with the formula of sectoral employment of labour (2.9), our laws for the changes of the price system lead to the following laws of employment. First, we find from (iii) that a fall in the relative wage rate w'_i results in an increase in the employment of labour in sector i, after taking into account all repercussions upon prices. This means that a relatively low wage rate in a sector causes disguised unemployment to be absorbed in that sector. Second, it follows from (i) that a fall in the wage rate in some other sector j will induce a decrease in the employment of labour in sector i by lowering the prices of all goods. In this case, the disguised unemployment is transferred from sector i to j. Thus we may conclude that if there is one sector where the wage rate is very low in comparison with the wage rates in other sectors, disguised unemployment is concentrated in that sector, while if there are several sectors paying workers at low rates, disguised unemployment is distributed among them.

The above argument for Model I *mutatis mutandis* holds for Model II. That is to say, differentiating (2.15′) with respect to log w'_i, we have equations similar to (2.18). Solving, we get

$$
\begin{pmatrix} e_{i1} \\ e_{i2} \\ \vdots \\ e_{in} \end{pmatrix} = (J^*)^{-1} \begin{pmatrix} 0 \\ \vdots \\ \gamma_i \\ \vdots \\ 0 \end{pmatrix} = \begin{pmatrix} J_{i1}^* \gamma_i \\ J_{i2}^* \gamma_i \\ \vdots \\ J_{in}^* \gamma_i \end{pmatrix}, \tag{2.19′}
$$

where J_{ik}^* is the (k, i)th element of the inverse of J^*. J and J^* have similar properties. Therefore, we finally get the same laws of prices and laws of employment that we have derived for Model I.

5. EFFECTS OF AN INCREASE IN FINAL DEMAND ON DISGUISED UNEMPLOYMENT

Assuming implicitly that there prevails an equilibrium relative wage structure, Keynes was concerned with unemployment of labour due to a deficiency of effective demand. As relative wage rates are set at the

---

[1] W. W. Leontief, *The Structure of American Economy, 1919–39* (New York: Oxford University Press, 1951), pp. 192–201, and M. Morishima, *Equilibrium, Stability and Growth*, p. 21.

equilibrium levels, there is no disguised unemployment; and if the homo-geneity of degree zero in prices and wage rates prevails, the absolute level of money wage rates has no effect on employment. Unemployment, if it existed, could be removed only by increasing final demand, say through investment. It is expected from the formula of sectoral employment (2.9) or (2.9′) that this Keynesian policy would remain effective in our system, where the actual relative wage structure might deviate from the equilibrium one. However, in addition to the direct effects of an increase in final demand, there will also be secondary effects upon employment, through the price changes which it will bring about. We may then ask two questions: (i) Does an increase in final demand stimulate employment, even if all the secondary repercussions upon prices are allowed for? (ii) Is it efficacious in decreasing disguised unemployment?

The effect of an increase in final demand D_k upon employment in sector i, z_i, is obtained by differentiating (2.9) with respect to D_k:

$$\frac{\partial z_i}{\partial D_k} = \frac{\gamma_i}{w_i'}\left(b_{ik}p_k' + \sum_j b_{ij}D_j\frac{\partial p_j'}{\partial D_k}\right), \tag{2.21}$$

which may be rewritten, by virtue of (2.9) and (2.17), in the elasticity form:

$$\epsilon_{i(k)} = \xi_{ik} + \sum_j \xi_{ij}e_{j(k)}, \tag{2.22}$$

where

$$\epsilon_{i(k)} = \frac{D_k}{z_i}\frac{\partial z_i}{\partial D_k} \quad \text{and} \quad e_{j(k)} = \frac{D_k}{p_j'}\frac{\partial p_j'}{\partial D_k}.$$

The formula (2.22) gives the elasticity of employment z_i with respect to the final demand D_k, split up into two terms: the first represents the partial elasticity of z_i with respect to D_k at constant prices and the second the secondary effects due to induced price changes. The elasticities of prices, $p_1', \ldots, p_n'$, with respect to the final demand, D_k, denoted by $e_{1(k)}, \ldots, e_{n(k)}$, respectively, are determined by simultaneous equations (2.15). Differentiating them with respect to $\log D_k$, we get

$$\begin{bmatrix} 1-(\alpha_{11}+\alpha_1\xi_{11}+\beta_1\eta_1) & \cdots & -(\alpha_{n1}+\alpha_1\xi_{1n}+\beta_1\eta_n) \\ \vdots & & \vdots \\ -(\alpha_{1n}+\alpha_n\xi_{n1}+\beta_n\eta_1) & \cdots & 1-(\alpha_{nn}+\alpha_n\xi_{nn}+\beta_n\eta_n) \end{bmatrix}$$
$$\times \begin{pmatrix} e_{1(k)} \\ e_{2(k)} \\ \vdots \\ e_{n(k)} \end{pmatrix} = \begin{pmatrix} \alpha_1\xi_{1k} \\ \alpha_2\xi_{2k} \\ \vdots \\ \alpha_n\xi_{nk} \end{pmatrix}, \tag{2.23}$$

because $m_{jk} = b_{jk}D_k$ by definition. Solving,

$$\begin{pmatrix} e_{1(k)} \\ \vdots \\ e_{n(k)} \end{pmatrix} = J^{-1} \begin{pmatrix} \alpha_1 \xi_{1k} \\ \vdots \\ \alpha_n \xi_{nk} \end{pmatrix}. \tag{2.24}$$

Now, it is first seen from (2.17) that

$$\xi_{jk} = \frac{b_{jk} p'_k D_k}{\Sigma b_{ji} p'_i D_i}. \tag{2.25}$$

Because the b_{ji}s are elements of the Leontief inverse of the indecomposable non-negative matrix A fulfilling the Hawkins–Simon conditions, they are all positive. Therefore, the ξ_{jk}s are positive and less than one, as the D_is are positive. Secondly, all α_js are positive and less than one. Finally, $I - J$ is also an indecomposable, non-negative matrix fulfilling the Hawkins–Simon conditions, so that all elements of J^{-1} are positive. Thus, all elements appearing on the right-hand side of (2.24) are positive; and hence the prices have positive elasticities with respect to any final demand.

This result enables us to answer our first question definitely. In (2.22), the direct effect of an increase in final demand in sector k on employment in sector i given by the first term is positive and is reinforced by repercussions upon prices, because the effects of final demand on prices are positive and the effects of prices upon employment are also positive. As this holds for any prescribed, actual wage structure, we may conclude that the Keynesian employment policy of increasing final demand is efficacious in encouraging actual employment, even though the wage structure is in disequilibrium.

As for our second question, it must be noted that the above is also true for the equilibrium wage structure. An increase in final demand in sector k stimulates both actual and equilibrium employment in each sector; consequently, nothing can be said on an *a priori* basis about disguised unemployment, which is defined as the excess of the former over the latter, if the secondary effects through price changes are allowed for. However, if they are neglected and the analysis is confined to the direct effect of D_k on disguised unemployment in sector i, we have from (2.21)

$$\frac{\partial(z_i - \bar{z}_i)}{\partial D_k} = \frac{\gamma_i}{w'_i} b_{ik} p'_k - \frac{\gamma_i}{\bar{w}'_i} b_{ik} \bar{p}'_k,$$

where $\bar{w}'_i$ represents the equilibrium relative wage rate in sector i, and $\bar{z}_j$ and $\bar{p}'_j$, $j = 1, ..., n$, are the equilibrium levels of employment and prices which are associated with the wage structure $\bar{w}'_1, ..., \bar{w}'_n$. Suppose now that only w'_i differs from $\bar{w}'_i$, other w'_js being equal to $\bar{w}'_j$. Then there is disguised unemployment in sector i if w'_i is lower than $\bar{w}'_i$; i.e. $z_i - \bar{z}_i > 0$ if $w'_i < \bar{w}'_i$.

In this case we have $p'_k < \bar{p}'_k$ for all ks, as stated by proposition (i) in section 4 above. Moreover, from proposition (iii) in the same section, it follows that p'_k/w'_i is greater than $\bar{p}'_k/\bar{w}'_i$ for all k. Hence

$$\frac{\partial(z_i - \bar{z}_i)}{\partial D_k} > 0, \tag{2.26}$$

which means that an increase in final demand in any sector k has an adverse effect upon disguised unemployment in sector i. As has been seen above, however, very restrictive premises are required in order to derive this result rigorously. For instance, if some secondary effects via price changes are not negligible, or if more than one w'_i deviate from their respective equilibrium values, (2.26) does not necessarily follow as a logical or deductive consequence. We may still ask whether the Keynesian employment policy of increasing final demand is efficacious in diminishing disguised unemployment or not. This problem has to be solved empirically, as we do in Chapter 4. We shall obtain a negative conclusion as far as our sample period is concerned.

3. *Data and estimates of the parameters*

The four Japanese input–output tables for the years 1951, 1955, 1960, and 1965 are different in the number of sectors. We aggregate the sectors of each table into twenty major industries. They are numbered as follows:

1. Agriculture, fishing & forestry,
2. Mining,
3. Food, beverages & tobacco,
4. Textiles & clothing,
5. Wood & wood products,
6. Pulp, paper & printing,
7. Leather & rubber products,
8. Chemical products,
9. Stone, pottery & glass,
10. Iron, steel & nonferrous metals,
11. General machinery & equipment,
12. Electrical machinery,
13. Ship-building & vehicles,
14. Precision machinery,
15. Other manufacturing,
16. Construction,
17. Electricity,
18. Distributive trades,
19. Transport & storage,
20. Communication, gas, water & business services.

There are some minor comments to be made at this point. First, in the 1951 table, the printing sector is separated from industry 6 and is aggregated with industry 7 (leather and rubber products) and industry 15 (other manufacturing) into one industry; so in 1951 industry 6 was producing only pulp and paper, whilst industry 15 was a hybrid industry consisting of the sectors 'printing and publishing', 'leather and rubber products' and 'other manufacturing'. There was no independent industry 7 producing leather and rubber products in the 1951 table, so that the table is 19 by 19, missing the seventh column and row. In the other three tables the above classification of industries is adopted.

Secondly, in the 1951 and 1955 tables inter-industrial input coefficients do not account for inputs of imported goods; so they do not represent at all accurately the amounts of goods technologically required per unit of the respective outputs and are subject to drastic change, since industries can easily substitute inputs of imported goods for those of domestic goods. The compilation of the table was revised with respect to this point at a later stage; the figures in the cells of the 1960 and 1965 tables include not only domestic but also imported inputs. Differences between input coefficients of any two tables may reflect technical changes occurring during the period, or may simply be due to different treatments of competitive imported inputs. Finally, it should be noted that throughout the four tables, our service industry 20 does not include the sector of 'public administration, defence, health and education'.

We begin by estimating the parameters of the production functions. In Model I for the 1951 and 1955 tables, the production function of each firm k is given by

$$x_j^k = G_j x_{1j,k}^{\alpha_{1j}} \dots x_{nj,k}^{\alpha_{nj}} y_{j,k}^{\beta_j} z_{j,k}^{\gamma_j} \quad (j = 1, \dots, n), \tag{3.1}$$

in which imported input is distinguished from inputs of domestic goods. Imported input is not disaggregated into goods; instead we take it as if each firm imported a single commodity which could not be produced in Japan at all. Also we assume that all firms belonging to the same industry are homogeneous, and that the marginal productivity conditions prevail. Then the indices, α_{ij}, of the Cobb–Douglas functions (3.1), or the elasticities of outputs with respect to the domestic inputs, are identified with Leontief's input coefficients, or factors' shares of output values, $p_i x_{ij}/p_j x_j$; the indices β_j, or the elasticities of outputs with respect to the imported inputs, with import coefficients, or imported inputs' shares of output values; and the indices γ_j, or the elasticities of outputs with respect to labour, with labour–input coefficients, or labour's shares of output values.

In Model II for the 1960 and 1965 tables, on the other hand, the imported inputs are disaggregated into goods, so that they do not appear in the production functions,

$$x_j^k = G_j x_{1j,k}^{\alpha_{1j}} \dots x_{nj,k}^{\alpha_{nj}} z_{j,k}^{\gamma_j} \quad (j = 1, \dots, n), \tag{3.1'}$$

as independent variables. The indices $\alpha_{1j}, \dots, \alpha_{nj}$ in (3.1') are redefined so as to include imported inputs of the respective sorts. Under the marginal productivity conditions for a competitive economy, we can, of course, again identify α_{ij}s or γ_js with Leontief's inter-industrial-input or labour-input coefficients.

There is thus an asymmetric treatment of imports between these two models. In Model I goods are imported by industries for their own use; so it is considered that they buy composite goods which have already been mixed in appropriate proportions in foreign countries. On the other hand, in Model II, it is assumed that only industry i can import good i, so that those industries which want to use imported good i must buy it from industry i. Since we do not distinguish between domestic and foreign goods, these industries which wish to buy imported goods can appear only in the domestic market. The import coefficient of good i, as industry i's propensity to import good i as the sole importing agent of good i, is given as the ratio of the value of imports of good i to the value of output of industry i, μ_i.

TABLE 6. The Leontief matrix for the Japanese economy, 1951

$(\alpha_{ij} \times 10^4,\ \beta_j \times 10^4,\ \gamma_j \times 10^4)$

i \ j	1	2	3	4	5	6	7	8	9	10	11	12	13	14	15	16	17	18	19	20
1	594	294	2311	276	4278	602	*	106	63	15	0	0	0	0	469	185	40	30	27	797
2	168	168	81	76	22	320	*	1043	1695	289	47	84	44	30	79	299	2511	5	597	14
3	213	0	1209	24	0	8	*	359	1	0	2	2	2	2	5	0	18	0	3	841
4	140	19	46	4331	26	138	*	28	72	27	43	63	76	14	844	24	18	44	169	416
5	14	89	40	9	1234	48	*	19	196	20	61	85	242	582	62	1400	197	138	103	66
6	10	0	118	127	18	3414	*	114	506	6	59	100	21	135	1371	38	9	138	36	67
7	*	*	*	*	*	*	*	*	*	*	*	*	*	*	*	*	*	*	*	*
8	487	244	99	254	120	271	*	2418	483	409	112	219	172	136	844	71	50	7	601	228
9	10	21	71	2	32	6	*	102	777	75	41	168	101	153	4	1185	26	0	23	52
10	24	611	113	17	53	102	*	216	241	5167	3976	3085	2685	2325	103	1864	499	90	355	361
11	18	96	0	36	3	2	*	2	1	31	1268	108	652	141	4	73	83	2	8	35
12	0	21	1	3	3	1	*	1	2	4	46	1141	503	4	15	94	0	0	47	57
13	9	0	0	0	0	0	*	0	0	0	0	0	659	0	0	0	0	0	208	56
14	56	104	14	50	7	127	*	39	48	10	0	0	0	997	0	140	33	23	2	23
15	0	0	0	0	0	0	*	0	0	0	101	54	413	76	706	0	0	64	175	178
16	0	0	0	0	0	0	*	0	0	0	0	0	0	0	0	0	0	0	0	184
17	14	324	62	47	120	146	*	181	176	97	50	61	61	71	47	3	118	11	107	57
18	162	112	168	184	117	193	*	216	235	104	239	366	394	278	334	647	198	63	136	504
19	48	161	140	46	410	297	*	232	346	85	99	102	113	94	145	420	302	104	206	547
20	310	1437	598	642	427	1076	*	1001	1332	1858	853	688	916	601	969	141	1660	2266	1458	1924
β_j	122	58	772	1875	188	341	*	1274	291	431	69	118	69	1	1275	44	52	29	179	187
γ_j	6505	3516	627	840	1667	1296	*	968	2093	802	1960	2285	1882	2757	1749	1207	2657	3443	3960	1244

TABLE 7. The Leontief matrix for the Japanese economy, 1955

$(\alpha_{ij} \times 10^4,\ \beta_j \times 10^4,\ \gamma_j \times 10^4)$

i \ j	1	2	3	4	5	6	7	8	9	10	11	12	13	14	15	16	17	18	19	20
1	1769	947	1783	571	4733	506	580	218	171	6	0	1	1	0	263	157	0	5	1	270
2	233	233	41	64	6	148	61	847	1291	304	20	21	20	5	38	355	1143	3	254	19
3	115	0	1046	26	13	80	0	190	2	0	1	1	1	2	30	0	0	0	0	685
4	53	5	9	4441	46	8	1095	8	3	16	16	8	50	93	279	14	23	6	30	121
5	66	80	26	0	900	0	0	0	82	10	77	75	335	351	327	1595	7	68	51	211
6	27	26	129	220	43	3622	34	41	298	10	72	29	3	18	558	9	26	5	39	289
7	1	42	4	17	10	34	842	19	5	10	30	54	479	148	562	10	34	4	69	112
8	437	226	241	319	133	257	441	2266	329	380	123	193	359	549	1484	120	83	5	720	266
9	11	16	43	1	13	8	41	66	520	53	35	234	103	127	54	1016	11	0	7	74
10	44	194	108	10	71	30	2	100	65	4681	1230	985	1085	230	533	1508	120	5	69	275
11	17	35	0	15	3	0	9	1	4	78	3529	128	277	0	14	89	42	0	0	45
12	1	0	0	0	0	0	0	0	0	3	277	2759	278	19	0	74	21	0	0	37
13	31	0	0	0	0	0	0	0	0	0	0	398	2612	230	0	0	0	0	168	57
14	0	0	0	0	0	0	48	0	0	0	0	0	0	1750	0	0	0	2	0	13
15	10	0	6	10	37	0	0	0	0	2	53	222	16	18	450	32	0	8	2	47
16	0	0	0	0	0	0	0	0	0	0	11	0	16	0	0	3	0	0	0	0
17	18	461	86	86	99	210	108	250	315	151	65	80	121	45	83	19	93	38	110	58
18	220	92	671	234	101	214	258	277	464	109	232	465	480	524	467	384	74	14	126	357
19	58	103	157	54	66	101	53	298	415	117	89	98	117	73	114	347	321	129	126	265
20	504	847	857	824	812	1342	2009	1528	1661	1626	667	790	300	829	1228	805	1832	2913	2266	1461
β_j	306	112	912	1234	396	107	2202	1387	307	526	150	122	157	171	149	53	58	19	176	91
γ_j	5027	4294	966	1103	1577	1875	1306	895	2091	893	2044	1643	1749	2217	1778	2841	2271	2881	3722	2161

TABLE 8. *The Leontief matrix for the Japanese economy, 1960*

$(\alpha_{ij} \times 10^4, \gamma_j \times 10^4, \mu_j \times 10^4)$

$i \backslash j$	1	2	3	4	5	6	7	8	9	10	11	12	13	14	15	16	17	18	19	20
1	1560	306	4246	1466	4344	434	1694	290	33	4	0	7	−5	239	358	81	0	−5	0	56
2	3	161	35	26	10	136	61	1445	1292	476	2	4	5	6	46	161	1125	0	98	79
3	397	0	1453	26	0	7	605	92	5	0	0	0	0	0	42	0	0	8	0	44
4	111	56	6	3862	66	53	1421	35	39	12	35	68	41	231	77	103	19	85	67	218
5	21	49	40	23	1179	164	6	105	33	16	68	81	110	60	437	1195	10	86	11	39
6	14	116	89	66	56	4038	30	363	348	39	76	91	31	217	459	58	23	248	53	304
7	6	0	2	107	10	2	446	5	1	10	82	106	700	187	78	11	0	1	8	33
8	604	285	286	1116	311	393	1100	2537	672	398	120	254	156	276	2755	245	763	205	803	289
9	12	6	104	0	18	6	74	38	847	72	45	153	71	107	18	922	20	−5	2	30
10	24	188	70	46	421	35	98	121	294	5756	2537	1852	1236	1058	576	1646	62	51	11	121
11	44	146	4	44	15	55	55	39	26	62	2298	212	1463	365	25	242	54	5	10	36
12	21	73	3	12	18	11	14	38	38	43	244	2596	415	27	7	524	562	0	2	82
13	44	32	3	0	18	0	0	0	21	6	42	35	1491	0	0	141	0	132	805	53
14	1	9	0	2	1	8	1	2	3	2	64	89	26	1496	3	25	2	12	3	72
15	23	14	23	19	45	11	173	9	6	2	58	203	59	72	150	93	2	11	3	83
16	50	183	32	20	36	22	33	48	87	25	25	28	34	36	27	10	405	122	83	260
17	19	567	39	101	70	325	111	253	396	170	65	72	75	56	91	15	105	91	137	93
18	108	191	400	381	393	293	476	301	509	187	179	268	263	285	445	487	105	158	177	195
19	80	157	163	108	239	284	148	255	593	155	162	155	143	178	193	355	320	280	368	235
20	158	824	469	345	297	575	371	715	575	342	615	692	592	927	820	529	300	832	833	1161
γ_j	5502	4267	503	1292	1552	1557	1463	769	1906	884	1396	1229	1609	1998	1332	1493	1479	3882	3421	2768
μ_j	1822	10040	471	47	47	161	93	978	108	529	616	122	205	735	112	1	8	54	−550	127

TABLE 9. *The Leontief matrix for the Japanese economy, 1965*

$(\alpha_{ij} \times 10^4, \gamma_j \times 10^4, \mu_j \times 10^4)$

i \ j	1	2	3	4	5	6	7	8	9	10	11	12	13	14	15	16	17	18	19	20
1	1555	128	4275	1048	3590	206	691	316	14	1	0	3	−5	153	325	24	0	0	0	86
2	2	96	23	4	0	46	27	1411	991	577	5	4	2	2	44	316	650	0	25	32
3	650	0	1199	25	16	8	540	92	1	0	0	0	0	0	45	0	0	5	0	2
4	115	25	7	3789	137	55	1227	12	9	9	25	40	36	144	196	101	6	16	58	68
5	14	41	43	45	1402	227	20	22	58	32	71	104	102	33	454	1039	12	40	19	47
6	18	110	131	104	91	3975	140	326	108	33	50	159	44	419	465	63	30	155	55	289
7	6	29	2	111	14	8	810	8	0	14	71	35	464	92	63	7	0	0	6	20
8	603	766	385	1164	321	336	1308	2433	728	408	107	240	134	212	2270	198	971	202	614	282
9	18	2	101	0	24	5	36	36	910	68	41	126	62	104	78	897	12	11	1	22
10	22	145	114	49	427	31	254	111	217	5144	1527	1781	1261	754	473	1361	7	62	14	70
11	58	149	28	44	42	48	78	75	155	80	2046	170	844	240	44	233	34	3	40	20
12	3	95	2	12	1	10	2	46	22	23	569	2249	254	71	9	432	313	0	4	56
13	51	131	11	5	17	3	21	9	33	19	26	10	2213	9	5	51	18	192	1024	16
14	1	13	1	5	3	12	2	5	7	3	52	31	55	1488	6	14	4	13	10	54
15	26	21	47	35	96	33	252	65	12	8	87	266	123	197	645	96	4	17	6	64
16	56	109	20	20	33	27	31	41	57	22	22	27	28	27	15	9	313	99	74	275
17	18	398	47	96	88	233	132	230	373	220	87	52	63	60	93	35	13	104	119	91
18	169	411	370	475	510	319	431	259	370	326	336	387	390	367	565	625	64	231	248	182
19	137	162	188	201	208	270	166	245	421	202	240	192	168	193	214	361	207	373	823	158
20	352	709	431	303	282	678	672	716	738	396	548	655	348	1046	494	416	523	1045	386	861
γ_j	5211	3292	711	1577	1650	1571	1879	732	1901	1061	2093	1608	1793	2276	1537	2201	1255	3560	3953	3135
μ_j	2007	14938	565	97	109	205	134	792	69	376	532	297	183	591	322	0	0	93	499	97

The point estimates of these parameters calculated from the available four input–output tables are presented, in matrix form, in Tables 6–9. In them and throughout the subsequent tables, industries and goods are numbered in the order given at the beginning of this chapter. It should also be noted that in the tables for 1951, column 7 and row 7 are missing for the reason stated above.

The labour-input coefficients of the industries other than 'agriculture' (industry 1) have been calculated according to the following formula. First, the wage rate of each industry is estimated simply by dividing the income from employment in that industry by the number of workers employed there. These figures are available in the input–output tables. Moreover, besides employees, a substantial number of unpaid family workers work in many industries such as 'food, beverages and tobacco', 'textiles and clothing', 'wood and wood products', 'other manufacturing', 'distributive trades' and 'communication, gas, water and business services', as well as in 'agriculture'. The income from their work is included in the gross profits and other trading income of the respective industries. However, the input–output tables do not provide the figures for the numbers of unpaid family workers; and the figures for industrial employees which are consistent with the available figures for unpaid family workers are inconsistent with the figures for industrial employees provided in the input–output tables. We have, therefore, made some adjustment to the figures for employees and unpaid family workers, and estimated the labour share of industry j, β_j, by dividing the product of industry j's wage rate (estimated above) and the total number of workers in j (i.e. the number of employees and the number of unpaid family workers in j, both adjusted) by industry j's value of output.

In the case of agriculture, not only family workers but also the heads of the farms are considered as workers; so the wage rate and the labour-input coefficient of 'agriculture' is calculated by dividing the sum of the income from employment and the gross profits and other trading income of 'agriculture' (after deducting from the former the gross profits and other trading income of the subsectors, such as agricultural services, forestry, deep-sea fishing and whaling) by the number of persons engaged in 'agriculture' and the value of agricultural output respectively.

2. CONSUMPTION FUNCTIONS

An average worker in the agricultural sector is assumed to have a different type of consumption behaviour from that of an average worker in non-agricultural sectors (industries 2 to 20). We have estimated the consumption functions in the following way. First, the farmers' total income is the sum of their farm and non-farm income and gifts and aid from others. The ratio of total income to farm and non-farm income, represented by ρ_1, is assumed to be constant. The cross-section data of consumption (per man) of farming households were regressed on the total income of farmers for the four years 1951, 1955, 1960, 1965, according to the formula,

$$\frac{C_1}{N_1} = c_1 \frac{I_1}{N_1} + d_1,$$

where C_1 denotes total consumption and I_1 total income, both per farming household, and N_1 the average number of members of the farming household. In estimating c_1 and d_1 of the above equation, the data were collected mainly from the *Statistical Yearbook of the Ministry of Agriculture* and the *Nohka Seikeihi Chohsa Hohkoku* of the Ministry of Agriculture and Forestry. The results are:

(i) 1951:

$$\frac{C_1}{N_1} = \underset{(0.037)}{0.523} \frac{I_1}{N_1} + \underset{(1585)}{11875}, \quad \bar{R}^2 = 0.80; \rho_1 = 1;$$

(ii) 1955:

$$\frac{C_1}{N_1} = \underset{(0.013)}{0.484} \frac{I_1}{N_1} + \underset{(796)}{20201}, \quad \bar{R}^2 = 0.99; \rho_1 = 1.06;$$

(iii) 1960:

$$\frac{C_1}{N_1} = \underset{(0.033)}{0.502} \frac{I_1}{N_1} + \underset{(2792)}{24414}, \quad \bar{R}^2 = 0.97; \rho_1 = 1.08;$$

(iv) 1965:

$$\frac{C_1}{N_1} = \underset{(0.018)}{0.454} \frac{I_1}{N_1} + \underset{(2684)}{52572}, \quad \bar{R}^2 = 0.99; \rho_1 = 1.10;$$

where $\bar{R}^2$ represents the measure of the goodness of fit adjusted for the degree of freedom, and the figure in parentheses below each estimated parameter is the standard error of the corresponding estimate.

Next, the total consumption C_1 is allocated among goods. The allocation depends, among other things, upon the level of income, as well as prices. However, we avoided complications by simply assuming that $e_{i1} = C_{i1}/C_1$, $i = 1, \ldots, 20$, were constant, C_{i1} being the expenditure on good i per farming household. The data are available only in purchaser prices in *Nohka Seikeihi Chohsa Hohkoku*, and they were converted into producer prices so as to be consistent with the figures in the input–output tables. We obtain the producer price if we deduct the transportation cost and the dealer's margin from

TABLE 10. *The marginal propensity to consume*

Good or industry	(1951) c_{i1}	c_i	(1955) c_{i1}	c_i	(1960) c_{i1}	c_i	(1965) c_{i1}	c_i
1	0.159	0.116	0.122	0.084	0.040	0.034	0.034	0.043
2	0	0.001	0	0.001	0.001	0.001	0.001	0.002
3	0.051	0.098	0.068	0.086	0.166	0.130	0.127	0.153
4	0.040	0.045	0.033	0.043	0.046	0.043	0.039	0.047
5	0.002	0.001	0.002	0.003	0.001	0.002	0.013	0.006
6	0.001	0.001	0.007	0.010	0.009	0.010	0.007	0.011
7	*	*	0.002	0.001	0.002	0.001	0.003	0.001
8	0.007	0.010	0.009	0.010	0.012	0.010	0.010	0.017
9	0.001	0.001	0.001	0.001	0	0.001	0.004	0.002
10	0.002	0.004	0.003	0.002	0	0.001	0.004	0.003
11	0	0	0	0	0.001	0.001	0.005	0.005
12	0	0	0.001	0.003	0.014	0.011	0.008	0.006
13	0.002	0.001	0.002	0.001	0.009	0.003	0.009	0.005
14	0	0	0.001	0	0.001	0.001	0.003	0.002
15	0.009	0.014	0.011	0.007	0.009	0.007	0.006	0.010
16	0	0	0	0	0	0	0	0
17	0.005	0.006	0.005	0.006	0.007	0.008	0.008	0.013
18	0.097	0.091	0.086	0.076	0.077	0.064	0.090	0.102
19	0.016	0.015	0.017	0.016	0.015	0.014	0.023	0.023
20	0.060	0.058	0.075	0.085	0.082	0.094	0.100	0.134
Total	0.454	0.461	0.444	0.435	0.494	0.436	0.497	0.585

the purchaser price. The dealers' margins and the transportation costs thus collected from C_{i1}, $i = 1, ..., 20$, were re-allocated between industries 18 and 19, 'distributive trades' and 'transport and storage'.

These procedures result in sectoral consumption functions of the form,

$$C_{i1}m = e_{i1}c_1\rho_1(W_1 + W_1') + e_{i1}d_1N_1m \quad (i = 1, ..., 20),$$

where m is the number of farming households, W_1 the total farm income, and W_1' the total non-farm income of farmers. The figures for the sectoral marginal propensities to consume, $c_{i1} = e_{i1}c_1\rho_1$, for the four sample years are listed in Table 10. In the following we assume that non-farm workers in 'agriculture' and farm family workers have the same tastes as actual farmers; and W_1 is extended so as to include non-farm wages from 'agriculture' as well as imputed wages to family workers on farms.

Next, workers employed by industries other than 'agriculture' are assumed to be homogeneous in their propensities to consume. The total consumption of a typical working household depends on its total income, which includes income from part-time jobs and other sources, as well as income from regular employment. We allowed for the size of the household in the same way as in the case of the farming household. Cross-section data taken from the *General Report on the Family Income and Expenditure Survey* and *Annual Report on the Family Income and Expenditure Survey* published by the Bureau of Statistics, office of the Prime Minister, were fitted to the formula,

$$\frac{C^*}{N^*} = c^* \frac{I^*}{N^*} + d^*,$$

where C^* represents total consumption and I^* total income, both per working household, and N^* the average size of working households. These data are available for the four years under investigation, but only for married workers in 28 representative cities, so that we had to make some adjustments to them by using the data for the whole country for the year 1959 in the *National Survey of Family Income and Expenditures*. The results are:

(i) 1951:

$$\frac{C^*}{N^*} = \underset{(0.021)}{0.474} \frac{I^*}{N^*} + \underset{(80)}{1362}, \quad \bar{R}^2 = 0.99; \rho^* = 1.05;$$

(ii) 1955:

$$\frac{C^*}{N^*} = \underset{(0.021)}{0.482} \frac{I^*}{N^*} + \underset{(236)}{2274}, \quad \bar{R}^2 = 0.97; \rho^* = 1.05;$$

(iii) 1960:

$$\frac{C^*}{N^*} = \underset{(0.013)}{0.471} \frac{I^*}{N^*} + \underset{(193)}{2599}, \quad \bar{R}^2 = 0.99; \rho^* = 1.05;$$

(iv) 1965:

$$\frac{C^*}{N^*} = \underset{(0.019)}{0.575} \frac{I^*}{N^*} + \underset{(352)}{2600}, \quad \bar{R}^2 = 0.98; \rho^* = 1.05;$$

where ρ^* represents the ratio of the working household's total income to its income from employment. We find that the marginal propensities to consume of the working households thus estimated are slightly lower than the corresponding estimates of farming households, except for 1965.

In exactly the same way as we calculated the farmer's marginal propensity to consume each good, we calculated the worker's. The data concerning the allocation of total expenditure among goods are available, with respect to the average household in the 28 cities, in the *General Report on the Family Income and Expenditure Survey*. They are available only in terms of purchaser prices; therefore we converted them into producer prices, so that they would be consistent with the figures in the input–output tables. We followed the same procedure as that which was applied to similar data for the farming households. Let C_i^* be the expenditure on good i of the average working household; let m^* be the number of working households in the economy. Define e_i^* as C_i^*/C^*. We then have

$$C_i^* m^* = e_i^* c^* \rho^* W^* + e_i^* d^* N^* m^*,$$

where W^* is the total income from employment of all working families.

It is now noticed that only a part, although a substantial part, of the total income from industrial employment goes to working families, the remaining being paid to farmers who have additional part-time jobs or work as seasonal workers in industry. Let W be the total wage payments of the industries $2, ..., 20$, other than 'agriculture' (industry 1); redefine W_1' (the total non-farm income of the farmers) as the sum which the workers in industry 1 receive in the form of wages for their additional jobs in industries $2, ..., 20$. Evidently, we have

$$W = W^* + W_1',$$

which holds true even if W, W_1', W^* are extended, as we have done in the present study, so as to include imputed wages to unpaid family workers. We assume the ratios, $\omega^* = W^*/W$ and $\omega_1 = W_1'/W$, are constant. Then a marginal increment in W induces an increase in demand for goods by workers and farmers in the amounts,

$$e_i^* c^* \rho^* \omega^* + e_{i1} c_1 \rho_1 \omega_1 \quad (i = 1, 2, ..., 20).$$

These give sectoral marginal propensities to consume, $c_i, i = 1, 2, ..., 20$. As a marginal increment in wages in any industry j ($j = 2, ..., 20$) has the same effect, the sectoral marginal propensities are equalized among industrial workers. Our estimates of c_is for the four years are given in Table 10. From the comparison with the results for farmers, it is interesting to note that farmers are consistently higher, throughout the four years, in the propensities to consume 'ship-building and vehicles' as well as the products of 'agriculture' than workers, whilst workers consumed more (though not much) 'pulp, paper and printing' and 'electricity' than farmers.

3. FINAL DEMANDS AND OTHERS

To estimate disguised unemployment in various industries we have to calculate the constant terms of final demand. The final demand for goods consists, as in usual input–output models, of current expenditure of consumers and public authorities, gross domestic capital formation and exports. Among them, only demands by farmers and workers are considered to depend upon endogenous variables, whilst all others are regarded as exogenous and constant. We denote the exogenous part of the final demand for good i in year t by $D_i(t)$, which may be equated, if the quantities of good i are measured so that its actual price in year t is unity, with the excess of the total value of the final demand for good i in t over the part of farmers' and workers' demand for good i which depends on their income, $c_{i1} W_1 + c_i W$. As we know the values of $c_{i1} W_1$ and $c_i W$, we can directly calculate the values of $D_i(t), i = 1, ..., 20$, from the input–output tables. Or alternatively, under the same assumption that appropriate units of measurement are taken such that $p_i = 1$ for all goods, we can calculate $D_i(t)$ by the formula,

$$
\begin{pmatrix} D_1(t) \\ D_2(t) \\ \vdots \\ D_{20}(t) \end{pmatrix} =
$$

$$
\begin{pmatrix} 1-\alpha_{11}-c_{11}\gamma_1 & -\alpha_{12}-c_{12}\gamma_2 & \cdots & -\alpha_{1,20}-c_{1,20}\gamma_{20} \\ -\alpha_{21}-c_{21}\gamma_1 & 1-\alpha_{22}-c_{22}\gamma_2 & \cdots & -\alpha_{2,20}-c_{2,20}\gamma_{20} \\ \vdots & \vdots & \cdots & \vdots \\ -\alpha_{20,1}-c_{20,1}\gamma_1 & -\alpha_{20,2}-c_{20,2}\gamma_2 & \cdots & 1-\alpha_{20,20}-c_{20,20}\gamma_{20} \end{pmatrix} \begin{pmatrix} X_1(t) \\ X_2(t) \\ \vdots \\ X_{20}(t) \end{pmatrix}
$$

in the case of the 1951 and 1955 tables, and by the formula,

$$
\begin{pmatrix} D_1(t) \\ D_2(t) \\ \vdots \\ D_{20}(t) \end{pmatrix} =
$$

$$
\begin{pmatrix} 1+\mu_1-\alpha_{11}-c_{11}\gamma_1 & -\alpha_{12}-c_{12}\gamma_2 & \cdots & -\alpha_{1,20}-c_{1,20}\gamma_{20} \\ -\alpha_{21}-c_{21}\gamma_1 & 1+\mu_2-\alpha_{22}-c_{22}\gamma_2 & \cdots & -\alpha_{2,20}-c_{2,20}\gamma_{20} \\ \vdots & \vdots & \cdots & \vdots \\ -\alpha_{20,1}-c_{20,1}\gamma_1 & -\alpha_{20,2}-c_{20,2}\gamma_2 & \cdots & 1+\mu_{20}-\alpha_{20,20}-c_{20,20}\gamma_{20} \end{pmatrix} \begin{pmatrix} X_1(t) \\ X_2(t) \\ \vdots \\ X_{20}(t) \end{pmatrix}
$$

in the case of the 1960 and 1965 tables; in the formulas $X_i(t)$s denote the actual values of outputs in year t. As Tables 6–10 provide the figures for $\alpha_{ij}, \gamma_j, \mu_j$ and c_{ij}, we can easily find the values of $D_i(t)$s corresponding to the actual outputs, $X_i(t)$s. In principle, these two methods obviously result in the same estimates of $D_i(t)$s, except for rounding errors. Our estimates by the second method are presented in Table 11.

Other parameters whose values are required for the estimation of disguised unemployment are the productivity coefficients of the production functions of (3.1) or (3.1′). Their values depend upon the units of measurement of the outputs and inputs. It is also noted that these coefficients are obtained by substituting the average output and inputs,

$$x_j/\theta_j, \; x_{1j}/\theta_j, \; ..., \; x_{nj}/\theta_j, \; y_j/\theta_j, \; z_j/\theta_j$$

(where θ_j is the number of firms in industry j) for the firm k's output and inputs $x_j^k, x_{1j,\,k}, ..., x_{nj,\,k}, y_{j,\,k}, z_{j,\,k}$, respectively, in (3.1) or (3.1′), so that the calculated productivity coefficients are $G_j \theta_j^{\alpha j}, j = 1, ..., 20$, where

$$\alpha_j = 1 - \Sigma\alpha_{ij} - \beta_j - \gamma_j \tag{3.2}$$

in the case of the 1951 and 1955 tables and

$$\alpha_j = 1 - \Sigma\alpha_{ij} - \gamma_j \tag{3.2′}$$

in the case of the 1960 and 1965 tables. The results are also presented in Table 11.

In addition to these, we need some statistics concerning the distribution of competitive imports. Let u_k be the total value of competitive imports of good k used by industries as current input. Each of $u_k, k = 1, ..., 20$, is divided by the sum of them; and the resultant ratios, n_ks, may be used as weights for calculating the price-index of imported goods,

$$q = \Sigma p_j n_j,$$

that is, a Laspeyre price index number. This formula enables us to eliminate the price of imported goods from Model I for 1951 and 1955. The weights n_j are shown in Table 11.

4. ESTIMATION OF DISGUISED UNEMPLOYMENT

We are now ready for the adventure. In the case of the 1951 and 1955 tables the main formulas are (2.15) and (2.9) in the preceding chapter. In (2.15) the values of the coefficients other than k_i, α_i, m_{ik} are directly given. α_is are at once calculated according to the formula (3.2), while m_{ik}s are elements of $(I - A)^{-1}\hat{D}$, where A has diagonal elements, $\alpha_{ii} + c_{ii}\gamma_i - \mu_i$ and off-diagonal

TABLE 11. *The exogenous part of final demand, the productivity coefficient and the distribution of competitive imports*

Good or industry	D_i				$G_i\theta_i^{\alpha_i}$				n_i	
	1951	1955	1960	1965	1951	1955	1960	1965	1951	1955
1	518.6	910.2	494.3	724.6	2.9	7.7	7.0	14.6	0.49	0.49
2	5.2	4.8	6.6	14.3	71.0	41.1	59.1	251.6	0.14	0.18
3	264.7	633.2	2,027.5	2,607.8	514.0	310.8	85.1	80.1	0.13	0.02
4	457.1	558.4	775.4	1,143.1	19.8	12.6	17.1	18.4	0.01	0.01
5	41.1	60.0	108.0	208.3	13.9	11.4	13.6	22.8	0	0
6	27.6	127.4	95.7	166.4	36.2	27.2	38.6	67.5	0.02	0.01
7	*	27.6	89.5	166.8	*	15.9	48.1	39.7	*	0
8	89.0	108.0	272.4	636.8	54.0	52.9	224.8	414.8	0.06	0.09
9	30.0	29.5	46.3	72.8	27.0	52.2	108.0	191.8	0	0
10	170.5	157.3	175.2	641.6	8.4	17.1	25.0	33.1	0.02	0.02
11	133.4	208.7	944.3	1,556.4	10.5	19.3	68.9	99.5	0.01	0.04
12	73.6	156.0	603.6	1,131.2	16.5	56.2	70.9	85.5	0	0.01
13	190.7	282.0	892.8	1,861.3	18.2	29.9	52.8	72.2	0.03	0.01
14	32.2	82.6	110.0	279.3	18.0	51.8	79.4	92.3	0.01	0.02
15	121.9	54.4	131.6	291.6	20.1	37.8	72.0	94.4	0	0
16	421.3	1,069.5	2,889.0	6,067.6	78.5	10.7	80.9	74.1	0	0
17	25.6	51.6	63.4	75.1	21.4	353.8	1,828.3	7,251.3	0	0
18	383.3	717.4	1,027.7	2,162.1	216.1	356.9	510.6	1,034.0	0	0
19	190.2	362.9	554.4	1,161.9	22.6	39.3	233.4	145.8	0	0
20	1,159.3	2,027.1	2,631.0	5,928.4	155.6	353.5	1,118.9	2,822.5	0.08	0.09

elements, $\alpha_{ij} + c_{ij}\gamma_j$, and $\hat{D}$ is the diagonal matrix with $D_1, \ldots, D_{20}$ on the diagonal. Finally, each k_i is given by (2.16) as a linear function of $\log w_i'$. The constant term $\log H_i$ is analysed into $\alpha_{1i}, \ldots, \alpha_{20, i}, \beta_i, \gamma_i$ and $G_i \theta_i^{\alpha_i}$, whose values are all known to us.

We now calculate the numbers of workers which Japanese industries would employ if the UK relative wage rates prevailed. Since we could not disaggregate the UK machinery industry into industries of 'general machinery and equipment', 'electrical machinery' and 'precision machinery' as we have in the Japanese input–output tables, we have to assume that the wage rates were equated to each other in these three industries in the UK in 1960. The UK relative wage rates shown in Table 4 are substituted into (2.16) to obtain the k_js which correspond to the UK relative wage rates and which, in turn, are substituted into (2.15). Equations (2.15) are then solved with respect to relative prices in terms of the wage rate in 'agriculture', $p_1', \ldots, p_{20}'$. Substituting these relative prices as well as the UK relative wage rates into the formula (2.9), we can calculated the 'normal' employment in each industry i, i.e. the number of workers which would be employed by industry i in Japan, if the 1960 UK relative wage rates prevailed in Japan, in 1951 or 1955. The 'normal' employment is compared with actual employment in each industry; if the latter is greater than the former, then the difference gives the magnitude of disguised unemployment in that industry. If, on the contrary, the former is greater than the latter in some industry, the workers employed in that industry might be considered as labour aristocrats, because, other things being equal, their actual wage rate would be higher than their equilibrium, UK rate, in the relative sense.

The same procedure as above applies to the calculation of disguised unemployment in 1960 and 1965. The only changes are to replace the formulas used above by the corresponding formulas numbered with primes, say, (2.15) by (2.15′).

The results are presented in Table 12. Column (1) of each year shows the actual employment of each industry, which is defined as the sum of the number of employees and the number of unpaid family workers who work in that industry. In each year, the total actual employment exceeds the total 'normal' employment, which is shown at the bottom of column (2) of the table. This shows that there has been a persistent tendency towards over-employment in Japan; in other words, Japan could have saved labour if she had had, instead of her wage system with big interindustrial differentials, relative wages as existed in the UK in 1960. From this point of view, the notorious Japanese wage system might be considered as having played the role of a buffer in mitigating the unemployment problem. However, the rate of over-employment to normal employment decreased drastically during

TABLE 12. *Employment and disguised unemployment in Japan, 1951–65*
(in million persons)

Industry	1951 Actual employment (1)	1951 Normal employment (2)	1951 Disguised unemployment (3)	1955 Actual employment (1)	1955 Normal employment (2)	1955 Disguised unemployment (3)	1960 Actual employment (1)	1960 Normal employment (2)	1960 Disguised unemployment (3)	1965 Actual employment (1)	1965 Normal employment (2)	1965 Disguised unemployment (3)
1	17.22	12.40	4.82	15.26	11.10	4.16	13.49	10.17	3.31	11.05	7.63	3.42
2	0.53	0.71	–	0.52	0.66	–	0.56	0.66	–	0.43	0.41	0.02
3	0.77	0.63	0.14	0.94	1.11	–	1.14	1.07	0.07	1.07	1.24	–
4	1.31	1.49	–	1.39	1.48	–	1.89	1.93	–	1.87	1.93	–
5	0.45	0.35	0.10	0.49	0.46	0.03	0.71	0.59	0.11	0.70	0.69	0.01
6	0.15	0.25	–	0.50	0.65	–	0.60	0.66	–	0.76	0.71	0.05
7	*	*	*	0.15	0.14	0.01	0.20	0.24	–	0.26	0.28	–
8	0.39	0.49	–	0.39	0.47	–	0.51	0.70	–	0.44	0.71	–
9	0.27	0.30	–	0.32	0.28	0.03	0.43	0.45	–	0.62	0.48	0.15
10	0.63	0.89	–	0.72	0.72	–	1.07	1.32	–	1.31	1.44	–
11	0.40	0.36	0.04	0.40	0.39	0.01	0.78	0.92	–	1.19	1.30	–
12	0.22	0.25	–	0.28	0.22	0.05	0.69	0.74	–	0.91	0.88	0.03
13	0.35	0.35	–	0.37	0.32	0.05	0.69	0.81	–	1.08	1.16	–
14	0.10	0.11	–	0.13	0.13	–	0.18	0.18	–	0.28	0.26	0.01
15	0.43	0.52	–	0.23	0.17	0.06	0.28	0.23	0.05	0.37	0.36	0.01
16	1.05	0.51	0.54	1.38	1.53	–	2.31	1.90	0.40	3.33	3.14	0.18
17	0.14	0.25	–	0.16	0.28	–	0.17	0.28	–	0.18	0.25	–
18	2.49	3.11	–	3.64	3.08	0.56	4.03	4.46	–	5.24	5.28	–
19	1.21	1.50	–	1.30	1.39	–	1.59	1.85	–	2.10	2.36	–
20	2.58	3.02	–	4.49	5.87	–	5.62	6.12	–	7.09	7.99	–
Total	30.69	27.48	5.64	33.03	30.45	4.96	36.93	35.27	3.94	40.27	38.49	3.88

1951–65. It is estimated at 11.7 per cent in 1951, and then at 8.5 per cent in 1955, 4.7 per cent in 1960 and 4.6 per cent in 1965.

Disguised unemployment also decreased sharply during the period. The ratio of disguised unemployment to actual employment is estimated at 18.4 per cent in 1951, which is lower than the figure insisted on by Marxian economists in Japan, but not far from it. The disguised unemployment ratio is then estimated at 15.0 per cent in 1955, 10.7 per cent in 1960 and 9.6 per cent in 1965. It is seen that there was a big improvement in the labour market in favour of workers, particularly in 1955–60. This result is consistent with the findings of other Japanese economists. For example, Minami found the turning point of the Japanese economy from the 'unlimited' to the 'limited supply of labour' type in the latter half of the 1950s.[1]

In 'agriculture', actual employment is taken as being equal to the total number of persons at work in that sector, because most agricultural enterprises have been of such a small scale that they have had as labourers only the self-employed and unpaid family workers. As is naturally expected, an enormous amount of disguised unemployment existed in 'agriculture'. During the period 1951–65, however, actual employment in 'agriculture' decreased in a striking way, at a speed faster than that at which 'normal' employment in 'agriculture' decreased. This migration from agriculture to industry resulted in a decrease of 1.4 million persons in disguised unemployment in 'agriculture' in these fifteen years. Nevertheless, this sector was still in a state of severe over-employment in 1965, disguised unemployment there amounting to 3.4 million persons.

Although, by virtue of an abnormal temporary increase in the wage rate, the 'construction' industry had no disguised unemployment in 1955, it was the second biggest reservoir of disguised unemployment in the other three years. Our investigation shows that in this industry too, disguised unemployment diminished rapidly during the period. However, the contrast between the parallel events in 'agriculture' and 'construction' is remarkable. In 'construction' the disguised unemployment was decreased, not by workers leaving the sector, but by employment being normalized within it. 'Construction' was one of the fastest-growing industries in the period 1951–65; its 'normal' employment grew at a greater rate than actual employment, so that the disguised unemployment which existed at the beginning was normalized during the period. Figure 1 compares the movements of actual and normal employment in the 'construction' sector with those in the 'agriculture' sector.

Finally, it is found that the sectors of 'wood and wood products' and

[1] R. Minami, 'The turning point in the Japanese economy', *Quarterly Journal of Economics*, vol. LXXXII, no. 3 (August 1968), pp. 380–402.

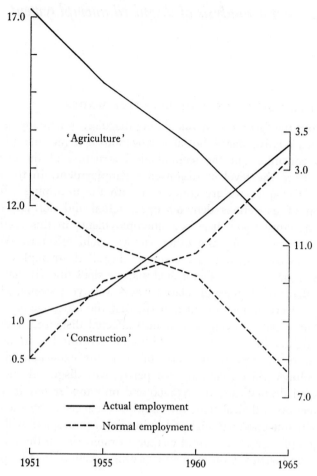

Figure 1

Actual and normal employment in 'agriculture' and 'construction' (in million persons).

'other manufacturing' were regular members of the group of disguised-unemployment-generating sectors. However, according to Table 12, 'other manufacturing' had no disguised unemployment in 1951. This is probably due to the fact that this sector in the 1951 table includes not only 'other manufacturing' proper, but also the subsectors of 'printing' and 'leather and rubber products', which are classified in industries 6 and 7 in the other tables; the pure result for 'other manufacturing' strictly defined is obscure in Table 12.

4. Factor analysis of disguised unemployment

I. THE DOMINANCE OF RELATIVE WAGES

It is clear from the formulas for calculating disguised unemployment that not only actual relative wages, but also exogenous demand, marginal propensities to consume and the technological structure of the economy, may all influence the level of disguised unemployment. In the second section of this chapter we are concerned with the multiplier effects of an expansion of exogenous demand upon actual and normal employment, and therefore upon disguised unemployment; in this section we investigate how powerfully the other factors could affect it. We shall examine the two contrasting decreases in disguised unemployment in 1955–60 and 1960–5 for the factor analysis; we shall find (i) that in the former the effects of changes in relative wages were very strong, whilst in the latter they were almost absent and (ii) that the other factors (except the level of aggregate exogenous demand) affected disguised unemployment only slightly in both periods. Although account has to be taken of the effects of changes in the level of aggregate exogenous demand, these two findings will explain, at least partly, why disguised unemployment decreased dramatically in 1955–60 and only moderately in 1960–5. The third section will deal with the multiplier effects of an increase in exogenous demand upon national and industrial incomes, and will supply an explanation of a great structural change – a rapid rise in the secondary and tertiary industries with a compensating decline in the primary industries.

A number of simulations were made for the analysis. First we calculated the 'actual employment' which would have prevailed in 1955 if the 1960 relative wages had prevailed instead of the actual 1955 wages. The figure for each industry was obtained in exactly the same way as we calculated normal employment in 1955; that is to say, we substituted into the formula, (2.9), the values of the relative prices obtained by assuming the 1960 relative wages in (2.15), with all other parameters being kept at their 1955 values. The disguised unemployment was then calculated by deducting the normal employment from the 'actual employment'. The results are compared, in Table 13, with the actual disguised unemployment in 1955 and that in 1960. The table shows that the industrial distribution of disguised unemployment in the 1955 economy would have been very similar, not to the actual

TABLE 13. *Disguised unemployment under different relative wages*
(in thousand persons)

Industry	(1) 1955 actual	(2) 1960 with 1955 wages	(3) 1955 with 1960 wages	(4) 1960 actual	(5) 1965 with 1960 wages	(6) 1960 with 1965 wages	(7) 1965 actual
1	4,157	4,164	2,768	3,311	2,968	3,727	3,420
2	–	–	–	–	–	10	20
3	–	–	107	68	155	–	–
4	–	–	–	–	35	–	–
5	28	23	58	113	144	–	10
6	–	–	–	–	–	24	54
7	6	1	–	–	–	–	–
8	–	–	–	–	–	–	–
9	31	33	–	–	–	123	147
10	–	–	–	–	–	–	–
11	14	–	–	–	–	–	–
12	52	135	–	–	–	2	26
13	52	93	–	–	–	–	–
14	3	–	–	–	–	5	13
15	59	81	22	45	81	–	10
16	–	–	180	403	670	69	182
17	–	–	–	–	–	–	–
18	556	700	–	–	–	–	–
19	–	–	–	–	–	–	–
20	–	–	–	–	–	–	–
Total	4,958	5,230	3,135	3,940	4,053	3,960	3,882

distribution in 1955, but to the one in 1960, if the 1960 relative wages had prevailed in 1955.

The same simulations were made for the 1960 economy by assuming 1955 and 1965 relative wages and for the 1965 economy by assuming 1960 relative wages. All the results are consistent with the above results for the 1955 economy; that is to say, the industrial distribution of disguised unemployment in the 1960 economy would have been very similar to the actual distribution in 1955 or 1965 if 1955 or 1965 relative wages had prevailed in 1960; and similarly, disguised unemployment would have been found in 1965 in those industries which actually had disguised unemployment in 1960, if there had been no change in relative wages between 1960 and 1965. As is seen from Table 13, the actual distribution of disguised unemployment among industries in 1955 was greatly different from that in 1960, both of which, in turn, were different from that in 1965. It is thus seen that the pattern of distribution of disguised unemployment among industries is highly sensitive to relative wages in the industries.

M T W

Table 13 offers more information. First, comparisons of columns (1) and (3) and of columns (2) and (4) both show that a change in the relative wages may, *ceteris paribus*, give rise to a great change not only in the distribution of disguised unemployment among industries but also in its total amount. From this one might think of the industrial wage structure as determining the aggregate amount of disguised unemployment too. However, comparison of column (1) with (2) and of column (3) with (4), especially the latter, shows that the total amount of disguised unemployment may differ greatly between two economies with the same relative wage structure, depending on the other structural parameters, such as the material- and labour-input coefficients, the marginal propensities to consume and the inter-industrial distribution and the absolute level of exogenous demand. We may thus conclude that, although it is true that the relative wage structure is the most powerful factor in the determination of the distribution of disguised unemployment among industries, it is not the sole dominant factor in the determination of aggregate disguised unemployment.

The effects of the other factors can easily be analysed into those of changes in the input coefficients and the marginal propensities to consume and the level of the aggregate exogenous demand, on the one hand, and those of a change in the distribution of exogenous demands among industries, on the other, by making the following additional simulations.

First, we calculated the 'actual' and 'normal' numbers of workers which would have been employed in the 1955 economy if the exogenous demands had been redistributed in the 1960 proportions. The disguised unemployment from these may be compared with actual disguised unemployment in 1955, to show the effects of a *ceteris paribus* change in the distribution of exogenous demand on disguised unemployment. Similarly the disguised unemployment in the 1960 economy under the 1955 distribution of exogenous demand, calculated in an analogous way, may be compared with actual disguised unemployment in 1960. Also, we calculated the 'actual' and 'normal' employment, and hence the disguised unemployment, which would have been obtained in the 1955 economy if there had prevailed the 1960 relative wages and the 1960 distribution of exogenous demand. These results are compared with those of the simulation in the 1955 economy with the 1960 relative wages and the actual 1955 exogenous demands. In the same way, the disguised unemployment calculated under the assumption that the 1955 relative wages and the 1955 distribution of exogenous demand prevailed in 1960 may be compared with the disguised unemployment in the 1960 economy with the 1955 relative wages and the 1960 distribution of exogenous demand.

The results are presented in Table 14. Four pairs of columns, (1) and (2),

TABLE 14. *Disguised unemployment under different distributions of exogenous demand*
(in thousand persons)

Industry	(1) a, d, w:[1] 1955	(2) a, w: 1955, d: 1960	(3) a: 1960, d, w: 1955	(4) a, d: 1960, w: 1955	(5) a, d: 1955, w: 1960	(6) a: 1955, d, w: 1960	(7) a, w: 1960, d: 1955	(8) a, d, w: 1960	(9) a, d, w: 1960	(10) a, w: 1960, d: 1965	(11) a: 1965, d, w: 1960	(12) a, d: 1965, w: 1960	(13) a, d: 1960, w: 1965	(14) a: 1960, d, w: 1965	(15) a, w: 1965, d: 1960	(16) a, d, w: 1965
1	4,157	3,699	4,287	4,164	2,768	2,632	3,380	3,311	3,311	3,070	3,228	2,968	3,727	3,424	3,755	3,420
2	–	–	–	–	107	160	50	68	68	–	–	–	10	25	11	20
3	–	–	–	–	–	–	–	–	–	80	145	155	–	–	–	–
4	–	–	–	–	–	–	–	–	–	5	2	35	–	–	–	–
5	28	27	12	23	58	79	82	113	113	129	127	144	–	1	3	10
6	–	–	–	–	–	–	–	–	–	–	–	–	24	41	37	54
7	6	3	–	1	–	–	–	–	–	–	–	–	–	–	–	–
8	–	–	–	–	–	–	–	–	–	–	–	–	–	–	–	–
9	31	29	24	33	–	–	–	–	–	–	–	–	123	137	133	147
10	–	–	–	–	–	–	–	–	–	–	–	–	–	–	–	–
11	14	–	–	–	–	–	–	–	–	–	–	–	–	–	–	–
12	52	74	78	135	–	–	–	–	–	–	–	–	2	10	17	26
13	52	49	56	93	–	–	–	–	–	–	–	–	–	–	–	–
14	3	–	–	–	–	–	–	–	–	–	–	–	–	8	8	13
15	59	65	70	81	22	31	35	45	45	35	71	81	5	2	3	10
16	–	–	–	–	180	294	259	403	403	472	576	670	69	97	139	182
17	–	–	–	–	–	–	–	–	–	–	–	–	–	–	–	–
18	556	505	703	700	–	–	–	–	–	–	–	–	–	–	–	–
19	–	–	–	–	–	–	–	–	–	–	–	–	–	–	–	–
20	–	–	–	–	–	–	–	–	–	–	–	–	–	–	–	–
Total	4,958	4,451	5,230	5,230	3,135	3,196	3,806	3,940	3,940	3,791	4,149	4,053	3,960	3,745	4,106	3,882

[1] a = the input coefficients and the marginal propensities to consume, d = distribution of exogenous demand, w = relative wages.

TABLE 15. *The ratio of disguised unemployment to total employment under various conditions*

A

	1955a[1]	1960a		B	1960a		1965a	
	1955w[1]	1960w	1955w 1960w		1960w 1965w		1960w 1965w	
1955d[1]	15.0%	10.0%	12.7% 9.4%	1960d	10.7% 10.7%		10.1% 10.0%	
1960d	14.7%	10.9%	13.9% 10.7%	1965d	10.6% 10.5%		10.0% 9.6%	

[1] For the definitions of a, d, and w, see note 1 to Table 14.

(3) and (4), (5) and (6), and (7) and (8), all show that a change in the distribution of exogenous demand, *ceteris paribus*, has no significant effects in either direction on the distribution and the absolute level of disguised unemployment. It is not surprising to see that we obtained very similar figures for aggregate disguised unemployment in the three pairs other than the first, because the exogenous demands, even though they were redistributed, were unchanged in the total sum within each pair. Table 14 also shows similar results between 1960 and 1965; and a comparison of column (7) with (10) will lead us to the same conclusion.

By taking different pairs of columns in Table 14, we can reveal the effects of changes in the material- and labour-input coefficients and the marginal propensities to consume. Compare, for example, columns (2) and (4). In both cases relative wages take on the actual values in 1955 and exogenous demand is distributed among industries in the 1960 proportions; differences are, however, found in the assumed input coefficients and marginal propensities to consume and the absolute level of exogenous demand. In column (2), we assumed the input coefficients and marginal propensities of 1955 and total exogenous demand at the 1955 level, while in column (4) all of these are fixed at their 1960 values. Therefore differences between the corresponding figures in columns (2) and (4) show the effects of changes in the input coefficients and marginal propensities to consume *plus* the multiplier effects of an expansion of the level of exogenous demand upon industrial and national disguised unemployment. Since the same relative wages are assumed in both cases, the interindustrial distribution of disguised unemployment is of the same pattern in both, but because the level of exogenous demand is expanded from the 1955 to the 1960 level, the total amount of disguised unemployment is clearly increased from column (2) to (4).

We may then compare column (1) with (3), (2) with (4), (5) with (7), and (6) with (8) in the same way and obtain the same result as above. That is to say, in both cases for each pair, disguised unemployment is similarly distributed among industries at two significantly different levels. It will, however, be found, by making similar comparisons between 1960 and 1965, that this cannot be a conclusion of general applicability. In fact, as the latter half of Table 14 (i.e. columns (9)–(16)) shows, the difference between the total amounts of disguised unemployment in any paired cases (say, columns (13) and (15)) is not very large, in spite of a big difference between the total amount of exogenous demand in 1960 and 1965. This leads us to conjecture that the multiplier effects of an expansion of aggregate exogenous demand upon the aggregate amount of disguised unemployment became very small in the period 1960–5, whereas they had been very large in 1955–60. One of the purposes of the next section is to provide econometric evidence for this conjecture.

Finally, let us briefly review the above results concerning the absolute amount of aggregate disguised unemployment in terms of its ratio to total employment. Our results are summarized in Table 15. First, comparing the figures in the first row of Table *A* (or *B*) with the corresponding figures in the second row of the same table, we observe that a change in the distribution of exogenous demand in 1955–60 and 1960–5 had *ceteris paribus* no clear effects on the percentage of disguised unemployment. Secondly, comparing the first column with the second, and the third with the fourth, we find from Table *A* that a change in relative wages from the 1955 to the 1960 ratio had the effect, *ceteris paribus*, on aggregate disguised unemployment of substantially reducing it in relation to total employment whereas Table *B* shows that a change in relative wages had only a negligible effect on the percentage of disguised unemployment in 1960–5. We may also compare the first column with the third, and the second with the fourth, in order to find the effects of changes in the input coefficients and the marginal propensities to consume.

2. EMPLOYMENT AND DISGUISED UNEMPLOYMENT MULTIPLIERS

In the standard economic models like Keynes', workers are unemployed if they are not 'normally' employed. There is only one multiplier concerning employment (or unemployment), since actual employment can never deviate from the normal level. In our model, however, they may differ and the difference between them, if it is positive, gives disguised unemployment. We have two kinds of multipliers, one on actual employment and the other on 'normal' employment, the multiplier on disguised unemployment being given by the difference between them. If the multiplier on disguised unemployment is estimated to be positive, the expansion of exogenous demand which would be recommended by Keynesians produces disguised unemployment as well as some 'normal' employment. The Keynesian policy for full employment is insufficient in economies with a 'dual' structure – some additional measures, especially revision of the inter-industrial wage structure, must be undertaken for normalization of the workers in the situation of disguised unemployment.

The main formulas from which the formulas of the multiplier effects are derived are again equations (2.9) and (2.15) (or (2.9') and (2.15')). They are reproduced here, respectively, as

$$z_i = \frac{\gamma_i}{w_i'} \sum_j b_{ij}(p_j' D_j) \quad (i = 1, \ldots, n), \tag{4.1}$$

$$\begin{bmatrix} 1-\alpha_{11} & -\alpha_{21} & \cdots & -\alpha_{n1} \\ -\alpha_{12} & 1-\alpha_{22} & \cdots & -\alpha_{n2} \\ \vdots & \vdots & & \vdots \\ -\alpha_{1n} & -\alpha_{2n} & \cdots & 1-\alpha_{nn} \end{bmatrix} \begin{bmatrix} \log p_1' \\ \log p_2' \\ \vdots \\ \log p_n' \end{bmatrix}$$

$$= \begin{bmatrix} k_1 + \alpha_1 \log\left(\sum_j p_j' b_{1j} D_j\right) + \beta_1 \log\left(\sum_j p_j' n_j\right) \\ k_2 + \alpha_2 \log\left(\sum_j p_j' b_{2j} D_j\right) + \beta_2 \log\left(\sum_j p_j' n_j\right) \\ \vdots \\ k_n + \alpha_n \log\left(\sum_j p_j' b_{nj} D_j\right) + \beta_n \log\left(\sum_j p_j' n_j\right) \end{bmatrix}, \tag{4.2}$$

where z_i = employment in industry i,

D_j = exogenous demand for good j,

p_j' = price of good j in terms of the wage rate in industry 1,

w_j' = wage rate in industry j in terms of the wage rate in industry 1,

α_{ij} = input coefficient of good i of industry j,

β_j = imported-input coefficient of industry j,

γ_j = labour-input coefficient of industry j,

$\alpha_j = 1 - \sum_i \alpha_{ij} - \beta_j - \gamma_j$,

n_j = the ratio of the competitive imports of good j to total competitive imports,

b_{ij} = the (i,j) element of $(I-A)^{-1}$, where $A = (\alpha_{ij} + c_{ij}\gamma_j)$ and c_{ij} is the marginal propensity to consume commodity i of the workers in industry j,

$k_j = -\log H_j + \gamma_j \log w_j'$, where H_j is a constant given by equation (2.12) or (2.12').

It should be noted that in Model I for 1951 and 1955 the imported-input coefficients β_j may be positive, whilst in Model II for 1960 and 1965 they must vanish because the input–output tables for these years are so constructed.

Now, with given w_i', $i = 1, ..., n$, we first differentiate (4.2) with respect to D_k. Defining

$$\rho_{ik} = \alpha_i p_k' b_{ik} / (\sum_j p_j' b_{ij} D_j), \tag{4.3}$$

$$\theta_{ij} = \alpha_{ij} + \alpha_i p_j' b_{ij} D_j / (\sum_h p_h' b_{ih} D_h) + \beta_i p_j' n_j / (\sum_h p_h' n_h), \tag{4.4}$$

then we have

$$\begin{bmatrix} 1-\theta_{11} & -\theta_{21} & \cdots & -\theta_{n1} \\ -\theta_{12} & 1-\theta_{22} & \cdots & -\theta_{n2} \\ \vdots & \vdots & & \vdots \\ -\theta_{1n} & -\theta_{2n} & \cdots & 1-\theta_{nn} \end{bmatrix} \begin{bmatrix} \mathrm{d}\log p_1'/\mathrm{d}D_k \\ \mathrm{d}\log p_2'/\mathrm{d}D_k \\ \vdots \\ \mathrm{d}\log p_n'/\mathrm{d}D_k \end{bmatrix} = \begin{bmatrix} \rho_{1k} \\ \rho_{2k} \\ \vdots \\ \rho_{nk} \end{bmatrix}, \tag{4.5}$$

or, in more concise form,

$$[I-\Theta](\mathrm{d}\log p'/\mathrm{d}D_k) = \rho_k. \tag{4.5}$$

Solving, we obtain

$$\mathrm{d}p'/\mathrm{d}D_k = \hat{p}'[I-\Theta]^{-1}\rho_k, \tag{4.6}$$

where $\hat{p}'$ is the diagonal matrix with p_i' on the diagonal.

Next, differentiating (4.1) with respect to D_k, we get

$$\frac{\mathrm{d}z_i}{\mathrm{d}D_k} = \frac{\gamma_i}{w_i'}\left[\sum_j b_{ij}\frac{\mathrm{d}p_j'}{\mathrm{d}D_k}D_j + p_k'b_{ik}\right].$$

Substituting for $\mathrm{d}p_j'/\mathrm{d}D_k$ from (4.6), this becomes

$$\frac{\mathrm{d}z_i}{\mathrm{d}D_k} = \frac{\gamma_i}{w_i'}[\sum_j b_{ij}(\sum_h p_j'\eta_{jh}\rho_{hk})D_j + p_k'b_{ik}], \tag{4.7}$$

where η_{jh} is the (j, h) element of $[I-\Theta]^{-1}$. This gives the effect of a change in the exogenous demand for good k upon employment in industry i.

It is seen from (4.3) and (4.4) that θ_{ij} and ρ_{hk} depend on p_j' as well as D_j, $j = 1, ..., n$; therefore, (4.7) depends on p_j' and D_j, $j = 1, ..., n$, and w_i'. When these take on the actual values which prevailed in some year, (4.7) gives the multiplier effect on actual employment in industry i in that year. On the other hand, the multiplier on 'normal' employment is obtained by substituting into (4.7) the 'normal' relative wage rate w_i' (i.e. the relative wage rate in industry i in the UK, 1960) and the equilibrium prices p_j', $j = 1, ..., n$, corresponding to the normal wage rates. Obviously, the multiplier on actual employment may be different from that on normal

TABLE 16. *Employment multiplier: effect of a unit increase in exogenous demand for good j upon actual employment (A), normal employment (N) and disguised unemployment (U)*

Good j	1951 (A)	1951 (N)	1951 (U)	1955 (A)	1955 (N)	1955 (U)	1960 (A)	1960 (N)	1960 (U)	1965 (A)	1965 (N)	1965 (U)
1	19.39	17.52	3.12	11.91	11.76	1.13	7.13	7.22	0.54	3.76	3.79	0.36
2	12.61	10.63	2.67	8.21	7.03	1.61	3.28	3.03	0.36	1.77	1.70	0.16
3	12.28	10.82	2.41	6.90	6.35	1.21	5.74	5.62	0.64	2.97	2.90	0.39
4	8.18	7.73	1.28	6.59	6.27	0.90	6.07	5.83	0.67	3.34	3.23	0.33
5	16.96	15.42	2.87	9.86	9.30	1.32	6.59	6.49	0.70	3.48	3.41	0.35
6	11.32	9.60	2.61	7.15	6.32	1.35	5.04	4.77	0.55	2.89	2.77	0.28
7	*	*	*	6.07	5.74	0.82	5.74	5.49	0.73	3.21	3.07	0.32
8	9.96	8.91	1.91	6.10	5.63	1.00	4.33	4.01	0.54	2.35	2.21	0.28
9	12.29	10.88	2.22	7.72	7.00	1.24	5.05	4.77	0.49	3.12	3.00	0.34
10	10.69	9.39	2.16	6.52	5.18	1.29	4.50	4.21	0.50	2.71	2.57	0.25
11	12.01	10.77	2.15	7.35	6.32	1.24	4.67	4.32	0.51	2.94	2.76	0.27
12	11.68	10.31	2.11	7.50	6.56	1.33	4.96	4.66	0.50	3.00	2.85	0.26
13	11.85	10.54	2.09	7.35	6.47	1.24	4.89	4.54	0.55	2.98	2.81	0.28
14	12.70	11.22	2.23	7.71	6.85	1.19	4.97	4.68	0.50	3.00	2.87	0.27
15	10.24	9.27	1.89	7.71	7.04	1.32	5.23	4.95	0.50	2.87	2.73	0.28
16	14.37	12.82	3.21	7.90	6.97	1.39	5.52	5.24	0.64	3.20	3.08	0.30
17	11.26	9.12	2.69	6.43	5.40	1.37	4.45	4.08	0.67	2.39	2.25	0.26
18	11.09	9.82	2.00	7.57	7.02	1.12	5.22	4.97	0.57	3.02	2.89	0.22
19	11.28	9.72	2.17	7.03	6.35	1.03	5.17	4.82	0.45	2.84	2.63	0.27
20	11.95	10.53	2.40	6.97	6.21	1.28	5.03	4.75	0.53	2.83	2.66	0.27
Average[1]	12.50	11.14	2.34	7.76	7.10	1.21	5.34	5.09	0.57	3.01	2.87	0.29

[1] The average of the elements of the corresponding column with weights D_i/D, $i = 1, 2, ..., 20$.

employment; the difference between them, if it is positive, gives the disguised unemployment caused in industry i by a marginal increase in the exogenous demand for good k. However, if actual employment is lower than normal employment in industry i before the increase, then this marginal disguised unemployment will be absorbed, so that it will not be actualized as disguised unemployment. We denote the multiplier on actual employment by $(\mathrm{d}z_i/\mathrm{d}D_k)^A$ and that on normal employment by $(\mathrm{d}z_i/\mathrm{d}D_k)^N$. The differences between $(\mathrm{d}z_i/\mathrm{d}D_k)^A$ and $(\mathrm{d}z_i/\mathrm{d}D_k)^N$, $i = 1, \dots, n$, are summed over all those industries in which there is some disguised unemployment. The sum, which may be denoted by

$$\sum_{i \mid z_i^A > z_i^N} \left[\left(\frac{\mathrm{d}z_i}{\mathrm{d}D_k} \right)^A - \left(\frac{\mathrm{d}z_i}{\mathrm{d}D_k} \right)^N \right], \tag{4.8}$$

gives the multiplier effect on aggregate disguised unemployment.

The formula (4.7) has been applied to the data to calculate the multipliers on actual and normal employment. The results are shown in Table 16. For each year, the figure in the kth row in column (A) represents the effect on actual total employment of an increase in the exogenous demand for good k, i.e. $\sum_i (\mathrm{d}z_i/\mathrm{d}D_k)^A$, and the corresponding figure in column (N) shows the similar effect on normal total employment, i.e. $\sum_i (\mathrm{d}z_i/\mathrm{d}D_k)^N$. (In these two expressions the summation is, of course, taken over all industries.) In column (U) there appears the sum (4.8) in the kth row, showing the effect on disguised unemployment. At the bottom of the table are the averages of the multipliers on actual or normal employment, or on disguised unemployment, with weights, D_k/D, $k = 1, \dots, 20$, i.e.

$$\sum_k \left[\sum_i \left(\frac{\mathrm{d}z_i}{\mathrm{d}D_k} \right)^A \right] \frac{D_k}{D}, \quad \sum_k \left[\sum_i \left(\frac{\mathrm{d}z_i}{\mathrm{d}D_k} \right)^N \right] \frac{D_k}{D}$$

$$\text{or} \quad \sum_k \left(\sum_{i \mid z_i^A > z_i^N} \left[\left(\frac{\mathrm{d}z_i}{\mathrm{d}D_k} \right)^A - \left(\frac{\mathrm{d}z_i}{\mathrm{d}D_k} \right)^N \right] \frac{D_k}{D} \right)$$

for the four years, 1951, 1955, 1960 and 1965, where D is the sum of D_k over all goods $k = 1, \dots, 20$. These give the effects on actual or normal employment, or on disguised unemployment, when an additional unit of aggregate exogenous demand, D, is distributed among goods in the actual proportions D_k/D, in the respective years.

From the table it is seen that the multipliers on actual employment were greater than the corresponding multipliers on normal employment, so that an increase in exogenous demand usually generated, in these years, not only normal employment but also disguised unemployment. This may explain, to some extent, the already observed tendency towards over-employment in Japan. It is also seen that all the multipliers were in declining trends, because of the increases in the productivity of labour which occurred during the period covered. Thirdly, the ratio of the multiplier on aggregate disguised unemployment to the multiplier on actual total employment was also in a declining trend; it was 18.8 per cent in 1951, and then 15.6 per cent in 1955, 10.7 per cent in 1960 and 9.6 per cent in 1965. This means that 18.8 per cent of the increased employment (due to an expansion of exogenous demand) was in the form of disguised unemployment in 1951, but only 9.6 per cent in 1965. When this ratio becomes negligible, we can ignore disguised employment, as Keynes did, as far as the incremental employment is concerned, although we still have some disguised unemployment in the economy. In order for disguised unemployment to vanish entirely from the economy, we must have negative multipliers on disguised unemployment. Though we did not obtain negative multipliers for the years we investigated, we may expect them for some years after 1965. Finally, the figures in Table 16 may be considered as sufficient evidence for our conjecture that the multiplier effects of an increase in the level of aggregate exogenous demand upon disguised unemployment in 1960–5 are significantly smaller than those in 1951–5.

3. INCOME MULTIPLIERS

This final section is devoted to a study of the effects of an expansion of exogenous demand upon sectoral and national real incomes. We are only concerned with the case where all exogenous demands are increased in the existing proportions, i.e. $dD_k/dD = D_k/D$ for all $k = 1, ..., n$. Income from industry j, that is gross output of industry j minus inputs of industry j other than its labour input, is given by

$$Y_j = (1 - \Sigma\alpha_{ij} - \beta_j)p_j x_j. \tag{4.9}$$

It is again noted that the interindustrial input coefficients α_{ij} cover only domestic inputs in the 1951 and 1955 tables although they all include imported inputs in the 1960 and 1965 tables, so that the imported-input coefficients, β_j, may be positive only in the first two tables; p_j is the price of output j; x_j denotes the physical output of industry j. When $D_k, k = 1, ..., n$, change proportionately, incomes $Y_j, j = 1, ..., n$, are affected, with constant prices, as

$$\frac{dY_j}{dD} = (1 - \Sigma\alpha_{ij} - \beta_j)p_j \sum_k \frac{dx_j}{dD_k} \frac{D_k}{D}. \tag{4.10}$$

It must be noted that in deriving (4.10) from (4.9) prices p_j are purposely held constant, so that dY_j/dD gives the real effect of D on Y_j obtained when nominal effects due to changes in prices are eliminated. Actually, however, a change in D induces changes in prices which have repercussions upon physical outputs, so that in calculating dx_j/dD_k, price changes must be taken into account.

Dividing the ith input–output equation, (2.7) or (2.7'), by p_i, we get

$$(1 + \mu_i) x_i = \sum_j (\alpha_{ij} + c_{ij} \gamma_j) \frac{p_j}{p_i} x_j + D_i \quad (i = 1, ..., n), \qquad (4.11)$$

or in matrix form

$$(I + \hat{\mu}) x = \hat{p}^{-1} A \hat{p} x + \{D\}, \qquad (4.11)$$

where $A = (\alpha_{ij} + c_{ij} \gamma_j)$; $\hat{\mu}$ and $\hat{p}$ are the diagonal matrices with diagonal elements μ_i and p_i, respectively; x and $\{D\}$ are column vectors. The μ_is, which stand for the import coefficients, may be non-zero only in the 1960 and 1965 tables, because the tables have been so constructed. In this physical input–output system, $\alpha_{ij}, c_{ij}, \gamma_j$ and μ_i are considered as constant. (4.11) implies that x may be affected directly by D_k and indirectly by changes in prices caused by D_k, which are given by (4.6). We have from (4.11)

$$(I + \hat{\mu}) \frac{dx}{dD_k} = \hat{p}^{-1} A \hat{p} \frac{dx}{dD_k} + \hat{p}^{-1} \left[A \frac{d\hat{p}}{dD_k} x - \hat{p}^{-1} \frac{d\hat{p}}{dD_k} A \hat{p} x \right] + \Delta_k,$$

where Δ_k is the column vector having 1 as the kth component and 0 in all other places. Substituting for dp/dD_k from (4.6), the above equation can be solved with respect to dx/dD_k. The dx_i/dD_k, $i = 1, ..., n$, thus obtained are further substituted into (4.10), to derive the effect on the 'real' income from industry j. Finally, by summing dY_j/dD over all industries we get the effect on the real national income.

The results of the application of the formula just established to the data are shown in Table 17, in which the effects on the real national income are presented in the bottom row. The figures are comparable with those for the UK economy given in Part II of this book. It is seen that the marginal effects on the real income from individual industries changed greatly during the period 1951–65; for example, the multiplier on the real income from 'agriculture' decreased from 0.37 to 0.16, and that from the construction industry increased from 0.04 to 0.09; nevertheless, rather surprisingly, the aggregate multiplier on real national income remained very stable throughout the period, being confined within the range 1.15–1.20. By aggregating the industries 'agriculture, fishing and forestry' and 'mining' into the primary industry, the industries 'distributive trades', 'transport and

TABLE 17. *Income multiplier: effect of a proportional increase in exogenous demand upon the real income from industry j*

Industry	1951	1955	1960	1965
1	0.37 ⎱ 0.41	0.27 ⎱ 0.30	0.21 ⎱ 0.24	0.16 ⎱ 0.17
2	0.04 ⎰	0.03 ⎰	0.02 ⎰	0.01 ⎰
3	0.07	0.07	0.07	0.06
4	0.06	0.04	0.04	0.04
5	0.02	0.02	0.02	0.02
6	0.02	0.03	0.02	0.03
7	*	0.01	0.01	0.01
8	0.03	0.03	0.04	0.04
9	0.01	0.01	0.02	0.01
10	0.04 ⎱ 0.37	0.04 ⎱ 0.35	0.06 ⎱ 0.47	0.05 ⎱ 0.49
11	0.01	0.02	0.04	0.04
12	0.01	0.01	0.03	0.03
13	0.02	0.01	0.03	0.04
14	0.01	0.01	0.01	0.01
15	0.02	0.01	0.01	0.01
16	0.04	0.05	0.07	0.09
17	0.01	0.02	0.02	0.01
18	0.15 ⎱ 0.43	0.13 ⎱ 0.50	0.14 ⎱ 0.45	0.16 ⎱ 0.54
19	0.08	0.06	0.07	0.08
20	0.21 ⎰	0.31 ⎰	0.24 ⎰	0.30 ⎰
Total	1.20	1.15	1.16	1.20

storage' and 'communication, gas, water and business services' into the tertiary industry, and all others into the secondary industry, we obtain multipliers at the medium level of aggregation. Table 17 shows that the multiplier for the real income from the primary industry steadily decreased from the 1951 level of 0.41 to the 1965 level of 0.17, in compensation for an increase in the multiplier for the real income from the secondary and tertiary industries. The fact is worth emphasizing that in the same period as Japan succeeded in developing her economy at a miraculous rate, her economic structure was changed so as to be very favourable for the expansion of the secondary and tertiary industries.

Finally, dividing the multiplier for the real national income by the multiplier for actual employment, we can calculate the marginal (not partial but total) productivity of labour. It is found that it increased steadily during the period 1951–65. The annual compound rate of growth of the marginal productivity of labour is calculated at 11.3 per cent in 1951–5, 8.0 per cent in 1955–60, and 12.8 per cent in 1960–5 on average. It is not surprising to find such high rates of growth of the marginal total productivity of labour underlying the high actual rates of growth of the gross national product in Japan.

APPENDIX

An estimation of the international trade
multiplier, 1954–1965

by M. Morishima and Y. Murata

1. *Introduction*

In other parts of this volume we estimate the multiplier effects of an increase in government expenditure or other exogenous variables on GNP, national income or other endogenous variables, for the USA, the UK and Japan. These effects are 'one-way' in the sense that they allow for leakages of purchasing power to foreign countries but not for any feedback to the country where the original increase takes place, through the channels of exports to other countries. True foreign trade multipliers which recognize the entire network of international trade have been proposed by Metzler,[1] but there have so far been few attempts to estimate the values of the Metzlerian multipliers statistically. Beckerman's study may be considered outstanding in this field of research, in spite of its rather crude estimation of import coefficients.[2] The propensities to import of individual countries have been estimated by many economists such as Chang, Neisser and Modigliani, Polak, and Adams *et al.* but their results have not been incorporated into a consistent econometric model of world trade.[3] The purpose of this appendix is confined to giving the Metzler theory a statistical coating, in the hope that by replacing the simply estimated consumption functions of our model by more elaborate macroeconometric national models developed in various countries, international trade multipliers will be estimated more accurately in future.

In this study the world is taken to consist of the following ten regions: (i) the European Economic Community (EEC), (ii) the United Kingdom, (iii) the rest of Western Europe (RWE), (iv) USA, (v) Canada, (vi) Latin America (LA), (vii) free Asia (FA), (viii) Japan, (ix) Australia, New Zealand, and the Republic of South Africa (ANZA), and (x) the rest of the world. The rest of Western Europe includes Austria, Denmark, Finland, Greece, Iceland, the Republic of Ireland, Norway, Portugal, Spain, Sweden,

---

[1] L. A. Metzler, 'A multiple region theory of income and trade', *Econometrica*, vol. 18, 1950, pp. 329–54.

[2] W. Beckerman, 'The world trade multiplier and the stability of world trade, 1938 to 1953', *Econometrica*, vol. 24, 1956, pp. 239–52.

[3] T. C. Chang, *Cyclical Movements in the Balance of Payments*, Cambridge University Press, 1951; H. Neisser and F. Modigliani, *National Incomes and International Trade* (University of Illinois Press, 1953); J. J. Polak, *An International Economic System* (George Allen and Unwin Ltd, 1954); F. G. Adams, H. Eguchi and F. Meyer-zu-Schlochtern, *An Econometric Analysis of International Trade* (Paris: OECD Publications, 1969).

Switzerland, Turkey and Yugoslavia. Latin America includes Argentina, Brazil, Chile, Colombia, Costa Rica, Dominican Republic, Ecuador, Guatemala, Honduras, Mexico, Nicaragua, Panama, Paraguay, Peru, Uruguay and Venezuela. Free Asia includes Burma, Ceylon, Malaya (excluding Singapore), the Philippines, South Korea, Taiwan and Thailand only. Those countries for which national accounts data are not available have been omitted. For this reason Cambodia, India, Pakistan, Bolivia and El Salvador, for which only partial data are available, are included in the rest of the world, together with the socialist and communist countries, where the national accounting system is different from that used in the capitalist countries. Also, those countries for which data are unavailable for only one or two years in the period 1953–65, are treated in the estimation of the consumption and imports functions as if they had not existed in these particular years. For example, in the estimation of the consumption function of LA, Nicaragua in 1954, Paraguay in 1965 and Uruguay in 1954 and 1965 do not appear in the sample for this reason. Thus, we arrange for countries to have places in the estimation of the parameters, as long as their national accounts data are available; so the coverage of our sample is more than 75 per cent of the whole of world trade.

We estimate regional consumption functions and inter-regional imports functions by applying the simple least-squares method to the data from 1953 to 1965.[1] The main source of the data are United Nations' publications.[2] The consumption per capita of region i in period t is explained by the GNP per capita of i in period t and the consumption per capita of i in period $t-1$. The aggregate imports of region i from region j in period t are explained not only by the GNP of i at t and its variation from $t-1$ to t but also by the terms of trade of region j relative to the other regions.

The parameters estimated enable us to calculate the values of the international trade multipliers: impact multipliers, long-run multipliers and supermultipliers. First of all, on the basis of a theoretical analysis, it is found that each of these multipliers is bounded from above by the corresponding closed-economy multiplier and from below by the corresponding one-way foreign trade multiplier. These inequalities are tested econometrically. It is shown that for some countries the upper and lower bounds are close to each other, but that for others the ranges set by them are fairly large. It is also shown that the true foreign trade multipliers differ numerically very little

[1] The data for 1953 are used only for estimating the effect of lagged consumption on current consumption.

[2] They are *Yearbook of National Accounts Statistics*, for consumption, personal income and GNP; *Yearbook of International Trade Statistics*, for exports and imports; *Demographic Yearbook*, for population; and *Statistical Yearbook*, for prices.

from the corresponding one-way foreign trade multipliers. Although it cannot of course be claimed that our econometric results are accurate, our findings give grounds for believing that differences between true and one-way multipliers are a matter of second approximation.

On the other hand it is found that some of the cross-effects from one country to another are reasonably large, while others are negligible. On the basis of the estimated import functions, it is seen that the world economy is nearly decomposable into three blocs: (i) USA, (ii) LA, EEC, RWE, UK, Canada, and (iii) ANZA, Japan, FA. Thus the econometric significance of the Metzler theory lies in elaborating cross-country income propagations instead of making the one-way foreign trade multipliers more accurate.

Finally, the actual GNP of a country is analysed into a dissipative part, a stationary part determined by the long-term multipliers and a trend part determined by the Brown–Jones supermultipliers;[1] and the relative magnitudes of these parts are calculated for each of the nine endogenous regions. It is found that the ratio of the stationary part to the actual GNP was very high for each country in 1964; the sum of the other parts hardly exceeded a fifth of the actual GNP. It is also found that investment and government expenditures have much stronger effects on the GNP than other factors (prices, or the terms of trade, and the exports and imports of the exogenous countries) determining the multiplicands of the long-run multipliers.

[1] M. Brown and R. Jones, 'Economic growth and the theory of international income flow', *Econometrica* (January 1962).

2. *A modified Metzler model*

Although we make a number of modifications, our model is basically the Metzler–Brown–Jones model of international trade, which is an important extension of Keynes' savings-investment model of income determination into the case of multiple countries trading with each other. It consists of equations, as many as the number of countries, each giving the GNP of a country as the sum of consumption, investment, government expenditure and the excess of exports over imports, of that country. We modify the model by taking current consumption as being influenced not only by current income but also by the previous year's consumption. We also deviate from these authors, especially from Metzler, in assuming that imports in any year depend on prices and on the difference between the income of that year and the previous year, in addition to current income, which has been taken into account by Metzler.

Investment and government expenditure of each country are regarded as autonomous. Exports of a country are imports of other countries from it, so that they are influenced by the terms of trade of that country, and current incomes and income changes of other countries. Thus, through imports and exports, countries are coupled with each other directly or indirectly; in fact, if the world is 'indecomposable', an autonomous increase in the aggregate effective demand in one country increases the level of income in every country in the world.

The 'world' is described in abstract terms as follows. There are n endogenous and one exogenous country in the system. For each country i, we denote the gross national product by Y_i, private consumption expenditure by C_i, investment and government expenditures by G_i, total imports by M_i, total exports by X_i, imports of i from j by M_{ij}, imports of i from the exogenous country by M_{in+1} and exports of i to the exogenous country by X_{in+1}, the terms of trade (prices of exporting country i relative to prices of other countries) by p_i, population by N_i, population in the initial year by $\bar{N}_i$, and the rate of growth of population by $\rho_i - 1$ (or $\rho_i = 1 +$ the rate of growth of population). We write $y_i = Y_i/N_i$ and $c_i = C_i/N_i$, which are income and consumption, both per capita, respectively.

For each country the following identities hold in each year:

$$Y_i = C_i + G_i + X_i - M_i, \tag{2.1}$$

$$M_i = \sum_j M_{ij} + M_{in+1}, \qquad (2.2)$$

$$X_i = \sum_j M_{ji} + X_{in+1}. \qquad (2.3)$$

(2.1) implies the Keynesian income determination that the GNP of country i is determined so that it equals consumption *plus* investment and government expenditures *plus* exports *minus* imports of country i. (2.2) and (2.3) simply state that the total imports and the total exports of country i are the sum of her imports from the endogenous and exogenous countries and the sum of her exports to them, respectively. Consumption functions are given in terms of per capita consumption and per capita income:

$$c_i = \alpha_i y_i + \beta_i c_{i,-1} + \gamma_i \quad (i = 1, ..., n), \qquad (2.4)$$

where the second subscript of the variable $c_{i,-1}$ indicates a one-year time lag and α_i, β_i and γ_i are constant. Assuming a constant rate of growth of population, we may write (2.4) in terms of aggregate consumption and income as

$$C_i = c_i N_i = \alpha_i Y_i + \beta_i \rho_i C_{i,-1} + \gamma_i \rho_i^t \bar{N}_i \quad (i = 1, ..., n), \qquad (2.5)$$

in which the effect of an increase in population on aggregate consumption is explicit. Import functions may be written as

$$M_{ij} = \mu_{ij} Y_i + \lambda_{ij} \Delta Y_i + \pi_{ij} p_j + \theta_{ij} \quad (i, j = 1, ..., n), \qquad (2.6)$$

where ΔY_i is the difference in aggregate income, $Y_i - Y_{i,-1}$, and the coefficients are assumed to be constant. (2.6) is the most general form of the import functions. Those countries for which some coefficients λ_{ij} or π_{ij} are found not to be statistically significantly different from zero have import functions of a degenerate form:

$$M_{ij} = \mu_{ij} Y_i + \lambda_{ij} \Delta Y_i + \theta_{ij}, \text{ or } \mu_{ij} Y_i + \pi_{ij} p_j + \theta_{ij}, \text{ or } \mu_{ij} Y_i + \theta_{ij},$$

the first being Brown and Jones' form, while the last two are Metzler's. Finally, the exports and imports of the exogenous country are regarded as autonomous.

Next let

$$\mu_i = \sum_j \mu_{ij}, \quad \bar{\mu}_i = \mu_i - \mu_{ii}, \quad \lambda_i = \sum_j \lambda_{ij}, \quad \bar{\lambda}_i = \lambda_i - \lambda_{ii}.$$

For each single country μ_{ii} and λ_{ii} are zero, so that $\bar{\mu}_i = \mu_i$ and $\bar{\lambda}_i = \lambda_i$. But for a hybrid country, such as the EEC, import coefficients within the region are not necessarily zero; and the gross aggregate import propensities μ_i and λ_i may be different from the net propensities $\bar{\mu}_i$ and $\bar{\lambda}_i$ which describe the true propensities to import by the 'country' from 'abroad'. We define the five matrices as

$$
M = \begin{bmatrix} -\bar{\mu}_1 & \mu_{21} & \cdots & \mu_{n1} \\ \mu_{12} & -\bar{\mu}_2 & \cdots & \mu_{n2} \\ \multicolumn{4}{c}{\dotfill} \\ \mu_{1n} & \mu_{2n} & \cdots & -\bar{\mu}_n \end{bmatrix}, \quad
L = \begin{bmatrix} -\bar{\lambda}_1 & \lambda_{21} & \cdots & \lambda_{n1} \\ \lambda_{12} & -\bar{\lambda}_2 & \cdots & \lambda_{n2} \\ \multicolumn{4}{c}{\dotfill} \\ \lambda_{1n} & \lambda_{2n} & \cdots & -\bar{\lambda}_n \end{bmatrix},
$$

$$
A = \begin{bmatrix} \alpha_1 & 0 & \cdots & 0 \\ 0 & \alpha_2 & \cdots & 0 \\ \multicolumn{4}{c}{\dotfill} \\ 0 & 0 & \cdots & \alpha_n \end{bmatrix}, \quad
B = \begin{bmatrix} \beta_1 & 0 & \cdots & 0 \\ 0 & \beta_2 & \cdots & 0 \\ \multicolumn{4}{c}{\dotfill} \\ 0 & 0 & \cdots & \beta_n \end{bmatrix},
$$

$$
R = \begin{bmatrix} \rho_1 & 0 & \cdots & 0 \\ 0 & \rho_2 & \cdots & 0 \\ \multicolumn{4}{c}{\dotfill} \\ 0 & 0 & \cdots & \rho_n \end{bmatrix}.
$$

Combining equations (2.1)–(2.6) and viewing the definitions of the matrices, we have simultaneous equations which are written in matrix form as

$$
(I - A - M - L)\, Y = [BR(I - M - L) - L]\, Y_{-1} \\
+ BRLY_{-2} + T + U, \tag{2.7}
$$

where Y, T, U are n dimensional vectors with elements, Y_i, $i = 1, \ldots, n$,

$$
T_i = \gamma_i \rho_i^t \bar{N}_i \quad (i = 1, \ldots, n),
$$

$$
U_i = (\textstyle\sum_j \pi_{ji})\, p_i - \sum_j \pi_{ij} p_j - \beta_i \rho_i [(\sum_j \pi_{ji})\, p_i - \sum_j \pi_{ij} p_j]_{-1}
$$
$$
+ G_i - \beta_i \rho_i G_{i,-1}
$$
$$
+ (X_{in+1} - M_{in+1}) - \beta_i \rho_i (X_{in+1} - M_{in+1})_{-1}
$$
$$
+ (1 - \beta_i \rho_i)(\textstyle\sum_j \theta_{ji} - \sum_j \theta_{ij}) \quad (i = 1, \ldots, n),
$$

respectively.

It is noted that elements of the vector T grow at rates which are equal to the rates of growth of population of the respective countries, while those of U depend upon prices, investment and government expenditures of the endogenous countries, and the exports and imports of the exogenous country. Those are considered to be determined outside the system. Then the fundamental equation (2.7) can be solved with respect to current incomes Y, because the lagged incomes Y_{-1} and Y_{-2} have been determined in the past. The impact international trade matrix multiplier is simply calculated by inverting the extended Metzler matrix $(I - A - M - L)$.

The impact multipliers give the short-term effects of a unit increase in an autonomous outlay of a country on aggregate incomes of the countries in the system. They allow not only for the direct effects through consumption but also for all repercussions through the network of mutual trade flows among countries. They may be compared, on the one hand, with the simplest Keynesian multiplier for a closed country, $(1 - \alpha_i)^{-1}$, which is obtained when the foreign market is completely inaccessible to country i, and on the other hand, with the one-way foreign trade multiplier, $(1 - \alpha_i + \bar{\mu}_i + \bar{\lambda}_i)^{-1}$, which takes account of the leakage of income abroad through the home country's imports but ignores repercussions from the other countries.

Let us now assume that the propensity to consume of each country is less than one but greater than its propensity to import, i.e.

$$1 > \alpha_i > \bar{\mu}_i + \bar{\lambda}_i > 0 \quad \text{for all } i. \tag{2.8}$$

Since off-diagonal elements of M and L are non-negative and A is diagonal, the matrix $A + M + L$, denoted by Q hereafter, is a non-negative matrix. Moreover, since the column sums of M and L are all null because of the definitions of $\bar{\mu}_i$ and $\bar{\lambda}_i$, the column sums of Q are all less than unity; therefore, as is now familiar among economists, we have

$$H = (I - Q)^{-1} > 0, \tag{2.9}$$

if Q is indecomposable.

Let E be a row vector which has unities as elements. As

$$E(I - Q) = (1 - \alpha_1, 1 - \alpha_2, ..., 1 - \alpha_n),$$

we have

$$E = (1 - \alpha_1, 1 - \alpha_2, ..., 1 - \alpha_n)H,$$

from which it follows, in view of (2.9), that the ith diagonal element of the impact multiplier matrix H is smaller than $(1 - \alpha_i)^{-1}$ for all i. Further, one of the Frobenius properties concerning non-negative matrices implies that all elements of H increase when an element of Q increases; that is to say, the diagonal and cross-multiplier effects become larger, the larger are the elements of Q. Therefore we find that the ith diagonal element of H is greater than $(1 - \alpha_i + \bar{\mu}_i + \bar{\lambda}_i)^{-1}$, because the former is reduced to the latter when all off-diagonal elements of $M + L$ vanish. Thus we may say that the Keynesian multipliers overestimate the true diagonal multiplier effects which, in turn, are underestimated by the one-way foreign trade multipliers due to Harrod, Samuelson and others.[1]

Next, the diagonal (or own) impact multipliers are compared with the

[1] R. Harrod, *International Economics* (Cambridge University Press, 1939), pp. 131–4. P. A. Samuelson, 'The simple mathematics of income determination', in L. A. Metzler *et al. Income Employment and Public Policy: Essays in Honor of Alvin Hansen*, 1948.

corresponding cross-impact multipliers. An off-diagonal element, say the jth, of the ith row of H represents the effect of an increase in the autonomous outlay of country j on the income of country i. It is necessarily smaller than i's own multiplier because we assume moderate propensities to import for all countries such that they satisfy (2.8). In fact, as has been seen, Q is then a non-negative matrix with column sums being all less than one, so that the Metzler theorem may be applied in order to establish that the diagonal elements of H are greater than the off-diagonal elements of the corresponding rows.[1]

The concept of impact (instantaneous or 0-year) multipliers is extended to a more general concept of dynamic (later-years) multipliers, which give the effects of a sustained unit increase in a parameter (e.g. the autonomous outlay or the rate of growth of population of country i) on the incomes of all the trading countries after t years, $t = 1, 2, 3, \ldots$. For this purpose we assume that the terms of trade p_i, government expenditure G_i, the exports and imports of the exogenous country X_{in+1} and M_{in+1} and the rate of growth of population are all constant. Then in (2.7), the elements of the vector U remain unchanged and those of T grow at the rates $\rho_1, \ldots, \rho_n$ from period to period. The general solution to (2.7) may be given in the form of the sum of a particular solution to

$$S_0 Y + S_1 Y_{-1} + S_2 Y_{-2} = U, \tag{2.10}$$

a particular solution to

$$S_0 Y + S_1 Y_{-1} + S_2 Y_{-2} = T, \tag{2.11}$$

and the general solution to the reduced equation,

$$S_0 Y + S_1 Y_{-1} + S_2 Y_{-2} = 0, \tag{2.12}$$

where

$$\left. \begin{array}{l} S_0 = I - Q = I - A - M - L, \\ S_1 = -BR(I - M - L) + L, \\ S_2 = -BRL. \end{array} \right\} \tag{2.13}$$

A particular solution (a stationary one) to (2.10) is found by assuming $Y = Y_{-1} = Y_{-2}$ and solving (2.10) with respect to Y, which is

$$Y = (S_0 + S_1 + S_2)^{-1} U. \tag{2.14}$$

The matrix multiplier $(S_0 + S_1 + S_2)^{-1}$ gives the long-term effects of an

[1] L. A. Metzler, 'A multiple-country theory of income transfers', *Journal of Political Economy* (1951), pp. 14–29, and 'Taxes and subsidies in Leontief's input–output model', *Quarterly Journal of Economics* (1951), pp. 433–8. See also M. Morishima, *Equilibrium, Stability and Growth*, pp. 18–19.

autonomous increase in an element of U upon incomes. In view of the definitions of S_is, we may put (2.14) in the form,

$$Y = [I - A - BR - (I - BR)M]^{-1} U. \qquad (2.15)$$

Thus each long-run multiplier effect is independent of the accelerator coefficients of imports, λ_{ij}.

Let us now assume that[1]

$$\alpha_i + \beta_i \rho_i < 1 + (1 - \beta_i \rho_i)\bar{\mu}_i \quad \text{for all } i. \qquad (2.16)$$

Then $A + BR + (I - BR)M$ is a non-negative matrix with column sums being less than one; therefore we obtain

$$J = [I - A - BR - (I - BR)M]^{-1} > 0.$$

Next, let us partition M into M^1 and M^2 so that

$$M^1 = - \begin{bmatrix} \bar{\mu}_1 & 0 & \cdots & 0 \\ 0 & \bar{\mu}_2 & \cdots & 0 \\ \multicolumn{4}{c}{\dotfill} \\ 0 & 0 & \cdots & \bar{\mu}_n \end{bmatrix} \quad \text{and} \quad M^2 = \begin{bmatrix} 0 & \mu_{21} & \cdots & \mu_{n1} \\ \mu_{12} & 0 & \cdots & \mu_{n2} \\ \multicolumn{4}{c}{\dotfill} \\ \mu_{1n} & \mu_{2n} & \cdots & 0 \end{bmatrix}.$$

We have from $J > 0$, $M^2 \geqq 0$, and $1 > \beta_i \rho_i \ (i = 1, \ldots, n)$

$$[I - A - BR - (I - BR)M^1]J > I,$$

which implies

the ith diagonal of $J > (1 - \alpha_i - \beta_i \rho_i + (1 - \beta_i \rho_i)\bar{\mu}_i)^{-1}$

for all i. Evidently, the right-hand side of the above expression stands for the long-run one-way multiplier which is obtained when country i is not affected by repercussions from abroad. The same inequality as has been seen concerning the impact multipliers holds for the long-run multipliers: the long-run diagonal multiplier is larger than the long-run one-way multiplier, for each country.

It is also seen that the long-run diagonal multipliers are smaller than the corresponding long-run closed-economy multipliers. Taking $EM = 0$ (i.e. each column sum of M is zero) into account, we have

$$E(I - BR)^{-1}(I - A - BR - (I - BR)M)$$
$$= [(1 - \beta_1 \rho_1)^{-1}(1 - \alpha_1 - \beta_1 \rho_1),$$
$$\ldots, (1 - \beta_n \rho_n)^{-1}(1 - \alpha_n - \beta_n \rho_n)],$$

[1] Our estimates of α_i, β_i, etc. satisfy (2.16), together with (2.16′) and (2.21) below, as well as (2.8).

so that

$$[(1-\beta_1\rho_1)^{-1}, ..., (1-\beta_n\rho_n)^{-1}]$$
$$= [(1-\beta_1\rho_1)^{-1}(1-\alpha_1-\beta_1\rho_1),$$
$$..., (1-\beta_n\rho_n)^{-1}(1-\alpha_n-\beta_n\rho_n)]\,J. \qquad (2.17)$$

We now strengthen conditions (2.16) into

$$\alpha_i+\beta_i\rho_i < 1 \quad \text{for all } i. \qquad (2.16')$$

Since $J > 0$ and $1 > \beta_i\rho_i$ for all i, we then have from (2.17)

$$(1-\beta_i\rho_i)^{-1} > (1-\beta_i\rho_i)^{-1}(1-\alpha_i-\beta_i\rho_i)$$
$$\times \text{the } i\text{th diagonal element of } J \text{ for all } i;$$

hence, the ith long-run diagonal multiplier (the ith diagonal element of J) is smaller than the ith long-run closed-economy multiplier, $(1-\alpha_i-\beta_i\rho_i)^{-1}$.

We now turn to (2.11) which gives what Brown and Jones called the foreign-trade supermultipliers.[1] Suppose (2.11) has a solution of the type $Y = KT$, where K is an unknown $n \times n$ matrix with constant elements. Substituting from this, (2.11) can be written as

$$S_0KT+S_1KT_{-1}+S_2KT_{-2} = T. \qquad (2.18)$$

The matrix K is determined in the following way. Since T is the sum of n vectors,

$$T^i = \begin{bmatrix} 0 \\ \vdots \\ 0 \\ \gamma_i\rho_i^t\overline{N}_i \\ 0 \\ \vdots \\ 0 \end{bmatrix} \quad (i = 1, ..., n),$$

(2.18) may be decomposed into n sets of n equations

$$S_0KT^i+S_1KT^i_{-1}+S_2KT^i_{-2} = T^i \quad (i = 1, ..., n), \qquad (2.19)$$

the ith set determining the ith column of K. Eliminating $\beta_i\rho_i^t\overline{N}_i$ from (2.19) and denoting the ith column of K by K^i and $S_0+\rho_i^{-1}S_1+\rho_i^{-2}S_2$ by V_i, we have

$$V_iK^i = I^i,$$

where I^i stands for the ith column of the $n \times n$ identity matrix. We have

$$K^i = V_i^{-1}I^i \quad (i = 1, ..., n).$$

[1] M. Brown and R. Jones, *op. cit.* p. 90. As they recognize, the supermultiplier was first discussed and so named by Hicks. Morishima and Kaneko also discussed a multi-sectoral version of the supermultiplier: M. Morishima and Y. Kaneko, 'On the speed of establishing multi-sectoral equilibrium', *Econometrica* (1962), pp. 818–23.

Hence, the foreign-trade supermultipliers are given, in matrix form, as

$$K = (V_1^{-1}I^1, V_2^{-1}I^2, ..., V_n^{-1}I^n). \qquad (2.20)$$

We now assume

$$\rho_i > 1 \quad (i = 1, ..., n). \qquad (2.21)$$

The inequalities (2.16'), together with (2.21), imply that

$$V_i = S_0 + \rho_i^{-1}S_1 + \rho_i^{-2}S_2$$
$$= (I - A - \rho_i^{-1}BR) - \rho_i^{-1}(\rho_i I - BR)(M + (1 - \rho_i^{-1})L) \qquad (2.22)$$

has positive diagonal elements and non-positive off-diagonal elements. Moreover, we obtain

$$E(\rho_i I - BR)^{-1}V_i$$
$$= [(\rho_i - \beta_1\rho_1)^{-1}(1 - \alpha_1 - \beta_1\rho_1/\rho_i),$$
$$..., (\rho_i - \beta_n\rho_n)^{-1}(1 - \alpha_n - \beta_n\rho_n/\rho_i)] \qquad (2.23)$$

that is to say, the column sums of V_i with positive weights $E(\rho_i I - BR)^{-1}$ are all positive (because of (2.16') and (2.21) again). Hence, we find that the supermultipliers are positive:

$$V_i^{-1} > 0 \quad (i = 1, ..., n). \qquad (2.24)$$

Therefore, from

$$E(\rho_i I - BR)^{-1}$$
$$= [(\rho_i - \beta_1\rho_1)^{-1}(1 - \alpha_1 - \beta_1\rho_1/\rho_i),$$
$$..., (\rho_i - \beta_n\rho_n)^{-1}(1 - \alpha_n - \beta_n\rho_n/\rho_i)] V_i^{-1},$$

we obtain

$$1 > (1 - \alpha_i - \beta_i) \times \text{the } i\text{th diagonal element of } V_i^{-1}. \qquad (2.25)$$

We can show that $(1 - \alpha_i - \beta_i)^{-1}$ is the closed-economy supermultiplier of country i, so that (2.25) implies that each country's diagonal foreign-trade supermultiplier is smaller than its closed-economy supermultiplier. Finally, it follows from $V_i^{-1} > 0$ and the fact that the off-diagonal elements of each column of V_i are non-positive and at least one of them is negative, that the product of a diagonal element of V_i^{-1} and the corresponding diagonal element of V_i is greater than one; we have, in particular, for the ith diagonal element,

the ith diagonal element of V_i^{-1}

$$> \text{the reciprocal of the } i\text{th diagonal element of } V_i, \qquad (2.26)$$

the latter being $[1 - \alpha_i - \beta_i + (1 - \beta_i)(\bar{\mu}_i + (1 - \rho_i^{-1})\bar{\lambda}_i)]^{-1}$. Consequently,

(2.26) implies that country i's diagonal foreign-trade supermultiplier is greater than its one-way foreign-trade supermultiplier.

We are now able to conclude that, as far as the diagonal elements are concerned, the impact, the long-run and the supermultipliers are bounded from above by the corresponding closed-economy multipliers and from below by the corresponding one-way foreign-trade multipliers. Most of the multipliers calculated by Goldberger, Evans and others, as well as by us in the other parts of this volume, are examples of one-way foreign multipliers, so that they tend to underestimate the true values.

The long-term multipliers and the supermultipliers are meaningless if the general solutions to the reduced equation (2.12) are unstable, because the general solutions to the original equation (2.7) do not approach the moving equilibrium determined by the long-term multipliers and the super-multipliers. The necessary and sufficient conditions for stability are that the characteristic equation

$$|\xi^2 S_0 + \xi S_1 + S_2| = 0$$

has solutions $\xi_1, ..., \xi_{2n}$, each of which is smaller than one in modulus. Instead of calculating the characteristic roots directly, we may examine S_0, S_1, S_2 to find out whether they satisfy sufficient conditions for stability. For this aim we rewrite the above characteristic equation as

$$|\xi^2 S_0 + \xi S_1 + S_2| = |S_0(\xi^2 I + \xi S_0^{-1} S_1 + S_0^{-1} S_2)|$$
$$= |S_0| \, |\xi I + W| = 0,$$

where

$$W = \begin{bmatrix} S_0^{-1} S_1 & S_0^{-1} S_2 \\ -I & 0 \end{bmatrix}.$$

Therefore, the characteristic roots $\xi_1, ..., \xi_{2n}$ are the roots of

$$|\xi I + W| = 0$$

and, hence, of

$$|\xi^t I + W^t| = 0$$

(by a theorem due to Frobenius). It is now easily seen that if W^t tends to 0 as t tends to infinity, then the characteristic roots, $\xi_1, ..., \xi_{2n}$, are all less than unity in modulus. By simple calculations we can test whether the stability condition, $\lim_{t \to \infty} W^t = 0$, is satisfied or not. In our case, it is satisfied by the parameters accepted and listed in the next chapter.

Let us now set the supermultiplier effects at zero and analyse dynamically the effects of a sustained increase in U on incomes of all the trading countries in consecutive years. Suppose the autonomous outlay of country i is increased by ΔG_i in period o and remains constant at the new level after o. Let

$$\Delta G = \begin{bmatrix} o \\ \vdots \\ o \\ \Delta G_i \\ o \\ \vdots \\ o \end{bmatrix};$$

then in view of the definitions of U we have from (2.7) for periods o, 1 and 2

$$S_0 \Delta Y_0 = \Delta G, \tag{2.27}$$

$$S_0 \Delta Y_1 + S_1 \Delta Y_0 = \Delta G - BR\Delta G, \tag{2.28}$$

$$S_0 \Delta Y_2 + S_1 \Delta Y_1 + S_2 \Delta Y_0 = \Delta G - BR\Delta G, \tag{2.29}$$

respectively, where Y_t denotes the vector Y in period t. Noting $H = S_0^{-1}$, we may write, by eliminating ΔY_0 and ΔY_1,

$$\Delta Y_1 = H(I - S_1 H - BR)\Delta G, \tag{2.30}$$

$$\Delta Y_2 = H(I - S_1 H(I - S_1 H - BR) - S_2 H - BR)\Delta G, \tag{2.31}$$

which give one-year and two-year multipliers, respectively.

As S_1 is neither non-positive nor non-negative, the signs of the elements of $I - S_1 H - BR$ are indeterminate. However, in the case of the elements of L being small enough, we can show that the one-year matrix multiplier is positive, that is

$$H(I - S_1 H - BR) > o. \tag{2.32}$$

To see this, we put $L = o$ in the following discussion. Then, bearing the definitions of S_1 and H in mind, we have

$$-S_1 = BR(I - A - M) + BRA \quad \text{and} \quad H = (I - A - M)^{-1};$$

therefore,

$$-S_1 H = BR + BRAH. \tag{2.33}$$

Hence, from (2.27) and (2.30) we obtain

$$\Delta Y_1 = \Delta Y_0 + BRAH\Delta G. \tag{2.34}$$

As $H > o$ and $\Delta G \geq (\neq) o$, the second term on the right-hand side of (2.34) is obviously positive. Thus the one-year multipliers are positive and greater than the corresponding zero-year multipliers.

Under the same assumption that L is zero, the two-year multipliers are similarly shown to be positive and greater than the one-year multipliers.

Because of (2.33), the one-year and two-year multipliers (2.30) and (2.31) are reduced to

$$\Delta Y_1 = H(I+BRAH)\Delta G, \tag{2.30'}$$

$$\Delta Y_2 = H[I+(I+BR+BRAH)BRAH]\Delta G, \tag{2.31'}$$

respectively. Comparing them, we find that

$$\Delta Y_2 = \Delta Y_1 + H(BR+BRAH)BRAH\Delta G. \tag{2.35}$$

The second term on the right-hand side is again positive; so we have $\Delta Y_2 > \Delta Y_1 > 0$. In the same way we have, for the three-year multipliers,

$$\Delta Y_3 = \Delta Y_2 + H(BR+BRAH)^2 BRAH\Delta G$$

and for the general $(t+1)$ year multipliers,

$$\Delta Y_{t+1} = \Delta Y_t + H(BR+BRAH)^t BRAH\Delta G.$$

They are increasing:

$$\Delta Y_{t+1} > \Delta Y_t \quad \text{for each } t. \tag{2.36}$$

Therefore, the sequence $\{\Delta Y_t\}$ converges if it can be shown to be bounded from above. To do this, we require some conditions for stability. As we neglect L, we obtain stability under rather generous conditions. One of such sets of sufficient conditions might be

$$\alpha_i + \beta_i \rho_i (1+\bar{\mu}_i) < 1 \quad (i = 1, ..., n), \tag{2.37}$$

that is, the sum of the marginal propensity to consume, α_i, and the coefficient of the lagged consumption, $\beta_i \rho_i$, multiplied by $1 +$ the propensity to import, $\bar{\mu}_i$, is less than one for each country.

The fact that ΔY_t is bounded from above can easily be shown. Premultiplying (2.28) or (2.29) by E (the row vector consisting of unities), we obtain, since $L = 0$,

$$E(I-A)\Delta Y_t = EBR(I-M)\Delta Y_{t-1} + E(I-BR)\Delta G \tag{2.38}$$

where the term $M\Delta Y_t$ disappears because the column sums of M vanish. In view of the fact that the off-diagonal elements of M are non-negative and ΔY_{t-1} is positive but less than ΔY_t, we have from (2.38)

$$E\Delta Y_t \leqq EA\Delta Y_t + EBR(I+\bar{M})\Delta Y_t + E(I-BR)\Delta G, \tag{2.39}$$

where $\bar{M}$ is the diagonal matrix with diagonal elements $\bar{\mu}_i, i = 1, ..., n$. We obtain further from (2.39)

$$E\Delta Y_t \leqq [\alpha^* + \beta^* \rho^* (1+\bar{\mu}^*)] E\Delta Y_t + E(I-BR)\Delta G,$$

where $\alpha^* + \beta^* \rho^* (1 + \overline{\mu}^*)$ is the maximum of $(\alpha_i + \beta_i \rho_i (1 + \overline{\mu}_i)), i = 1, ..., n$ and is less than one by virtue of (2.37). Therefore, $E\Delta Y_t$ is bounded from above:

$$E\Delta Y_t \leq \frac{1}{1 - (\alpha^* + \beta^* \rho^* (1 + \overline{\mu}^*))} E(I - BR)\Delta G.$$

As $\Delta Y_t > 0$, each element of ΔY_t is also bounded. Hence, we have the convergence.

Even though $L \neq 0$, the above result holds as long as its elements are small enough.

3. Estimation of parameters and multipliers

I. MARGINAL PROPENSITIES TO CONSUME AND COEFFICIENTS OF LAGGED CONSUMPTION

Our world comprises four thoroughbreds (Canada, Japan, UK, USA) and five hybrids (EEC, RWE, LA, ANZA, FA). Each of them has a consumption function of the form

$$c_i = \alpha_i y_i + \beta_i c_{i,-1} + \gamma_i \quad (i = 1, \dots, 9), \qquad (3.1)$$

where c_i and $c_{i,-1}$ are the current and the lagged consumption per capita of region i, and y_i the current GNP per capita of i. (They are all given in terms of the dollar.) In the case of a region which consists of a single country, the coefficients, α_i, β_i, γ_i, are estimated in the following way. Using cross-section data, we first estimate

$$c_i = a_i y_{p,i} + b_i \quad \text{or} \quad \log c_i = a_i \log y_{p,i} + b_i \qquad (3.2)$$

where $y_{p,i}$ denotes the personal income per man of country i. Then a statistical relationship between the personal income and the GNP, both per man,

$$y_{p,i} = h_i y_i + k_i, \qquad (3.3)$$

is estimated by the use of time-series data. (3.2) and (3.3) enable us to calculate dc_i/dy_i which is the product $a_i h_i$ in the case of (3.2) being linear. This value, or in the case of (3.2) being log-linear, the value of dc_i/dy_i evaluated at the point of the sample means, is taken as the estimate of α_i of (3.1). The remaining coefficients, β_i and γ_i, of (3.1) are so determined that the sum of squared deviations of $c_i - \alpha_i y_i$ from the line $\beta_i c_{i,-1} + \gamma_i$ is minimized; in this final regression time-series data are used.

The cross-section consumption function (3.2) was estimated in the linear form for Canada, 1962, and the UK, 1964, but in the log-linear form for Japan, 1965, and the USA, 1961. The complete results of the estimation are as follows:

Canada:

$$c = 0.606 y_p + 418.7, \qquad \bar{R}^2 = 0.96, \; n = 10,$$
$$\quad (0.041)$$

$$y_p = 0.715 y + 81.7, \qquad \bar{R}^2 = 0.98, \; d = 1.32, \; n = 8,$$
$$\quad (0.043)$$

$$c = 0.434 y + 0.292 c_{-1} + 71.3, \qquad \bar{R}^2 = 0.95, \; d = 2.32, \; n = 7;$$
$$\quad (0.089)$$

Japan:

$$\log c = 0.496 \log y_p + 2.36, \qquad \bar{R}^2 = 0.99, \, n = 16,$$
$${}_{(0.010)}$$

$$y_p = 0.728y + 14.6, \qquad \bar{R}^2 = 0.99, \, d = 1.27, \, n = 12,$$
$${}_{(0.020)}$$

$$c = 0.278y + 0.466c_{-1} + 19.6, \qquad \bar{R}^2 = 0.99, \, d = 2.14, \, n = 12;$$
$${}_{(0.013)}$$

UK:

$$c = 0.525y_p + 568.3, \qquad \bar{R}^2 = 0.99, \, n = 8,$$
$${}_{(0.023)}$$

$$y_p = 0.853y - 38.2D - 21.2, \qquad \bar{R}^2 = 0.99, \, d = 2.81, \, n = 10,$$
$${}_{(0.031)} {}_{(7.4)}$$

$$c = 0.448y + 0.306c_{-1} + 17.8, \qquad \bar{R}^2 = 0.86, \, d = 1.33, \, n = 12;$$
$${}_{(0.053)}$$

USA:

$$\log c = 0.646 \log y_p + 2.5, \qquad \bar{R}^2 = 0.99, \, n = 9,$$
$${}_{(0.010)}$$

$$y_p = 0.774y + 73.2, \qquad \bar{R}^2 = 0.99, \, d = 2.34, \, n = 6,$$
$${}_{(0.028)}$$

$$c = 0.396y + 0.376c_{-1} + 20.5, \qquad \bar{R}^2 = 0.88, \, d = 1.39, \, n = 7.$$
$${}_{(0.062)}$$

The numbers in parentheses under the coefficients are estimated sampling errors. The measure of goodness of fit $\bar{R}^2$ is adjusted for degree of freedom. d represents the Durbin–Watson statistic and n the number of samples. The dummy variable D which appears in the second equation for the UK takes on values of unity for the years 1954–8 and zero for 1961–5. (It is noted that in the estimation of that equation, the years 1959 and 1960 were excluded from the sample period.)

The consumption functions of the hybrid regions are estimated by a completely different method, which is well illustrated by the procedures we took for EEC. For each of the five countries (France, Germany, Italy, Netherlands and Belgium–Luxembourg) in the EEC region, the data concerning current and lagged consumption per capita and current GNP per capita in each year in the period 1954–65 were collected. To the 60 sets of observations thus obtained, the following regression equation was fitted:

$$c_i = \alpha_i y_i + \beta_i c_{i,-1} + \gamma_i + \epsilon_{iF} D_F + \epsilon_{iI} D_I + \epsilon_{iB} D_B,$$

where D_F, D_I, and D_B are dummy variables for France, Italy, and Belgium–Luxembourg respectively, which take on unity in the case of the respective countries concerned and zero otherwise. German was taken as the base country and the Netherlands' dummy coefficient was concluded not to be significantly different from zero, so that the constant term for these two countries was given by γ_i, but those for France, Italy and Belgium–Luxembourg were $\gamma_i + \epsilon_{iF}$, $\gamma_i + \epsilon_{iI}$, and $\gamma_i + \epsilon_{iB}$ respectively. (In the following we retained only those dummy coefficients which were found to be statistically significantly different from zero.)

We obtained the following results:

EEC:

$$c = 0.403y + 0.363c_{-1} - 17.8 + \text{dummies}, \quad \bar{R}^2 = 0.99, n = 60,$$
$$\underset{(0.038)}{} \quad \underset{(0.065)}{} \quad \underset{(6.9)}{}$$

the dummy coefficients: France = 44.2; Germany = 0; Italy = 32.5; Netherlands = 0; Belgium–Luxembourg = 54.0;

RWE:

$$c = 0.323y + 0.513c_{-1} - 3.9 + \text{dummies}, \quad \bar{R}^2 = 0.99, n = 154,$$
$$\underset{(0.029)}{} \quad \underset{(0.046)}{} \quad \underset{(3.8)}{}$$

the dummy coefficients: Austria = 0; Denmark = 22.1; Finland = −14.8; Greece = 34.1; Iceland = 16.8; Ireland = 40.5; Norway = −38.2; Portugal = 20.8; Spain = 15.8; Sweden = −28.9; Switzerland = 0; Turkey = 11.0; Yugoslavia = 0;

LA:

$$c = 0.499y + 0.349c_{-1} + 16.5 + \text{dummies}, \quad \bar{R}^2 = 0.99, n = 183,$$
$$\underset{(0.059)}{} \quad \underset{(0.070)}{} \quad \underset{(7.6)}{}$$

the dummy coefficients: Argentina = −26.5; Brazil = −20.6; Chile = 0; Colombia = −16.9; Costa Rica = −18.0; Dominican Republic = −23.7; Ecuador = −19.0; Guatemala = 0; Honduras = −13.3; Mexico = 0; Nicaragua = −12.7; Panama = −10.4; Paraguay = −15.1; Peru = −18.2; Uruguay = −12.9; Venezuela = −130.9;

ANZA:

$$c = 0.310y + 0.397c_{-1} + 138.3 + \text{dummies}, \quad \bar{R}^2 = 0.99, n = 36,$$
$$\underset{(0.067)}{} \quad \underset{(0.129)}{} \quad \underset{(74.5)}{}$$

the dummy coefficients: Australia = 0; New Zealand = 0; Republic of South Africa = −93.2;

FA:

$$c = 0.355y + 0.427c_{-1} + 9.2 + \text{dummies}, \quad \bar{R}^2 = 0.99, n = 80,$$
$$\underset{(0.056)}{} \quad \underset{(0.093)}{} \quad \underset{(2.1)}{}$$

the dummy coefficients: Burma = −6.0; Ceylon = 0; South Korea = 5.2; Malaya = 0; Philippines = 16.4; Taiwan = −3.7; Thailand = 0.

As has been seen in Chapter 2, the marginal propensity to consume, α_i, and the coefficient of lagged consumption, β_i, give the closed-economy impact multiplier of country i as $1/(1-\alpha_i)$, the closed-economy long-run multiplier of i as $1/(1-\alpha_i-\beta_i\rho_i)$, and the closed-economy supermultiplier of i as $1/(1-\alpha_i-\beta_i)$, which are greater than the true impact multiplier, long-run multiplier and supermultiplier which would work in the actual world with international markets. On the basis of our estimates of α_i and β_i above and the rates of growth of population, ρ_i-1, listed at the bottom of Table 1, the three kinds of closed-economy multipliers were estimated at the respective values presented in the first three rows of Table 1. It is evident from the formulas that a high impact multiplier does not necessarily imply a high

TABLE I. *Closed-economy multipliers and rates of growth of population*

Multiplier	USA	LA	EEC	RWE	UK	Canada	ANZA	Japan	FA
Impact	1.66	1.99	1.68	1.48	1.81	1.77	1.45	1.38	1.55
Long-term	4.52	7.05	4.35	6.33	4.12	3.74	3.52	3.97	4.85
Supermultiplier	4.39	6.56	4.28	6.09	4.07	3.65	3.41	3.90	4.59
Population-growth rate	1.6%	3.0%	1.1%	1.2%	0.8%	2.3%	2.3%	1.0%	2.8%

long-run multiplier, and vice versa; in fact, RWE has a low impact and a high long-run multiplier, whilst Canada has a high impact and a low long-run multiplier. On the other hand, since the effect of population growth is negligible, it is observed that there is a strong parallelism between the long-run multiplier and the supermultiplier.

2. IMPORT FUNCTIONS

Imports are assumed to depend on the GNP of the importing country, its increase (i.e. the difference between the current and the previous GNP), and the terms of trade (i.e. the prices of the exporting country relative to the prices of other countries). The linear equations,

$$M_{ij} = \mu_{ij}Y_i + \lambda_{ij}\Delta Y_i + \pi_{ij}p_j + \theta_{ij} \quad (i,j = 1, ..., 9), \qquad (3.4)$$

were first fitted to the collected time-series data; in cases where the results were not satisfactory, the log-linear equations,

$$\log M_{ij} = \mu'_{ij}\log Y_i + \lambda'_{ij}\log\Delta Y_i$$
$$+ \pi'_{ij}\log p_j + \theta'_{ij} \quad (i,j = 1, ..., 9), \qquad (3.4')$$

were tried and, if successful, were linearized at the respective sample means. In (3.4) or (3.4'), coefficients of Y_i and ΔY_i are expected to be positive, and that of p_j negative. If some coefficients were found not to be of the proper sign by the so-called 't-ratio' tests, they were equated to zero and then the remaining coefficients were re-estimated. We regarded imports between i and j as exogenous only if no effort resulted in a tolerable estimation of (3.4) or (3.4'). (Hereunder the coefficients of Y_i, ΔY_i, and p_j in the linear approximation to (3.4') are denoted by μ_{ij}, λ_{ij}, and π_{ij}, respectively.)

Our results are summarized in Tables 2*a*, 2*b*, and 2*c*. In each of them, the italicized figures were obtained by fitting the log-linear equation (3.4') and then linearizing; the other figures were the results of linear estimation.

TABLE 2*a*. *Import coefficients:* μ_{ij}^1

j	*i* USA	LA	EEC	RWE	UK	Canada	ANZA	Japan	FA
USA	–	–	0.026	0.023	0.026	0.071	0.067	0.024	0.051
LA	0.003	0.007	0.011	0.008	0.005	0.019	0.002	0.006	–
EEC	0.009	0.028	0.173	0.145	0.051	0.015	0.038	0.007	–
RWE	0.003	0.003	0.029	0.052	0.039	0.005	0.010	0.002	–
UK	0.001*	0.006	0.021	0.036	–	0.026	0.038	0.003	0.013
Canada	0.009	0.005	0.004	0.002	0.009	–	0.008	0.004	–
ANZA	0.002	0.001	0.005	0.004	0.014	0.003	0.012	0.011	0.012
Japan	0.011	0.006	0.003	0.008	0.008	0.010	0.035	–	0.072
FA	0.001	–	0.002	0.001	–	0.002	–	0.013	0.049
Total	0.038	0.055	0.274	0.278	0.153	0.151	0.210	0.069	0.196

[1] *i* represents the importing country and *j* the exporting country.

TABLE 2*b*. *Import coefficients:* λ_{ij}^1

j	*i* USA	LA	EEC	RWE	UK	Canada	ANZA	Japan	FA
USA	–	0.298	–	–	0.098	0.180*	–	0.048*	–
LA	–	0.053	–	–	–	0.020	–	–	–
EEC	–	–	–	–	0.021	–	–	0.010	–
RWE	–	–	–	–	0.050	–	–	0.003	–
UK	0.006*	–	–	–	–	–	–	–	–
Canada	–	–	–	–	0.024*	–	–	0.008	–
ANZA	–	–	–	–	–	–	–	0.019	–
Japan	–	–	–	–	–	–	–	–	–
FA	–	–	–	–	–	–	–	–	–
Total	0.006	0.350	–	–	0.173	0.199	–	0.082	–

[1] *i* represents the importing country and *j* the exporting country.

TABLE 2*c*. *Import coefficients:* π_{ij}^1

j	*i* USA	LA	EEC	RWE	UK	Canada	ANZA	Japan	FA
USA	–	–	–	–	–	–	−4.09	–	–
LA	−4.27	–	–	–	−1.67	–	–	–	–
EEC	−19.27	−3.04*	–	−10.95*	–	−1.61	–	–	–
RWE	–	−0.76	−2.88	–	–	–	–	–	–
UK	–	–	−8.29	–	–	–	–	–	−2.08
Canada	−4.20*	–	−2.54	–	–	–	–	–	–
ANZA	−0.98	–	−0.64	−0.28	–	−0.04	−0.22	–	−0.28
Japan	–	−1.28	−0.63	–	–	–	–	–	–
FA	–	–	–	–	–	–	–	–	–

[1] *i* represents the importing country and *j* the exporting country.

TABLE 3. *Import coefficients:* $\mu_{ij} + \lambda_{ij}$[1]

j	USA	LA	EEC	RWE	UK	Canada	ANZA	Japan	FA
USA	–	0.30	0.03	0.02	0.12	0.25	0.07	0.07	0.05
LA	*[2]	0.06	0.01	*	*	0.04	*	*	–
EEC	*	0.03	0.17	0.15	0.07	0.02	0.04	0.02	–
RWE	*	*	0.03	0.05	0.09	*	0.01	*	–
UK	*	*	0.02	0.04	–	0.03	0.04	*	0.01
Canada	*	*	*	*	0.04	–	*	0.01	–
ANZA	*	*	*	*	0.01	*	0.01	0.01	0.03
Japan	0.01	*	*	*	*	0.01	0.04	–	0.07
FA	*	–	*	*	–	*	–	0.01	0.05

[1] *i* represents the importing country and *j* the exporting country.
[2] * stands for a number being less than 0.01.

Figures with an asterisk are significantly different from zero at the 12.5 per cent significance level but not at the 5 per cent level. All other figures are significant at the 5 per cent level, most of them being so even at the level of 2.5 per cent.

As $\Delta Y_i = Y_i - Y_{i,-1}$, an increase in Y_i affects M_{ij} through the channels of the first and second terms of (3.4) or (3.4′). If we neglect those coefficients μ_{ij} and λ_{ij} such that $\mu_{ij} + \lambda_{ij} < 0.01$, we obtain Table 3 of $\mu_{ij} + \lambda_{ij}$.[1] It is seen that the world economy is indecomposable at this level of accuracy. Especially, EEC, RWE and the UK are strongly interrelated. Also, coupling between LA and EEC, between UK and Canada, between UK and ANZA, between USA and Japan, and among ANZA, Japan and FA are noticeable, though not strong. However, if we neglect the three coefficients concerning imports of USA from Japan (0.011), of UK from ANZA (0.014), and of Canada from Japan (0.010), then the world may be found to be decomposable into three blocs: (i) USA, (ii) LA, EEC, RWE, UK, Canada, and (iii) ANZA, Japan, FA. The third bloc is (almost) independent of the first two, and the second of the first. As we shall see below, because of this almost complete decomposability, the impact multipliers of the countries in the third bloc with respect to an increase in the final demand for GNP of the countries in the first and second blocs are very small, and similarly, the impact multipliers of the countries in the second bloc with respect an autonomous change in the USA are also small.

[1] The short-run and long-run marginal propensities to import are given by $\sum_j \mu_{ij} + \sum_j \lambda_{ij}$ and $\sum_j \mu_{ij}$ respectively. Our estimates of the short-run propensities are more or less comparable with Chang's estimates for the period 1924–38, although we estimate the long-run propensities at considerably lower values. (T. C. Chang, *op. cit.* p. 24.)

3. INTERNATIONAL MULTIPLIERS

We are now able to estimate various international multipliers. First, aggregate import coefficients, $\sum_j \mu_{ij}$ and $\sum_j \lambda_{ij}$, are given at the bottom of Tables 2*a* and 2*b*. Subtracting the corresponding elements, μ_{ii} and λ_{ii}, from them, we obtain $\bar{\mu}_i$ and $\bar{\lambda}_i$. Then the one-way foreign trade impact multipliers, which neglect repercussions via imports of foreign countries, can be calculated by the use of the formula,

$$(1 - \alpha_i + \bar{\mu}_i + \bar{\lambda}_i)^{-1} \quad (i = 1, ..., 9),$$

and the one-way foreign trade long-run multipliers by the formula,

$$(1 - \alpha_i - \beta_i \rho_i + (1 - \beta_i \rho_i)\bar{\mu}_i)^{-1} \quad (i = 1, ..., 9).$$

They give the lower bounds of the true, two-way foreign trade impact and long-run multipliers respectively, and may be compared with the closed-economy multipliers which are the upper bounds of the true multipliers. Our results are presented in Table 4. It is evident that for the USA the upper and lower bounds are close because of that country's low import coefficients, but for the other countries the ranges set by them are fairly large. For example, LA, UK and Canada have closed-economy impact multipliers which are greater than 1.6 times their one-way foreign trade multipliers. However, it may be noticed that in the case of the long-run multiplier the range is not wide for the LA region, because its large $\bar{\lambda}_i$ does not contribute to lowering the value of its one-way foreign trade multiplier.

Also the true foreign trade supermultipliers are bounded by the closed-economy and one-way foreign trade supermultipliers, from above and below respectively. The latter,

$$[1 - \alpha_i - \beta_i + (1 - \beta_i)(\bar{\mu}_i + (1 - \rho_i^{-1})\bar{\lambda}_i)]^{-1},$$

is reduced to the former,

$$(1 - \alpha_i - \beta_i)^{-1},$$

if $\bar{\mu}_i$ is zero and either ρ_i equals unity or $\bar{\lambda}_i$ equals zero. But even in the case of ρ_i being different from one, the effect of $\bar{\lambda}_i$ is negligible, because ρ_i is still very close to one. It is again found that the one-way foreign trade super-multiplier of the USA approximates well its closed-economy supermultiplier. It is also seen that LA has a small difference between its closed-economy and one-way foreign trade supermultipliers, because its $\bar{\mu}_i$ is small and its large $\bar{\lambda}_i$ makes no significant contribution to the difference.

The true foreign trade multipliers, impact, long-term and super, are listed, together with cross-multipliers, in Tables 5, 6, and 7. It is at once seen

TABLE 4. *One-way foreign trade multipliers*

Multiplier	USA	LA	EEC	RWE	UK	Canada	ANZA	Japan	FA
Impact	1.54	1.18	1.43	1.11	1.14	1.09	1.13	1.15	1.26
Long-term	4.08	5.78	3.40	3.75	2.86	2.68	2.49	3.47	3.47
Supermultiplier	3.97	5.29	3.36	3.65	2.83	2.60	2.43	3.41	3.31

TABLE 5. *Impact multiplier matrix*

	USA	LA	EEC	RWE	UK	Canada	ANZA	Japan	FA
USA	1.56	0.56	0.08	0.07	0.26	0.46	0.14	0.15	0.12
LA	0.01	1.18	0.02	0.02	0.01	0.05	0.01	0.01	0.00
EEC	0.02	0.06	1.45	0.24	0.15	0.04	0.08	0.04	0.01
RWE	0.01	0.01	0.05	1.12	0.12	0.01	0.02	0.01	0.00
UK	0.02	0.02	0.04	0.05	1.15	0.04	0.05	0.01	0.02
Canada	0.02	0.01	0.01	0.01	0.05	1.10	0.01	0.02	0.00
ANZA	0.00	0.00	0.01	0.01	0.02	0.01	1.13	0.04	0.02
Japan	0.02	0.02	0.01	0.01	0.02	0.02	0.05	1.15	0.11
FA	0.00	0.00	0.00	0.00	0.00	0.00	0.00	0.02	1.27

TABLE 6. *Long-term multiplier matrix*

	USA	LA	EEC	RWE	UK	Canada	ANZA	Japan	FA
USA	4.11	0.05	0.27	0.34	0.26	0.51	0.48	0.24	0.50
LA	0.06	5.80	0.16	0.18	0.09	0.21	0.05	0.09	0.02
EEC	0.10	0.38	3.51	1.27	0.41	0.14	0.27	0.08	0.04
RWE	0.03	0.06	0.20	3.85	0.23	0.05	0.08	0.03	0.02
UK	0.02	0.10	0.17	0.33	2.91	0.15	0.21	0.03	0.10
Canada	0.07	0.06	0.04	0.04	0.06	2.70	0.05	0.03	0.01
ANZA	0.01	0.01	0.03	0.04	0.07	0.02	2.50	0.06	0.07
Japan	0.09	0.07	0.04	0.08	0.06	0.07	0.18	3.49	0.48
FA	0.01	0.00	0.02	0.02	0.00	0.01	0.01	0.09	3.48

TABLE 7. *Supermultiplier matrix*

	USA	LA	EEC	RWE	UK	Canada	ANZA	Japan	FA
USA	4.01	0.16	0.26	0.33	0.26	0.52	0.46	0.24	0.47
LA	0.06	5.30	0.15	0.17	0.09	0.20	0.05	0.08	0.02
EEC	0.10	0.34	3.46	1.22	0.40	0.14	0.26	0.08	0.04
RWE	0.03	0.05	0.19	3.74	0.23	0.05	0.08	0.02	0.01
UK	0.02	0.09	0.16	0.32	2.88	0.15	0.20	0.03	0.10
Canada	0.07	0.06	0.04	0.04	0.06	2.62	0.05	0.03	0.01
ANZA	0.01	0.01	0.03	0.04	0.07	0.02	2.43	0.06	0.07
Japan	0.08	0.07	0.04	0.08	0.06	0.07	0.17	3.43	0.44
FA	0.01	0.00	0.02	0.02	0.00	0.01	0.01	0.09	3.32

that they are much nearer to the lower bounds than to the upper bounds; in fact, differences between the true and the one-way foreign trade multipliers are almost negligible. This means that as far as the diagonal effects are concerned, the gains from making the model complex by taking all the feedbacks via imports of other countries into account are too small to justify doing so. In addition to this, if cross-multipliers were found to be of very small magnitudes, we might conclude that replacing the simple Harrod–Machlup model by Metzler's did not produce any significant improvement in our estimates of the direct multipliers. However, as is seen in Tables 5–7, some of the cross-effects (such as the USA's impact multipliers with respect to an autonomous change in LA or Canada, and the EEC's long-run multiplier and supermultiplier with respect to a change in RWE) are quite high. If we consider the fact that in the case of the diagonal multipliers, the original increase in the final demand is included in the final values of the multipliers, whilst in the case of the cross-multipliers it is not, we may say that cross-impact multipliers are very high if they are greater than 0.2 and cross long-term multipliers and supermultipliers are fairly high if they are between 0.4 and 1 and very high if they exceed 1. The number of high cross-multipliers found in Tables 5–7 ensure for Metzler's model its *raison d'être*.

It has been seen in the previous section that the general solution to the modified Metzler model (2.7) is given as the sum of the general solution to the reduced dynamic equation (2.12) and

$$JU + KT,$$

where J is the long-term multiplier matrix, K the supermultiplier matrix, and U and T are vectors defined there. The first part of the general solution is dissipating, and in the last part the ith element of T is given as γ_i times the population in region (or country) i. γ_i is the constant term of the consumption function of i, which is usually a small positive number and may for some i, even take on a negative value. For example, in the case of Canada, γ_i is 71.3 (in 1958 US dollars) but Canadian GNP per man, y_i, is more than 2,000 dollars. Therefore, KT cannot be the principal component of the solution. On the other hand, it is clear from the definition of U that the second part, JU, of the general solution depends *inter alia* on imports and exports between the endogenous and exogenous countries and therefore is affected by international political affairs. Keynes and Metzler emphasized that a part of JU depended upon government expenditures. It may be controllable to some extent, in spite of the fact that the long-run level of government expenditure in a country is restrained by its gross national product, its balance of trade and other economic aggregates.

Let us define

$$u_{i1} = (\sum_j \pi_{ij}) p_i - \sum_j \pi_{ij} p_j - \beta_i \rho_i [(\sum_j \pi_{ji}) p_i - \sum_j \pi_{ij} p_j]_{-1}$$
$$+ (1 - \beta_i \rho_i)(\sum_j \theta_{ji} - \sum_j \theta_{ij}),$$

$$u_{i2} = G_i - \beta_i \rho_i G_{i,-1},$$

$$u_{i3} = (X_{in+1} - M_{in+1}) - \beta_i \rho_i (X_{in+1} - M_{in+1})_{-1},$$

and write

$$U_1 = \begin{pmatrix} u_{1,1} \\ \vdots \\ u_{9,1} \end{pmatrix}, \quad U_2 = \begin{pmatrix} u_{1,2} \\ \vdots \\ u_{9,2} \end{pmatrix}, \quad U_3 = \begin{pmatrix} u_{1,3} \\ \vdots \\ u_{9,3} \end{pmatrix}.$$

Also, let GDS stand for the general solution to the reduced dynamic equation (2.12). Then the actual GNP of country i may be analysed into the five components as

$$Y_i = (JU_1)_i + (JU_2)_i + (JU_3)_i + (KT)_i + (GDS)_i. \tag{3.5}$$

On the right-hand side the first term represents the long-run multiplier effects of prices, the second the long-run multiplier effect of investment and government expenditure, the third the long-run multiplier effect of trade with exogenous countries, the fourth the supermultiplier effect of population and the fifth the dynamic effect, which fluctuates from period to period. On the basis of the actual 1963 and 1964 values of p_i, G_i, X_{in+1}, M_{in+1} and N_i, the ratios of the five components to the actual 1964 GNP were calculated for each country. The results are presented in Table 8, which shows that the long-run multiplier effect of investment and government expenditure is by far the largest in each country. As the dynamic effects are dissipated because of the stability of the long-run equilibrium, we may neglect them in the long-run analysis. For each country i, the sum of the first four terms of (3.5), represented by Y_i^*, is given at the bottom of Table 8. The figures of the last row approximate to the long-run equilibrium values of the gross national products of the nine endogenous 'countries' which will prevail if there are no changes in the terms of trade, investment and government expenditures of the endogenous countries, or in their trade with the exogenous countries.[1] It is seen from Table 8 that Japan has the greatest ratio of long-run equilibrium GNP to actual 1964 GNP. This means that the long-run equilibrium which Japan would eventually approach is relatively high, explaining, at least to some extent, the miraculous growth of Japan in recent years.

Finally, let H^i and J^i be the ith column vectors of the impact and long-term

---

[1] The true long-run equilibrium values would differ from these figures, since there would be additional effects of population growth in the future.

TABLE 8. *Contributions of long-run multiplier effect, supermultiplier effects and dynamic effects to the actual 1964 GNP[a]*

	USA	LA	EEC	RWE	UK	Canada	ANZA	Japan	FA
Y_i	586,500	57,450	219,399	93,510	81,224	44,237	31,085	60,946	21,498
$(JU_1)_i$	21,711 (3.7)	−10,728 (−18.7)	−7,722 (−3.5)	6,624 (7.1)	2,715 (3.3)	−1,625 (−3.7)	869 (2.8)	−11,945 (−19.6)	408 (1.9)
$(JU_2)_i$	574,656 (98.0)	70,315 (122.4)	245,772 (112.0)	105,333 (112.6)	87,811 (108.1)	43,312 (97.9)	25,527 (82.1)	77,635 (127.4)	16,755 (77.9)
$(JU_3)_i$	2,978 (0.5)	7,829 (13.6)	−2,479 (−1.1)	−1,460 (−1.6)	−2,174 (−2.7)	1,386 (3.1)	127 (0.4)	1,206 (2.0)	29 (0.1)
$(KT)_i$	19,601 (3.3)	−2,293 (−0.4)	6,204 (2.8)	2,997 (3.2)	4,163 (5.1)	4,159 (9.4)	6,951 (22.4)	8,280 (13.6)	6,207 (28.9)
$(GDS)_i$	−32,446 (−5.5)	−7,673 (−13.3)	−22,376 (−10.2)	−19,984 (−21.3)	−11,291 (−13.8)	−2,995 (−6.7)	−2,389 (−7.7)	−14,230 (−23.4)	−1,901 (−8.8)
Y_i^*	618,946 (105.5)	65,123 (113.3)	241,775 (110.2)	113,494 (121.3)	92,515 (113.8)	47,232 (106.7)	33,474 (107.7)	75,176 (123.4)	23,399 (108.8)

[a] Unit: million US dollars at 1958 prices. The figures in parentheses represent the percentage contributions.

TABLE 9. *Effect of a unit increase in government expenditure in a region upon its own trade balance*

	USA	LA	EEC	RWE	UK	Canada	ANZA	Japan	FA
Impact	−0.07	−0.41	−0.13	−0.25	−0.37	−0.38	−0.22	−0.17	−0.19
Long-run	−0.15	−0.28	−0.30	−0.83	−0.41	−0.40	−0.49	−0.23	−0.52

multiplier matrices, H and J, respectively; let M_i and L_i be the ith row vectors of the import coefficient matrices, M and L (defined in Chapter 2). Then the impact and long-run net effects of a unit increase in region i's government expenditures on its own trade balance are given by $(M_i + L_i) H^i$ and $M_i J^i$. Table 9 presents the estimated effects for the nine regions. It is interesting to see that the UK suffers a relatively large adverse effect on her trade balance, whilst Japan experiences only a small one, in the long run as well as in the short run.

Bibliography

Adams, F. G., Eguchi, H. and Meyer-zu-Schlochtern, F., *An Econometric Analysis of International Trade* (OECD Publications, 1969).

Ando, A. and Modigliani, F., 'The relative stability of monetary velocity and the investment multiplier', *American Economic Review* (September 1965).

Arrow, K. J., Chenery, H. B., Minhas, B. S. and Solow, R. M., 'Capital labour substitution and economic efficiency', *Review of Economics and Statistics* (August 1961).

Ball, R. J. and Drake, P. S., 'The relationship between aggregate consumption and wealth', *International Economic Review* (January 1964).

Balopoulos, E. T., *Fiscal Policy Models of the British Economy* (North-Holland Publishing Co. 1967).

Barrett, C. R. and Walters, A. A., 'The stability of Keynesian and monetary multipliers in the United Kingdom', *Review of Economics and Statistics* (November 1966).

Beckerman, W., 'The world trade multiplier and the stability of world trade, 1938 to 1953', *Econometrica* (July 1956).

Blumenthal, T., 'The determination of wage differentials in the Japanese economy', *Discussion Paper No. 41*, The Institute of Social and Economic Research, Osaka University (1965).

Bodkin, R. G., *The Wage–Price–Productivity Nexus* (University of Pennsylvania Press, 1966).

Bodkin, R. G. and Klein, L. R., 'Nonlinear estimates of aggregate production functions', *Review of Economics and Statistics* (February 1967).

Broadbridge, S., *Industrial Dualism in Japan* (Frank Cass and Co. 1966).

Bronfenbrenner, M. and Mayer, T., 'Liquidity functions in the American economy', *Econometrica* (October 1960).

Brown, A. J., 'Interest, prices, and the demand schedule for idle money', *Oxford Economic Papers* (May 1939).

—, *The Great Inflation: 1939–51* (Oxford University Press, 1955).

Brown, E. C., 'Fiscal policy in the 'thirties: a reappraisal', *American Economic Review* (December 1956).

Brown, M. and Jones, R., 'Economic growth and the theory of international income flow', *Econometrica* (January 1962).

Chang, T. C., *Cyclical Movements in the Balance of Payments* (Cambridge University Press, 1951).

Chow, G. C., *Demand for Automobiles in the United States: A Study in Consumer Durables* (North-Holland Publishing Co. 1957).

Christ, C., 'A test of an econometric model for the United States, 1921–47', in *Conference on Business Cycles* (National Bureau of Economic Research, 1951).

Cochrane, D. and Orcutt, G. H., 'Application of least squares regressions to relationships containing auto-correlated error terms', *Journal of the American Statistical Association* (March 1949).

Cohen, L., 'An empirical measurement of the built-in flexibility of the individual income tax', *American Economic Review* (May 1959).

David, P. A. and Klundert, Th. van de, 'Biased efficiency growth and capital–labor substitution in the U.S., 1899–1960', *American Economic Review* (June 1965).

Dhrymes, P. J., 'A comparison of productivity behavior in manufacturing and service industries', *Review of Economics and Statistics* (February 1963).

Duesenberry, J. S., Fromm, G., Klein, L. R. and Kuh, E., *The Brookings Quarterly Econometric Model of the United States* (North-Holland Publishing Co. 1965).

Evans, M. K. and Klein, L. R., *The Wharton Econometric Forecasting Model*, 2nd ed. (University of Pennsylvania, 1968).

Fabricant, S., *Basic Facts on Productivity Change*, Occasional Paper 63 (National Bureau of Economic Research, 1959).

Friedman, M., *A Theory of Consumption Function* (Princeton University Press, 1957).

Fromm, G. and Taubman, P., *Policy Simulations with an Econometric Model* (North-Holland Publishing Co. 1968).

Gale, D. and Nikaido, H., 'The Jacobian matrix and global univalence of mappings', *Mathematische Annalen*, vol. 159 (1965).

Georgescu-Roegen, N., 'Some properties of a generalized Leontief model', *Activity Analysis of Production and Allocation*, ed. T. C. Koopmans, (John Wiley and Sons, Inc. 1951).

Goldberger, A. S., *Impact Multipliers and Dynamic Properties of the Klein–Goldberger Model* (North-Holland Publishing Co. 1959).

Goldsmith, R. W., *A Study of Saving in the United States* (Princeton University Press, 1956).

—, *The National Wealth of the U.S. in the Postwar Period* (Princeton University Press).

Gorman, W. M., 'Separable utility and aggregation', *Econometrica* (July 1959).

Griliches, Z., Maddala, G. S., Lucas, R. and Wallace, N., 'Notes on estimated aggregate quarterly consumption function', *Econometrica* (July 1962).

Gurley, J. G., 'Excess liquidity and European monetary reforms, 1944–1952', *American Economic Review* (March 1953).

Haavelmo, T., 'Multiplier effects of a balanced budget', *Econometrica* (October 1945).

Hansen, B., *Fiscal Policy in Seven Countries, 1955–65* (OECD, 1969).

Harberger, A. C., ed., *The Demand for Durable Goods* (University of Chicago Press, 1960).

Harrod, R. F., *International Economics* (Cambridge University Press, 1939).

—, *Towards a Dynamic Economics* (Macmillan, 1948).

Hicks, J. R., *Value and Capital* (Oxford University Press, 1939; second edition 1946).

Houthakker, H. S. and Taylor, L. D., *Consumer Demand in the United States, 1929–1970* (Harvard University Press, 1966).

Kendrick, J. W., *Productivity Trends in the United States* (Princeton University Press, 1961).

Keynes, J. M., *The General Theory of Employment, Interest and Money* (Macmillan, 1936).

Klein, L. R., *Economic Fluctuation in the United States, 1921–41* (John Wiley and Sons, 1950).

—, 'On the interpretation of Professor Leontief's system', *Review of Economic Studies* (1952–3).

—, 'The empirical foundations of Keynesian economics', in *Post Keynesian Economics*, K. K. Kurihara, ed. (George Allen and Unwin, 1955).

Klein, L. R. and Goldberger, A. S., *An Econometric Model of the United States, 1929–1952* (North-Holland Publishing Co. 1955).

Klein, L. R. and Kosobud, R. F., 'Some econometrics of growth: great ratios of economics', *Quarterly Journal of Economics* (May, 1961).

Klein, L. R. and Shinkai, Y., 'An econometric model of Japan, 1930–59', *International Economic Review* (January 1963).

Klein, L. R. *et al.*, *Contributions of Survey Methods to Economics* (Columbia University Press, 1954).

Kuznets, S., *Capital in the American Economy: Its Formation and Financing* (Princeton University Press, 1961).

Lebergott, S., 'Annual estimates of unemployment in the United States, 1900–1950', *The Measurement and Behavior of Unemployment* (Princeton University Press, 1957).

Leontief, W. W., *The Structure of American Economy, 1919–39* (Oxford University Press, 1951).

Lusher, D. W., 'The stabilizing effectiveness of budget flexibility', *Conference on Policies to Combat Depressions* (National Bureau of Economic Research, 1956).

Mansfield, E., 'Comment on Marc Nerlove's "Recent empirical studies of the CES and related production functions",' *The Theory and Empirical Analysis of Production*, ed. by Murray Brown (National Bureau of Economic Research, 1967).

Marx, K., *Capital: A Critical Analysis of Capitalist Production*, vol. 1, translated by S. Moore and Edward Aveling (Moscow, 1965).

Massell, B. F., 'A disaggregated view of technical change', *Journal of Political Economy* (December 1961).

Metzler, L. A., 'A multiple region theory of income and trade', *Econometrica* (October 1950).

—, 'A multiple-country theory of income transfers', *Journal of Political Economy* (February 1951).

—, 'Taxes and subsidies in Leontief's input–output model', *Quarterly Journal of Economics* (1951).

Minami, R., 'The turning point in the Japanese economy', *Quarterly Journal of Economics* (August 1968).

Miyazawa, K., 'Foreign trade multiplier, input–output analysis and the consumption function', *Quarterly Journal of Economics* (February 1960).

Miyazawa, K. and Masegi, S., 'Interindustry analysis and the structure of income-distribution', *Metroeconomica* (1963).

Miyasawa, K. and Sakiyama, K., *An Input–Output Analysis of the Japanese Heavy and Chemical Industries* (Shōwa-36-nen Sangyō-renkanhyō no Sakusei niyoru Wagakuni Jūkagakukōgyō no Bunseki), (Nippon Sangyōkōzō Kenkyūsho, 1964).

Moore, H. L., *Synthetic Economics* (Macmillan, 1923).

Morishima, M., *Equilibrium, Stability, and Growth: A Multisectoral Analysis* (Oxford: Clarendon Press, 1964).

—, *Theory of Economic Growth* (Oxford University Press, 1969).

Morishima, M. and Kaneko, Y., 'On the speed of establishing multi-sectoral equilibrium', *Econometrica* (October 1962).

Musgrave, R. A., 'On measuring fiscal performance', *Review of Economics and Statistics* (May 1964).

Musgrave, R. A. and Miller, M. H., 'Built-in flexibility', *American Economic Review* (March 1948).

Neisser, H. and Modigliani, F., *National Incomes and International Trade* (University of Illinois Press, 1953).

Office of the Prime Minister, *Japan Statistical Year Book* (*Nippon Tōkei Nenkan*), (Office of the Prime Minister, 1966).

Patinkin, D., *Money, Interest, and Prices* (Harper and Row, 1965).

Polak, J. J., *An International Economic System* (George Allen and Unwin Ltd, 1954).

Prais, S. J. and Houthakker, H. S., *The Analysis of Family Budgets* (Cambridge University Press, 1955).

Rhomberg, R. R., 'A three-region world trade and income model, 1948–60', paper presented at the Summer Meeting of the Econometric Society, Ann Arbor, September 1962.

Robinson, J., *Essays in the Theory of Employment* (Macmillan, 1937).

Samuelson, P. A., *Foundations of Economic Analysis* (Harvard University Press, 1948).

—, *Economics: An Introductory Analysis*, 6th ed. (McGraw-Hill, 1964).

—, 'The simple mathematics of income determination', in L. A. Metzler *et al. Income Employment and Public Policy: Essays in Honor of Alvin Hansen* (1948).

—, 'Abstract of a theorem concerning substitutability in open Leontief models', *Activity Analysis of Production and Allocation*, ed. T. C. Koopmans (John Wiley and Sons, Inc. 1951).

—, 'An extension of the LeChatelier principle', *Econometrica* (April 1960).

Samuelson, P. A. and Solow, R. M., 'Analytical aspects of anti-inflation policy', *American Economic Review, Papers and Proceedings* (May 1960).

Sato, R., 'Fiscal policy in a neo-classical growth model: an analysis of time required for equilibrating adjustment', *Review of Economic Studies* (February 1963).

Selden, R. T., 'Monetary velocity in the United States', in *Studies in the Quantity Theory of Money*, M. Friedman, ed. (University of Chicago Press, 1956).

Smith, P. E., 'A note on the built-in flexibility of the individual income tax', *Econometrica* (October 1963).

Solow, R. M., 'Technical change and the aggregate production function', *Review of Economics and Statistics* (August 1957).

Stone, R., 'Private savings in Britain, past, present and future', *The Manchester School of Economics and Social Studies* (May 1964).

Stone, R. and Rowe, D. A., 'The market demand for durable goods', *Econometrica* (July 1957).

Stone, R. and Stone, W. M., 'The marginal propensity to consume and the multiplier', *Review of Economic Studies* (October 1938).

Stone, R. *et al. The Measurement of Consumers' Expenditure and Behaviour in the United Kingdom, 1920–38*, vol. 1 (Cambridge University Press, 1954).

Suits, D. B., 'Forecasting with an econometric model', *American Economic Review* (March 1962).

Theil, H., *Economic Forecasts and Policy*, 2nd ed. (North-Holland Publishing Co. 1965).

—, *Applied Economic Forecasting* (North-Holland Publishing Co. 1966).

Tilanus, C. B. and Rey Guido, 'Input–output volume and value predictions for the Netherlands, 1948–1958', *International Economic Review* (January 1964).

Torii, Y., 'Economic development and labor supply (Keizai-hatten to Rōdō-kyōkyū-shutai no Kinkō-zushiki)', *Keizaigaku Nempō* (Keiōgijuku-keizaigakkai, 1966).

Ueno, H. and Kinoshita, S., 'A simulation experiment for growth with a long-term model of Japan', *International Economic Review* (February 1968).

United States Department of Commerce, *The National Income and Product Accounts of the United States, 1929–65* (A Supplement to the Survey of Current Business), (Department of Commerce, 1966).

Valavanis-Vail, S., 'An econometric model of growth, U.S.A., 1869–1953', *American Economic Review, Papers and Proceedings* (May 1955).

Walras, L., *Elements of Pure Economics*, translated by W. Jaffé (Richard D. Irwin, 1954).

Walters, A. A., 'Production and cost functions: an econometric survey', *Econometrica* (January–April 1963).

Zellner, A., 'The short-run consumption function', *Econometrica* (October 1957).

Index

Adams, F. G., 303, 330
adaptable-accelaration principle, *see* investment function
Ando, A., 38, 330
Arrow, K. J., 16–17, 330

balanced budget, *see* multiplier
Ball, R. J., 92–3, 330
Balopoulos, E. T., 134, 223, 330
Barett, C. R., 37, 330
Beckerman, W., 303, 330
Blumenthal, T., 154, 330
Bodkin, R. G., 16–17, 19, 21, 330
Broadbridge, S., 247, 252, 330
Bronfenbrenner, M., 8n, 13, 330
Brookings model, 3, 199
Brown, A. J., 11n, 13, 330
Brown, M., 305, 312, 330
built-in flexibility of personal taxes; Cohen measure, 133; longer-term, 137–40; Musgrave–Miller measure, 131–3, 136, 221, 223–4, 226–7; short-term, 131–6

Chang, T. C., 303, 323n, 330
Chenery, H. B., 16–17, 330
Chow, G. C., 178n, 331
Christ, C., 8, 10n, 19, 331
Christ–Phillips–Lipsey curve, 16, 20–1, 154
Cochrane, D., 173, 331
Cochrane–Orcutt method, 173–4
Cohen, L., 132–3, 331
comparative statical laws; Hicks laws, 96–9, 189, 264; Metzler law, 97, 310; Samuelson–LeChatelier law, 97, 99–102
complementarity, gross, 189
consumption function, 7–12, 78–80, 151–2, 171–8, 277–81, 307, 318–20; Duesenberry–Modigliani effect, 8, 80, 87, 90–3, 103, 151–2, 318–20; Pigovian effect, 8–10, 33

David, P. A., 17, 331
depreciation equation, 23
Dhrymes, P. J., 170, 331
disguised unemployment, 244–6, 286; its calculation, 263–4; in agriculture, 286; in the construction industry, 286; effect of a change in: the final demand, 266–9, 294, the marginal 'propensity to consume,

291–2, relative wages, 288–90, technological coefficients, 291–2; *see also* multiplier
disposable income; its subsistence level, 90–1
Drake, P. S., 92–3, 330
Duesenberry, J. S., 73n, 80, 87, 331
Duesenberry–Modigliani coefficient, *see* consumption function
Durbin–Watson statistics, 7, 174, 319

Eguchi, H., 303, 330
Engel curve, 7
Evans, M. K., 38, 199n, 314, 331
ex post forecasting; the final method, 26; the total method, 26–7

Fabricant, S., 41n, 331
fiscal and monetary policies; marginal rate of substitution between, 43–5; *see also* multiplier
Friedman, M., 13n, 41n, 331
Fromm, G., 73n, 199n, 331
full employment and price stability, 20–2, 54–6, 61

Gale, D., 261, 331
Georgescu-Roegen, N., 147, 331
Goldberger, A. S., 8, 10n, 13n, 14, 25–6, 33, 36, 38, 46, 73–5, 106–8, 132–4, 199n, 222–3, 314, 331
Goldsmith, R. W., 8, 10n, 11n, 331
Gorman, W. M., 152, 331
government expenditure; efficiency of a global budget, 112–13; a marginal budget, 113–15
Great Depression, 4, 40, 59, 62, 65, 67
Griliches, Z., 8, 10n, 331
growth, full-employment–full-capacity, 16
growth equilibrium; its existence, 48–51; its stability, 51–3
Gurley, J. G., 11n, 331

Haavelmo, T., 74, 123–4, 331
Hansen, B., 134, 223, 332
Harberger, A. C., 178n, 332
Harrod, Sir Roy, 4, 309, 332
Harrod–Machlup model, 326
Hawkins–Simon condition, 260, 262, 268
Hicks, Sir John, 4, 102, 147, 149, 150, 181, 189, 312n, 332